Agile Information Systems

Conceptualization, Construction, and Management

Edited By
Kevin C. Desouza
The Information School
University of Washington
Seattle, WA

LONDON AND NEW YORK

First published 2007 by Butterworth-Heinemann

This edition published 2011 by Routledge
2 Park Square, Milton Park, Abingdon, Oxfordshire OX14 4RN
711 Third Avenue, New York, NY 10017, USA

First issued in hardback 2017

Routledge is an imprint of the Taylor & Francis Group, an informa business

Library of Congress Cataloging-in-Publication Data

Desouza, Kevin C., 1979-
Agile information systems : conceptualization, construction, and management / Kevin C. Desouza.
p. cm.
Includes bibliographical references and index.
ISBN 0-7506-8235-3 (alk. paper)
1. Information technology–Management. 2. Management information systems.
I. Title.
HD30.2.D466 2006
658.4′038011–dc22

2006040569

British Library Cataloguing-in-Publication Data
A catalogue record for this book is available from the British Library.

ISBN 13: 978-1-138-16423-9 (hbk)
ISBN 13: 978-0-7506-8235-0 (pbk)

This book is dedicated to our families.

Table of Contents

Preface xi

Acknowledgements xviii

About the Editor..xx

About the Contributors xxi

1

Strategizing for Agility: Confronting Information Systems Inflexibility in Dynamic Environments 1
Robert D. Galliers

2

Agile Information Systems for Agile Decision Making............16
William B. Rouse

3

The Logic of Knowledge: KM Principles Support Agile Systems 31
William E. Halal

4

Producing and Consuming Agility 41
Anders Mårtensson

5

Business Agility: Need, Readiness and Alignment with IT Strategies 52
Marcel van Oosterhout, Eric Waarts, Eric van Heck, and Jos van Hillegersberg

6

Achieving Economic Returns from IS Support for Strategic Flexibility: The Roles of Firm-Specific, Complementary Organizational Culture and Structure 70
Michael J. Zhang

7

Balancing Stability and Flexibility: The Case of the California Energy Commission 83
Miguel Gabriel Custodio, Alan Thorogood, and Philip Yetton

8

Enabling Strategic Agility Through Agile Information Systems: The Roles of Loose Coupling and Web Services Oriented Architecture 97
John G. Mooney and Dale Ganley

9

Agile Information Systems as a Double Dream 110
Silvia Gherardi and Andrea Silli

10

Degrees of Agility: Implications for Information Systems Design and Firm Strategy 122
Tsz-Wai Lui and Gabriele Piccoli

11

Integration Management for Heterogeneous Information Systems 134
Joachim Schelp and Robert Winter

12

Investigating the Role of Information Systems in Contributing to the Agility of Modern Supply Chains..........150
Adrian E. Coronado M. and Andrew C. Lyons

13

Clumsy Information Systems: A Critical Review of Enterprise Systems 163
Sue Newell, Erica L. Wagner, and Gary David

14

Enterprise Information Systems and the Preservation of Agility..........178
Anthony Wensley and Eveline van Stijn

15

Interpretative Flexibility and Hosted ERP Systems 188
Sarah Cadili and Edgar A. Whitley

16

Agile Drivers, Capabilities and Value: An Over-Arching Assessment Framework for Systems Development..........207
Kieran Conboy and Brian Fitzgerald

17

Vigilant Information Systems: The Western Digital Experience 222
Robert J. Houghton, Omar A. El Sawy, Paul Gray, Craig Donegan, and Ashish Joshi

18

Coors Brewing Point of Sale Application Suite: An Agile Development Project 239
Jack Buffington and Donald J. McCubbrey

19

Organizational Agility with Mobile ICT? The Case of London Black Cab Work 250
Silvia Elaluf-Calderwood and Carsten Sørensen

20

Co-Evolution and Co-Design of Agile Organizations and Information Systems Through Agent-Based Modeling 266
Mark E. Nissen and Yan Jin

Index....................285

Preface

The concept of agility continues to grow in popularity in the management and technology literatures. On the management front, organizations are facing greater pressures to demonstrate agile behavior. Simply put, taking a reactive stance to changes in the environment is not an acceptable option. On the technology front, devices deployed to manage information are becoming more nimble and flexible. Moreover, our methods (for example, system development methodologies) for crafting these technologies are also undergoing fundamental transformations. The days of lengthy waterfall systems development life cycles are being replaced by agile and extreme programming methods. While the concept of agility continues to dominate the management and technology literatures, this growth can be characterized as being in silos or independent of each other. There is very little literature that examines the concept of agility in an integrated manner, i.e., examining the management and technological aspects in concert.

Agile Information Systems is a compilation of the most eclectic, profound, and provocative thinking on how we create, manage, and deploy information systems in an agile manner and in a manner that leads to organizational agility. One of the goals of the book is to bring together both the management and technological concepts in an integrated manner to shed light on the concept of agility. As the editor of the book, I am humbled and honored to present this book to you. All praises for the book belong solely to the authors of the various chapters. These individuals have demonstrated their kindness, eagerness, professionalism, and intellect in the preparation of their chapters. It has been my pleasure to work with every one of these distinguished individuals.

A cursory glance at the table of contents will reveal that I have not authored (or coauthored) a single chapter in the book. There is a very important reason behind this. I did write a chapter for the book, with my colleague Yukika Awazu.[1] We even thought that the chapter was quite good and sent it to our colleagues for comments. However, upon reading all the chapters I received from the contributors, I realized that I could not afford not to publish their chapters. My goal was to have twenty of the best ideas on agile information systems in one book, not twenty-one. I hence opted to keep my chapter out of the book. I will use some of the concepts that were contained in that chapter to introduce the chapters of this book.

---

[1] A preliminary version of our chapter, "Designing Agile Information Organizations: Information, Knowledge, Work, Technology," was presented at the International Federation for Information Processing (IFIP) Working Group 8.2 on Information Systems in Organizations—Organization and Society Information Systems (OASIS) 2005 Workshop, in Las Vegas, Nevada, USA, during December 2005.

The Agile Organization

How do we know an organization is agile? Being agile will result in the ability to (1) sense signals in the environment, (2) process them adequately, (3) mobilize resources and processes to take advantage of future opportunities, and (4) continuously learn and improve the operations of the organization. Furthermore, the preceding activities need to occur in quick time cycles and with minimal cost and effort. If these are the desired abilities of an agile organization, the next question becomes: How do we build agile organizations?

Before answering this question, it is important to consider the terms *agile organizations* and *agile information systems*. Are agile organizations and agile information systems distinct, or do they signify the same thing? Well, it depends. On the one hand, we can consider them as one and the same. After all, a system is an organization of some sorts. A system is an organized collection of parts and processes, tied with inputs and outputs. Moreover, since information is managed within and across organizations, the concept of *agile information systems* can be used to denote an *agile organization*. Information makes for the basis of organization and is the outcome of organized work.

On the other hand, we can consider them as being distinct with "agile information systems" used to denote instantiations of technological solutions, mostly computer-based, that help in the processing of information, and agile organizations representing the physical (people, processes, technology assets) and logical (information, knowledge) organization, in which technology (i.e., the agile information system) is all but one component.

If we consider the first perspective, where the agile organization is an agile information system, then we are really asking how we build an "agile information organization." I prefer this perspective as it is more comprehensive and integrated. Thinking about constructing Agile Information Organizations (AIOs) forces one to think about the entire spectrum of issues that influence organizational agility and not just focus on a technocentric view.

In order to construct AIOs, we need to focus on four critical components: (1) information, (2) knowledge, (3) work, and (4) technologies. First, you need to have the information. Information helps the organization manage itself by receiving and sending signals to its environment. Second, the organization needs to have a knowledge base that helps it conduct work. A main task of this knowledge base is to help manage the remaining three components—information, work, and technology. For example, without the requisite knowledge base in place, an organization may not able to process incoming signals or even structure work processes. Third, work represents the routines that an organization does in response to information and also to provide information, products, and services to its environment. Finally, we have technology. These can be thought of as artifacts that help automate the work and enhance the work practices. Taken together, these need to be managed in an integrated manner if we are to create AIOs. It is important to pay attention to the concept of balance here. It is not wise to focus on one or more components at the expense of others. For example, a highly, technologically savvy organization may have limited gains in agility if it does not have flexible organizational processes or a nimble and superior knowledge base in place.

Each of the above components has undergone fundamental transformations in recent times. Information requirements for the organization have changed. It is difficult to plan for all possible information one might need to process. Hence, it is quite difficult to build "robust" systems. One must hence focus on dealing with emergent information and move toward the design of agile systems. Emergent systems accept the fact that it is impossible to predict all information needs a priori and are open in their ability to intake unspecified information. Such systems often sacrifice efficiencies for effectiveness. In addition, information, especially when we are dealing with the processing of images, videos, voice, and so forth, have less structure than just the simple processing of numbers. The volume of information has increased over the last few years and is going to continue to increase. Finally, we have high varieties of information—different types from voice and video, for example, that need to be integrated and managed in a collective manner.

Knowledge required by an organization has also gone through transformations. Today, no organization has all knowledge in its midst. It is just too expensive to keep all resources needed in-house. Hence, organizations resort to a distributed model for knowledge management. Knowledge needs are met by engaging with external entities. In the past, one would just source out work (e.g., manufacturing) to external entities; today, knowledge work and even knowledge is purchased and outsourced to external entities. Moreover, organizations are moving away from the specialist models of operations to one where the organization serves as an integrator of cross-disciplinary knowledge. Finally, knowledge management has moved from the push-model (supply-based) to the pull-model (demand-based). Knowledge is sought in real time for specific needs, utilized, and often abandoned or moved to other areas upon achievement of objectives.

Work in organizations has also been undergoing fundamental transformations. Today, we have knowledge workers who for the most part work on nonroutine tasks and complex efforts. Emergent work practices are become common rather than prescripted projects. Most of the simple tasks have been automated or soon will be. People work in distributed and heterogeneous contexts, and many times in transfunctional roles. The AIO must be able to support this. In order to work in an agile manner, the worker must be able to access information in an agile manner as well.

Finally, we have changes to technology artifacts. Technological devices have become ubiquitous and pervasive in organizations. We have seen great advances in mobile computing efforts. Today, technological devices can cut across heterogeneous environments, integrate information from multiple sources, deliver information in multiple manners, and can even be personalized and customized by users to meet their needs. Finally, system development methods have been undergoing rapid transformations. The days of extended system development approaches and large software projects are coming to an end. Today, designers of information systems and technologies must rely on leaner, agile, and flexible design methodologies. Many of these involve bringing the customer into the design cycles, engaging in rapid prototyping, and so forth.

While integrating the changes in each of the components, we can see some high-level trends taking place in organizations. First, there are greater pressures on organizations to be agile in how they manage each component. This requires an organization to move from long-term planning models to a mode of constant adjustment and realignment. An interesting thing I envision is that in the near future the concept of organizational goals as we know it will disappear. Defining goals a priori and even settling on operating strategies may limit an organization's ability to take advantage of opportunities in an uncertain and constantly changing environment. The future organization will be one where emergent strategies are devised on the fly for specific short-term endeavors, and then a process of reconfiguration goes on to see how best to mobilize resources for the next task.

Second, we are already witnessing the movement toward a renting rather than an owning model for resource management. I expect this trend to continue, with increased focus on renting processes and information. Today, we see an abundance of renting in terms of knowledge and technology components. Knowledge components are rented through outsourcing efforts, especially when one considers the outsourcing of software development and research and development efforts. Technology renting has been under way since the days of Application Service Provision (ASP) efforts and outsourcing of the management of information technology functions, such as outsourcing of technology maintenance and updates. Of recent interest is the outsourcing of entire business processes, for example, outsourcing of logistics and distribution functions to FedEx or UPS. While business processing outsourcing has been under way for sometime, what has changed is the intensity of such efforts and the boldness in organizations to outsource processes previously considered corporate treasures. For example, pharmaceutical companies are beginning to outsource some aspects of their research and development functions. Finally, we must consider the renting of information. If we expect the premise that an organization will need to pay attention to emergent information and will not be able to pre-specify all their information needs a priori, then the concept of renting information becomes salient. Just like we would not want to hoard physical raw materials and would instead focus on building a just-in-time model for inventory management, I could imagine similar situations in terms of information management. We would rent information as needed from organizations who were known to be "specialized information managers." For example, today, especially in the case of marketing and competitive intelligence assignments, it is natural to purchase information reports from third parties who are in the business of collecting, analyzing, and presenting the needed information. Renting information will pose interesting challenges and opportunities for organizations. On the opportunity side, it will redefine the nature of information processing and resource allocation in the organization, while, on the challenge side, it will require organizations to carefully consider how to manage outsourcing of information so as not to become wholly dependent on external parties for information so as to cripple the organization.

The final change we need to be cognizant about is the move from organizational maintenance toward organizational transformation. Maintaining organizations, a reactive stance, requires an organization to make constant adaptations to changes in the environment. Reacting to changes, as we all know, is not an ideal competitive move. Transforming organization requires an organization to be proactive and lead redefinition and redesign efforts without succumbing to environmental pressures. The benefit of leading transformation efforts is that one has the advantage of pre-emption. However, this is no panacea. Being pre-emptive is only of value if the pre-emption turns out to be an advantage for the organization and not a liability. In order for preemption to work, an organization must have a viable information management program in place. Information (i.e., the signals), both from within and outside organizational quarters, must be used to make sense of the environment, identify opportunities, and take action. Action will also need to be bold and risky rather than always playing the safest route. The very nature of how we strategize, manage, and deploy organizational resources will undergo radical changes in the next few years.

Introducing the Stars

Agile Information Systems contains 20 chapters. Chapters are ordered by their unit of focus. The first few chapters are focused on agility at the organizational level and the role of information systems in them. The chapters in the middle of the book focus on issues at both the organizational and technology levels. Finally, the chapters at the end of the book take a focused look at issues surrounding technologies, and relate these back to organizational considerations.

The book begins with a chapter by Bob Galliers. I have always enjoyed exchanging ideas with Bob and have come to truly appreciate his writings on strategic management of information systems, this chapter being no exception. Bob discusses the concept of agile IS strategizing and its implications in terms of building agile information systems. One of the many salient points raised in the chapter is the issue of embracing emergence and the complexity of the environment in which organizations operate. I would like to quote the closing line from Bob's chapter as it succinctly describes what we need to pay attention to: "Let's not lament fragmentation, provisionality, or incoherence, but rather take it as a given. If we can't predict the future, then let's not pretend that we can. Rather, let's enjoy the incongruities, the range of stances we take, and emergence—the new knowledge that arises from the confluence of ideas emanating from our different worldviews, our different 'futures' and scenarios. Agility in our thinking, in our reactions to change—and in our IS—will follow."

In Chapter 2, William Rouse, from Georgia Tech, ties the concept of agile information systems with agile decision making. An organization's agility is displayed in its ability to make effective decisions in an efficient manner, both in a pre-emptive and adaptive manner. Unless information is used in an agile manner to enable for superior decision making, the true value of agile information systems will not be realized. William Halal's chapter is a nice follow-up to the concepts raised by Rouse. Halal discusses, through the use of vivid examples, the need to be more creative in how we think about organizing and managing knowledge. Taken together, Chapters 2 and 3 provide a good coverage of the issues involved in managing information and knowledge components of the AIO. In Chapter 4, Anders Mårtensson discusses how agility is produced and consumed in organizations. He highlights what gives rise to agility in organizations, how to manage the level of agility required by an organization, and what consumes agility. This chapter serves as a good conclusion for the first step of chapters in the book that discuss the organizational aspects of agility.

To start the second section of the book, we begin with Chapter 5 by Marcel van Oosterhout and colleagues who examine the business case for agility. In particular, they focus on two questions: What are the contributing factors requiring organizations to be agile? What is the relative importance of these factors? Furthermore, which of these factors are related to information technologies and how do these technologies enable or hinder the required level of agility? Next, Michael Zhang presents findings from a field study that assessed the performance impacts of IS support for strategic flexibility. His research found that IS support for strategic flexibility was positively associated with two common measures of profitability (Return on Sales and Return on Assets) only when IS were complemented by firm-specific organizational culture and structure. In Chapter 7, drawing on a case study of the California Energy Commission (CEC), Gabi (Miguel Gabriel Custodio), Alan Thorogood, and Philip Yetton explore how to balance between stability and flexibility. They describe how the CEC, repositioned its Information Technology Services Branch as an agile provider of IT services, balancing between the two seemingly contradictory demands of being stable and being agile. In Chapter 8, John Mooney and Dale Ganley explore the concept of Web Services Oriented Architecture (wSOA) as agile information systems. wSOA architecture has several desirable benefits that make them ideal candidates for agile information systems.

In Chapter 9, Silvia Gherardi and Andrea Silli take us through an interesting discussion of whether agile information systems are a double dream. While designers of information systems may want to build information systems that are agile, their very focus during the design process is to stabilize the information systems, thereby giving rise to the double dream. Chapter 10 by Tsz-Wai Lui and Gabriele Piccoli explores the notion of degrees of agility. Grounded in socio-technical theory, they use fuzzy logic to define and compute the measures of agility.

Beginning with Chapter 11, we start the third and final section of the book. Chapter 11 discusses issues of integration among heterogeneous information systems. To be agile, it is imperative that information systems be able to connect and integrate with peer systems. Joachim Schelp and Robert Winter rightly argue that integration and decoupling of applications have to be managed if we are to construct agile information systems. In Chapter 12, Adrian E. Coronado M. and Andrew C. Lyons describe the role played by information systems in the development of agile supply chains. The authors draw on their examination of supplier parks in the automobile sector to examine the implications of information systems in the supply chain.

Chapter 13, by Sue Newell and colleagues, outlines the clumsy nature of Enterprise Information Systems. The business and academic literatures have seen their fair share of stories dealing with failures in enterprise system projects. Sue and her colleagues acknowledge that these systems are difficult to implement, and go a step further to explore how these systems are problematic, even if their implementations were successful. Their chapter has several implications that need to be carefully considered, especially by those who think that Enterprise Systems are the Holy Grail in terms of information systems. Chapter 14, by Anthony Wensley and Eveline Van Stijn, also explores the negativities of Enterprise Systems in terms of how agility and flexibility are impaired through the implementation and use of enterprise systems. In Chapter 15, Sarah Cadili and Edgar A. Whitley argue that ERP systems can be viewed through multiple lenses rather than through a single deterministic vision of what the system can or cannot do. This chapter serves a good complement to the ideas put forth in Chapters 13 and 14.

In Chapter 16, Kieran Conboy and Brian Fitzgerald discuss agile information systems development methods. The authors construct a framework drawing on the management, organizational behavior, and manufacturing literature to assess the level of agility inherent in information systems development projects. Chapters 17 to 19 provide case studies of agile information systems. Chapter 17, by Bob Houghton, Omar A. El Sawy, Paul Gray, Craig Donegan, and Ashish Joshi, discusses how Western Digital benefited from the development of a specific type of agile information systems—vigilant information systems. Chapter 18, by Jack Buffington and Donald J. McCubbrey, explores how the Coors Brewing Company developed a Point-of-Sale system in what can be considered as an agile systems development project. In Chapter 19, Silvia Elaluf-Calderwood and Carsten Sørensen explore the concept of mobility in agile information systems by an examination of London Black Cab operations. The book ends with a chapter by Mark Nissen and Yan Jin who discuss how we might go about designing agile information organizations and agile information systems through the use of agent-based modeling techniques. Agent-based techniques are ideal for building agile systems as they avoid the pitfall of the common reductionist techniques and allow the researcher to study emergent behavior in complex systems.

Closing Thoughts

It is my sincere hope that you will appreciate the ideas and insights presented in the pages that follow. One note of caution is in order. I purposely did not screen chapters in an *academic* sense. I wanted authors to explore their ideas in a free and open manner. As a result, some of the material that follows is quite provocative and novel, and you will find a good mix of ideas and well-tested concepts, and even some ideas applied on well-tested concepts. Think through the material presented in an *agile* and *open* manner rather than in a *rigid* and *closed* manner, and you will truly come away with interesting practices to experiment with, interesting ideas to ponder, interesting research spaces to explore, and probably most importantly, interesting people to contact for further discussions on this important topic.

Kevin C. Desouza
Seattle, Washington, USA

Acknowledgements

This book would not have been possible if not for the contributors. It is always a pleasure to work with a distinguished set of writers and thinkers. I would like to thank each of them personally—Bob Galliers, Bill Rouse, Bill Halal, Anders Mårtensson, Marcel van Oosterhout, Eric Waarts, Eric van Heck, Jos van Hillegersberg, Michael Zhang, Gabi Custodio, Alan Thorogood, Philip Yetton, John Mooney, Dale Ganley, Silvia Gherardi, Andrea Silli, Tsz-Wai Lui, Gabriele Piccoli, Joachim Schelp, Robert Winter, Adrian Coronado, Andrew Lyons, Sue Newell, Erica Wagner, Gary David, Anthony Wensley, Eveline van Stijn, Sarah Cadili, Edgar Whitley, Kieran Conboy, Brian Fitzgerald, Bob Houghton, Omar El Sawy, Paul Gray, Craig Donegan, Ashish Joshi, Jack Buffington, Donald McCubbrey, Silvia Elaluf-Calderwood, Carsten Sørensen, Mark Nissen, and Yan Jin—thank you! Some of the contributors are on their second tour of duty with me. Sue Newell, Carsten Sørensen, and Mark Nissen contributed to my earlier book, *New Frontiers of Knowledge Management*. I thank you for joining me on yet another project. Bob Galliers and Omar El Sway also deserve special thanks for participating in my panel on *Information Systems Research that Really Matters* at the Twenty-Sixth International Conference on Information Systems. I hope that I can count on all you for future collaborative efforts.

Generous resources were made available to me for this project by the Engaged Enterprise, and its think-tank, the Institute for Engaged Business Research. I would like to acknowledge the support received from Yukika Awazu who currently serves as the president of the Engaged Enterprise. I would like to thank the staff of the Engaged Enterprise, especially Alec, Pierre, Sandra, Matsumoto, and Giovanni for their tireless efforts in handling all administrative tasks regarding this book project. I would also like to thank my assistant at the Engaged Enterprise, Sophie Stiles, for all her work in coordinating the project schedule and keeping me on time.

I would like to acknowledge the warm welcome extended to me by my new colleagues at the Information School of the University of Washington. I am proud to be part of this intellectual community and to be associated with a distinguished set of colleagues. I would like to thank my graduate assistant at the University of Washington, Melinda Snarr, for assistance in proofreading the chapters and ensuring that all references were complete and accurate.

I thank Karen Maloney of Butterworth-Heinemann for seeing the value of the book and crafting a fruitful working relationship. Karen helped me bring this book to fruition from a two-paged proposal to the completed manuscript that is before you.

Finally, for the last few months as I prepared this book, I have had an unusually busy travel schedule. During this time, I have been on over 40 flights all of which have been on United Airlines. I did most of the work for this book while on flight, and it is only fitting that I extend my sincere warm gratitude to all of the airhostesses who made my travels safe, calm, and peaceful. I would not have completed this book on time if not for their generosity and kindness.

Thank you one and all.

Kevin C. Desouza
Seattle, Washington, USA

About the Editor

Kevin C. Desouza is on the faculty of the Information School at the University of Washington. His immediate past position was the Director of the Institute for Engaged Business Research, a think-tank of the Engaged Enterprise, a strategy consulting firm with expertise in the areas of knowledge management, crisis management, strategic deployment of information systems, and government and competitive intelligence assignments. He has authored *Managing Knowledge with Artificial Intelligence* (Quorum Books, 2002), co-authored *The Outsourcing Handbook—How to Implement a Successful Outsourcing Process* (Kogan Page, 2006), *Managing Information in Complex Organizations* (M. E. Sharpe, 2005) and *Engaged Knowledge Management* (Palgrave Macmillan, 2005), and edited *New Frontiers of Knowledge Management* (Palgrave Macmillan, 2005). In addition, he has published over 70 articles in prestigious practitioner and academic journals. His work has also been featured by a number of publications such as the Washington Internet Daily, Computerworld, KM Review, and Human Resource Management International Digest. Desouza has advised major international corporations and government organizations on strategic management issues ranging from knowledge management, to competitive intelligence, and crisis management. Desouza is frequently an invited speaker on a number of cutting-edge business and technology topics for national and international, industry and academic audiences. Desouza received his BSc from the University of Illinois at Chicago, an MBA from the Illinois Institute of Technology, and a doctorate from the University of Illinois at Chicago. He is a fellow of the Royal Society of the Arts.

About the Contributors

Jack Buffington is Director of Business Process Improvement, Coors Operations, Molson Coors Brewing Company, where he is responsible for leading transformational change initiatives within Coors Brewing Company Operations and some initiatives internationally. Prior to this, he was one of the leaders of a large supply chain systems initiative to consolidate all of Coors' operations/logistics systems into one enterprise resource planning tool. He joined Coors in 2001 as Director of e-Business, following a career in industry and consulting. He started his career in finance and became a Controller of USF+G, a large Property and Casualty insurance company. He later joined KPMG as a manager in their Financial Services consulting practice, while concurrently working on his dissertation studying the "corporate productivity paradox."

Sarah Cadili studied Information Systems at the London School of Economics and Political Science. She has a BSc (Hons) in Information Systems from Royal Holloway, University of London, and an MSc in Information Systems from the LSE.

Prior to joining NUI, Galway, *Kieran Conboy* worked for Accenture Consulting across many industrial sectors, such as financial services, communications, and the public sector. These engagements involved organizations across the United Kingdom, central Europe, the Nordics, and the United States. Kieran is a member of the Chartered Institute of Management Accountants, and is now completing a PhD at the University of Limerick.

Adrian E. Coronado M. is a Research Fellow on the Future Supply Innovations—FUSION, a project at the University of Liverpool Management School. The aim of the research is to design an information and materials flow architecture that will achieve total supply chain customization and synchronous materials flow. Adrian's research interests concern the analysis and evaluation of supply chains in supplier parks and industrial clusters, management and evaluation of information systems, mass customization, and manufacturing agility. Adrian is a member of the Association for Computing Machinery—SIGMIS.

Miguel Gabriel Custodio is a PhD candidate and the principal researcher of the government and industry-funded National eProcurement Research Project Australia (NeRPA) at the University of Sydney. Before proceeding to academics, he had many years of senior management and technology consulting experience in IS/IT operations of several Fortune 500 companies in the United States. As Senior Enterprise Solutions Architect at Best Buy Company, Inc., he helped establish the operations of www.bestbuy.com, where he holds a patent for inventing its web-based software deployment and management system. He has an MBA from the University of Dallas, Executive Education from the Wharton School, and an Oracle Master Architect Certificate in Application and Database Design.

Gary David is Associate Processor of Sociology, Bentley College, US. He has a BS (in sociology and psychology) and an MA (in sociology), Central Michigan University;

and a PhD (in sociology), Wayne State University (1999). His research focuses on the role that interpersonal interactions play in the formation of intergroup relations, as well as ethnographic studies of the workplace. He has conducted research primarily in workplace settings where intercultural/intergroup interactions take place on a regular basis. Past studies include the analysis of interactions between workers and customers in Arab-owned convenience stores in Metropolitan Detroit. Present projects include examining globally distributed collaborative software development teams, focusing on the role of information and communication technologies. Other workplace research includes examinations of enterprise system design and implementation. Dr. David also specializes in Arab-American studies, and ethnic identity research.

Craig Donegan is Business Solutions Manager at Western Digital Corporation. The majority of his 30 years of experience (20 years at Western Digital) in the high-tech industry has been dedicated to Inventory management, Supply Chain optimization, and Data warehousing. Craig's work experience has been divided equally between Business Operations and Information Technology. Prior to joining Western Digital Corporation, he was Senior MRP Project Manager at Comdial Corporation.

Omar A. El Sawy is Professor of Information Systems in the Information and Operations Management department at the Marshall School of Business, and Director of Research at the Center for Telecom Management (CTM). He also teaches managing global e-Business in the IBEAR MBA Program. His interests include redesigning electronic value chains, collaborative integration and business process redesign in e-Business, and knowledge management and vigilance in fast-response environments. Before assuming his position at CTM in 2001, his research projects have been sponsored by the RosettaNet Consortium and by Carnegie-Mellon University. As Director of Research at CTM, he oversees and leads an industry-sponsored research program that focuses on critical infrastructure management, e-Business collaborative integration, and wireless mobility. El Sawy holds a PhD from Stanford Business School, an MBA from the American University in Cairo, and a BSEE in Telecommunications from Cairo University. Prior to joining USC in 1983, he worked as an engineer and manager for twelve years, first at NCR Corporation, and then as a manager of computer services at Stanford University. He has lectured, consulted, and carried out research in four continents, has been an information systems advisor to the United Nations Development Programme in Egypt, and a Fulbright scholar in Finland. El Sawy is the author of over 70 papers, and his writings have appeared in both information systems and management journals. He is the author of the book Redesigning Enterprise Processes for e-Business, 2001. He serves on six journal editorial boards, and is a six-time winner of SIM's Paper Awards Competition.

Silvia Elaluf-Calderwood is a Computer Engineer (BSc and MSc). She has worked in the telecommunications industry in the United Kingdom and the Netherlands (CCNP). She is currently studying at the PhD program at the Information Systems department at the LSE. Her area of specialization is mobile technology and mobile workers.

Brian Fitzgerald holds the Frederick A. Krehbiel II Chair in Innovation in Global Business and Technology at the University of Limerick, Ireland, where he also is a Research Fellow and Science Foundation Ireland Principal Investigator. Having worked in industry prior to taking up an academic position, he has more than 20 years of experience in the software field. This experience has gained a range of sectors in several countries including Ireland, the United Kingdom, Belgium, and Germany.

Robert D. Galliers joined Bentley in July 2002 as Provost and Vice President for Academic Affairs. Previously Professor of Information Systems and Research Director in the Department of Information Systems at the London School of Economics, he retains his connection with the LSE as a Visiting Professor. Before joining LSE, Dr. Galliers served as Lucas Professor of Business Management Systems and Dean of the Warwick Business School in the United Kingdom, and earlier as Foundation Professor and Head of the School of Information Systems at Curtin University in Australia. Dr. Galliers holds an AB in Economics from Harvard University, as well as an MA in Management Systems from Lancaster University, a PhD in Information Systems from the London School of Economics, and an Honorary Doctor of Science degree awarded by the Turku School of Economics and Business Administration in Finland in 1995 for his contributions to European Information Management research. He is a Fellow of the Royal Society of Arts, the British Computer Society, and the Association for Information Systems, of which he was President in 1999. He has chaired previous ICIS and ECIS conferences, and has been a keynote speaker at ECIS and ACIS, among others. He is editor-in-chief of the Journal of Strategic Information Systems and on the editorial boards of a number of other major journals. He has authored over 60 journal articles and a number of books, the most recent being *Exploring Information Systems Research Approaches* (Routledge, 2006), with Lynne Markus and Sue Newell, and the third edition of the best-selling *Strategic Information Management* (Butterworth-Heinemann, 2003), with Dorothy Leidner.

Dale Ganley is a Research Associate for the Department of Telecommunication, Information Studies and Media at Michigan State University. She received her PhD from the University of California, Irvine, with a focus on information technology and global economics. She also has degrees in economics, information systems, and mathematics, and has over fifteen years of experience in the information systems and telecommunications industries. She has presented work in several peer-reviewed conferences, and in journals such as Electronic Markets and the Journal of the Association of Information Systems. Her research interests are in the diffusion of computing in the global context and the impact of trade and policy mechanisms on computing in developing environments.

Silvia Gherardi is Full Professor of Sociology of Organization at the Faculty of Sociology of the University of Trento, Italy, where she coordinates the Research Unit on Communication, Organizational Learning, and Aesthetics (www.soc.unitn.it/rucola). Areas of interest include the exploration of different "soft" aspects of knowing in organizations, with a peculiar emphasis for cognitive, emotional, symbolic, and linguistic aspects of organizational learning. She can be contacted at: silvia.gherardi@soc.unitn.it.

Paul Gray is Professor Emeritus and Founding Chair of the School of Information Science at Claremont Graduate University. His current interest in information systems include business intelligence, knowledge management, data warehousing, and electronic commerce. Before coming to Claremont in 1983, he was a professor at Stanford University, the Georgia Institute of Technology, the University of Southern California, and Southern Methodist University where he taught in departments of industrial engineering and management science. Prior to his academic career, he worked for 18 years in research and development organizations, including nine years at SRI International. He is currently a Visiting Professor at the University of California at Irvine and is affiliated with its Center for Research on Information, Technology and Organization (CRITO). He is editor-in-chief of the electronic journal *Communications of the*

Association for Information Systems. Gray is the author of three "first papers" in group decision support systems, telecommuting, and analysis of crime in transportation. He was recognized with the LEO award for lifetime achievement by the Association for Information Systems; the Kimball Medal of INFORMS; and the EDSIG Outstanding Information Systems Educator 2000. He is a fellow of both AIS and INFORMS. He was president of the Institute of Management Science in 1992. His PhD is in Operations Research from Stanford University.

William E. Halal is Professor of Science, Technology, and Innovation at George Washington University, Washington, D.C. An authority on emerging technology, strategic planning, knowledge, and institutional change, he has worked with General Motors, AT&T, SAIC, MCI, Blue Cross/Blue Shield, International Data Corporation, the Department of Defense, the Asian Development Bank, foreign companies, and various government agencies. Bill recently substituted for Peter Drucker in giving a talk to 2000 managers at the Los Angeles Coliseum. Halal's work has appeared in journals such as *Nature/BioTechnology, California Management Review, Strategy & Business, Knowledge Management Review, Academy of Management Executive, Journal of Corporate Citizenship, Human Relations, Systems & Cybernetics*, and *Technological Forecasting*. He has also published in popular media like *The New York Times, Christian Science Monitor, Toronto Globe & Mail, Advertising Age, Executive Excellence*, and *The Futurist*. He has produced five books: *The New Capitalism* (Wiley, 1986), *Internal Markets* (Wiley, 1993), *The New Management* (Berrett-Koehler, 1996), *The Infinite Resource* (Jossey-Bass, 1998), and *21st Century Economics* (St. Martin's Press, 1999). Halal is the founder of TechCast, a Web-based system that pools the knowledge of experts to forecast breakthroughs in all technical fields—"A Virtual Think-Tank Tracking the Technology Revolution." He also cofounded the Institute for Knowledge & Innovation as a collaborative effort between the GW School of Business and the School of Engineering. Bill studied engineering, economics, and the social sciences at Purdue University and U.C. Berkeley. Previously, he was a major in the U.S. Air Force, an aerospace engineer in the *Apollo* Program, and a Silicon Valley business manager. He serves on advisory boards of AMD Corporation, the World Future Society, and other organizations. His work has received prominent recognition. One paper, "Beyond the Profit-Motive," won the 1977 Mitchell Prize and an award of $10,000, and he received a medal from the Freedom Foundation for Excellence in the Study of Enterprise. Macmillan's Encyclopedia of the Future ranked him among "The World's 100 Most Influential Futurists," including H. G. Wells, Arthur C. Clarke, Alvin Toffler, and Daniel Bell.

Eric van Heck is Professor of Information Management and Markets at RSM Erasmus University. He can be contacted at: evanheck@rsm.nl.

Jos van Hillegersberg is Professor of Information Systems at School of Business, Public Administration and Technology, University of Twente. He can be contacted at: j.vanhillegersberg@utwente.nl.

Robert J. Houghton returned to Western Digital in 2000 as chief information officer and vice president, information technology. With more than 26 years in the IT field, Houghton previously served Western Digital from 1998 to 1999 as director of information services. Reporting to Matt Massengill, chairman and chief executive officer, Houghton is responsible for all aspects of Western Digital's information technology infrastructure worldwide, including information services, network infrastructure, and technical operations, to provide a best-of-class information environment and help drive the company's expanding business objectives. Previously, he was CIO and vice president of MIS and network operation centers at Zland.com, where he was responsible for worldwide and co-location hosting data centers. He also served such companies as Adaptec, Jennings Corporation, RWD Technologies, and Litton Systems in IT management functions. Houghton earned his bachelor's degree in criminal justice and sociology from the University of Maryland, and information systems management certifications from the University of Maryland and University of California at Davis, as well as under the American Management Association program. He currently is a member of many professional groups, including the Southern California Chapter of SIM (Society of Information Managers); the Southern California Chapter of CIOs, Orange County; WINPOPRO.NET (World Information Professional Network, CIOs); Advisory Board for Proof Point Ventures; and Oracle Leaders Circle.

Yan Jin is Associate Professor of Aerospace and Mechanical Engineering at the University of Southern California, Director of USC IMPACT Laboratory, and a Visiting Professor at Stanford University. He received his PhD in Naval Engineering from the University of Tokyo in 1988. Since then, Dr. Jin has done research on design theory, knowledge-based systems, distributed problem solving, organization modeling, along with their applications to computer-integrated manufacturing, collaborative engineering, and project management. Prior to joining USC faculty in fall 1996, Dr. Jin worked as a senior research scientist at Stanford University for five years. His current research interests include design methodology, agent-based collaborative engineering, and computational organization modeling. Dr. Jin is a recipient of National Science Foundation CAREER Award (1998), TRW Excellence in Teaching Award (2001), Best Paper in Human Information Systems (5th World Multi-Conference on Systemics, Cybernetics and Informatics, 2001), and Xerox Best Paper Award (ASME International Conference on Design Theory and Methodology, 2002). He is currently heading a research program at IMPACT Lab aiming at building knowledge infrastructure to support collaborative engineering.

Ashish Joshi has over nine years of experience in Information Technology. He currently serves as Manager of Business Applications for Western Digital Corporation. Ashish has been with Western Digital since 1997 often working in the factories and developing systems for production use.

Tsz-Wai Lui is a PhD candidate at the School of Hotel Administration at Cornell University and interested in Information Systems. She graduated from the Cornell University with a Master of Management in Hospitality degree in 2005.

Andrew C. Lyons is Lecturer at the Management School of the University of Liverpool, responsible for the EPSRC FUSION research project. This program aims to develop and prototype innovative business models that provide supply networks with new levels of performance. He has undertaken a wide range of research, consultative, and teaching projects in the automotive industry.

Anders Mårtensson is Assistant Professor at the Stockholm School of Economics. His research deals with the management of IT, especially technology adoption and abandonment, application sourcing, and issues concerning IT governance and strategies. Anders studies the financial industry, primarily securities trading, where he also has extensive experience from working with exchanges, banks, and technology providers.

Donald J. McCubbrey, PhD, is a Clinical Professor in the Department of Information Technology and Electronic Commerce and Director of the Center for the Study of Electronic Commerce in the Daniels College of Business at the University of Denver. He joined the Daniels College faculty in 1984 after a career in information systems consulting with Andersen Consulting/Arthur Andersen & Co. Since then, he has concentrated his teaching and research in the areas of strategic information systems and electronic commerce. He is a cofounder and board member emeritus of the Colorado Software and Internet Association. He has coauthored five textbooks and has published papers in several academic and practitioner journals. He has been an associate editor of Communications of Information Systems since its inception.

John G. Mooney is Associate Professor of Information Systems at Pepperdine University's Graziadio School of Business and Management, where he teaches the core "Information and Process Systems" course on the MBA program. He is also a Research Associate at the Center for Research on Information Technology and Organizations at the University of California, Irvine. Prior to joining the faculty at the Graziadio School, he served as the Associate Dean for Information and Learning Technology at the University College Dublin (UCD) Business Schools, and was a visiting professor of Information Systems at the University of California at Irvine. Dr. Mooney's current teaching and research interests include the management of information technology resources and services, e-Business transformation, and IT outsourcing. Dr. Mooney holds a BSc in Computer Science and a Masters in Management Science both from University College Dublin, Ireland, and a PhD in Information Systems from the University of California, Irvine. He was a founding member of ISWorld Net, and created and managed the ISWorld email list of over 3,500 Information Systems academics from around the world from 1994 to 1999. He is Vice President for Chapters and Affiliated Organizations at the Association for Information Systems (AIS), and was an AIS council member from 1998 to 2001 representing Information Systems academics in Europe, the Middle East, and Africa. He is a member of the editorial boards of *MISQ Executive*, the *eService Journal*, and the *Journal of Strategic Information Systems*, and formerly served on the editorial board and as associate editor for the *Communications of the AIS*. He was a member of the Executive Committee of the International Conference on Information Systems (ICIS) from 2001 to 2004, cochaired the ICIS Doctoral Consortium in December 2003, and served on the ICIS Site Selection Committee from 2002 to 2003. He consults to senior management on e-Business, information management, and IT management. Former consulting and executive coaching clients include AIB, Bank of Ireland, IDA Ireland, KPMG Ireland, and PriceWaterhouseCoopers Ireland. He is a current or former member of the Boards of Directors/Advisers of RealExPayments (which he cofounded), Orbism, eWare, and the Educational Multimedia Corporation. He has been honored with a number of teaching, research, and service awards. From 2001 to 2003, Dr. Mooney was Visiting Associate Professor of Information Systems at the Graduate School of Management, University of California, Irvine. Prior to that, he was on the faculty of the Smurfit Graduate and Quinn Undergraduate Schools of Business at University College Dublin (UCD), where he was Associate Dean for Information and Learning Technologies from 1998 to 2001. During this time, he developed the blueprint for the school's IT strategy and enabling infrastructure, and he secured funding for its implementation. In addition, he developed the core technology-enabled education and learning concept for the new undergraduate campus that opened in fall 2002.

Sue Newell is the Camrarata Professor of Management, Bentley College, U.S. and Visiting Professor of Management at Royal Holloway, University of London, UK. BSc (econ), PhD (Psychology), Cardiff University, UK. She has worked previously at Aston, Birmingham, Nottingham Trent and Warwick Universities, all in the United Kingdom. Sue's research focuses on understanding the relationships between innovation, knowledge, and organizational networking, primarily from an organizational theory perspective. Her research emphasizes a critical, practice-based understanding of the social aspects of innovation, change, knowledge management, and interfirm network relations.

Mark E. Nissen is Associate Professor of Information Systems and Management at the Naval Postgraduate School. His research focuses on knowledge dynamics. He views work, technology, and organizations as an integrated design problem, and has concentrated recently on the phenomenology of knowledge flows, culminating in a new book entitled *Harnessing Knowledge Dynamics: Principled Organizational Knowing & Learning* (IRM Press, 2006). Mark's publications span information systems, project management, organization studies, knowledge management, and related fields. In 2000, he received the Menneken Faculty Award for Excellence in Scientific Research, the top research award available to faculty at the Naval Postgraduate School. In 2001, he received a prestigious Young Investigator Grant Award from the Office of Naval Research for work on knowledge-flow theory. In 2002 and 2003, he was Visiting Professor at Stanford, integrating knowledge-flow theory into agent-based tools for computational modeling. In 2004, he established the Center for Edge Power for multi-university, multidisciplinary research on the military terms *command amd control*. Before his information systems doctoral work at the University of Southern California, he acquired over 12 years of management experience in the aerospace and electronics industries.

Marcel van Oosterhout, MSc is a Project Manager/Scientific Researcher specialized in Business Agility and e-Business at RSM Erasmus University (moosterhout@rsm.nl).

Gabriele Piccoli is Assistant Professor of Information Systems at the School of Hotel Administration at Cornell University. His research and teaching expertise is in strategic information systems and the use of network technology to support customer service. Gabe's research has appeared in *MIS Quarterly*, *Decision Sciences Journal*, *MIS Quarterly Executive*, *Communications of the ACM*, *Harvard Business Review*, *The DATABASE for Advances in Information Systems*, *The Cornell Hotel and Restaurant Administration Quarterly*, as well as other academic and applied journals. He also serves on the editorial board of *The Cornell Hotel and Restaurant Administration Quarterly* and *Decision Sciences Journal*.

William B. Rouse is Executive Director of the Tennenbaum Institute at the Georgia Institute of Technology. This universitywide center pursues a multidisciplinary portfolio of initiatives focused on research and education to provide knowledge and skills for enterprise transformation. He is also a professor in the College of Computing and School of Industrial and Systems Engineering. Rouse has over thirty years of experience in research, education, management, marketing, and engineering. His expertise includes individual and organizational decision making and problem solving, as well as design of organizations and information systems. In these areas, he has consulted with over one hundred large and small enterprises in the private, public, and nonprofit sectors, where he has worked with several thousand executives and senior managers. Rouse has written hundreds of articles and book chapters, and has authored many books, including most recently *Essential Challenges of Strategic Management* (Wiley, 2001) and the award-winning *Don't Jump to Solutions* (Jossey-Bass, 1998). He is coeditor of *Organizational Simulation: From Modeling & Simulation to Games & Entertainment* (Wiley, 2005) and the best-selling *Handbook of Systems Engineering and Management* (Wiley, 1999). He is also editor of the eight-volume series *Human/Technology Interaction in Complex Systems* (Elsevier). Among many advisory roles, he has served as Chair of the Committee on Human Factors of the National Research Council, a member of the U.S. Air Force Scientific Advisory Board, and a member of the DoD Senior Advisory Group on Modeling and Simulation. Rouse is a member of the National Academy of Engineering, as well as a fellow of the Institute of Electrical and Electronics Engineers (IEEE), the Institute for Operations Research and Management Science, and the Human Factors and Ergonomics Society. He has received the Joseph Wohl Outstanding Career Award and the Norbert Wiener Award from the IEEE Systems, Man, and Cybernetics Society; a Centennial Medal and a Third Millennium Medal from IEEE; and the O. Hugo Schuck Award from the American Automation Control Council. He is listed in *Who's Who in America, Who's Who in Engineering,* and other biographical literature, and has been featured in publications such as *Manager's Edge*, *Vision*, *Book-Talk*, *The Futurist*, *Competitive Edge*, *Design News*, *Quality & Excellence*, *IIE Solutions*, and *Engineering Enterprise*. Rouse has served in a variety of leadership roles in several companies and on the faculty of the University of Illinois at Urbana–Champaign. He also has served in visiting positions on the faculties of Delft University of Technology in the Netherlands and Tufts University. He received his B.S. from the University of Rhode Island, and his SM and PhD from the Massachusetts Institute of Technology.

Joachim Schelp is Lecturer at University of St. Gallen (HSG). He received a Masters degree and a doctorate in economics from Ruhr-University, Bochum, Germany. After a year as a researcher at the University of Duisburg, Germany, he came to St. Gallen in late 2000. He was responsible for HSG's Competence Center's Application Integration Management and Integration Factory. Consequently, his research interests focus on integration management, architecture management, and service management.

Andrea Silli is Assistant Researcher at Research Unit on Communication, Organizational Learning, and Aesthetics and earned his PhD in Information Systems and Organization at the University of Trento, conducting a research project on ethnography of information systems.

Carsten Sørensen is Senior Lecturer in Information Systems at the London School of Economics and Political Science, United Kingdom. He holds a BSc in mathematics, an MSc in computer science, and a PhD in information systems from Aalborg University, Denmark. Carsten is studying how ICT shapes and is shaped by emerging working practices and organizational forms and has most recently studied the organizational use of mobile technologies. He has been involved in research on mobile computing since the mid-1990s, where he was one of the founding members of the Internet Project. In 2001, he initiated the mobility@lse research network in mobile interaction (http://mobility.lse.ac.uk/), which aims at drawing together academics and practitioners. Carsten has extensive EU research project experience from 1992 and international project experience from 1990. He is actively engaged with executive education and has consulted for a range of organizations. His homepage is located at http://personal.lse.ac.uk/sorensen/.

Eveline van Stijn is a PhD candidate at the School of Business, Public Administration and Technology, University of Twente, the Netherlands. She received her MSc degree in Industrial Engineering from the University of Twente where she specialized in information management as well as logistics. Her current research is in the areas of complex information systems such as Enterprise Resource Planning (ERP), organizational practices, and knowledge management.

Alan Thorogood is researching theoretical frameworks to assist management thinking with regard to IT flexibility, outsourcing, and project management. In the research, he draws on nearly two decades of wide-ranging global industry experience. He is a PhD candidate in Professor Philip Yetton's Information Systems area of the Australian Graduate School of Management (AGSM) and is the IT course leader on the AGSM's MBA programs. His AGSM MBA was awarded in 2003 with the Australian Business Limited Prize for the top academic performance and the BCG Prize in Strategy.

Eric Waarts is Professor of Marketing & Competition at RSM Erasmus University. He can be contacted at: ewaarts@rsm.nl.

Erica L. Wagner is an Assistant Professor of Information Systems at Cornell University's School of Hotel Administration. She earned her PhD from the London School of Economics. Her research interests focus on the ways software is "made to work" within different organizational contexts, with particular emphasis on narrative articulations of action, negotiation, and compromise and temporal practices during post-implementation phases of project work.

Anthony Wensley is an Associate Professor of Information Systems at the University of Toronto. He has a PhD from the University of Waterloo and various other degrees in philosophy and business. His research interests concern the implementation and use of complex information systems, knowledge management, decision support, and the nature and management of intellectual property.

Edgar A. Whitley is a Reader in Information Systems at the London School of Economics and Political Science. He has a BSc (Econ) Computing and a PhD in Information Systems, both from the LSE. He is coeditor for *Information Technology & People* and an associate editor for *MIS Quarterly*. His work looks at how information technology and society interact most recently exploring how information and communications technologies are regulated.

Robert Winter is full professor of information systems at University of St. Gallen (HSG), director of HSG's Institute of Information Management, and academic director of HSG's Executive MBA program in Business Engineering. He received a masters degrees in business administration and business education as well as a doctorate in social sciences from Goethe University, Frankfurt, Germany. After eleven years as a researcher and deputy chair in information systems, he was appointed chair of information management at HSG in 1996. His research interests include business engineering methods and models, information systems architecture/architecture management, and integration technologies/integration management.

Philip Yetton is AGSM Professorial Research Fellow and Commonwealth Bank of Australia Chair at the Australian Graduate School of Management, University of New South Wales. He is the author of numerous articles in journals as different as *MIS Quarterly, Journal of Management Information Systems, Journal of Accounting Research, Accounting, Organizations and Society, Organizational Behavior and Human Decision Processes, Journal of Applied Psychology, Journal of Management Studies, Sloan Management Review,* and *IEEE Transactions on Software Engineering.*

He is also a member of a number of Editorial Boards. He was coawarded the Kenneth R. Ernst Thought Leadership Award in 2001 by Accenture. His major research interests are multidisciplinary, focusing on the management of information technology, project management, IT-based strategic change, strategic leadership, and decision making. Philip is a graduate of Cambridge, Liverpool, and Carnegie-Mellon Universities.

Michael J. Zhang is an assistant professor of management in the Department of Management at Sacred Heart University. He received his Doctor of Business Administration degree from Cleveland State University. His current research focuses on the strategic roles of information systems in supporting a number of key distinctive organizational capabilities, including strategic flexibility, knowledge management, organizational learning, top management capabilities, and organizational innovation. Dr. Zhang has published in *Journal of Management*, *Journal of Managerial Issues*, *Journal of Engineering and Technology Management*, and *Technovation*.

1

Strategizing for Agility: Confronting Information Systems Inflexibility in Dynamic Environments[1]

Robert D. Galliers

Over the relatively short history of Information Systems (IS) planning and strategy,[2] a major principle that has been taken as axiomatic in the mainstream literature relates to the concept of *alignment*. In this context, this often means that Information and Communication Technology (ICT) systems should somehow align with an organization's business strategy. This is surely a "self-evident truth." When we come to examine this truth, however, we begin to uncover a number of problems and issues that need to be addressed. One such relates to the dynamic nature of an organization's business environment and the consequent need for flexible—or agile—IS. A second issue relates to our inability to foresee the future and the changing business information requirements that will come with it. A third issue relates to the role that information can play in informing agile responses to changing circumstances and imperatives—a proactive, rather than reactive, role for IS.

This chapter aims to make a contribution to this book by addressing these issues and identifying what this means for agile IS strategy, or more appropriately, IS *strategizing*. Thus, this chapter will take an alternative perspective to the norm. The perspective will focus more on the *process* of IS strategizing rather than on the *outcome* of the process—the IS strategy itself. As I hope to demonstrate, benefit is gained from a more inclusive, exploratory, postmodernist approach to the IS strategy process. This perspective can be contrasted with the common view, which is more concerned with exploiting the potential of ICT systems for business gain. I will attempt to synthesize the arguments arising from a consideration of the problems associated with the somewhat mechanistic treatment of alignment found in the mainstream literature by utilizing concepts of architecture and infrastructure (e.g., Star and Ruhleder, 1996), and of knowledge creation and sharing (e.g., Cook and Brown, 1999; von Krogh, et al., 2000) with a view to refining the IS strategizing framework, introduced in Galliers (2004; 2006a). By means of setting a context for the arguments that follow, the chapter begins with a critique of concepts of alignment, competitive advantage, enterprise systems, and knowledge management. The issues discussed above will then be considered, in turn, with the arguments being synthesized into a revised IS strategizing framework—a framework aimed at strategizing for agile IS.

Alignment, Competitive Advantage, Enterprise Systems, and Knowledge Management: A Critique

As indicated above, a key aspect of IS strategy theory and practice over the years has been the concept of alignment. This concept has had a number of different forms and interpretations. For example, some thirty years ago, McLean and Soden (1977) compared the theoretical need for a "strong link" between an organization's business and IS plans with its then current practice. They found this link in a minority of cases in their U.S. study. Earl (1983) reported a similar result in the UK. Building on this early work, Earl (1989) introduced the important conceptual distinction between an Information Systems (IS) strategy and an Information Technology (IT) strategy. He argued that the IS strategy is concerned with identifying the information needed to support the business and the information services that need to be provided. Thus, the IS strategy is demand-oriented. Conversely, Earl depicted the IT strategy as being supply-oriented since it focuses on what is and could be made available in terms of IT infrastructure, applications, and services. His argument was that IS and IT strategies should be aligned. Other proponents of alignment include, for example, Parker, et al. (1988), MacDonald (1991), Baets (1992), Henderson and Venkatraman (1992), and Peppard and Ward (2004). These different alignment perspectives make a telling point: What is being aligned with what? The above examples from the literature refer to alignment between the business and IT strategies, between IS and IT strategies, between business performance and IT acquisitions, between an organization's internal and external environments, and between IS capability and organizational performance.

While the alignment concept may be intuitively appealing, an issue that has remained relatively unchallenged and unquestioned[3] is how to align a relatively fixed ICT that is implemented in an organization with a business strategy and associated information requirements that are in constant need of adjustment, while keeping in line with the dynamic nature of the organization's business imperatives. In other words, the issue is how to make IS agile. Despite the useful distinction made between IS and IT strategies, Earl's (1989) model, for example, is relatively static and does not account adequately for the *changing* information requirements of organizations in line with a *changing* business strategy. While a subset of these information requirements undoubtedly remain relatively constant over time, the dynamic nature of the compet-

[3] Sabherwal, et al. (2001) are an exception. These authors refer to the concept of *punctuated equilibrium* in noting the natural tendency of organizations' Information Systems strategies and business strategies falling in and out of alignment over time.

itive, collaborative, and regulatory environments in which organizations conduct their business dictates the need for constant and careful attention to this ever-changing nature of information need. In addition, as I have pointed out elsewhere (Galliers, 1991; 1993; 1999), information is needed to *question* whether an existing strategy continues to remain appropriate, given the changing environmental context, or *external* considerations, and the lessons learned from the unintended consequences of actions taken and IT systems implemented (Robey and Boudreau, 1999), which are classified as *internal* considerations.

This issue leads to the conclusion that information itself may usefully be perceived as a medium through which alignment might take place, with necessary information being provided "top-down" in support of the business strategy and "bottom-up" in terms of learning from on-the-ground realities associated with the use made and impact of existing systems and platforms. Indeed, this is implied by Earl's (1989) model. Alignment between the internal and external environments is an additional dimension to be incorporated into the alignment debate, as noted above. Here, an "inside-out" perspective would also need to be taken. It should be noted, however, that from the perspective of information as the alignment medium, the focus in practice and in the mainstream literature has been on getting the most out of such artifacts as IT and the strategic plan, for bottom-line business benefit. There are, however, those whose approach is more focused on *exploration* rather than *exploitation* (cf. March 1991). The former approach has been identified as coming from the processual school (e.g., Whittington, 1993) and is more concerned with the process of strategizing than with the resultant strategy itself.

This brings us to the issue of *emergence*—a topic of debate in the business strategy literature for the past twenty years or so (e.g., Mintzberg and Waters, 1985). In practice, IS strategy approaches tend to be based on a rational analysis of need, either in response to an extant business strategy and/or an analysis of current ICT capability, or in a proactive manner, based on a "clean slate" approach. The latter was at the heart of the Business Process Reengineering (BPR) movement, the argument being that revolutionary change would lead to "order of magnitude" business benefits (e.g., Hammer, 1990; Venkatraman, 1991; Davenport, 1993). The BPR approach was essentially to identify and streamline key business processes and customer requirements, and then to identify how ICT might support (and often automate) these processes and requirements. The objective was to improve efficiency and effectiveness, and cut costs. The downside to BPR, which is often glossed over, was that it involved quite some risk (Galliers, 1997) and often led to what was euphemistically called "downsizing," with many middle managers being "let go." This had a consequent, unintended (cf. Robey and Boudreau, 1999), and deleterious effect on organizational memory and available expertise (Davenport, 1996; Galliers and Swan, 1999).

What is perhaps both surprising and disappointing about the faddishness of much of the literature on IS strategy is that many key lessons were soon forgotten as new technologies or movements emerged. Thus, for example, Leavitt's (1965) argument that organizations could usefully be viewed as complex socio-technical systems comprising four elements (objectives, structure, technology, and people) seems to have become lost in the excitement, the *zeitgeist*, if you will. Even one of the founding fathers of the BPR movement proclaimed that it had become "the fad that forgot people" (Davenport, 1996).

The focus in the age of BPR was primarily on ICT and processes, and in the age of Enterprise Systems, it appears to be primarily on a technological architecture that actually *dictates* how processes should be undertaken. The formal and informal roles that people play in organizations—the role of informal information (Land, 1982)—and the role of knowledge sharing between people and projects (Newell, et al., 2003) have become sidelined.

In some respects, recent developments in ICT, such as Enterprise Systems, have had a negative impact on agility and sustained competitiveness rather than the positive impact most often expounded in the mainstream literature. Companies that have attempted to utilize ICT to increase efficiency and reduce costs may have lost agility in the process. Companies adopting this approach run the risk of reducing their effectiveness, dexterity, and innovative capacity. Unless they can develop the ambidexterity of which Tushman and O'Reilly (1996) speak, they face the common dilemma of gaining efficiency at the expense of innovation (March, 1991). They also run the risk of losing their capacity for organizational learning.

Enterprise Systems are often promoted as a means of transferring "best-practice" knowledge. An Enterprise System's built-in processes require the adopting organization to adapt its existing processes to the exigencies of the software. The argument is that, since these built-in processes are based on best-practice industry standards, the organization concerned will automatically benefit as a result. However, vendors of Enterprise Systems make much of the consultancy services they offer during and after implementation. Presumably, these services are provided in order for the best-practice solution to become "better," and the off-the-shelf solution to be customized. Research undertaken by Wagner (Scott and Wagner, 2003; Wagner and Newell, 2004) demonstrates how these so-called best practices have to be molded and adapted to the realpolitik of organizations, *despite* the services of the vendor. In addition, and in relation to the earlier discussion on alignment, Enterprise Systems are often implemented to replace legacy systems, which presumably have drifted out of alignment to become legacy systems in their own right over time.

Moreover, by advocating the copying of best practices to improve efficiency, organizations are potentially running the risk of reducing their ability to create the new knowledge needed to innovate and respond creatively to changing imperatives. Given that this is a key concern of business strategy, and that knowledge management systems (KMS) are meant to support and inform the process of strategizing, it appears that we may have another problem. ICT such as Enterprise Systems can then be seen as a force for *standardization*, thus speeding competitive convergence, given that the technology is more or less common—and increasingly commoditized—irrespective of the organization implementing it.

But what of innovation and serendipity? As indicated above, there is a school of thought that argues for the *emergent* nature of strategic processes. In the field of IS, Ciborra used terms such as *bricolage* (after Lévi-Strauss, 1966), *drift*, and *tinkering* (Ciborra, 1992; 2000; 2002) to propose a more incremental, ad hoc approach to strategizing. He argued that even in situations in which a strategic advantage had been gained from the astute application of ICT, the resultant gain was by no means always expected and in no way preordained. Rather, the organizations concerned had benefited from creating an environment—or infrastructure—in which innovation might emerge. The approach advocated by Ciborra smacks of *playfulness*. Others see benefit in combining incremental and radical change. The idea of "ambidextrous" organizations, introduced by Tushman and O'Reilly (1996), has already been noted. He and Wong (2004) confirm the utility of this view in an empirical study of more than two hundred manufacturing firms (see also Gibson and Birkinshaw, 2004).

All in all then, the question of alignment is a vexed one. I posed the question, "What is being aligned with what?" There is also the question of "alignment with whom?" Given the advent of inter-organizational systems and the Internet, alignment is also presumably required along the virtual value chain, with such relationships as those with suppliers and customers needing to be a key consideration. Thus, we need to take into account human interaction, rather than almost totally relying on the rational analysis of a reified *organizational* need or on ICT per se. If we incorporate the emerging field of knowledge management in this discussion, we might consider the need for "boundary-spanning" (Tushman and Scanlan, 1981) and "boundary objects" (Carlile, 2002), understanding and trust (Newell and Swan, 2000), and the natural development of "communities of practice" (Lave and Wenger, 1991; Brown and Duguid, 2001)—both within and between organizations—in order for new knowledge to emerge.

We have seen that alignment has been considered from different perspectives and that alignment between *what* and *whom* are key questions. However, a more basic point to consider is the conceptual link that appears to be missing between what is a conceptual business strategy and ICT—a physical, technological artifact. I pondered whether the missing ingredient might be information, and it is certainly a reasonable argument. In addition, however, it should be remembered that organizations often comprise many technologies and many—often dispersed—individuals. Increasingly, these individuals are "organized" on a project-by-project basis, thereby adding increased dynamism to the mix, and compounding the issue of alignment still further. Hansen (1999) talks of the need for weak ties across organizational subunits. Gerardi and Nicolini (2000) call for the establishment of safety for individuals to form communities of practice for sharing understanding and knowledge. The processes of developing weak ties and safe communities are learned—and these learning processes are as important as the content knowledge itself (Newell, et al., 2003).

Knowledge, or *knowing* (Blackler, 1995), is considered by many to be a key organizational resource, and the knowledge management movement that followed the BPR era has encouraged organizations to attempt to exploit more strategically their knowledge assets (e.g., Kogut and Zander, 1992; Grant, 1996). Companies are thus lured by the suggestion that they can gain and maintain competitive advantage by managing their knowledge assets more astutely, and in particular, by transferring knowledge across individuals, groups, and organizational units, using ICT to achieve this end. Having said that, there is a relative lack of such considerations in mainstream IS strategy discourse. This is surprising, given the common view that knowledge is a strategic organizational resource, and that ICT systems are means by which such knowledge can be transferred across time and space.

KMS emerged in the 1990s. The popular view was that ICT-based KMS can store and transfer knowledge. Thus, existing knowledge can be collected and reused, utilizing ICT. From this perspective, knowledge is "out there," ready to be mined and harvested. The mythology surrounding best practice underpins much of this kind of thinking. Presumably, for such knowledge to be worth reusing, knowledge of what *is* best practice is required.[4] Let us consider some basic principles here. Checkland (1981) reminds us that, while ICT can be exceptionally powerful and proficient in processing data, it is human beings who apply meaning (their knowledge) to selected data in order to make sense of these data (cf. Weick, 1995) for a specific purpose. Data may

---

[4] Nonaka and Takeuchi (1995) define knowledge as "justified true belief," following Plato. Given adherence to the social construction of reality (cf. Berger and Luckman, 1966), knowledge here might better be interpreted as "justified belief."

therefore be context-free, while information can only be informative (i.e., adding to or challenging existing knowledge) within a particular context. ICT systems are therefore data-processing systems; they are nothing more and nothing less (Galliers and Newell, 2003b). *Information* systems require the presence of human beings who apply their knowledge to turn data into information. Knowledge is therefore tacit (cf. Polanyi, 1966) and embedded. "It resides within our brains, and enables us to make sense of the data we [choose to] capture" (Galliers, 2004: 253). It is also "sticky" (Szulanski, 1996; Szulanski and Jensen, 2004) in that its contextual nature means that it is less easily transferred than the KMS perspective might otherwise suggest.

Responsibility for the misconception that codified knowledge can be captured in ICT systems can, partially at least, be laid at the doorstep of Nonaka (e.g., Nonaka and Takeuchi, 1995). Their model depicts the transformation of tacit knowledge into codified knowledge and is widely known and frequently cited. An alternative perspective has also appeared on the scene, however, which is much more in line with the perspective adopted in this chapter. Blackler (1995), Boland and Tenkasi (1995), Tsoukas (1996), and Cook and Brown (1999), among others, raise issues of knowledge transfer and *knowing* rather than knowledge capture and codification. Individuals working with colleagues in organizations learn (e.g., Bogenreider and Nooteboom, 2004) from their interactions with each other and their interactions with formal (and informal) data-processing systems (cf. Land, 1982). Similarly, Wenger (1998) talks of situated learning in the context of communities of practice, while Sole and Edmondson (2002) develop the concept further in relation to geographically dispersed teams. The contrast between these perspectives on knowledge and knowing, on capture and creation, and on explicit and tacit knowledge is similar to the personalization-codification distinction of Hansen, et al. (1999), and the community-codification distinction made by Scarbrough, et al. (1999). In taking the more processual perspective, I would argue that there is potentially considerably more to be gained from the process of knowing, of knowledge creation, of learning and human interaction, and, in the context of this chapter, the process of strategizing,[5] than the mere transfer of "knowledge" (sic.) per se.

Thus, the issue of alignment is a vexed one, and not the self-evident truth that may first have been thought. Following a consideration of the three problematic aspects introduced earlier, a revised model for IS strategizing will be developed as a conclusion to this contribution. This framework will attempt to address the issues and problems with the concept of alignment, and will draw on aspects of architecture and infrastructure, of knowing, of communities of practice, and of exploration in its further development.

Incorporating Considerations of Environmental Dynamism, Future Information Needs, and the Proactive Role of Information in Strategizing

In line with the arguments above, it would seem that to be agile, IS and IS strategies need to take into account the dynamic nature of an organization's business environment, some means of assessing and meeting future information requirements (and the role that information can play in informing a business strategy that incorporates

[5] Cummings and Angwin (2004) use the metaphor of the Chimera to discuss potential future developments in strategic thinking.

agile responses to changing circumstances and imperatives), and the lessons that are learned from experience. Let us take each of these considerations in turn.

Business strategy literature provides some means of coming to grips with dynamic business environments. For example, an analysis of a firm's competitive environment may be assisted by approaches advocated by Porter, such as an analysis of competitive forces, and of the firm's extended[6] value chain (Porter, 1980; 1985), with a view to identifying environmental threats and opportunities.[7] Additional analytical techniques include PEST (political, economic, social and technological) factors,[8] the 4 *P*s (issues associated with product, place, promotion, price),[9] and the balanced scorecard[10] approach (Kaplan and Norton, 1992). Rockart (1979) links such analyses to surface key information requirements by the identification of critical success factors (CSF),[11] while Lincoln's (1980) constraints analysis assists in identifying feasible strategies, given an organization's capability for change. All of these techniques are typical of rational, deliberate strategic analysis, and are certainly helpful in formulating views as to potential developments and initiatives. In order to be ambidextrous, however, organizations need to complement such approaches with more emergent forms of strategizing. A consideration of alternative "futures," or scenarios, falls into the latter category.

Despite Ackoff's (1981) claims to *create* the future, we live in a highly dynamic, unpredictable world. How, then might we produce agile IS in such an environment as this? One approach that holds some promise is the creation of scenarios. In other words, one can build on the concept of alternative interpretations of the same data to build alternative "futures" (cf. Galliers, 1993, 1995). Based on these different views of the future, organizations can consider alternative business strategies and then identify the information required to support and question each one. A proportion of this information need will likely be common to each scenario/strategy; a proportion might be unique. Figure 1.1, which is an amendment to Galliers (1993: 209), illustrates the point. A business judgment can then be made as to the information and related IS that should be made available. It is likely, for example, that information associated with the overlapping areas of each scenario would be well worthy of collection. In addition, absolutely key information unique to a particular future might well be considered to be so strategic in nature as to require collection in addition. An approach to scenario creation used by the French consultancy, Sema Prospective, was to identify facts (e.g., a university is—and will remain—in the business of higher education and research, and not in the production of widgets, throughout the planning period), major trends over which minimal or no control can be applied (e.g., demographic trends and realities), and issues (e.g., whether to expand into executive education or how to deal with decreasing public funding).

The proactive role that information can play in questioning the appropriateness or utility of a business strategy tends to be underemphasized in the mainstream literature.

---

[6] I.e., to include a firm's suppliers and customers.

[7] Environmental threats and opportunities can then be matched against the organization's strengths and weakness to round out so-called SWOT analyses.

[8] See, for example, Bowman and Asch, 1996; 27–33.

[9] Extended by Doyle (1994; 85) to include distribution, services, and staffing considerations.

[10] Recent applications of the Balanced Scorecard approach can be found on the Balanced Scorecard Institute's Web site: http://www.balancedscorecard.org/

[11] The CSF approach can be augmented to include the identification of critical failure factors (Galliers, 1993; 207), critical decisions, critical people, and critical processes (Ward, 1990).

Figure 1.1

Alternative Futures and Their Associated Information Requirements

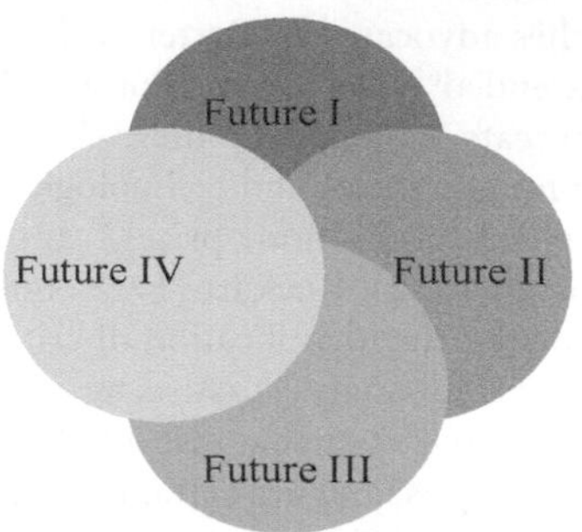

Information to support the business strategy is often identified in a somewhat mechanistic approach, common to many of the aforementioned techniques. Notwithstanding, lessons learned from the unintended consequences of actions taken (cf. Robey and Boudreau, 1999), and of surprising events, as well as from a review of ongoing organizational activity, can play an important role in informing the business strategy and questioning its relevance in changed and changing circumstances. Ongoing assessment and review thus plays a critical role in IS strategizing (Galliers, 1993) and in informing the scenario (re)building process. While exploiting an organization's key human, technological, and informational assets are key components, so are the more exploratory components associated with knowledge sharing, informal information collection, cross-project learning, and human interaction.

Synthesis: Toward a Framework for Information Systems Strategizing

In this final section, I will attempt to bring together the aspects of the foregoing arguments as a basis for the development of a framework for IS strategizing. With regard to the topic of alignment, we have noted, *inter alia*, that there are vexed issues associated with aligning dynamic information needs with a relatively static technology. We also raised the issues of alignment with what and with whom. Competitive advantage on the back of an increasingly commoditized technology also presents us with something of a conundrum, with the importance of ICT use and capability, and with the key (proactive) role of information each being highlighted. In addition, it has been argued that means of identifying information need in relation to alternative futures/scenarios can be helpful in developing agile IS. In relation to knowledge management and KMS, questions have been raised as to whether ICT systems could in fact capture and transfer knowledge, with the *process* of knowing and knowledge creation being privileged in my thinking over knowledge capture and transfer. In extending the argument, the idea was introduced that organizations could be ambidextrous (cf. the arguments introduced earlier, based on the work of Tushman and O'Reilly, 1996) in combining an ability both to exploit current capability and to explore new possibilities.

In attempting to synthesize these arguments with the aim of developing an integrated framework for IS strategizing, the socio-technical concept of an information architecture or infrastructure has proven to be a useful building block (e.g., Star and Ruhleder, 1996; Monteiro, 1998; Ciborra, 2000; Hanseth, 2004), as argued in Galliers (2004). Modes of exploitation and exploration, I argue, may be facilitated by a socio-technical environment—an information infrastructure or architecture—that provides a supportive context for learning and interaction. The framework, a further refinement of that which was introduced in Galliers (2004: 256), is illustrated below as Figure 1.2. It should not be used prescriptively but as a sense-making (cf. Weick, 1995) device. The framework is not meant to be a prescriptive tool, or to provide a solution. It is meant to be used more as an *aide memoir*, to raise questions and facilitate discussion concerning the strategizing elements and connections that may or may not be in place in any particular organization. I shall now take each component of the framework in turn in order to facilitate comprehension of its component parts.

The process of *exploitation* adopted in the framework bears many of the hallmarks of mainstream thinking on IS strategy. This is the deliberate (as compared to the emergent) strategy of which Mintzberg speaks so eloquently (Mintzberg and Waters, 1985). A deliberate attempt is made to identify and develop ICT applications that both support and question the organization's strategic vision, and its current need for information and expertise. Here, we find both the IS and IT strategies that Earl (1989) proposes. It is likely that Enterprise Systems, so-called KMS, and standardized

Figure 1.2

A Framework for Information Systems Strategizing

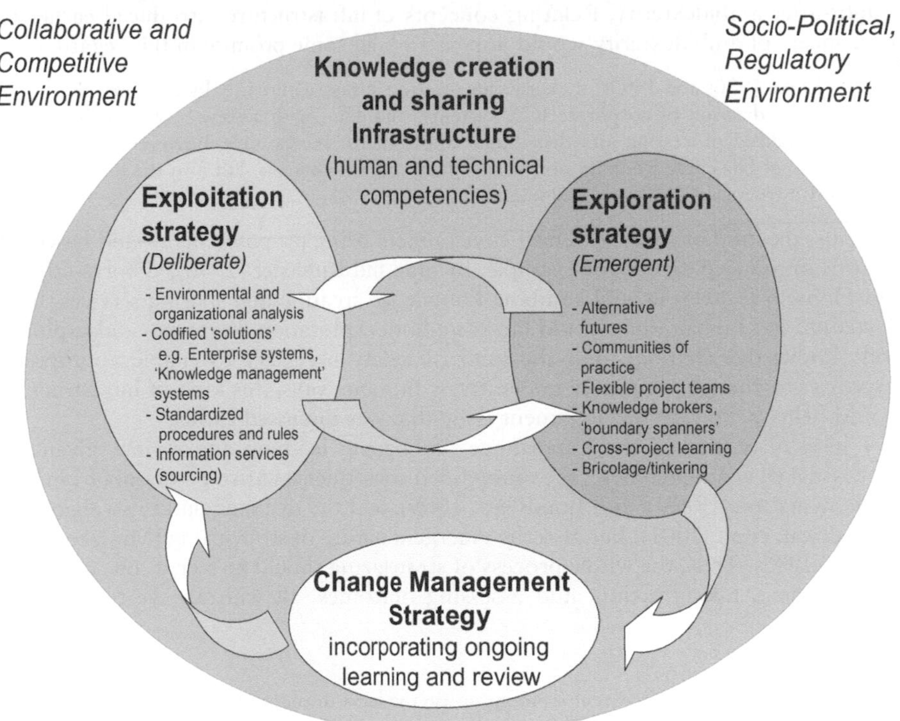

procedures for adopting ICT products, hiring ICT personnel, and developing customized applications will each contribute to this exploitation strategy. And in line with the models introduced in Galliers (1991; 1999), an aspect of this strategy will relate to the organizational arrangements for IS/IT services, including sourcing considerations (cf. Lacity and Willcocks, 2000, for example).[12] Policies on such issues as risk, security, and confidentiality will also need to be considered in this context (e.g., Backhouse, et al., 2005).

With respect to the *exploration* aspects of strategizing, here the emphasis is much more on issues associated with situated learning, communities of practice, and cross-project learning. Ciborra and colleagues (Ciborra, 2000) talk of drift in this context as against control, but there is nonetheless a sense of direction and purpose associated with this activity. I therefore prefer the term *emergence* in this regard. Having said that, there is certainly a sense of bricolage (cf. Lévi-Strauss, 1966) and tinkering at play here, to return to terms favored by Ciborra (1992). In addition, organizations are increasingly reliant on project teams whose membership may well be in flux and distributed. Considerations of trust (Sambamurthy and Jarvenpaa, 2002) and learning from one project to another (e.g., Scarbrough, et al., 2004) are key features that need to be incorporated in this regard. The role of communities of practice (e.g., Wenger, 1998) is crucial in knowledge creation as we have seen, as is the role of boundary spanning individuals (Tushman and Scanlan, 1981), or what we might term *knowledge brokers* (see also, Lave and Wenger, 1991; Hansen, 1999).

While the concept of the ambidextrous organization has been postulated (Tushman and O'Reilly, 1996) and some empirical research has been conducted to test the notion (e.g., He and Wong, 2004), there remains little in the literature that might be of assistance in providing an enabling, supportive environment that might foster this sought-after ambidexterity. Relating concepts of infrastructure introduced earlier to the concept of ambidexterity would appear to hold some promise in this regard.

> "In the 1980s and 1990s, the term information infrastructure usually connoted the standardization of corporate ICT, systems, and data, with a view to reconciling centralized processing and distributed applications. Increasingly, however . . . the concept has come to relate not just to data and ICT systems, but also the human infrastructure." (Galliers, 2004; 256)

Thus, the kind of socio-technical environment being proposed here—and based on notions introduced earlier, for example, by Star and Ruhleder (1996), Ciborra (2000), and Hanseth (2004)—would combine knowledge creation and sharing services, both electronic and human, that would facilitate both exploration (knowing) and exploitation (knowledge sharing), and the kind of agility necessary to enable appropriate responses to changing business imperatives. In some ways, this kind of infrastructure would help circumvent the alignment issue that was discussed earlier.

I have also stressed the importance of ongoing learning and review, given the processual view adopted here, the unintended consequences arising not only from ICT implementations (Robey and Boudreau, 1999), and the dynamic nature of alignment (Sabherwal, et al., 2001), but also the emergent nature of strategizing (Mintzberg and Waters, 1985). Thus, the whole process of strategizing should be seen as one of visioning, planning, taking action, and assessing outcomes, all with an eye to changing

[12] An information *management* strategy to use the term introduced by Earl (1989) and clarified by Galliers (1993).

circumstance and imperatives, *and* the actions of individuals and groups outside, and notwithstanding, any formal strategy or plan. There are countless books on breakthrough change management focusing on the role of ICT (e.g., Lientz and Rea, 2004) and on so-called transformational leaders (e.g., Anderson and Anderson, 2001). The major features of this genre include prescriptive, deliberate approaches that suggest guaranteed, order-of-magnitude gains. Organizational realities suggest an alternative, incremental approach more akin to "muddling through" (Lindblom, 1959), however. What is being envisaged here is the incremental exploration of possibilities—the tinkering (Ciborra, 1992) and bricolage (Lévi-Strauss, 1966)—along with the more deliberate, analytical approaches that incorporate oversight of implementations and review of outcomes (e.g., Willcocks, 1999).

I will make one final point in closing. The fact that I continue to refer to the strategizing framework as one concerned with IS (as opposed to either ICT at one pole or knowledge sharing and creation at the other) is deliberate. There are two primary reasons for this. The first reason relates to the earlier discussion concerning the nature of data, information, and knowledge (cf. Galliers and Newell, 2003b). The sociotechnical infrastructure depicted in Figure 1.2 comprises human beings who can make sense of data provided by both formal and informal systems (cf. Land, 1982) via the application of their (situated) knowledge. In doing so, they turn data into purposeful information. The second reason is to provide an otherwise missing link between the literature on IS/IT strategy, on knowledge management, and on organizational strategies for change. Too often viewed as discrete, an underlying argument to be found in this chapter is that the concepts emerging from this literature should be viewed as complimentary, synergistic, and mutually constituted. In addition, agility is more likely to emerge from a creative process of exploration, and not from mechanistic, prescriptive, and commoditized techniques and technologies. As argued in Galliers (2006b) in relation to recent debates on the academic field of IS, much of the mainstream literature on IS strategy is premised on a view that there is unity and coherence in the world "out there." In contrast, I take a postmodernism stance. We should not lament fragmentation, provisionality, or incoherence, but rather take it as a given. If we can't predict the future, we should not pretend that we can. Rather, let's enjoy the incongruities, the range of stances we take, and emergence—the new knowledge that arises from the confluence of ideas emanating from our different worldviews, our different "futures" and scenarios. Agility in our thinking, in our reactions to change—and in our IS—will follow.

References

Ackoff, R. L. (1981). *Creating the Corporate Future: Plan or Be Planned For*. New York: Wiley.

Anderson, D. and Anderson, L. A. (2001). *Beyond Change Management: Advanced Strategies for Today's Transformational Leaders*. San Francisco: Jossey-Bass/Pfieffer.

Backhouse, J., et al. (2005). Risk management in cyberspace. In *Trust and Crime in Information Societies* (R. Mansell and B. Collins, eds.). Cheltenham: Edward Elgar, pp. 349–379.

Baets, W. (1992). Aligning Information Systems with business strategy. *Journal of Strategic Information Systems,* 1 (4), September, 205–213.

Berger, P. L. and Luckman, T. (1966). *The Social Construction of Reality*. Garden City, NY: Doubleday.

Blackler, F. (1995). Knowledge, knowledge work and organizations: An overview and interpretation. *Organization Studies*, 16 (6), 1020–1047.

Bogenreider, I. and Nooteboom, B. (2004). Learning groups: What types are there? A theoretical analysis and an empirical study in a consultancy firm. *Organization Studies*, 25 (2), 287–313.

Boland, R. J. and Tenkasi, R. V. (1995). Perspective making and perspective taking in communities of knowing. *Organization Science*, 6 (4), 350–372.

Brown, J. S. and Duguid, P. (2001). Knowledge and organization: A social-practice perspective. *Organization Science*, 12 (2), 198–213.

Bowman, C. and Asch, D. (1996). *Managing Strategy*. Basingstoke, UK: Macmillan.

Carlile, P. (2002). A pragmatic view of knowledge and boundaries: Boundary objects in new product development. *Organization Science*, 13 (4), 442–455.

Checkland, P. B. (1981). *Systems Thinking: Systems Practice*. Chichester, UK: Wiley.

Ciborra, C. U. (1992). From thinking to tinkering: The grassroots of IT and strategy. *Information Society*, 8, 297–309.

Ciborra, C. U. (2000) (ed.). *From Control to Drift: The Dynamics of Corporate Information Infrastructures*. Oxford, UK: Oxford University Press.

Ciborra, C. U. (2002). *The Labyrinths of Information: Challenging the Wisdom of Systems*. Oxford, UK: Oxford University Press.

Cook, S. D. and Brown, J. S. (1999). Bridging epistemologies: The generative dance between organizational knowledge and organizational knowing. *Organization Science*, 190, 381–400.

Cummings, S. and Angwin, D. (2004). The future shape of strategy: Lemmings or Chimeras? *The Academy of Management Executive*, 18 (2), 21–36.

Davenport, T. H. (1993). *Process Innovation: Re-engineering Work through Information Technology*. Boston: Harvard Business School Press.

Davenport, T. H. (1996). Why re-engineering failed. The fad that forgot people. *Fast Company*. Premier Issue, 70–74.

Doyle, P. (1994). *Marketing Management and Strategy*. London, UK: Allyn & Bacon.

Earl, M. J. (1983). Emerging trends in managing new Information Technologies. Oxford Centre for Management Studies, Management Research Paper, 83 (4). Reproduced in *The Management Implications of New Information Technology* (N. Piercey, ed.). London, UK: Croom Helm, 1986, pp. 189–215.

Earl, M. J. (1989). *Management Strategies for Information Technology*. London, UK: Prentice Hall.

Galliers, R. D. (1991). Strategic Information Systems planning: Myths, reality and guidelines for successful implementation. *European Journal of Information Systems*, 1 (1), 55–64.

Galliers, R. D. (1993). Towards a flexible information architecture: Integrating business strategies, Information Systems strategies and business process redesign. *Journal of Information Systems*, 3 (3), 199–213.

Galliers, R. D. (1995). Reorienting Information Systems strategy: Integrating Information Systems into the business. In *Information Systems Provision: The Contribution of Soft Systems Methodology* (F.A. Stowell, ed.). London, UK: McGraw-Hill, pp. 51–74.

Galliers, R. D. (1997). Against obliteration: Reducing risk in business process change. In *Steps to the Future: Fresh Thinking on the Management of IT-Based Organizational Transformation* (C. Sauer, P. W. Yetton, and Associates, eds.). San Francisco: Jossey-Bass, pp. 169–186.

Galliers, R. D. (1999). Towards the integration of e-business, knowledge management and policy considerations within an Information Systems strategy framework. *Journal of Strategic Information Systems*, 8 (3), 229–234.

Galliers, R. D. (2003). Change as crisis or growth? Towards a transdisciplinary view of Information Systems as a field of study. *Journal of the Association for Information Systems*, 4 (6), 360–376.

Galliers, R. D. (2004). Reflections on Information Systems strategizing. In *The Social Study of Information and Communication Technology: Innovation, Actors, and Contexts* (C. Avgerou, C. Ciborra, and F. Land, eds.). Oxford, UK: Oxford University Press, pp. 231–262.

Galliers, R. D. (2006a). On confronting some of the common myths of Information Systems strategy discourse. In *Oxford Handbook on Information and Communication Technologies* (R. E. Mansell, et al., eds.). Oxford, UK: Oxford University Press (in press).

Galliers, R. D. (2006b). "Don't worry, be happy . . ." A post modernist perspective on the Information Systems domain. In *Information Systems: The Need for a Discipline?* (J. King and K. Lyytinen, eds.). Chichester, UK: Wiley 2006.

Galliers, R. D. and Newell, S. (2003a). Strategy as data + sense making. In *Images of Strategy* (S. Cummings and D. C. Wilson, eds.). Oxford, UK: Blackwell, pp. 164–196.

Galliers, R. D. and Newell, S. (2003b). Back to the future: From knowledge management to the management of information and data. *Information Systems and e-Business Management*, 1 (1), 5–13.

Galliers, R. D. and Swan, J. A. (1999). Information Systems and strategic change: A critical review of business process re-engineering. In *Rethinking Management Information Systems: An Interdisciplinary Perspective* (W. L. Currie and R. D. Galliers, eds.). Oxford, UK: Oxford University Press, pp. 361–387.

Gherardi, S. and Nicolini, D. (2000). The organizational learning of safety in communities of practice. *Journal of Management Inquiry*, 9 (1), 7–18.

Gibson, C. B. and Birkinshaw, J. (2004). The antecedents, consequences, and mediating role of organizational ambidexterity. *The Academy of Management Journal*, 47 (2), 209–226.

Grant, R. (1996). Prospering in dynamically-competitive environment: Organizational capability as knowledge integration. *Organization Science*, 7, 375–387.

Hammer, M. (1990). Don't automate, Obliterate. *Harvard Business Review*, 68 (4), 104–112.

Hansen, M. T. (1999). The search transfer problem: The role of weak ties in sharing knowledge across organizational sub-units. *Administrative Science Quarterly*, 44, 82–111.

Hansen, M., Nohria, N., and Tierney, T. (1999). What's your strategy for managing knowledge? *Harvard Business Review*, 77 (2), 106–116.

Hanseth, O. (2004). Knowledge as architecture. In *The Social Study of Information and Communication Technology: Innovation, Actors, and Contexts* (C. Avgerou, C. Ciborra, and F. Land, eds.). Oxford, UK: Oxford University Press, pp. 103–118.

He, Z-L and Wong, P-K (2004). Exploration vs. exploitation: An empirical test of the ambidexterity hypothesis. *Organization Science*, 15 (4), 481–494.

Henderson, J. and Venkatraman, N. (1992). Strategic alignment. In *Transforming Organizations* (T. A. Kochan and M. Useem, eds.). New York: Oxford University Press.

Howcroft, D., Newell, S., and Wagner, E. (eds.) (2004). Special issue: Understanding the contextual influences on enterprise system design, implementation, use and evaluation. *Journal of Strategic Information Systems*, 13 (4), 271–419.

Kaplan, R. S. and Norton, D. (1992). The Balanced Scorecard: Measures that drive performance. *Harvard Business Review*, 70 (1), 71–79.

Kogut, B. and Zander, U. (1992). Knowledge of the firm, combinative capabilities, and the replication of technology. *Organization Science*, 3, 383–397.

Kriebel, C. H. (1968). The strategic dimension of computer systems planning. *Long Range Planning*, September, 7–12.

Lacity, M. C. and Willcocks, L. (2000). *Global Information Technology Outsourcing: In Search of Business Advantage*. Chichester, UK: Wiley.

Land, F. (1982). Adapting to changing user requirements. *Information & Management*, 5, 59–75. Reprinted in *Information Analysis: Selected Readings* (R. D. Galliers, ed.) (1987). Sydney, Australia: Addison-Wesley, pp. 203–229.

Lave, J. and Wenger, E. (1991). *Situated Learning: Legitimate Peripheral Participation*. Cambridge, UK: Cambridge University Press.

Leavitt, H. J. (1965). Applying organizational change in industry: Structural, technological and humanistic approaches. In *Handbook of Organizations* (J. G. March, ed.). Chicago: Rand McNally.

Leidner, D. E. (ed.) (2000). Special issue: Knowledge management and knowledge management systems. *Journal of Strategic Information Systems*, 9 (2–3), 101–261.

Lévi-Strauss, C. (1966). The Savage Mind. London: Weidenfeld & Nicolson.

Lientz, B. P. and Rea, K. P. (2004). *Breakthrough IT Change Management: How to Get Enduring Change Results*. Oxford, UK: Elsevier Butterworth Heinemann.

Lincoln, T. J. (1975). A strategy for Information Systems development. *Management Datamatics*, 4 (4), 121–128.

Lincoln, T. J. (1980). Information Systems constraints: A strategic review. In *Information Processing 80* (S. H. Lavington, ed.). Amsterdam: North-Holland.

Lindblom, C. (1959). The science of muddling through. *Public Administration Review*, 19 (2), 79–88.

MacDonald, H. (1991). Business strategy development, alignment and redesign. In *The Corporation of the 1990s* (M. Scott Morton, ed.). New York: Oxford University Press.

March, J. (1991). Exploration and exploitation in organizational learning. *Organization Science*, 2 (1), 71–86.

McFarlan, F. W. (1971). Problems in planning the Information System. *Harvard Business Review*, 49 (2), 75–89.

McLean, E. R. and Soden, J. V. (1977). *Strategic Planning for MIS*. New York, NY: Wiley.

Mintzberg, H. and Waters, J. A. (1985). Of strategies, deliberate and emergent. *Strategic Management Journal*, 6 (3), 257–272.

Monteiro, E. (1998). Scaling information infrastructure: The case of the next generation IP in Internet. *The Information Society*, 14 (3), 229–245.

Newell, S. and Swan, J. (2000). Trust and inter-organizational networking. *Human Relations*, 53 (10), 1287–1328.

Newell, S., et al. (2003). "Best Practice" development and transfer in the NHS: The importance of process as well as product knowledge. *Journal of Health Services Management*, 16, 1–12.

Nonaka, I. and Takeuchi, H. (1995). *The Knowledge-Creating Company: How Japanese Companies Create the Dynamics of Innovation*. Oxford, UK: Oxford University Press.

Parker, M., Benson, R., and Trainor, E. (1988). *Information Economics: Linking Business Performance to Information Technology*. Englewood Cliffs, NJ: Prentice Hall.

Peppard, J. and Ward, J. (2004). Beyond strategic Information Systems: Towards an IS capability. *Journal of Strategic Information Systems*, 13 (2), 167–194.

Polanyi, M. (1966). *The Tacit Dimension*. Garden City, NY: Doubleday.

Porter, M. E. (1980). *Competitive Strategy: Techniques for Analyzing Industries and Competitors*. New York: The Free Press.

Porter, M. E. (1985). *Competitive Advantage: Creating and Sustaining Superior Performance*. New York: The Free Press.

Robey, D. and Boudreau, M. C. (1999). Accounting for the contradictory organizational consequences of Information Technology: Theoretical directions and methodological implications. *Information Systems Research*, 10 (2), 167–185.

Rockart, J. F. (1979). Chief executives define their own data needs. *Harvard Business Review*, 57 (2), 238–241.

Sabherwal, R., Hirschheim, R., and Goles, T. (2001). The dynamics of alignment: Insights from a punctuated equilibrium model. *Organization Science*, 12 (2), 179–197.

Sambamurthy, V. and Jarvenpaa, S. (eds.) (2002). Special issue: Trust in the digital economy. *Journal of Strategic Information Systems*, 11 (3–4), 183–346.

Scarbrough, H., Swan, J., and Preston, J. (1999). *Knowledge Management and the Learning Organization*. London: IPD.

Scarbrough, H., et al. (2004). The processes of project-based learning: An exploratory study. *Management Learning*, 35 (4), 491–506.

Scott, S. V. and Wagner, E. L. (2003). Networks, negotiations, and new times: The implementation of Enterprise Resource Planning into an academic administration. *Information & Organization*, 13 (4), 285–313.

Sole, D. and Edmondson, A. (2002). Situated knowledge and learning in dispersed teams. *British Journal of Management*, 13, S17–S34.

Star, S. L. and Ruhleder, K. (1996). Steps towards an ecology of infrastructure: Design and access to large information spaces. *Information Systems Research*, 7 (1), 111–134.

Szulanski, G. (1996). Exploring internal stickiness: Impediments to the transfer of best practice within the firm. *Strategic Management Journal*, 17 (1), 27–44.

Szulanski, G. and Jensen, R. J. (2004). Overcoming stickiness: An empirical investigation of the role of the template in the replication of organizational routines. *Managerial and Decision Economics*, 25 (6–7), 347–363.

Tsoukas, H. (1996). The firm as a distributed knowledge system: A constructionist approach. *Strategic Management Journal*, 17, 11–25.

Tushman, M. L. and O'Reilly, C. (1996). Ambidextrous organizations: Managing evolutionary and revolutionary change. *California Management Review*, 38 (1), 8–30.

Tushman, M. L. and Scanlan, T. (1981). Boundary spanning individuals: Their role in information transfer and their antecedents. *Academy of Management Journal*, 24 (2), 289–305.

Venkatraman, N. (1991). IT-induced business reconfiguration. In *The Corporation of the 1990s: IT and Organizational Transformation* (M. S. Scott Morton, ed.). New York: Oxford University Press, pp. 122–158.

Von Krogh, G., Ichijo, K., and Nonaka, I. (2000). *Enabling Knowledge Creation. How to Unlock the Mystery of Tacit Knowledge and Release the Power of Innovation*. New York: Oxford University Press.

Wagner, E. and Newell, S. (2004). "Best" for Whom?: The tension between best practice ERP packages and the epistemic cultures of an Ivy league university. *Journal of Strategic Information Systems*, 13 (4), 305–328.

Wagner, E., Howcroft, D., and Newell, S. (eds.) (2005). Special issue: Understanding the contextual influences on enterprise system design, implementation, use and evaluation, Part II. *Journal of Strategic Information Systems*, 14 (2), 91–242.

Ward, B. (1990). Planning for profit. In *Managing Information Systems for Profit* (T. Lincoln, ed.). Chichester, UK: Wiley, pp. 103–146.

Weick, K. E. (1995). *Sensemaking in Organizations*. Thousand Oaks, CA: Sage.

Wenger, E. (1998). *Communities of Practice: Learning, Meaning, and Identity*. Cambridge, UK: Cambridge University Press.

Whittington, R. (1993). *What Is Strategy? And Does It Matter?* London, UK: Routledge.

Willcocks, L. (1999). Managing Information Technology evaluation: Techniques and processes. In *Strategic Information Management: Challenges and Strategies in Managing Information Systems, 2nd ed.* (R. D. Galliers, D. E. Leidner, and B. S. H. Baker, eds.). Oxford, UK: Butterworth-Heinemann, pp. 271–290.

Young, R. C. (1967). Systems and data processing departments need long-range planning. *Computers and Automation*, May, 30–33, 45.

Agile Information Systems for Agile Decision Making

2

William B. Rouse

Agile information systems are intended to enable agile enterprises. Agility is often defined in terms of effective and efficient execution of business processes (Schrage, 2004; Baskerville, et al., 2005). This might imply needs for ERP-like information systems. However, the merit of such "solutions" depends on the constancy of business processes, and the advantages that such constancy brings to an enterprise's competitive position.

Another view of agility can be expressed in terms of an enterprise's abilities to continually improve business processes. A yet broader view characterizes agility in terms of an enterprise's ability to transform itself, to fundamentally change to address experienced or anticipated value deficiencies (Rouse, 2006). Constancy of business processes can impede transformation.

This suggests that agile information systems should provide sufficient flexibility to respond to disruptions of "business as usual," either due to opportunities, threats, or unforeseen events. Such flexibility may limit the possibilities of optimization to maximize efficiency in any given period. In fact, the need for flexibility suggests reformulation of approaches to optimization to include consideration of resiliency across disparate and uncertain time periods.

To address agility more specifically, we need to consider whose information needs are to be served. Needs in the executive suite are quite different from needs at the enterprise's call center. The decisions made, and the information needed to support these decisions, vary considerably across the various domains of the enterprise. To illustrate this point, the next section of this chapter compares information seeking in three rather different domains. A subsequent section provides a deeper view of one domain—strategic management. This provides a context for addressing, in a final section, desired characteristics of agile information systems to support strategic management.

Comparison of Domains

As noted in the introduction, the desired characteristics of agile information systems depend on the nature of the users of such systems. In an earlier paper (Rouse,

Table 2.1

Types of Information vs. Domains of Use			
Type of Information	**Research**	**Design**	**Management**
Nature of underlying phenomena	e.g., previous studies of phenomena of interest	e.g., compilation of data and equations	e.g., company case studies and lessons learned
Nature of critical issues and tradeoffs	e.g., interactions among key variables	e.g., cost vs. performance tradeoffs	e.g., cross-company comparisons
Estimates and projections of important variables	e.g., tabulations of properties	e.g., operating curves and conditions	e.g., financial performance = function (R&D investment)
Suggestions and characteristics of alternatives	e.g., alternative theories of phenomena	e.g., alternative technologies and processes	e.g., alternative strategies and tactics
Inputs to tradeoff analyses and optimization	e.g., computational requirements	e.g., technology maturity, production learning curves	e.g., projections of risks and returns of portfolio
Identity and assessment of competitors	e.g., publications of competing investigators	e.g., competitors' product characteristics	e.g., market players, competitive positions
Forecasts of tangible and intangible impacts	e.g., reports of limiting conditions	e.g., test data and usability studies	e.g., market size and share, impact of uncertainties

2002), I provided a detailed comparison of three domains of information use—research, design, and management—drawing upon over 20 years of research. While this chapter primarily focuses on management, it is useful to briefly summarize this comparison across domains to gain insights into the generality of the conclusions argued here.

Table 2.1 illustrates the range of information[1] of interest for the domains of research, design, and management. This representative set of examples portrays the great variety of needs of researchers, designers, and managers. Table 2.2 compares information seeking across these three domains. There are clearly very substantial differences among researchers, designers, and managers. It is unlikely that the same information sources and support will meet the needs of all three of these types of users.

[1] It can be useful to distinguish between information and knowledge (Rouse, 2002). However, this distinction is not maintained in this chapter and a broad interpretation of "information" is intended.

Table 2.2

Comparison of Information Seeking Across Domains			
Characteristics of Domains	**Research**	**Design**	**Management**
New, fundamental knowledge must be created	Inherent	Occasional	Seldom
New knowledge must reference past knowledge	Inherent	Seldom	Seldom
New forms of representation must be formulated	Common	Occasional	Seldom
Existing forms of representation must be populated with information	Occasional	Common	Common
Formal sources of information must be considered	Common	Occasional	Seldom
Manipulation of representation constitutes the overall task	Inherent	Occasional	Seldom
Optimal answer is the overriding goal	Common	Common	Seldom
Satisfactory answer is the overriding goal	Occasional	Common	Common
Results of manipulation provide sufficient argument	Common	Occasional	Seldom
Results must be "sold" to a wide range of stakeholders	Seldom	Occasional	Common
Nontechnical organizational considerations have a major impact	Seldom	Occasional	Common
Personal commitment to implications of results must be argued	Seldom	Occasional	Common

On the other hand, many studies have shown that there are underlying phenomena in common (Rouse and Rouse, 1984; Rouse, 1994b; Rouse, 2002):

- Human information seeking, in all three domains, is affected by the nature of questions and associated uncertainties.
- The extent and structure of information in a domain affects how people search and the success of their searches.
- The group-oriented nature of most organizational processes in these domains also affects information needs and sources.
- External and internal drivers associated with markets, technologies, and organizations also affect information-seeking behaviors.

Information seeking, in general, is made difficult by humans' poor abilities to specify value. This lack of ability is greatly compensated for by people's excellent abilities to recognize value. Incompatible representations across domains and disciplines also cause problems. Lack of time and the difficulty of convening groups are also problematic. Finally, the primacy of immediate and mandatory requirements often pre-empts access and use of valuable information.

Figure 2.1

Information Value Space

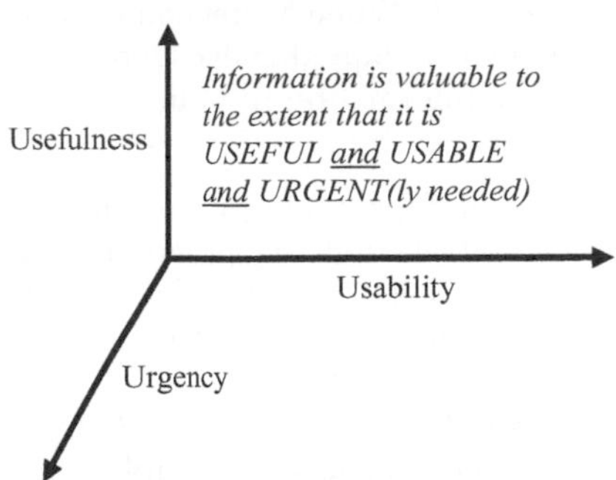

Our studies have also shown that the value of information appears to be conceptually similar in all three domains (Rouse and Rouse, 1984; Rouse, 1986; Rouse, 2002). As shown in Figure 2.1, usefulness, usability, and urgency are the primary dimensions of value. These dimensions can be defined as follows:

- Usefulness: Extent to which information helps users to pursue their intentions
- Usability: Extent to which information is easily accessed, digested, and applied
- Urgency: Extent to which information helps users to pursue near-term plans

A later discussion will consider the implications of the value space in Figure 2.1 for supporting users with high-value information. First, however, we need to address management information seeking in more detail.

Strategic Management

Agile information systems are intended to support an enterprise's business processes that enable the work of the enterprise. This raises a central question. What do enterprises do? There are lots of meetings, much typing and filing, and many things are lifted and stacked. There are innumerable tasks and activities. It is important that this work be productive, safe, and rewarding. However, we cannot approach strategic management at this level.

We need to begin with the work of the enterprise as a system, rather than the jobs, tasks, and activities of the many people that work in the enterprise. To an extent, we need to conduct a work domain analysis of an enterprise (Rasmussen, et al., 1994; Vicente, 1999). This analysis should begin with consideration of the goals and objectives of the work of enterprises.

Goals and objectives might be considered in terms of revenues, profits, market share, and so on, for the private sector, and budgets, constituencies served, and so on for the public sector. However, this level of analysis tends to be idiosyncratic. Instead, we should begin with the recognition that all enterprises face similar strategic challenges.

Essential Challenges

All enterprises face the essential strategic challenges shown below. These challenges must be appropriately understood and addressed for enterprises to succeed (Rouse, 2001).

- Growth: Increasing Impact, Perhaps in Saturated/Declining "Markets"
- Value: Enhancing Relationships of Processes to Benefits and Costs
- Focus: Pursuing Opportunities and Avoiding Diversions
- Change: Competing Creatively While Maintaining Continuity
- Future: Investing in Inherently Unpredictable Outcomes
- Knowledge: Transforming Information from Insights to Programs
- Time: Carefully Allocating the Organization's Scarcest Resource

There is a variety of ways of approaching these challenges (Collins and Porras, 1994; Collins, 2001; Rouse, 2001). Despite the pronouncements of a plethora of management gurus, there is no "silver bullet" that handles all of these challenges. Strategic management involves understanding which challenges are central and adopting a reasonable approach among the many possibilities.

As shown in Figure 2.2, *growth* has to be the goal. Growth can be cast in terms of economic, behavioral, and/or social impacts, or possibly in terms of improved quality, service, and responsiveness. The key point is that growth is a must—the only alternative is decline. Enterprise stasis is not a stable state. Hence, growth must be pursued or decline is assured.

It should be emphasized that share price, earnings per share, revenues, market share, and so on reflects only one perspective on growth. Impact can be measured in many ways. Enterprises can improve the quality of their offerings, the benefits of their services for their constituencies, and/or the influence of their activities and communications without necessarily growing financially or in terms of staff and facilities. Indeed, in some situations, growth of impacts may have to be pursued while such human, financial, and physical resources are declining.

There are, admittedly, situations in which graceful decline may be the appropriate goal. In such cases, the enterprise transformation of interest might be from providing value to providing nothing, perhaps in the sense of doing no harm in the process. Ideally, one might like to assure a "soft landing" for the enterprise's stakeholders. This unusual, though not improbable, case involves many concerns beyond pursuit of

Figure 2.2

Relationships Among Essential Challenges

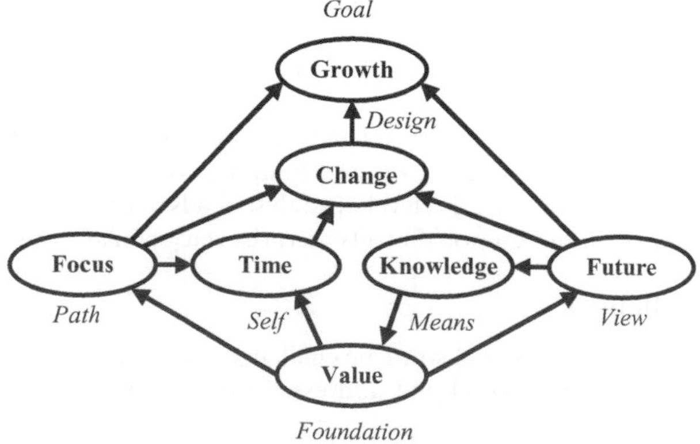

negative growth, e.g., liability and tax implications of ceasing operations, which are beyond the scope of this discussion.

Value provides the foundation for growth. Understanding the nature of value, its evolution or migration, and the consequent growth opportunities are critical elements of this challenge (Slywotsky, 1996; Slywotsky and Morrison, 1997). One of course, must then devise a value proposition and associated business processes to secure this growth. Understanding and enhancing the value streams that provide value to constituencies are keys to successful growth (Womack and Jones, 1996).

Focus provides the path to growth. Pursuit of opportunities and avoidance of diversions can be quite difficult (Rouse, 1998a), particularly in the presence of significant organizational learning disabilities (Senge, 1990), or when the organization is trapped in single-loop learning (Argyris and Schon, 1978). Equally difficult is *change* in terms of designing the enterprise to pursue this path (Rouse, 1993). Both focus and change can create enormous organizational and cultural change problems (Collins and Porras, 1994; Collins, 2001). Strong leadership is crucial during such transitions (Charan and Colvin, 1999; Bennis and O'Toole, 2000; Rouse, 2001; George, 2003).

The nature of the *future*, especially the long-term future, exacerbates the difficulties of focus and change. Not only are the magnitudes and timing of investment returns uncertain—the very nature of the returns is uncertain (Burke, 1996). Further, most large enterprises have difficulty taking advantage of new ideas, even when they are due to their original investments (Christensen, 1997).

The uncertainties and risks associated with an enterprise's view of the future create needs for hedges against downsides, while still being focused on the upsides. Option-based thinking can provide the needed balance between these two perspectives (Luenberger, 1998; Amram and Kulatilaka, 1999; Boer, 1999, 2002). Options provide ways for addressing an enterprise's future, contingent opportunities, and needs (Rouse and Boff, 2004).

Knowledge is the means by which enterprises increasingly address these challenges. It can be quite difficult to transform data, information, and knowledge into programs of action and results (Whiting, 1999; Zack, 1999). This involves both understanding the roles of information and knowledge in problem solving and decision making in different domains (Rouse, 2002), as well as the ways in which archival knowledge and people with knowledge can meet these needs (Cook and Brown, 1999; Brown and Duguid, 2000).

Time is an overarching challenge for leaders of enterprises. To a great extent, leaders define themselves by how they spend their time (Rouse, 1994a, 2001). Transformational leadership involves devoting personal time to those things that will create lasting value (Kouzes and Posner, 1987; George, 2003). Time is the scarcest of leaders' resources, much more than financial and physical resources. Nevertheless, leaders often report being trapped by urgent but unimportant demands for their time (Covey, 1989; Miller and Morris, 1999). This is a classic challenge for senior management (Oncken and Wass, 1974; Mintzberg, 1975).

Considering the nature of the above challenges, what do executives or teams of executives do? One might imagine that they spend time creating models, analyzing tradeoffs, and attempting to optimize allocations of resources. However, the fact is that executives and managers spend their time reacting to their environments, negotiating compromises, and "satisficing" much more than optimizing (Simon, 1957, 1969; Mintzberg, 1975). In general, they have to consider and balance the perceptions, concerns, and desires of the many stakeholders in their enterprises.

Figure 2.3

Strategic Management Tasks and Tools

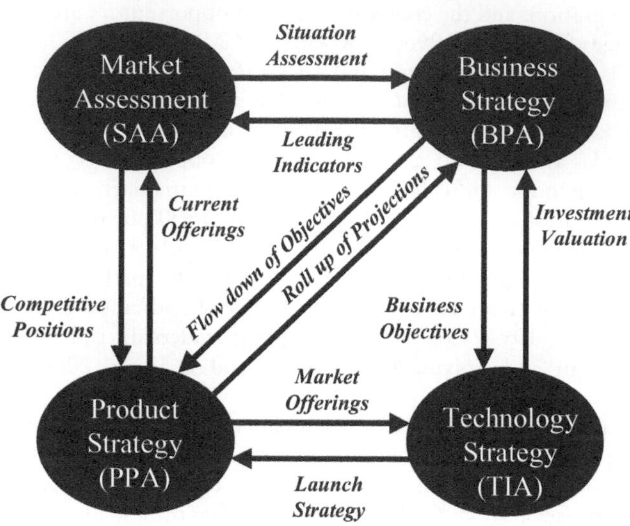

There is a wide variety of ways to address the essential challenges just outlined (Collins and Porras, 1994; Collins, 2001; Rouse, 2001). Process improvements and other incremental changes may be sufficient for a particular enterprise's challenges. However, in some cases, addressing these strategic challenges may involve enterprise transformation, i.e., fundamental changes in terms of relationships to markets, product and service offerings, market perceptions, and/or cost pressures (Hammer and Champy, 1993; Rouse, 2006). As indicated in the Introduction, truly agile information systems should be able to support change ranging from process improvements to enterprise transformation.

Strategic Management Tasks

To understand the nature of strategic management, we worked with several thousand executives and senior managers from over 100 enterprises. The methods used included interviews, questionnaires, and especially notes from working sessions. Figure 2.3 summarizes our findings (Rouse, 2001). There are logical orderings among the four interrelated tasks, yet they often also occur asynchronously.

Assessment of market situations informs business strategies, for which leading indicators enable evaluating the extent of their current and emerging success. Market assessments also provide indications of competitive positions and influence offerings of products and services. Product strategy is also affected by the flow down of business objectives, and yields roll ups of projected outcomes. Product offerings may require new technologies, the nature and availability of which affects launch strategies. Strategic business objectives and investment valuations also affect the extent of technology investments.

To support this range of strategic management tasks, we developed a suite of four software tools to address the issues depicted in Figure 2.3. These tools included:

- ***Product Planning Advisor*** for product strategy (Rouse, 1991)
- ***Business Planning Advisor*** for business strategy (Rouse, 1992)
- ***Situation Assessment Advisor*** for market assessment (Rouse, 1996)
- ***Technology Investment Advisor*** for technology strategy (Rouse, et al., 2000).

All four of these tools are discussed in *Essential Challenges of Strategic Management* (Rouse, 2001).

An obvious question concerns the impact of such tools on the senior management teams with which they were typically used. We addressed this question by compiling managers' observations from the first 100 (of many hundreds) of the planning and consensus-building sessions we conducted with these tools.

Typical product planning sessions focused on satellite communications networks, or new lines of passenger vehicles, or next generation microprocessors. Example business planning sessions included formation of a health information systems enterprise, diversifying in markets for commercial aircraft systems, and orienting R&D toward internal markets. Illustrative consensus building sessions addressed abilities to convert from defense to commercial markets, impacts of impending environmental regulations, and success of ongoing total quality programs.

In the course of these sessions, we asked management teams what they wanted from computer-based tools for supporting collaborative planning and consensus building (Rouse, 1998b). Managers responded with four types of desires. First, from a process perspective, planning teams want tools to provide a clear and straightforward process to guide their decisions and discussions, with a clear mandate to depart from this process whenever they choose. They want support, but not constraints.

Second, planning teams want tools to capture the information compiled, decisions made, and linkages between these inputs and outputs so that they can communicate and justify their decisions, as well as reconstruct decision processes. They want to avoid recreating wheels because no one remembered previous issues and decisions.

Third, planning teams want computer-aided facilitation of group processes via management of the nominal decision-making process using computer-based tools and large-screen displays. They reported that the extent to which tools externalize issues—on the screen rather than between individuals—they felt better able to address and resolve conflicting perceptions.

Finally, they expect surprises. Planning teams want tools that digest the information that they input, see patterns or trends, and then provide advice or guidance that the group perceives they would not have thought of without the tools. Otherwise, they question the "overhead" of feeding the tools all the information required to build the models that the tools manipulate.

Thus, management teams want process, information, facilitation, and surprises. Tools that provide these benefits will be perceived as valuable as long as the cost of use—mainly effort—is acceptable. This was usually assured by using trained facilitators who were highly skilled in use of the software tools.

In the many hundreds of planning sessions we have conducted since this initial study, several additional insights have emerged. Initially, we conducted strategy seminars with an emphasis on management training. In recent years, this has become untenable. Training is now only viable in context of doing real work, rather than just learning. Consequently, pressing problems and real decisions frame the typical agenda. Managers learn new methods and tools while also getting high-priority work done.

Summary

This section, as well as the preceding section, provides an overview of the context in which agile information systems should support executives and senior managers. The difficulty of the essential challenges and the interdependent nature of strategic management tasks suggest a very expansive view of the desired nature of agility. This is further complicated by the often asynchronous nature of how these challenges are addressed and tasks performed.

Information Systems

It seems reasonable to argue that agile information systems should provide valuable information that meets the needs of targeted user populations. In this section, we first review the implications of the value space discussed earlier. We then discuss additional considerations when the targeted users are executives and senior managers. This leads to discussion of the characteristics of agility.

Providing Value

Revisiting the information value space in Figure 2.1, it is clear that choices among information sources provided should be tailored to users' intentions. Forms of information provided should be tailored to users' expertise and preferences. Choices among useful information sources should be tailored to users' near-term plans.

Thus, mechanisms are needed to enable easy assessment of users' intentions, expertise, preferences, and plans. While users could provide these assessments, this is often unreasonable. Instead, users' intentions, expertise, preferences, and plans must be inferred from what they do. Google provides an excellent example of doing this well, albeit within a very constrained task domain, i.e., information seeking as an end in itself (Battelle, 2005).

Beyond tailoring information sources selected to users' intentions, expertise, preferences, and plans, an agile information system should enhance information seeking and use. Aid should be provided to exploit the structure of information. Aid should also support generalization of specific instances of value recognized by users. Finally, aid should facilitate the transformation of terminology, representations, and so on across domains and disciplines.

In addition to these basic principles, there are implications for functionality of information systems. These systems should enhance decision processes and not be premised on the notion that seeking and use of information are ends in themselves. Support should be provided for tracking and capturing information generated throughout decision-making processes. Information systems should facilitate collaboration—across space and time—of multidisciplinary teams.

Finally, to assure indisputable value, support systems should digest information captured in the context of processes and teams and provide insights that would otherwise not be possible. This could range from consistency checks of user-created models, to generalization of specific examples provided by users, to generation of new alternatives by piecing together numerous relationships articulated by users. We have experienced all of these types of computer-initiated "surprises" and seen the very positive effects such surprises have on teams.

The desired enhancements and support functionality outlined above is a "tall order." There is, however, one more requirement. All of the above has to be provided for near-zero cost/benefit. People increasingly expect information and associated support for minimal, if any, cost. They expect support to be on target, timely, and free. While they have never experienced this nirvana, their expectations are very high. In light of the rich set of results reviewed here, I expect that on target and timely is quite possible; free may be much more difficult. Of course, there are lots of ways to pay for things. So, I am sure that this nut will also be cracked.

Supporting Management

The above observations are relevant to many domains of information use, at the very least the three domains discussed earlier. There are additional considerations for information systems for executives and senior managers. First and foremost, the value of the information provided must be undeniably very high. Further, the ease of use in consuming this information and knowledge must be excellent. This often dictates involving highly skilled facilitation.

Easy-to-learn powerful models, methods, and tools can be important. Knowledgeable facilitation can be key here also. Facilitators with strong domain knowledge can accelerate the overall process. The value of these models, methods, and tools should not depend on any user follow up; nothing can be "left to the student." This requires reaching definitive conclusions while facilitation is still available.

We have found that virtually all executives and senior managers have one representation in common—spreadsheets. Consequently, we learned to stage all analyses in spreadsheets. Data and parameters could then be ported to tools such as depicted in Figure 2.3. Results could then be ported back to the spreadsheet. The resulting spreadsheet provides the "minutes" of all the analyses.

This spreadsheet assures a level of comfort for participants. Everything is there in a familiar format. The next step is to create a presentation, e.g., in PowerPoint, as a report of the planning session(s). This enables participants to brief their stakeholders on the nature and results of the session(s), as well as the basis of any action items that emerged. With the spreadsheet and presentation, participants have all they need to know to proceed.

Characteristics of Agility

Based on the foregoing arguments and summary of research results, it seems reasonable to conclude that executives and senior managers will judge information systems to be agile to the extent that they do the following:

- Tailor information sources selected to targeted users
- Employ representations familiar to targeted users
- Provide aiding to enhance information seeking and use
- Manage the process that information is intended to support
- Glean insights from the flow of information sought and used
- Epitomize excellent ease of learning and use
- Adapt all of the above to evolving intentions of targeted users

An information system with these characteristics would enable executives and senior managers to be agile decision makers. Any particular executives and senior managers might, for other reasons, not be agile decision makers. But these behaviors would not be constrained by their information systems.

It is important to note that typical ERP, CRM, SFA, and SCM information systems score poorly on these characteristics. As Schrage indicates (2004), most of these systems enforce consistency rather than support agility. Three examples are useful to illustrate both this tendency and the nature of the above characteristics of agile information systems.

Financial Management

The first example relates to experiences in adapting to a well-known ERP system to meet senior managers' needs for financial information. This example illustrates a lack of agility, as well as its cost.

Managers wanted to assure each month that revenue and costs associated with each of the accounts they managed were correct. They also wanted to be able to project revenues and costs to manage annual budgets. Their overall needs were for a one-page summary of revenue and costs by account, with the ability to drill down to see the components of any particular revenue or cost item of interest.

To generate this one-page summary, they had to access five reports from the ERP system and a legacy system for each account, reconcile numbers across reports, and re-enter information that enabled generating the one-page overall summary. These five reports included reports for direct and indirect labor (across staff members), planned staffing and staff payroll charges (per staff member), nonlabor costs, and encumbrances. The two systems (the ERP and legacy system) handled cross–fiscal-year projections differently, requiring another reconciliation process.

This state-of-the-art financial management system was not agile in terms of the first two characteristics listed above. Information sources were not tailored to users; everybody received everything. The representations were not tailored to users either. Multiple incompatible formats, inconsistencies across reports, and errors due to multiple re-entries of the same data across systems resulted in confused users and, in many cases, financial management simply being ignored until year-end when unexpected deficits prompted scrambling to balance accounts.

The cost of this lack of agility also included investments in a variety of "shadow" financial management systems to duplicate what the ERP was intended to provide. This persisted for over five years until the various kinks in the system were resolved. Managers still get five reports per account, which can total 100 pages or so per manager. They still have to winnow all this information into the one page they need. However, at least they can now count on the accuracy of the information produced by this very rigid (non-agile) information system.

Investment Modeling

This example concerns valuation of "big bet" investments such as acquisitions, capacity expansions, and large R&D initiatives (Rouse, et al., 2000; Rouse and Boff, 2004). This valuation is accomplished by constructing option-based financial models that project the probability distributions of returns, thereby enabling construction of risk-return portfolio diagrams where alternative investments can be compared.

From an information perspective, a major issue is identifying and accessing information that will enable estimation of parameters of models associated with market/technology maturity, production learning, and price volatility. Finance and accounting systems can seldom provide all of this information. Additional information must be sourced from marketing, sales, engineering, and manufacturing. All of the information from the various sources must be mapped into a common representation.

The tool developed to support this process (Rouse, et al., 2000) provides several alternative ways to construct and exercise models, as well as management of these processes for completeness and consistency. This illustrates the fourth characteristic on the above list, with elements of the third. Without this support, managers would be overwhelmed by the task of assimilating information from disparate sources and formulating interconnected models.

Of many experiences in this area, one stands out as particularly agile. The working team included roughly ten people from finance, operations, and technology organizations. The workroom allowed everyone to be networked, providing access to each other, enterprise information sources, and email. Everyone also had cell phones for immediate access to other members of the enterprise. As a result, identification and access of information sources was very rapid, with new information arriving in email attachments within minutes to hours.

The agility enabled by this combination of human expertise with information and communications technology led to completion of the investment valuation project in five days instead of the weeks or months often required. This speed allowed many "What if?" iterations, providing the team with numerous insights into the impacts of assumptions and uncertainties. The methods and tools employed helped them to glean insights (fifth in the above list) that resulted in unexpected conclusions from the overall process.

Product Planning

Product planning is concerned with deciding what new products and services to provide to existing and new markets. This involves formulating and manipulating market and product models that relate customers and other stakeholders to attributes of interest and, in turn, product and service functionality that can be bundled as new offerings (Rouse, 1991; Rouse, 2001). This process involves identification, access, and use of a wide variety of information.

People are central elements of the process of identifying and accessing information. Typical questions are:

- Who knows about topic X?
- When are they available? Are they available now?
- How can they be accessed?

Sources of interest include people in marketing, sales, engineering, manufacturing, finance, product support, and so on, as well as customers, suppliers, distributors, and more formal sources such as consultants, industry groups, and government agencies.

An agile information system can identify and access sources of "who knows what," assist in the selection of potentially high value sources, retrieve and represent valuable information, and support manipulation of these representations—and thereby embody the first three characteristics in the above list. It can also support the process of formulating and manipulating market and product models, as well as using these models to identify alternative innovations with potentially high competitive advantage—and thereby embody the fourth and fifth characteristics on the list.

Information systems and associated tools can aid users by assessing the completeness and consistency of representations, assuring that the process is yielding useful outcomes. Support can also be provided for the distributed, asynchronous nature of the planning process across enterprise functions, international locations, and numerous time zones. One feature that we have found that users highly value is the ability to log in and ask the system, "What has happened since I was last here?" The system knows who they are and when they were last there. It also knows—perhaps by observation and learning (the seventh characteristic in the list)—what elements of the process are of interest to them. It can, therefore, provide summaries of relevant activities since their last involvement. Our experience is that users view such support as highly agile relative to their intentions and needs.

Conclusion

The value of information systems being agile depends on the benefits agility affords to the users of the information provided by these systems. Thus, to address agility more specifically, we need to consider whose information needs are to be served. The decisions made by different types of users, and the information needed to support these decisions, vary considerably across the various domains of the enterprise.

This chapter briefly addresses three domains—research, design, and management—and then focuses on the challenges and tasks central to strategic management. This discussion leads to proposing a set of characteristics of agile information systems to support executives and senior managers. Three real-life examples are used to illustrate these characteristics. This set of characteristics portrays information systems that reach far beyond ERP-like systems and truly enable agile decision making. This, of course, is the ultimate reason for having agile information systems.

References

Amram, M. and Kulatilaka, N. (1999). *Real Options: Managing Strategic Investment in An Uncertain World*. Boston: Harvard Business School Press.

Argyris, C. and Schon, D. A. (1978). *Organizational Learning: A Theory of Action Perspective*, Vol. 1. Reading, MA: Addison-Wesley.

Baskerville, R., et al. (eds.) (2005). *Business Agility and Information Technology Diffusion: IFIP TC8 WG 8.6 International Working Conference*, May 8–11, 2005. Atlanta, Georgia, U.S.A. New York: Springer.

Battelle, J. (2005). *The Search: How Google and Its Rivals Rewrote the Rules of Business and Transformed Our Culture*. New York: Portfolio.

Bennis, W., and O'Toole, J. (2000). Don't hire the wrong CEO. *Harvard Business Review*, 78 (3), 171–176.

Boer, F. P. (1999). *The Valuation of Technology: Business and Financial Issues in R&D*. New York: Wiley.

Boer, F. P. (2002). Financial management of R&D: 2002. *Research Technology Management*, 45 (4), 23–35.

Brown, J. S. and Duguid, P. (2000). Balancing act: How to capture knowledge without killing it. *Harvard Business Review*, 78 (3), 73–80.

Burke, J. (1996). *The Pinball Effect: How Renaissance Water Gardens Made the Carburetor Possible and Other Journeys through Knowledge*. Boston: Little, Brown.

Charan, R. and Colvin, G. (1999). Why CEOs fail. *Fortune*, 139 (12), 69–78.

Christensen, C. M. (1997). *The Innovator's Dilemma: When New Technologies Cause Great Firms to Fail*. Boston: Harvard Business School Press.

Collins, J. C. (2001). *Good to Great: Why Some Companies Make the Leap and Others Don't*. New York: Harper Business.

Collins, J. C. and Porras, J. I. (1994). *Built to Last: Successful Habits of Visionary Companies*. New York: Harper Business.

Cook, S. D. N. and Brown, J. S. (1999). Bridging epistemologies: The generative dance between organizational knowledge and organizational knowing. *Organization Science*, 10 (4), 381–400.

Covey, S. R. (1989). *The Seven Habits of Highly Effective People: Restoring the Character Ethic*. New York: Simon and Schuster.

George, B. (2003). *Authentic Leadership: Rediscovering the Secrets to Creating Lasting Value*. San Francisco: Jossey-Bass.

Hammer, M. and Champy, J. (1993). *Reengineering the Corporation: A Manifesto for Business Revolution*. New York: Harper Business.

Kouzes, J. M. and Posner, B. Z. (1987). *The Leadership Challenge: How to Get Extraordinary Things Done in Organizations*. San Francisco: Jossey-Bass.

Luenberger, D. G. (1998). *Investment Science*. New York: Oxford University Press.

Miller, W. L. and Morris, L. (1999). *Fourth Generation R&D: Managing Knowledge, Technology, and Innovation*. New York: Wiley.

Mintzberg, H. (1975). The manager's job: Folklore and fact. *Harvard Business Review*, (July/August), 53 (4), 49–61.

Oncken, W. Jr. and Wass, D. L. (1974). Management time: Who's got the monkey. *Harvard Business Review*, 52 (6), 75–80.

Rasmussen, J., Pejtersen, A. M., and Goodstein, L. P. (1994). *Cognitive Systems Engineering*. New York: Wiley.

Rouse, W. B. (1986). On the value of information in system design: A framework for understanding and aiding designers. *Information Processing and Management*, 22 (3), 217–228.

Rouse, W. B. (1991). *Design for Success: A Human-centered Approach to Designing Successful Products and Systems*. New York: Wiley.

Rouse, W. B. (1992). *Strategies for Innovation: Creating Successful Products, Systems, and Organizations*. New York: Wiley.

Rouse, W. B. (1993). *Catalysts for Change: Concepts and Principles for Enabling Innovation*. New York: Wiley.

Rouse, W. B. (1994a). *Best Laid Plans*. Englewood Cliffs, NJ: Prentice-Hall.

Rouse, W. B. (1994b). Human-centered design of information systems. In *Expanding Access to Science and Technology: The Role of Information Technology, Proceedings of the Second International Symposium on the Frontiers of Science and Technology*, Kyoto, Japan, 12–14 May 1992 (J. Wesley-Tanaskovic, J. Tocatlian, and K. H. Roberts, eds.). Tokyo, Japan: United Nations University Press, pp. 214–223.

Rouse, W. B. (1996). *Start Where You Are: Matching Your Strategy to Your Marketplace*. San Francisco: Jossey-Bass.

Rouse, W. B. (1998a). *Don't Jump to Solutions: Thirteen Delusions that Undermine Strategic Thinking*. 1st ed. San Francisco: Jossey-Bass.

Rouse, W. B. (1998b). Computer support of collaborative planning. *Journal of the American Society for Information Science*, 49 (9), 832–839.

Rouse, W. B. (2001). *Essential Challenges of Strategic Management*. New York: Wiley.

Rouse, W. B. (2002). Need to know: Information, knowledge and decision making. *IEEE Transactions on Systems, Man, and Cybernetics—Part C Applications and Reviews*, 32 (4), 282–292.

Rouse, W. B. (Ed.) (2006). *Enterprise Transformation: Understanding and Enabling Fundamental Change*. New York, NY: Wiley.

Rouse, W. B. and Boff, K. R. (2004). Value-centered R&D organizations: Ten principles for characterizing, assessing and managing value. *Systems Engineering*, 7 (2), 167–185.

Rouse, W. B. and Rouse, S. H. (1984). Human information seeking and design of information systems. *Information Processing and Management*, 20 (1–2), 129–138. (Reprinted in W. A. Katz, ed., 1986, *Reference and Information Services*. Metuchen, NJ: Scarecrow Press.)

Rouse, W. B., et al. (2000). Technology investment advisor: An options-based approach to technology strategy. *Information · Knowledge · Systems Management*, 2 (1), 63–81.

Schrage, M. (2004). The struggle to define agility: It's all about the Execution. *CIO Magazine*, August 15. Available at: http://www.cio.com/archive/081504/schrage.html.

Senge, P. M. (1990). *The Fifth Discipline: The Art and Practice of the Learning Organization*. New York: Doubleday/Currency.

Simon, H. A. (1957). *Models of Man: Social and Rational; Mathematical Essays on Rational Human Behavior in Society Setting*. New York: Wiley.

Simon, H. A. (1969). *The Sciences of the Artificial*. Cambridge, MA: MIT Press.

Slywotzky, A. J. (1996). *Value Migration: How to Think Several Moves Ahead of the Competition*. Boston: Harvard Business School Press.

Slywotzky, A. J. and Morrison, D. J. (1997). *The Profit Zone: How Strategic Business Design Will Lead You to Tomorrow's Profits*. New York: Times Business.

Vicente, K. J. (1999). *Cognitive Work Analysis: Toward Safe, Productive, and Healthy Computer-Based Work*. Mahwah, NJ: Lawrence Erlbaum Associates.

Whiting, R. (1999). Knowledge management: Myths and realities. *Information Week*, November 22, 1999, 42–54.

Zack, M. H. (1999). Developing a knowledge strategy. *California Management Review*, 41 (3), 125–145.

Womack, J. P. and Jones, D. T. (1996). *Lean Thinking: Banish Waste and Create Wealth in Your Corporation*. New York and London: Simon and Schuster.

The Logic of Knowledge: KM Principles Support Agile Systems[1]

William E. Halal

The rise and fall of knowledge practices in the past few years was so dramatic that it mirrored the Dot Com boom. First organizational learning (OL) caught fire to cope with a world of change. Then knowledge management (KM) promised to harness the power of this hidden resource. Soon corporations were creating learning organizations, assessing their intellectual assets, storing it in knowledge repositories, and forming communities of practice. At the height of the boom, brochures flooded the mail announcing yet another conference that would reveal the secrets to managing knowledge. But in the corporate suites, CEOs began wondering about the payoff, and chief knowledge officers had little to offer that was convincing. The majority of projects failed to produce gains, and now most organizations have cut back their efforts.

Assuming this was not another fad, how will learning and knowledge play a more substantial role in the new economy? What organizational changes are needed to help managers put knowledge to work more effectively? How can the design of agile Information Systems (IS) better encourage the strategic use of this powerful resource?

I've been studying the knowledge economy for decades, and I've learned that knowledge is such a mysterious, fluid thing that it is easily misunderstood, much less controlled. The fact is that we can't really "manage" knowledge very well because its very nature eludes our grasp. One of the strongest trends today is the explosion of mobile wireless computing, forming a constantly shifting network of active users and smart devices. Think of the chirping propagation of smart cell phones with Internet access, speech recognition, and virtual displays, allowing people to blog, tag, and who knows what else in interactive, bottom-up knowledge systems that change constantly. All of this is creating a second generation "Web.2." that is impossible to control.

If you think about it, there is a fundamental ambiguity of information built into the universe at the quantum level where atomic particles can be two places at once and their speed and position cannot both be known. We can manage well-structured, artificially simple systems that do routine tasks, of course, such as *Windows*. But nature, organizations, markets, and knowledge systems are so complex and in perpetual motion that a different perspective is needed. As I will show, agile systems are better suited to the spontaneous creation of knowledge and guiding it to useful purposes (Halal, 1993; Wright, 1998; Manville, 1999; Leonard, 2001). Agile systems are built on entrepreneurial, bottom-up, interactive concepts, and they are dynamic enough to change constantly in an organic way.

eBay presents an instructive example. Rather than managing knowledge in the bureaucratic sense, eBay is growing 60 percent per year because it devised an "internal market economy" that brings together the creative ideas of countless entrepreneurs and the discriminating judgment of buyers around the world, spawning an entire industry that didn't exist before. The phenomenal growth of Craigslist is displacing newspaper classifieds by allowing advertisers to place their own ads online, while Flicker and Delicious allow people to swap photos and tags. "IT-immune systems" are being developed that destroy computer viruses by propagating automatically designed fixes in a viral fashion over the computer network, rather than using centralized security systems. Endless ventures are appearing that create value by pooling knowledge from diverse people in unpredictable ways, making the self-organizing knowledge system the emerging model of enterprise.

If we hope to make sense of these dynamic systems, we will have to understand the extraordinary way knowledge systems behave and the structural changes they are creating in organizations and the economy as a whole. To that end, we start this chapter by analyzing the unique logic that marks this special resource, the characteristic behavior that distinguishes a knowledge economy from a capital economy. As outlined in Table 3.1 below, the following sections describe 12 principles that define the way knowledge systems work. Drawing on the literature, copious examples, and my own insights, each principle is illustrated by trends in management and IS and their implications are explored. I do not claim that these principles are scientifically valid, and I'm sure there are many other ways to see this. But I think this approach serves as a foundation to tease out how knowledge systems are evolving.

Knowledge Can Be Created by Anyone

One of the most remarkable qualities about knowledge is that it can be created by anyone. A good example is Napster, the music-swapping software system that gained 50 million members in weeks. The invention of Napster was so clever that it established a dramatically different peer-to-peer architecture, which many claim will eclipse client-server architecture because it encourages bottom-up collaboration. Yet the inventor was a high school student. In a similar replay, BitTorrent was recently formed by another lone genius who designed a distributed P2P system able to break the logjam of bits waiting to transmit movies and TV on demand.

Similar examples abound in which people without advantage, resources, or status somehow gained the insight to produce creative innovations. This burst of creativity is clearly visible in the countless new ventures now being formed by people from all over the world, from all walks of life, and all ages. As we will see, individuals offer unique perspectives, however humble, that can contribute to our understanding.

The implication of this characteristic is that knowledge organizations should be driven from the bottom up using principles of entrepreneurship rather than those of hierarchy that continue to prevail. In a knowledge-centric world, we want to create the two entrepreneurial conditions that draw out talent: 1) encourage everyone to

Table 3.1

Characteristics and Implications of Knowledge	
Characteristic Principles	**Management Implications**
1. Created by anyone	• Fosters entrepreneurship
2. Distributed cheaply	• Increasing returns to scale
3. Increases when shared	• Cooperation is productive • Requires central organizer • Increases network size
4. Transmitted in networks	• Keeps people informed
5. Abhors a vacuum	• Provides transparency
6. Reduces conflict	• Distributed where needed
7. Changes value	• Leaks across boundaries
8. Acts as a fluid	• Can be sticky • Limited by smallest channel
9. Organized hierarchically	• Understanding is relative
10. Guided by spirit	• Limited by vision • Seeks awareness
11. Unique for individuals	• Differences are normal • Requires deep listening
12. An infinite resource	• Understands a complex world

introduce innovations, and 2) reward those who succeed. Yes, it will be messy, but innovation is a messy business.

Entrepreneurship also solves the difficult problem of evaluating IS and KM programs. The usual approach is to treat these as services subsidized by the CEO in cost-centers. This may be convenient, but line managers rightfully view cost-centers as a burden that increases overhead costs, and evaluating their productivity is difficult. If they are regarded as internal enterprises offering services selected by line managers from among competing providers, however, their value is easily recognized by the client's willingness to pay. The success and growth of these two important functions then rests on their ability to assist others.

Knowledge Is Distributed Cheaply

Once created and captured, knowledge can be duplicated and distributed easily, in contrast to the immutable properties of capital. The manufacture of physical goods may produce economies of scale up to a point, but the expansion to larger factories, longer supply chains, and multiple distribution channels eventually becomes too cumbersome and costly, resulting in *decreasing* returns to scale.

Growth of a knowledge-based enterprise, however, requires little additional complexity or cost, permitting *increasing* returns to scale (Arthur, 1996). The expenses incurred when creating an IS may be high, for instance, but the marginal cost of distributing additional copies is negligible. Better still, it can be simply transmitted online instantaneously. This explains why Microsoft enjoys huge operating margins on *Windows*, and why IBM considers utility computing a major strategic initiative.

The onset of increasing returns to scale has altered the behavior of modern knowledge economies. Witness the fierce competitive battles between start-ups struggling to gain "first mover" advantage, which permits dominance of a new industry through "lock in," creating a "winner take all" economy. To achieve critical mass, systems are designed to give away information, because its cost is negligible, and then reply on the growth of traffic to provide potential users of paying services. Google and the other search services profit by forming a heavily traveled media platform for ads. Apple's iTunes solved the entertainment industry's dilemma over distributing music online by pricing songs cheaply and reaping the benefits of huge global markets and the sale of iPods.

Knowledge Increases When Shared

Another striking feature is that knowledge can grow indefinitely, which is quite different from capital. Capital consists of tangible assets (factories, land, money) that are limited, but knowledge is an intangible asset that *increases* with use. Ray Smith, former CEO of Bell Atlantic who is often called the Father of the Information Age, said: "Unlike capital, knowledge can't be used up. The more you dispense, the more you generate" (Halal, 1998a).

Let's illustrate with a simple example. Physical assets, such as a car, can be used by only one owner at a time because they are finite. Cars can be sold, traded, and loaned, but the number of cars remains unchanged. However, an owner of valuable knowledge can share it with others in return for his or her knowledge. Both parties would then continue to own their original knowledge, while also having the new knowledge they gained, thereby increasing the total knowledge in use. Further, the integration of these different streams of knowledge may produce additional, higher-level knowledge, adding still more knowledge.

This leads to the striking implication that collaboration is now economically productive because it creates value. Collaboration was rare in the Industrial Age, which focused on manufacturing goods. But in an Information Age that focuses on creating knowledge, collaboration is widely encouraged because all parties can benefit. This new development in the nature of economics explains the wave of business alliances under way, even among competitors.

This also helps to understand the key to pooling knowledge. Few are altruistic enough to volunteer their time and effort to help others. Sharing may be noted on annual reviews, but the link to rewards is tenuous. And claims that cooperation can be encouraged by the right organizational culture usually are greeted with skepticism. Roughly 70 percent of managers think sharing knowledge is the biggest challenge in KM (Knowledge Management, 2001).

Rather than rely on good intentions, some type of mutual exchange is needed to make knowledge sharing a workable reality. Those sharing knowledge can also be rewarded with recognition, financial benefits, or anything else of value. When Xerox created its Eureka database of 30,000 technical articles, the contributing technicians declined financial awards in favor of having their names associated with each entry, like an author's byline. The type of rewards that motivate people can vary greatly, therefore, but some valuable incentive is essential to make sharing knowledge more than an empty piety. Ideally, the best exchange consists of the mutual assistance provided by collaborating together, which increases knowledge all around (Browne and Prokesch, 1997; Wright, 1998).

Knowledge Is Transmitted in Networks

The icon of the Information Age is the network because all nodes can reach other nodes directly and quickly, increasing the fidelity and scope of the system. How useful would the Internet be if you could only use it to contact a subset of sites and had to switch to another network for the others?

A central organizer is needed to create and maintain a network. Microsoft holds a near-monopoly in PC operating systems, for instance—not simply because it is powerful—but because a common network is needed to permit interchangeable applications and ease of communications. Other network organizers now permit the same advantages for music (iPods), tagging (RSS), social contacts (LinkIn), and product descriptions (RFID). It is expected that 1 trillion smart devices will interact around the globe by 2013.

This power of collaborative networks also lies behind the role of communities of practice (CoP). CoPs enhance understanding by increasing network interaction within the group, which drives tighter cohesion, increasing interaction again, and so on, to create an intense learning episode. A carefully nurtured process of this type helped the Navy "become alive with the fire of shared understanding" (Bennet, 1997).

Knowledge Abhors a Vacuum

Like Nature, knowledge abhors a vacuum because people feel a need to understand the world around them, and they will do whatever is needed to supply that understanding. If formal communication media are inadequate, people seek out spokespersons to inquire about pressing issues and they form grapevines of informal contacts.

But informal communications channels have a tendency to degrade. The accuracy of gossip, for instance, deteriorates with repetition, often spreading rumors that are unfounded. Systems function best if formal systems are transparent, allowing gossip, rumor, and hearsay to decline to minimal levels.

The power of transparency can be seen in the robust growth of open-source software design. It has been shown that *Linux* is easier to use and more error-free than *Windows* precisely because open access encourages wide participation to improve the system more easily than the top-down, secretive approach of Microsoft. The advantages are so great that open-source systems are appearing in scientific publications, drug development, and other fields. IBM is giving up its patents on commonly used systems for the same reason.

Knowledge Reduces Conflict

The principles above suggest that knowledge can reduce conflict. Consider the well-known two-person game, "Prisoner's Dilemma," often played in small groups to demonstrate principles of conflict versus cooperation. Two prisoners can win their freedom if both cooperate with each other in planning an escape. But if one agrees to cooperate and the other chooses conflict by snitching to authorities, the snitch gains rewards and the cooperating prisoner suffers. Conflict is encouraged in this game because the two parties' choices are unknown to each other, whereas if their intentions are visible, the possibility of being duped by a fellow prisoner disappears, encouraging cooperation.

Real situations are more complex, of course. However, this example illustrates how transparency of information can greatly reduce conflict by preventing one party from taking advantage of others. The 2003 Iraq invasion would have been much harder to justify, for instance, if the absence of Iraqi weapons of mass destruction were publicly known.

Even casual arguments can be alleviated by the enlightenment that knowledge confers. Most of us encounter daily misunderstandings with others, often attributing dark motives to the other party and fanning the flames of conflict. But when the facts are presented clearly by both parties, it is quite surprising to see how harmless the situation often is, dispelling animosity.

People may continue to provoke one another in the face of perfect knowledge, of course. However, a great deal of conflict can be readily dispelled simply by ensuring that transparency of knowledge aids accurate understanding.

Knowledge Changes Value

One of the most intriguing features of knowledge is that its value can change enormously. Consider the following anecdote demonstrating the powerful effects of knowledge:

> You're sitting at a sidewalk café, when you notice an attractive person of the opposite sex staring at you across the tables. Unsure of what this means, you glance around. When you look again, this person gives you a decided "wink." Well! This changes everything. So you walk over, say hello, and join this mysterious admirer. Who knows, your entire life could change. (Negroponte, 1995)

This modest story illustrates the power of knowledge. A "wink" is simply one bit—a 1 replaces a 0—yet it can have enormous value if the reward is of great importance, and the information is crucial in obtaining this reward. These factors can change enormously.

A good illustration can be seen in the Dot Com collapse. Analysts claim that 70 percent of the corporate assets involved were knowledge in the form of software, patents, employee skills, and marketing channels. The wild optimism that drove share prices to unsustainable levels reflected the bold prospects that Wall Street expected from the exploitation of these knowledge assets, while the subsequent collapse showed these expectations could not be sustained.

Thus knowledge exhibits a constant state of flux in which shifting assessments of its utility produce rises and declines in demand as people search for the best solutions to ever-changing problems. Little wonder the value of knowledge is so hard to quantify.

Knowledge Acts as a Fluid

It is common to recognize that knowledge behaves as a fluid. We often speak of communication channels as "pipes." "Leaks" occur because it is almost impossible to keep secrets fully secure. The difficulty of conveying personal understanding makes tacit knowledge "sticky." Knowledge is "congealed" in complex products that require intensive research.

Like all metaphors, there are limitations to considering knowledge a fluid. For instance, you can't simply mop it up after a spill. But the qualities of fluids often provide useful insights that enhance our understanding of this unusual resource. The speed of a complex information system, for instance, can be effectively gauged by noting that information, like any fluid, is limited by the choke point at its smallest channel.

The principles described above generally emphasize this fluidlike behavior. Unlike other resources, knowledge flows around obstacles, divides into multiple streams that may flow together again, and expands to cover the terrain—almost as though it possesses a life of its own. As broadband and digital convergence makes everything compatible, we are seeing the fluid movement of information among PCs, TVs, mobile phones, intelligent cars, and appliances.

Knowledge Is Organized Hierarchically

Like all else, knowledge is organized hierarchically. Cells are organized into bodies, people are organized into societies, and stars into galaxies. In a similar way, data, information, and knowledge form a hierarchy of understanding.

At the bottom, data are measurements that provide our link to reality: daily temperature, stock prices, SAT scores. Data are then aggregated into relationships we call information: "The average annual temperature in Mexico City is 20 degrees above Montreal." "The stock market has declined 30 percent." "SAT scores explain 60 percent of the variance in grades." Information, in turn, is organized into knowledge for solving problems to achieve some purpose: "If you want to avoid hot weather, live in Montreal." "This is a good time to invest in stocks." "A student with high SAT scores can expect to get good grades." Note that the distinctive feature that sets knowledge apart from data and information is that it is goal-oriented (Ackoff, 1994).

An interesting quality of this hierarchy is that the knowledge contained at a higher level subsumes that of lower levels, but the reverse is not true. The knowledge in the above examples reflects the information and data that went into it, for instance, but the data does not contain the information, and the information does not contain the knowledge. For a striking illustration, humans are able to understand the intricate workings of that wondrous colony of cells we call our bodies—but these cells have little conception of the larger system they comprise. Thus, understanding is relative to our position in the hierarchy of understanding.

Knowledge Is Guided by Spirit

At the top of this hierarchy of understanding lies "consciousness" or "spirit." I realize this is a bold claim that makes some uneasy, but it can be demonstrated logically. Knowledge is marked by a rational orientation to achieving goals, as we've just seen, and the very essence of goals introduces a vast domain of subjective concerns that lie *beyond knowledge:* values, purpose, beliefs, vision, choice, and so on. Note that this domain does not necessarily involve metaphysical phenomena, such as supernatural beings. Spirit can be adequately described as simply the "human spirit," that sense of consciousness or awareness we use to direct our lives.

Many philosophers claim that all life flows out of the spirit at the top of this hierarchy. For instance, Emmanuel Kant argued that "will" and "idea" form the basis of our perception of reality, while the Buddha summed it up more strongly in his famous aphorism, "With our thoughts, we make the world." Larry Prusak made the same point in conventional terms: "When it comes to managing knowledge, culture trumps all other factors" (Conference Board, 1997).

The failure to expand understanding is usually caused by limitations of spirit that pose obstacles to learning. For instance, fundamentalism, whether in Christian or

Islamic religions, is characterized by such tenacious adherence to a narrow faith that other sources of knowledge are excluded, distorting the learning process.

If knowledge rests on a spiritual foundation, the best way to improve understanding also lies at this level: seek awareness, question beliefs, set worthy goals, develop a sense of meaningful purpose, and remain open to inspiration and vision. Conversely, the lack of conscious awareness may explain why email, distance education, and other forms of IS communications are limited in conveying meaning effectively.

Knowledge Is Unique for Individuals

If knowledge flows out of the human spirit, the very nature of knowledge is unique because each individual inhabits a distinctively different perspective that is worthy in its own right. That's why the field of KM struggles with the challenge of making sense out of the diverse nature of tacit knowledge. There may be similarities in our thinking, influenced by common cultures and other social realities. But each human being is as individualized as the variety found in other aspects of nature.

Satellite radio Sirius is paying shock jock Howard Stern $500 million because his unique talent for raunchy humor has found a huge market. Stern claims that his performances are the only time he truly feels like himself. The field of biometrics is only possible because we all differ in small but distinctive ways.

One of the challenges in dealing with knowledge, therefore, is the realization that it is normal to find wide differences of opinion. This often results in severe conflict, but differences actually represent potential because they offer a richer interpretation than any one viewpoint. After all, it is differences that create the potential energy for all action. Different energy levels are necessary to power a mechanical engine, and price differences drive economic growth. Likewise, different viewpoints enlarge and heighten understanding.

Actually bridging such differences is difficult, of course, because it requires that we yield our grip on reality. To truly understand another's viewpoint, we must engage in "deep listening" that is so earnest it can only be achieved by momentarily entering the spirit of others, and thereby changing ourselves. This fusion of two unique souls is the source of profound new levels of insight needed to resolve conflict, create innovations, foster loving relationships, and most other worthy human accomplishments.

The present conflict between Islamic fundamentalism and Western modernism, for instance, could possibly be resolved if both parties became open to understanding one another. Islam could possibly recognize the value of modern science and economics in improving human welfare, while conversely, the West could recognize the need to reorient global capitalism toward serving human values.

Knowledge Is an Infinite Resource

The possibilities are vast because the principles described above drive the frontier of understanding to expand relentlessly. As we have seen, knowledge is created by countless people everywhere. It can be copied and distributed endlessly, and it encourages cooperation rather than conflict, creating still more knowledge. Networks facilitate this expansion, people absorb knowledge readily, and they focus on knowledge of greatest value. To facilitate this process, knowledge flows through a variety of channels, it leaks across boundaries, and it is drawn upward to more powerful understanding and awareness. And because we each view the world differently, the scope of this vast resource is almost unlimited.

Economics has traditionally been called the "dismal science" because it presumed *limited* resources that *decrease* when shared to produce a world of *scarcity*. But the above principles introduce a world of *unlimited* resources that *increase* when shared to produce a world of *abundance*. In short, knowledge is "The Infinite Resource" because it represents boundless power to manage a world of boundless potential. When Andrew Grove was CEO of Intel, he claimed that knowledge will become "practically free and practically infinite" (Schlender, 1996).

This vast potential is even now making knowledge the focus of entire societies. The world in 2003 employed 1 billion PCs, mostly used by the knowledge workers who dominate modern economies. And their output of new ideas permits countless entrepreneurs to create IT products that spread knowledge more easily still. The result is a virtuous cycle in which knowledge spurs innovation, which spurs knowledge, which spurs innovation again, on and on endlessly. As the HP ads proclaim, "Everything is possible."

From Knowledge *Management* to Knowledge *Nurturing*

To realize this potential, a new approach is needed to design knowledge systems more effectively. Rather than struggle to *manage* this illusive resource, knowledge systems should be *intrinsically designed to create and guide knowledge toward productive use*. Think of it as a move from Knowledge *Management* to Knowledge *Nurturing* (KN). Gordon Petrash, CKO at Dow Chemical, said: "We will be successful when knowledge management is everyone's job."

Despite the management innovations of the nineties, most systems remain focused on managing rather than nurturing. One exception is the transformation of the U.S. Military to "network-centric, information warfare," which raised the accuracy of air strikes by a factor of 10, making the United States almost invincible militarily. Generally, however, much work is needed before the average organization can design systems to mine the wealth of entrepreneurial skill lying dormant at the bottom and the understanding of constituencies outside its walls (Halal, 1998b).

The examples cited throughout this chapter suggest that more sophisticated knowledge systems are being developed now. A recent study showed that entire supply chains, customer relations, and employee collaboration are going online, transforming organizations into total information systems co-managed by all stakeholders in real time (Halal, 2005).

It is estimated that the rapid adoption of broadband, wireless, smart phones, networks, utility computing, and more sophisticated computer interfaces involving speech recognition and AI are driving various forms of e-commerce into the economic mainstream. Over the next five to ten years, B2B, Etailing, telemedicine, virtual education, entertainment-on-demand, online publishing, and e-government are likely to reach the 30 percent adoption level. Most of these services now account for a scant 5 to 10 percent of their markets, but they should blossom into major new forces and proliferate into a rich and creative new economic sector.

This coming confluence of the e-organization and a wave of mobile, intelligent, interactive knowledge markets suggest a watershed in the way we think about IT and organizations. The old deterministic, top-down, mechanical systems seem to be splintering into an organic network better suited for the dynamic nature of modern economies. It's as though the power of IT and knowledge are laying the foundation for an intricate global web of collective intelligence, a central nervous system for intelligent organizations and societies (Halal, 1998c).

Like the human brain, this newly emerging form of social intelligence requires the self-organizing, bottom-up, parallel processing qualities found in nature. Web sites should not focus on handing down lofty pronouncements from above, akin to Moses descending from the mountain with the 12 commandments, but should create flexible structures that pool knowledge from the bottom and distribute it. Corporate Intranets should allow lots of user involvement, much like the Internet. Knowledge sharing may work best using true markets that buy and sell intellectual property. Support systems should be based on an entrepreneurial model in which each business unit is an internal enterprise. Rather than hunching over a keyboard, intelligent computer interfaces should simply talk to people in a convenient, conversational mode.

There are undoubtedly many other design features to be discovered, and, of course, the old top-down architectures will always play an important role organizing all of this. To cut through the confusion and uncertainty when planning agile knowledge systems, I think it would be wise to keep in mind the basic principles that govern the unique logic outlined earlier in this chapter. I suspect that the basic reason the Dot Com and KM booms failed is that they lost sight of these first principles.

References

Ackoff, R. (1994). The content of learning. *Unpublished paper,* Ackoff Center for Systems Analysis, University of Pennsylvania.

Arthur, B. W. (1996). Increasing returns and the new world of business. *Harvard Business Review,* 74 (4), 100–109.

Bennet, A. (1997). Knowledge, limits and reality. *Unpublished paper,* U.S. Navy Department.

Browne, J. and Prokesch, S. (1997). Unleashing the power of learning: An interview with British Petroleum's John Browne. *Harvard Business Review,* 75 (5), 147–168.

Conference Board. (1997). *Managing knowledge for business success. Conference Board Report.* New York City.

Halal, W. (1993). *Internal Markets: Bringing the power of free enterprise inside your organization.* New York: Wiley.

Halal, W. (1998a). *The Infinite Resource: Creating and leading the knowledge enterprise.* San Francisco: Jossey-Bass.

Halal, W. (1998b). *The New Management: A Guide to the Parallel Revolutions in Technology, Business, and Leadership.* San Francisco: Berrett-Koehler.

Halal, W. (1998c). Organizational intelligence. *Knowledge Management Review*, 1 (2), 45–53.

Halal, W. (2001). The collaborative enterprise: A Stakeholder Model Uniting Profitability and Responsibility. *Journal of Corporate Citizenship*, 1 (2), 27–42.

Halal, W. (2005). Institutional change. *On The Horizon*, 13 (1), 20–23.

Knowledge Management. 2001. "The Price of Knowledge" (August), 31–36.

Leonard, D. (2001). An organic learning system at chaparral steel. *Knowledge Management Review*, 3 (4), 24–29.

Manville, B. (1999). A complex, adaptive approach to KM. *Knowledge Management Review,* 2 (3), 33–39.

Negroponte, N. (1995). *Being Digital.* New York: Knopf.

Schlender, B. (1996). A conversation with the lords of Wintel. *Fortune,* 134 (1), July 8, 1996.

Wright, P. (1998). Do incentive schemes promote knowledge sharing? *Knowledge Management Review*, 1 (3), 4–6.

Producing and Consuming Agility

4

Anders Mårtensson

In the last few years, the concept of agility has become popular. The "agile enterprise" has rapidly become something to strive for. Business agility has been defined as "the capacity to anticipate changing market dynamics, adapt to those dynamics and accelerate enterprise change faster than the rate of change in the market, to create economic value" (Melarkode, From-Poulsen, and Warnakulasuriya, 2004, p. 46). Sambamurthy, Bharadwaj, and Grover (2003) define agility as "the ability to detect and seize market opportunities with speed and surprise" (p. 238).

These definitions (and others) of agility bring a time perspective—agility is about "change faster" or "speed and surprise." Thus, acting agilely is about doing things in the short run, such as responding to changing market conditions. This chapter will discuss the long-term aspects of agility, or agile Information Systems (IS). How do companies prepare in order to be able to act agilely? What are the long-term consequences when a company acts agilely?

Business agility has many sources, one of them being the agility of the Information Technology (IT) portfolio of the company. On a general level, there is abundant support that information system capabilities are translated into business capabilities (e.g., Piccoli and Ives, 2005; Ray, Muhanna, and Barney, 2005). Furthermore, it is quite well-established that agile information systems contribute to business agility (e.g., Weill, Subramani, and Broadbent, 2002; Ahsan and Ye-Ngo, 2005). Sambamurthy, Bharadwaj, and Grover (2003) state that IT "can be an enabler of agility by virtue of the differences between digital economics and the (traditional) economics of physical components" (p. 243).

So, business agility is good and agile information systems can contribute to such agility. The natural questions then become, what is information systems agility and can it be acquired? This chapter will primarily deal with the latter of these questions, even though initially the concept of information systems agility will be discussed. The chapter will then move on to discuss where such agility comes from, i.e., how it can be produced. It will then analyze how agility is used or consumed in different ways.

By providing insights into the "agility life cycle" this chapter aims at increasing our understanding of the mechanisms that lead organizations to have varying levels of IS agility. Applying a life cycle approach to IS agility is in line with Sambamurthy,

Bharadwaj, and Grover (2003) who identify two strategic processes for leveraging IT for competitive advantage: capacity-building and entrepreneurial action processes. In this chapter, the two corresponding processes are producing and consuming agility.

What Is Agility?

This chapter takes on a resource-based view (Barney, 1991). This means that IS agility is considered a capability that companies can possess to a varying extent—the capability of acting agilely. It is important not to equate agility, or agile information systems, with flexibility, or flexible information systems. The concepts are related, but different.

Given the assumption that flexibility is (positively) correlated with complexity, a Laffer type curve can be constructed illustrating the relationship between agility and flexibility/complexity on a conceptual level (Figure 4.1). With no flexibility, there will be no agility, while with excessive flexibility, and thus excessive complexity, agility will also decline. The reason for this decline is that the flexibility (with its associated complexity) becomes hard to actually use. In this sense, agility can be seen as flexibility in use.

Contrasting Agile Action

Previous research has studied resource allocation efforts and categorized such effort in the matrix, as shown in Figure 4.2 (Mårtensson, 2006). This matrix uses two dimensions to categorize efforts within a company: time perspective and the type of goal expressed as pursuing opportunities or meeting obligations. This renders four different kinds of efforts, or projects, labeled agile action, firefighting, business transformation, and platform construction.

Agile action, or pursuing opportunities in a short-term perspective, means taking advantage of some opportunity while it lasts. Doing this in most cases requires having flexible and well-maintained IT solutions in the first place (Duncan, 1995). Such flexible solutions can either be having a well-maintained infrastructure or application portfolio in place or having a tradition of rapidly acquiring standard packages to pursue different business opportunities identified by the company.

Firefighting, or short-term projects to meet some obligation, is typically undertaken to solve technical problems reactively or fend off business threats. Firefights

Figure 4.1

Relating Agility, Flexibility, and Complexity

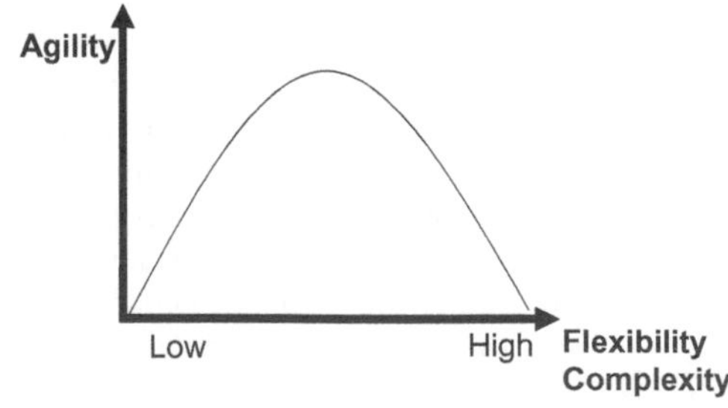

Figure 4.2

The Resource Allocation Matrix

	Short-term Perspective	**Long-term Perspective**
Pursuing Opportunities	Draw on existing flexibility *Agile action*	Technology-driven business development *Business transformation*
Meeting Obligations	React to everyday problems *Firefighting*	Well-planned orderly upgrade projects *Platform construction*

are often coupled with some sense of urgency. A typical firefighting issue could for instance be stability problems with a mission-critical Web site solution.

Business transformation, proactively pursuing long-term business opportunities, means that some business is transformed, either on a company or industry level. A company spinning off a software provider transforms its own business. It does not, however, transform the way business is done within the industry. A company may also undertake efforts that to some extent transform how business is done within the industry. Such efforts transform both the industry and, naturally, the company's own business. One example of business transformation is the Internet stock brokerages that transformed the traditional stock brokerage industry.

Platform construction, the long-term perspective on meeting obligations, refers to proactive projects that aim at creating a viable platform or infrastructure, essentially dissolving problems rather than solving them. By being well prepared in the long-term perspective, at least some future problems can be avoided. Examples can be updating a Web site and its structure in anticipation of increasing traffic, or replacing an existing legacy system with a more modern and adequate platform. Reddy and Reddy (2002) discuss legacy information systems and competitive agility.

It is important to note that a given project or activity obviously can cover more than one of these categories. Also, short-term efforts will build and shape the realized IT portfolio of a company, i.e., a portfolio will emerge in the absence of explicit platform construction efforts. If nothing else, a company's portfolio will be the aggregated consequences of the short-term activities that have been undertaken.

Characterizing Agility

One can be agile in different ways. Three different ways of acting agilely are by being versatile, by reconfiguration, and by reconstruction (cf. Mårtensson and Steneskog, 1996).

- Being versatile implies that an information system is flexible enough to cope with changing conditions as it is currently set up.

Table 4.1

Examples of Agility Characterization			
	Application	Portfolio	Network
Versatility	Use existing variety	Use existing variety	Use existing variety
Reconfiguration	Change parameters	Rearrange applications	Source activities differently between the companies
Reconstruction	Develop new functionality	Acquire new applications	Introduce (and/or remove) companies into network

- If current solutions are not versatile enough, reconfiguration will be needed. This can be interpreted as pent-up agility being released by a new configuration. In this case, the functionality scope that is available using a different configuration is agile enough for the new conditions.
- If reconfiguration is not enough, the information system must be reconstructed, i.e., changes or additions have to be made to it.

Moving beyond the individual application instance, the same logic can be applied also to the application portfolio within the company. In this case, versatility keeps its interpretation from above, while reconfiguration deals not with the individual application but instead with having the applications within the portfolio interact in a different way. In a similar fashion, reconstruction would imply reconstructing the portfolio, e.g., by replacing or adding an application within the portfolio. See Table 4.1 for examples of agility characterization.

Furthermore, the analogy can be extended beyond the application portfolio of a company to an interorganizational setting (see Morgan, 2004, for a discussion on inter-organizational agility). In such a setting, reconfiguration and reconstruction by analogy would refer to changing the role and contribution of different companies (reconfiguration) or changing what companies are included in the setting (reconstruction).

How Is Agility Produced?

Given that agility is an attractive property of a company's capabilities, it is now time to address the question of how it can be created. How does a company become agile? Agility has previously been discussed based on a framework of capability-building processes and entrepreneurial action processes (Sambamurthy, Bharadwaj, and Grover, 2003). Differentiating between capability-building and subsequent action is closely related to the idea of producing and consuming agility.

Thus, the level of agility at a company can be interpreted as the result of an agility production process to which resources are allocated (explicitly or implicitly), as shown in Figure 4.3. Given a production view on agility, the first question comes naturally, namely where does agility come from?

Where Does Agility Come From?

This is the first major question to be dealt with when discussing agility production. Why are certain companies (or with more of an IS perspective, certain application portfolios) more agile than others?

Figure 4.3

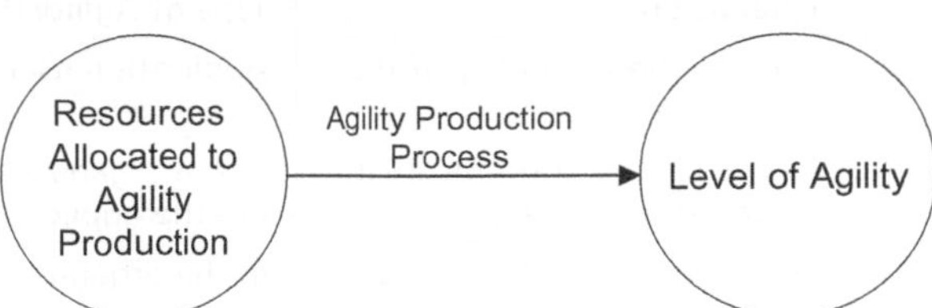

Using the framework presented above, it could be argued that using versatility to cope with changing conditions is more agile than having to use reconfiguration, which in turn is more agile than having to resort to reconstruction (Figure 4.4).

To produce agility then becomes a matter of increasing one's ability to cope with change by versatility, or possibly reconfiguration. It is important to keep in mind that this is not a question of information systems as such. Rather, it is about a company's ability to cope with changing conditions, implying a broader perspective (including not only information systems, but also organizational capabilities to use systems) in order to address the needs of some (internal or external) customer.

This can be interpreted in terms of the resource allocation matrix presented above in Figure 4.3. Platform construction is without a doubt the type of activity most prominently related to determining the capabilities of applications or application portfolios. Business transformation can be about increasing the level of agility if the transformation itself has to do with becoming more agile. Agile action is typically not about producing agility, but rather consuming it as will be discussed below. Firefighting has a more complex relation to the concept of agility. On one hand, it can be about producing badly needed agility, i.e., a hasty project to reconstruct or reconfigure existing solutions in order to accommodate new conditions. It can also consume agility as discussed below.

Thus, one important source of agility is the platform construction project, where application capabilities can be constructed that will allow coping with changing conditions using versatility, or potentially reconfiguration. However, as noted above, agility is not about flexibility alone. There are many ways of making solutions more agile as illustrated in Table 4.2.

Documentation refers both to documents that describe what functionality actually exists in an application or set of applications and to documents that increase the maintainability of the code base. Obviously, for in-house solutions this is done by the company, while for standard packages base documentation is delivered by the software

Figure 4.4

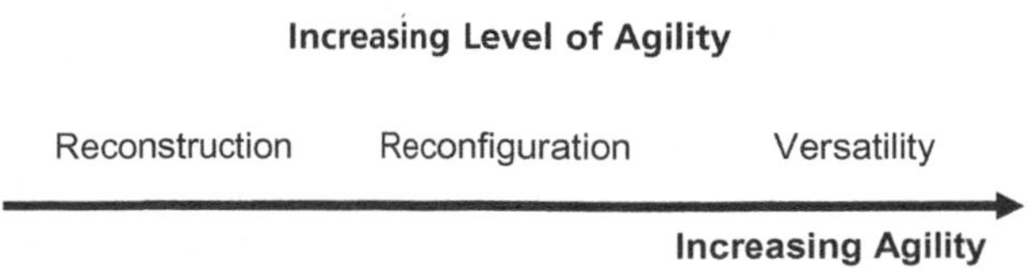

Table 4.2

Illustrating Ways of Producing Agility		
Example	**Explanation**	**Type of Agility Produced**
Adding flexibility	Increases the versatility of the application	Application itself
Improved documentation	Ensures that existing flexibility can be properly used	In the organization's ability to use the application
Improved testing capabilities	Ensures that reconfiguration and reconstruction can be done effectively	In the organization's ability to reconstruct the application

provider, even though company-internal documentation can be expected concerning deployment issues, appropriate usage, and so on.

Agility can also be increased by having proficient test tools making reconfiguration and reconstruction viable alternatives. In the absence of proper testing, making changes to existing setups is difficult, which will reduce agility. Developing a testing infrastructure is a good example of a platform construction project as described above. There are no direct benefits, but instead there are second order benefits in terms of better or cheaper testing in projects to come.

How Much Agility Is Needed?

Given that agility can be produced by for instance increasing application or organizational flexibility, a relevant question becomes how agile one should be. As always, when a property with positive connotations comes along, an easy but not overly insightful answer is "the more, the merrier."

First of all, there is no one absolute "right" level of agility. As is well-established within contingency theory, organizations must vary in order to cope with changing environments (e.g., Burns and Stalker, 1961; Lawrence and Lorsch, 1967). Some fifty years ago, Ashby formalized his law of requisite variety (Ashby, 1956), which basically states that "the variety within a system must be at least as great as the environmental variety against which it is attempting to regulate itself." In our case, this means that how much agility companies need will vary across companies, which is not all that surprising. The law of requisite variety also adds that a specific company will need enough agility to meet the variety in its environment. From a technology investment perspective, Weill and Broadbent (1998) note that "if a firm's strategy is different from those of its competitors, its information technology portfolio must also be different" (p. 30), which implies that different strategies will require different levels of agility.

Furthermore, producing agility requires an effort. The "cost" of producing a certain "amount" of agility, however, can vary significantly. A good design, for instance, does not necessarily involve more work than a bad one. To the extent that agility stems from good design, one could argue that the agility comes quite effortlessly. This, however, is typically not the norm.

Agility may be even more elusive than the eternal challenge of evaluating infrastructure projects, where at least costs can be properly estimated even though the benefits are difficult to calculate. A proper estimate of the production cost of agility would be to compare the cost added to a project in order to make the resulting solution more agile compared to some base case. In an information system setting, this would typically consist of adding flexibility to the solution or spending extra resources on properly documenting the solution.

Given that agility does not come for free, the optimum level of agility is when the company has exactly the agility needed to cope with the variety of its environment. Translating this theoretical statement into managerial implications is, however, non-trivial. The resource allocation matrix can be used to monitor the resource allocation concerning IT resources and thus provide some practical guidelines. Since there is no generically optimal allocation rule governing how resources should be divided among the different kinds of activities, the terms *overspending* and *underspending* are used in a relative sense. Both overspending and underspending on any type of initiative may evoke concerns as illustrated in Table 4.3 (see also Mårtensson, 2006). On a similar note as underspending, Weill, Subramani, and Broadbent (2002) note that "underinvesting reduces strategic agility and slows time to market" (p. 64).

Providing clearcut answers to these questions are in many cases next to impossible. They are, however, still useful as catalysts for discussion and to illustrate differences in opinion between different parties.

How Is Agility Consumed?

Turning to how agility is used, or consumed, it is useful to think in terms of the different economics of digital information and "traditional" goods where the concepts of "economy of information" and "economy of things" are sometimes used. "Economy

Table 4.3

Concerns with Overspending and Underspending		
Purpose	**Concerns with Overspending**	**Concerns with Underspending**
Firefighting	How did the company end up fighting fires? Is all the firefighting indicating lack of agility?	Are there fires not yet identified? Is the company excessively agile?
Agile action	Is the focus on reaping the rewards of yesterday's investments? Would more agility reduce these costs?	Are business opportunities lost? Is the company excessively agile?
Platform construction	Can viable business cases be presented for the resources spent on platform construction? Is too much spent on becoming agile?	Will there be nothing but firefights in the future? Will there be enough agility in the long run?
Business transformation	Are short-run issues sufficiently well catered for? Will the transformation be commercially viable?	Will the company be overrun? Will the industry change and make the company and its market offering obsolete?

of things" refers to normal goods, with traditional economic properties such as non-zero marginal production cost. "Economy of information" refers to digital information with well-known properties such as (practically) zero marginal production cost (e.g., Evans and Wurster, 2000).

Given the fact that an organization can "produce" agility, an interesting question then becomes whether agility abides by the economy of atoms or bits. Put more explicitly, if an organization has achieved a certain level of agility, will this agility be used up (atoms) or can it be endlessly copied (bits)?

Relating to Figure 4.5, a certain level of agility can be produced and be available when seizing business opportunities. Agility can then be consumed in various projects. When a business development effort is undertaken, the level of agility will affect this effort. A reasonable hypothesis is that a high level of agility will reduce the scope of the business development project. Similarly, a lack of agility will increase the scope of the business development project.

When moving on to discuss agility consumption, the difference lies in the strength of the negative feedback loop illustrated in Figure 4.5. The strength of this feedback indicates how much the company's agility is reduced by the business development effort. Put in another way, if this feedback is strongly negative, it is a costly form of agility compared to usage scenarios in which the negative feedback is smaller and the agility in a sense "costless." Of course, it would potentially be conceivable to have a positive feedback where the level of agility is increased as agility is consumed in the business development effort. More often than not, this feedback will, however, be negative.

Thus, in many situations, agility is reduced when consumed; the necessary agility is achieved, but at the cost of reduced future agility. Future agility can be reduced by the current change, reducing future options in how to use an application or having future

Figure 4.5

Relating Agility and Business Development

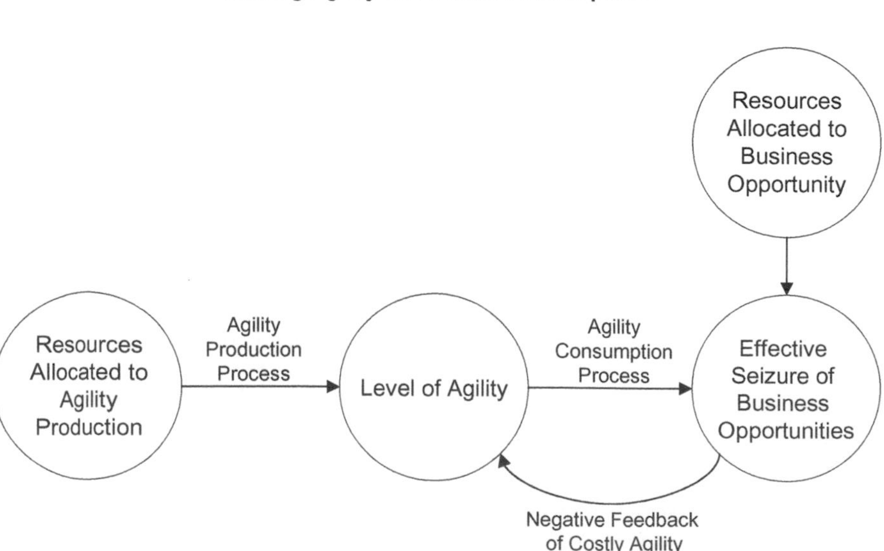

reconstruction efforts be more complicated, since there will be one more piece of existing functionality to consider when making changes. Future agility can also be indirectly reduced by, for instance, increasing maintenance costs, which in turn reduces the organization's ability to respond to new challenges. If the usage of the application in question becomes more complex, so will its maintenance. Increased maintenance costs will, in turn, put strains on available resources, making future changes harder to fit into existing budgets.

One example of costly agility is a brokerage firm that built an application to support the production of analyst reports by using advanced automation tools in their word processors, spreadsheets, and databases (Mårtensson, 2003). The capabilities of their tools and the skills of the analysts enabled an agile solution to the problem of easily populated analyst reports with already existing data. The research generator application was developed quite rapidly and was continually improved until it met the analysts' requirements.

The research generator, which was very successful, called for very strict standardization (on the level of printer drivers, for example). In terms of agility, it did, however, have some important implications. On one level, the office automation tools could, of course, continue to be used for whatever purpose, i.e., the analyst report support did not hamper the general use of the office automation tools. However, since the generator was quite fragile in the sense that it depended on a strictly standardized environment, it significantly reduced the agility to adopt new and enhanced office automation tools. When the rest of the brokerage firm upgraded to a new version, the research department was stuck with the old version since porting the application was quite complicated and thus expensive. This was troublesome, especially since the new version was not backward compatible. In fact, some analysts used two separate computers, one with the old version running the report generator and one with the new version for the rest of their work.

This report generator is merely one example of a project making use of the agility that is available to it, but while doing this also reduces future agility. The cost in terms of reduced future agility are often very difficult, if not impossible, to estimate even if one is aware of them. This difficulty should not, however, be used as an excuse for not considering them at all. If hard estimates are not possible, a qualitative analysis of the consequences of using existing agility is the least one can do.

In contrast with this costly agility, costless agility is also conceivable, i.e., agility that follows the economy of bits and is endlessly reproducible. It refers to situations in which agile action can be taken without adverse effects. The key issue is whether or not applying this agility to the problem at hand will reduce future agility by, for instance, reducing future versatility or increasing maintenance complexity. Similarly, if the agility is achieved by reconfiguration, what will be the future consequences of this reconfiguration?

Agility that stems from how information systems are used, and not from the system as such, is more likely to be costless. This relates to the fact that adding flexibility to an application tends to be quite difficult. To the extent that information systems as such can provide costless agility, infrastructure services would be the typical example, where existing infrastructures can cope with new applications without future agility being reduced. A current example of this is public Internet and telephony where companies such as Skype deliver a new service drawing on the capabilities of the public Internet and using its agility. Such services are, however, hardly detrimental to the future agility of the Internet, thus the negative feedback indicated in Figure 4.5 is quite weak.

Discussion

From an agility production perspective, it can be considered what options on future actions are exercised when a project is undertaken, and what options are potentially created. It can be concluded that such options will be necessary and what differs is the manner in which they are produced. If projects continuously make sure that the organization's agility is maintained, or even increased, such incremental efforts will together build the agility of the organization. The other approach to creating reasonable agility is to undertake larger-scale platform construction projects, i.e., specific renovation and/or construction projects, in which producing agility is a goal in itself, as illustrated in Figure 4.6.

From an agility consumption perspective, it seems better, all else equal, to avoid reducing one's future agility. The natural question then becomes how this can be done. Distinguishing between an application and its usage can provide parts of this answer. Agility stemming from an organization's ability to use an application in an agile way is less likely to reduce future agility than agility stemming from functionality inherent in the application. In fact, such organizational agility is probably the one area where the feedback loop in Figure 4.5 above can be expected to be positive since using, or consuming, organizational agility can be expected to have learning consequences, for example.

Concluding Remarks

The perspective chosen in this chapter emphasizes agility as a scarce resource. As such, it does not come for free, but has to be more or less diligently produced. In any project or effort, there is an important balance to be struck between consuming agility, i.e., to reap the benefits from the organization's capabilities, and producing agility, i.e., to sow the capabilities to be reaped later.

Apart from presenting a framework to manage agility from a life cycle perspective, this chapter presents two main conclusions:

- In every business development project, organizations should strive to make diligent trade-offs between agility production and agility consumption. To what extent should individual business development projects be allowed to reduce the agility level? To what extent should they contribute to the future level of agility?

Figure 4.6

Continuous versus Discrete Agility Production

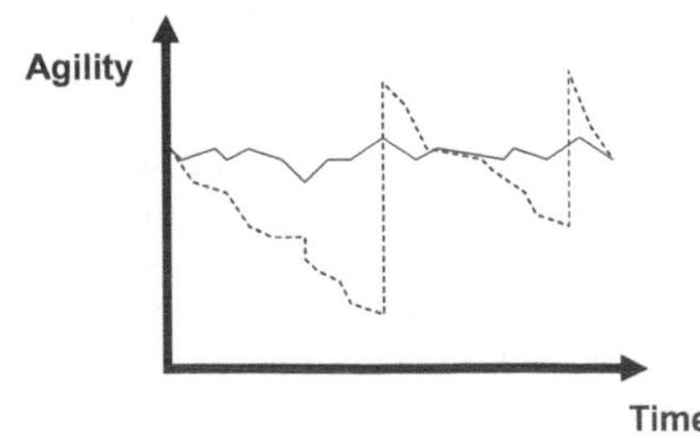

- Concerning agility consumption, organizational agility is often more likely to abide by the economy of bits than IS agility. This emphasizes the distinction between an application and its usage and also the importance of both building an agile organization in order to increase the level of agility when using information systems.

A final remark is that agility is by no means a panacea for traditional management challenges; instead, these challenges are more than likely to apply also when managing agility.

References

Ahsan, M. and Ye-Ngo, L. (2005). The relationship between IT infrastructure and strategic agility in organizations. In *Proceedings of the Eleventh Americas Conference on Information Systems* (N. C. Romano, Jr., ed.), Omaha, NE.

Ashby, W. R. (1956). *An introduction to cybernetics.* London, UK: Chapman & Hall.

Barney, J. (1991). Firm resources and sustained competitive advantage. *Journal of Management*, 17 (1), 99–120.

Burns, T. and Stalker, G. M. (1961). *The Management of Innovation.* London, UK: Tavistock.

Duncan, N. B. (1995). Capturing flexibility of information technology infrastructure: A study of resources characteristics and their measure. *Journal of Management Information Systems*, 12 (2), 37–57.

Evans, P. and Wurster, T. S. (2000). *Blown to Bits: How the New Economics of Information Transforms Strategy.* Boston: Harvard Business School Press.

Lawrence, P. R. and Lorsch, J. W. (1967). Differentiation and integration in complex organizations. *Administrative Science Quarterly*, 12 (1), 1–47.

Mårtensson, A. (2003). *Managing Mission-critical IT in the Financial Industry.* Stockholm, Sweden: Economic Research Institute (EFI).

Mårtensson, A. (2006). A resource allocation matrix approach to IT management. *Information Technology and Management*, 7 (1), 21–34.

Mårtensson, A. and Steneskog, G. (1996). Business process excellence—Some characteristics. In *Advancing your business—People and information systems in concert* (M. Lundeberg and B. Sundgren, eds.). Stockholm, Sweden: Economic Research Institute (EFI).

Melarkode, A., From-Poulsen, M., and Warnakulasuriya S. (2004). Delivering agility through IT. *Business Strategy Review*, 15, 45–50.

Morgan, R. (2004). Agile business relationships and technology. *Journal of General Management*, 29 (4), 77–92.

Piccoli, G. and Ives, B. (2005). IT-dependent strategic initiatives and sustained competitive advantage: A review and synthesis of the literature. *MIS Quarterly*, 29 (4), 747–776.

Ray, G., Muhanna, W., and Barney, J. (2005). Information technology and the performance of the customer service process: A resource-based analysis. *MIS Quarterly*, 29 (4), 625–652.

Reddy, S. and Reddy, R. (2002). Competitive agility and the challenge of legacy information systems. *Industrial Management + Data Systems*, 102 (1/2), 5–16.

Sambamurthy, V., Bharadwaj, A., and Grover, V. (2003). Shaping agility through digital options: Reconceptualizing the role of information technology in contemporary firms. *MIS Quarterly*, 27 (2), 237–263.

Weill, P. and Broadbent, M. (1998). *Leveraging the New Infrastructure: How Market Leaders Capitalize on Information Technology.* Boston, MA: Harvard Business School Press.

Weill, P., Subramani, M., and Broadbent, M. (2002). Building IT infrastructure for strategic agility. *MIT Sloan Management Review*, 44 (1), 57–65.

5

Business Agility: Need, Readiness and Alignment with IT Strategies[1]

Marcel van Oosterhout, Eric Waarts, Eric van Heck, and Jos van Hillegersberg

The concept of agility originated at the end of the eighties and in the early nineties in the manufacturing area in the United States. Agile Manufacturing was first introduced with the publication of a report entitled 21st Century Manufacturing Enterprise Strategy (Goldman et al., 1991). This was followed by a series of publications on agile manufacturing and agile corporations (Kidd, 1994; Kidd, 1995; Goldman, Nagel, and Preiss, 1995; Dove, 2001). The concept was extended to supply chains and business networks (Christopher, 1992; Mason-Jones and Towill, 1999; Van Hoek, Harrison, and Christopher, 2001; Swafford, 2003; Yusuf, Gunasekaran, Adeleye, and Sivayoganathan, 2004).

Despite the history of the concept, there is by far no consensus yet as to what exactly agility is. Nor is there a consensus on how one could assess and achieve agility (Schrage, 2004). Very few studies have attempted to empirically study the need for agility. What are the contributing factors requiring organizations to be agile, and what is the relative importance of these factors? Furthermore, which of these factors are related to Information Technology (IT) and how does IT enable or hinder the required level of agility?

The central question of this chapter is: *What are the contributing factors that require business agility, and what IT strategies can be implemented for enhancing business agility*? The sub-questions are:

- How can we define the concept of business agility?
- Do change factors that create a high business agility need to be generic or sector-specific?
- Is there a difference between various industry sectors on the perceived business agility readiness?

- Are there differences between three domains of business agility (operational, customer, and network) with regard to the need for business agility and the perceived readiness of organizations?
- Which IT strategies can be defined for enhancing business agility, depending on the business agility need and business agility readiness level?

Business Agility

Even though much has been said and written on agility, a consensus on a definition of agility has not yet emerged. Wadhwa and Rao (2003) describe the differences and overlap between flexibility and agility. Flexibility is defined as a predetermined response to a predictable change, while agility entails an innovative response to an unpredictable change. Flexibility is focused on single systems for low to medium rates of change, while agility is focused on groups of systems to deal with high rates of change. A variety of views on business agility can be found in the literature (Goldman et al., 1995; Sharifi and Zhang, 1999; Dove, 2001; Hooper et al., 2001; Ramasesh et al., 2001; Conboy and Fitzgerald, 2004). The definitions provide some common aspects.

Agility is a way to cope with external and internal changes, which are highly uncertain. Three types of perceived uncertainty can be distinguished: state uncertainty, effect uncertainty, and response uncertainty (Milliken, 1987). State uncertainty relates to unpredictability about whether or when a certain change will happen. Effect uncertainty relates to the inability to predict what the nature of the impact (i.e., effects) of a change will be on the organization. Some changes are quite predictable (e.g., deregulation in the telecom and energy sector); however, often the speed and exact requirements to the organization and processes are quite uncertain. Response uncertainty is defined as a lack of knowledge of response options and/or an inability to predict the likely consequences of a response choice.

Business agility can be implemented either proactively (leading or initiating a change—placing organizations in a leadership position) or reactively (responding to change, either opportunistic or degenerative, in order to retain competitiveness) (Canter, 2000). Dove (2001) highlights the importance of both sensing capabilities (detecting, anticipating) and responding capabilities (physical ability to act rapidly and with relative ease) (Dove, 2001). The concept of quickness and therefore speed is at the heart of agility—it is the capability of an organization to rapidly execute decision-making and operational cycles (Canter, 2000). Speed can be required in various areas, like time to market new products, time to process an order or service request, time to assemble a virtual business network for collaboration, time to reconfigure organizational processes and systems to react to certain changes, and so on.

Sambamurthy, Bharadwaj, and Grover (2003) distinguish three interrelated capabilities of agility: operational agility, customer agility, and partnering agility. For each capability, they describe the role and impact of IT. This distinction is in line with types of strategic agility as defined by Weill, Subramani, and Broadbent (2002), who make a distinction between business initiatives aimed at increasing strategic agility based on their position on the value net: demand-side initiatives (customer agility), supply-side initiatives (partnering agility) and internally focused initiatives (operational agility).

Taking all of the above considerations into account, the definition of business agility in this study will be:

> *Business agility is the ability to sense highly uncertain external and internal changes, and respond to them reactively or proactively, based on innovation of the*

internal operational processes, involving the customer in exploration and exploitation activities, while leveraging the capabilities of partners in the business network.

An Agility Framework

Building on the work by Sharifi and Zhang (1999) we constructed a framework to analyze business agility in detail (Figure 5.1).

The starting point of our model is the contributing factors, which are external and internal changes that can create a need for business agility (based on Sharifi and Zhang, 1999). In this chapter, we focus on the analyses of change factors, where a required response of the organization is related, directly or indirectly, to the organization's IT capability.

An organization's business agility readiness is determined by its business agility capabilities. Business agility capabilities are the means or barriers for a business to enhance its business agility. Business agility capabilities can be categorized based on the work of Sambamurthy, Bharadwaj, and Grover (2003) and Weill, Subramani, and Broadbent (2002). The business agility capabilities are the reasons behind the existence or nonexistence of agility gaps. If there is a mismatch between the businesses agility need and the business agility readiness, there is a business agility gap. This has implications for the business agility IT strategy.

In this chapter, we will report on the perceived business agility need (BAN) and the perceived business agility readiness (BAR) for external and internal change factors that are directly or indirectly related to the organization's IT. We will also discuss implications for business agility IT strategies to close the business agility gap (BAG).

Methodology

Based on the literature review, we constructed a questionnaire. We used feedback from experts and two workshops to test and improve the questionnaire. We chose to use multiple methods for data gathering in order to provide a rich description on the

Figure 5.1

Conceptual Framework*

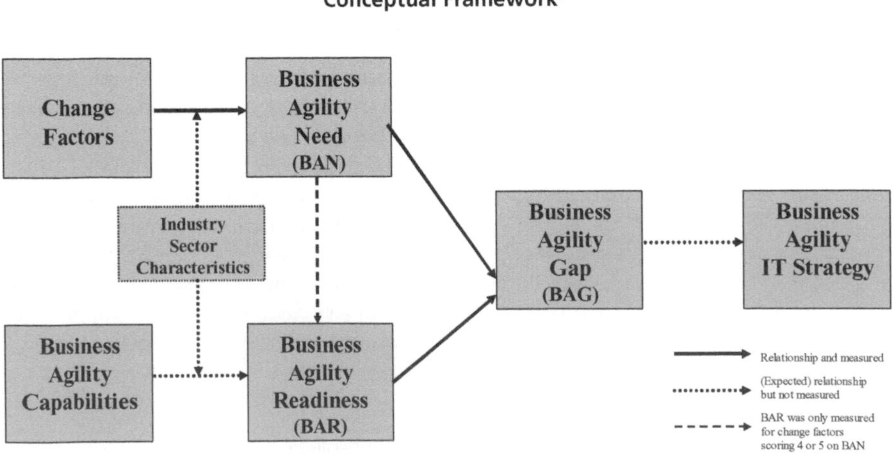

*** Adapted from Sharifi and Zhang, 1999.**

topic. We gathered quantitative data via an online questionnaire (110 respondents). This was complemented with in-depth qualitative data, gathered via interviews with 50 managers and workshop discussions. The results were validated by interviews with 14 sector experts.

Based on literature research and workshops with experts, we constructed a questionnaire containing 27 change factors, covering the three agility capabilities of our framework: factors requiring operational agility, factors requiring customer agility, and factors requiring business network and partnering agility. An overview of these change factors can be found in Table 5.1.[2]

Each change factor in the survey had to be scored on a Likert-5 scale. If the perceived BAN due to a certain change factor was high (score 4 or 5), a second question was posed regarding the perceived BAR (also on a Likert-5 scale). The BAG was measured as BAN minus BAR. In the next part of the questionnaire for the 10 change factors with the highest BAG score of the respondent, open questions were generated. For each BAG, the respondent was asked to elaborate on the bottleneck(s) and measures in the required business agility capabilities to deal with the BAG. This way, the questionnaire generated both quantitative as well as qualitative data on agility capabilities as enablers or disablers. We did a cross-check on possible survey fatigue which might bias our results. We found no difference in the variance of answers between the first half of the survey with the second half. Furthermore, we checked the number of responses to individual items in the second half of the questionnaire and compared it with the first half.

For the interviews with managers within each sector, a sample of organizations was selected. Criteria to select organizations were their position in the market (in the business sectors top market share players with considerable size). Within each organization, at least two managers were asked to fill out the survey, as a basis for the in-depth interviews. One interview was held to cover the general business or policy perspective (mainly with CEOs, marketing executives, and general managers) and one to cover the operations and IT perspective (mainly with COOs, CIOs, and CTOs). The average duration of the interview was 90 to 120 minutes. Basis for the interviews were the perceived agility gaps identified by the respondents in the survey. From each interview, minutes were taken and checked for accuracy with the interviewee.

We chose to study four business sectors and three public sectors in the Netherlands:

- Logistics (logistics service providers)
- Finance (retail banking)
- Utilities (distribution and sales of energy)
- Mobile telecom (mobile telecom operators)
- Central government (Dutch ministries)
- Higher education institutes
- Other public sectors (operational authorities such as tax authorities, local authorities, etc.)

These sectors constitute an important segment of the total Dutch business and public sector. Furthermore, these sectors are confronted with a wide variety of external and internal change factors, such as regulations, shifts in customer demands, reorganizations, and changes in IT.

[2] A copy of the full questionnaire can be obtained from the researchers.

Table 5.1

Business Agility Change Factor Scores					
Change Factors	**Absolute scores (Scale from 1 to 5)**			**Variance (Max-min score over 7 sectors)**	
Capability 1: Operational	**BAN**	**BAR**	**BAG**	**BAN variance**	**BAR variance**
1) Growing demand for financial transparency and accountability (Basel-2, IAS etc.)	3.40	2.93	0.47	1.80	0.72
2) New regulation at the national level	3.49	3.00	0.49	1.30	2.00
3) New security measures/IS security	3.35	2.42	0.93	1.10	1.00
4) Increased outsourcing of noncore business activities*	3.05	2.79	0.26	0.50	2.33
5) Increased outsourcing of IT-related systems and personnel*	3.28	2.83	0.45	0.80	1.10
6) Emerging price war (market focused on price)/shrinking margins	4.06	1.94	2.12	1.45	1.20
7) Need for lower-priced services	3.32	2.43	0.89	1.50	1.33
8) Changing requirements take too long to implement into the organization and systems*	3.30	2.01	1.29	1.26	1.62
9) Major organizational change (e.g., merger, acquisition)*	3.34	2.34	1.00	1.31	1.00
10) Digitalization of documents and e-signatures*	2.79	2.49	0.30	1.09	1.25
11) Increasing time and money spent on maintenance and support of existing IT infrastructure*	3.25	2.17	1.08	0.70	1.90
12) Desire to increase the levels of expertise of employees*	2.59	2.12	0.47	0.67	1.17
13) Reorganization of internal processes*	3.49	2.65	0.84	0.48	0.04

Capability 2: Customer	**BAN**	**BAR**	**BAG**	**BAN variance**	**BAR variance**
14) Shortening of competitors' time to market of new products and services	3.00	2.20	0.80	1.40	0.50
15) Decreasing loyalty of customers	3.18	2.46	0.72	1.97	1.70
16) Need to decrease delivery time of services toward customers	3.23	2.43	0.80	2.50	2.00
17) Need for (more) online facilities toward customers	3.50	2.98	0.52	1.53	0.91
18) Need for more customized/tailored services toward customers	3.30	2.65	0.65	0.63	1.93
19) Need for multichannel anytime anyplace access to information and services by customers	3.33	2.63	0.70	1.50	1.21
20) Need for quicker response to customer-service requests	3.62	2.75	0.87	1.50	0.83
21) Emerging technologies to easily connect to customers' information systems	3.45	2.20	1.25	1.10	1.10
Capability 3: Business Network and Partnering	**BAN**	**BAR**	**BAG**	**BAN variance**	**BAR variance**
22) Increasing number of partnerships	3.08	2.83	0.25	1.20	1.50
23) Complexity in processes due to increasing number of interdependencies with services of other organizational units	3.34	2.55	0.79	1.10	0.79
24) Information sharing in the network	3.40	2.91	0.49	1.20	1.47
25) Need for structured information exchange with other organizations/integration with systems of partners in network	3.25	2.72	0.53	2.60	1.90
26) Need for easier switching between suppliers of products and services	3.58	2.73	0.85	1.30	0.70
27) Accelerating rate of innovation of product technology	2.70	2.35	0.35	1.70	0.70
*Internal change factors are marked with an asterisk.	***3.28***	***2.54***	**0.75**		

Findings

We will present three types of findings. First, we will present an overview of the average scores on BAN, BAR, and BAG per sector and per dimension of business agility. Next, we will compare the public sectors with the business sectors on BAN, BAR, and BAG. Finally, we will analyze the importance of individual change factors per dimension of business agility.

Overall Differences between Sectors

Table 5.2 compares the seven sectors on BAN, BAR, and BAG per dimension of business agility. When we look at the overall BAN scores, logistics has the highest BAN (3.63) on all three dimensions. The lowest BAN is found in the education sector for the operational dimension (3.17), in the energy sector on the customer dimension (2.91), and in the finance sector on the network dimension (2.85).

When we look at the overall BAR scores, the energy sector has the lowest BAR on the operational dimension (2.08) and the customer dimension (1.91), while the lowest BAR is found in the other public sector on the network dimension (2.42). The highest BAR is found in the telecom sector on the operational dimension (2.91), in the government sector on the customer dimension (3.15), and in the logistics sector on the network dimension (3.07).

When we look at the overall BAG scores, the highest scores are found in the logistics (1.08) and energy (0.96) sectors, and on the operational (0.81) and customer (0.79) dimensions. On the operational dimension, the highest BAG scores are found within the logistics (1.33) and energy (1.21) sectors, on the customer dimension in the energy (1.00) and finance (0.96) sectors, and on the network dimension in the other public sector (1.15).

Public versus Business

When we compare the three public sectors with the four business sectors on BAN, BAR, and BAG, we find a few differences. BAN is about the same within public and business, only BAN on the business network dimension scores higher in public (3.41) compared to business (3.19). BAR is higher in public on the operational and customer dimensions, but slightly lower on the business network dimension. These differences are also found when we compare the BAG scores. Overall BAG scores within public are lower compared to business, with the exception of the average BAG score on the business network dimension, which is considerably larger within public (0.81) compared to business (0.51).

Importance of Individual Change Factors and the Role of IT

An analysis of the individual change factors will further clarify the differences between the seven sectors on changes which are related to the three dimensions of business agility. Table 5.1 presents the average scores on the 27 IT-related change factors on BAN, BAR, and BAG. Furthermore, we have included the variance between the seven sectors analyzed on BAN and BAR. The change factors have been grouped into the three major business agility capabilities: factors affecting operational agility, factors affecting customer agility, and factors affecting business network and partnering agility. We will now discuss the largest BAGs per agility capability category and the effects of IT on BAR, as found in our survey and discussed during the interviews. We will use examples from the different sectors to illustrate our findings.

Table 5.2

Sector Comparison on BAN, BAR, and BAG for the Three Business Agility Dimensions									
		government	**education**	**other public**	**finance**	**telecom**	**logistics**	**energy**	**average**
BAN	***average***	**3.29**	**3.25**	**3.40**	**3.29**	**3.36**	**3.63**	**3.10**	
	Operational	3.28	3.17	3.30	3.42	3.38	3.72	3.29	3.29
	Customer	3.26	3.38	3.48	3.43	3.40	3.54	2.91	3.33
	Network	3.36	3.30	3.57	2.85	3.28	3.62	3.02	3.22
BAR	***average***	***2.84***	***2.62***	***2.63***	***2.63***	***2.79***	***2.64***	***2.17***	
	Operational	2.68	2.55	2.69	2.50	2.91	2.38	2.08	2.47
	Customer	3.15	2.79	2.63	2.46	2.64	2.69	1.91	2.54
	Network	2.82	2.56	2.42	2.48	2.78	3.07	2.76	2.68
BAG	***average***	***0.45***	***0.63***	***0.77***	***0.80***	***0.58***	***1.08***	***0.96***	
	Operational	0.60	0.62	0.61	0.92	0.47	1.33	1.21	0.80
	Customer	0.11	0.59	0.85	0.96	0.76	0.92	1.00	0.79
	Network	0.54	0.74	1.15	0.37	0.50	0.81	0.38	0.60

Operational Business Agility

The change factor with the highest BAG (overall and within the operational dimension; BAG = 2.12) is the *emerging price war and shrinking margins (#6)*. This change factor influences all the business sectors analyzed and, to a lower degree, the public sectors. Companies have a lot of difficulties coping with the required changes in their internal processes. Lowering the prices requires changes in operational processes to cut costs as it influences the way companies are structured and operate. This is an important driver for *re-organizing the internal processes (#13)* and *major organizational change (#9)*. Many respondents mentioned the case of mergers and acquisitions as an example of major organizational change, where merging and integrating the various IT infrastructures was most time-consuming and caused the highest gaps.

Some of the deeper reasons behind the agility gaps in the operational agility capability can be found in the fact that *implementing changing requirements into the organization and IT systems takes too long (#8)*. Many respondents indicated that in many legacy systems business rules are embedded. There is no distinction between, data, applications, and business rules, which hampers BAR. Since *increasingly time and money is spent on maintenance and support of the existing IT infrastructure (#11)*, insufficient budget remains for investing in innovation and creating options for a more agility-enhancing architecture.

As a solution to the problems described, many organizations are considering or are already active in the *outsourcing of IT resources and personnel (#4 and #5)*. In our research, we saw a large variance between the sectors in the perceived BAR to deal with outsourcing (#4 BAR variance = 2.33). Lowest BAR was found in the other public sector segment (#4 BAR = 1.67), followed by the finance sector (#5 BAR = 2.10). Main reasons for outsourcing are reduction of costs, standardization of the IT infrastructure, and a focus on core competences. Respondents mentioned a number of difficulties involved in outsourcing. Strategic decisions need to be made on the degree of outsourcing. Furthermore, governance of the outsourcing provider creates new transaction costs. If part of the outsourcing deal is based on off-shoring, governance requires dealing with cultural issues and very clear and detailed specifications of change requests. In general, respondents provided both pros and cons for the proposition that outsourcing enhances BAR.

Another important change factor leading to a high BAN is *new regulation on national level (#2)* (BAN = 3.49) and specifically, *increasing demands from transparency and accountability regulation (#1)* (BAN = 3.40). Financial transparency and accountability causes the highest gap in the finance sector (BAG = 2.20). Examples of accountability regulation directly impacting organizations within finance are Basel 2, International Financial Reporting Standards (IFRS), International Accounting Standards (IAS), and Sarbanes Oxley. A lot of organizations within finance have IT systems, organized per product (group). This makes it difficult to comply with the transparency requirements from the new regulations, which are needed on a horizontal level crossing the various products groups.

Executives in all sectors that we studied perceive a high effect-and-response uncertainty with regard to government regulation measures. This leads to high BAN scores. The amount of new regulation, the problem of lack of implementation details, and the timing make it necessary to implement the required changes in a short time frame. This is causing BAGs within the energy (2.00), finance (1.20), and education (1.05) sectors. It is interesting to note that telecom organizations feel that they are overprepared

(#2 BAG = −1.3). Apparently, telecom organizations have found ways to deal with uncertainty in regulation.

Some change factors are dependent on the domain (business or public). Within the public sectors, we find two change factors that cause relatively large BAGs. *Digitization of documents and the usage of e-signatures (#10)* create BAGs within central government (1.26) and the other public sector (0.96). Digitalization of documents and signatures plays an important role to streamline policy decision making and transactions between citizens and government agencies, but has far-reaching impacts on the whole workflow throughout and between organizations, which explains the low BAR scores. Another BAG we found in all three public sectors (with average BAG = 0.97) is *increasing the levels of expertise of employees (#12)*. The information society and changing role of the public sector requires other types of expertise. Main factors hindering agility as found during our interviews were the aging workforce, insufficient change-oriented people, and a loss of expertise due to the usage of temporary external expertise, which insufficiently remains anchored in the organization.

Customer Business Agility

The change factor requiring customer business agility capability with the highest BAG (1.25) is *connecting to customers' information systems (#21)*. Connecting to customer information systems requires an IT architecture with quick-connect capabilities on the basis of open standards and the usage of middleware. A lot of organizations in our sample were insufficiently ready to handle these required quick-connect capabilities.

The second highest BAG is found for *responding quicker to customer service requests (#20)* (BAG = 0.87). Especially the logistics (BAG = 1.37), energy (BAG = 1.30), and other public (BAG = 1.04) sectors are insufficiently ready to deal with this agility need. For many organizations, these are large-scale processes, with many customer service requests. Especially public sector organizations and respondents in the energy sector (former public) need a redesign of their internal processes to become more customer-oriented.

Dealing with *shortening of competitors' time to market of new products and services (#14)* causes a BAG within the telecom sector (BAG = 1.30). There is a high pressure to bring new products and services onto the market within a short time frame. For instance, the introduction of new mobile payment models, data services, new content concepts based on increased bandwidth, and new location-based services require fundamental changes in the organization's procedures, systems, and partnerships.

Customization of services toward customers (#18) scores relatively equal on BAN over the seven sectors analyzed. Especially within energy there is a low BAR (BAR = 1.50). This is related to *decreasing loyalty of customers (#15)* in the energy sector, which scores high on BAN (4.30) and very low on BAR (1.30). Energy companies have been formed by mergers of various previously state-owned energy companies, which each had their own systems and procedures. Furthermore, inherited systems were never designed with a customer or service customization perspective. However, the open market requires customization to attract new customers or preserve existing customers. In the past, these companies did not have to worry about customers, since they did not have the possibility to switch to a competitor. Now this has changed, and fundamental changes are required into culture, processes, and IT systems.

The highest BAG within the finance sector on the customer dimension is caused by the *need for multi-channel any time any place access to information and services by customers (#19)* (BAG = 1.70). The original IT architectures of large financial institutes insufficiently support adding new channels for communication and transactions. Given the increasing importance of Internet banking and the opportunities of mobile payment, there is a high urgency to change IT architecture and systems to support the Internet and mobile devices as channels for communication and transactions.

Business Network and Partnering Agility

The highest BAG in the business network dimension is found in the *need for easier switching between suppliers of products and services (#26)* (BAG = 0.85). Especially within logistics (BAG = 1.5) and energy (BAG = 1.1), BAR is insufficient. To deal with this need, arrangements need to be made on business network level within the industry sector. In the energy sector, the energy clearinghouse has been set up by a number of energy companies to arrange information exchange on a standardized way to facilitate the switching of customers from one supplier to another. Defining the standards and connecting the different systems caused the most difficulties.

The second highest BAG is the *complexity in processes due to increasing number of interdependencies in the business network (#23)*. This change factor scores relatively high on BAN (3.34) and low on BAR (1.55). Especially respondents within the education (BAG = 1.30), other public (BAG = 1.34), and energy (BAG = 1.10) sectors find themselves insufficiently ready for this business network integration. This factor is closely related to *information sharing in the network (#24)*. Increasingly, public services are interdependent, and information needs to be shared between different organizations in the public sector. Public services more and more will make use of authentic registers, whereby distributed databases need to be coupled to provide a complete information profile on citizens for various types of services. Furthermore, government is working on a single portal for governmental services, a single window between citizens and the government for information exchange, information access, and services. In the back office, this means a lot of distributed databases need to be connected, which creates a lot of interdependencies.

The *need for structured information exchange (#25)*—think about EDI and XML—causes a high variety in BAN and BAR between the seven sectors analyzed. Highest BAG scores are found in logistics (BAG = 2.03) and other public (BAG = 0.94) sectors. In the logistics sector, the need for chain-wide tracking and tracing requires integration to partner information systems. Given the diversity in type of companies and size (a lot of Small-to-Medium Sized Enterprises (SMEs)), it is difficult to achieve chain-wide structured information exchange.

The lowest BAR is found in managing the *accelerating of innovation of product technology (#27)* (BAR = 1.35). Telecom companies are highly dependent on their mobile device and content partners to use this change factor as a way to innovate and distinguish from competitors. Especially within telecom, this causes a BAG (BAG = 1.2). New technologies in mobile devices; voice-over IP; emerging data services; and the merging of phone, Internet, and TV have resulted in a series of innovations in product technology. Customized products and services need to be put on the telecom market in ever shorter time.

Analyses

Figure 5.2 shows a plot of the relative scores on perceived BAN and perceived BAR for the 27 change factors analyzed. First, we calculated the overall average scores on BAN (3.28) and BAR (2.54). We then related the individual scores of the 27 change

Figure 5.2

Business Agility Change Factors Matrix

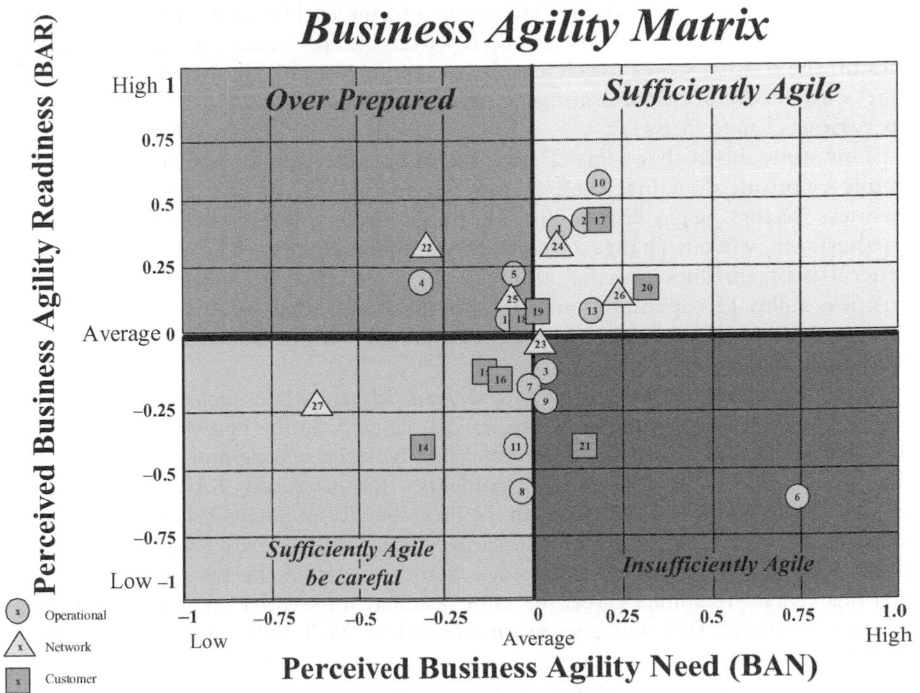

factors to this overall average score by subtracting the overall average score from the individual score. This way, we made the relative importance and relative scores of the 27 change factors on BAN and BAR explicit.

Based on their relative position on the Business Agility Matrix, factors can lead to a BAG. If BAN scores above average, and BAR below average, organizations are insufficiently agile and need immediate action to deal with the change factor. Most important change factors requiring immediate action as found in our research were *emerging price war and shrinking margins* (#6), followed by *connecting to customers' information systems (#21)* and *dealing with major organizational change (#9)*. A number of change factors need a careful watch. If the level of change increases, they also require immediate action. If BAN is below average and BAR is above average, organizations are more or less overprepared to deal with a change factor.

It is interesting to note that respondents find that their BAR to deal with change factors related to business network agility is relatively sufficient, compared to other factors. This can be explained by the fact that more attention is given to the internal operational business agility. Either there is yet insufficient awareness on the importance of the business network perspective, or solving internal problems still has priority over business network opportunities, or the business network is not found to be important.

Since Figure 5.2 only provides an overview of average scores over the total sample, the business agility matrix will look different per sector analyzed. As an example, we will show the business agility matrices for central government and finance (Figure 5.3).

Relative importance of change factors on a sector level becomes more explicit, with a wider range of scores on BAN and BAR. Given the differences between different sectors on the relative scores for change factors on BAN and BAR, sector-specific benchmarks are needed for organizations to assess and compare their BAN and BAR scores on various change factors.

This study shows that some change factors are generic, but some are dependent on public or private domains. These factors have a relatively similar type of BAN for all business sectors (e.g., #6) or for all public sectors (e.g., #10, #12, and #24). Furthermore, various change factors are sector-specific (e.g., #17 and #27). BAR in general is organization-specific, although the same types of challenges in increasing business agility IT capabilities are found in all organizations analyzed. Depending on the position of a change factor in the Business Agility Matrix, several IT strategies can be defined (Figure 5.4).

If an organization finds itself in the *Insufficiently Agile quadrant* for a certain change factor, two possible IT strategies can be used. In the first strategy, IT is used to increase the BAR. This includes increasing both the sensing and respond capabilities (Dove, 2001). A few general guidelines for increasing BAR were extracted from our interviews and confirmed in the literature. Respondents believe that IT architecture and standards should be managed centrally at enterprise level on the basis of a broadly enforced set of technology standards, while keeping room for local responsiveness. To some degree, the same accounts for security and risk and IT facilities management. This was also recommended by Weill, Subramani, and Broadbent (2002). Secondly, an infrastructure that is modular, service-based, and tailored to the enterprise's strategy (close alignment between business and IT) is expected to enhance business agility. Such an architecture is loosely coupled, based on modular reusable components in a scalable framework (Dove, 2001). A distinction between data, applications, and business rules creates the basis for more agility. Compatibility and integration can be achieved via standardized interfaces and connections, usage of standardized technology to store data (such as XML), and usage of interoperability and integration supporting standards and open protocols (e.g., XML and Web services) (Vervest and Dunn, 2000; Brown and Bessant, 2003). These are enablers for increasing the business network agility capability (van Hillegersberg, et al., 2005) as well as the internal operational business agility capability. A final guideline we found in the literature (Weill, Subramani, and Broadbent, 2002) is that the organization's infrastructure should be created via a series of incremental investments. Staged investment means partitioning a larger IT investment into stand-alone increments that build on the preceding ones, thereby creating strategic real options (Konsynski and Tiwana, 2004).

In the second strategy, IT is used to decrease the BAN. As an example, we take the *need to respond more quickly to customer service requests (#20)*. An IT strategy to lower BAN might be to create self-service environments where customers can help themselves or each other, based on access to their data, transactions, and intelligent decision support tools for solving problems. This can be extended to self-service environments, where customers are offered personalized products and services based on real-time product configurators and historic databases that match profiles to offers (like Amazon). By creating self-service environments, there will be less customer

Figure 5.3

Business Agility Change Factors Matrices: Central Government and Finance

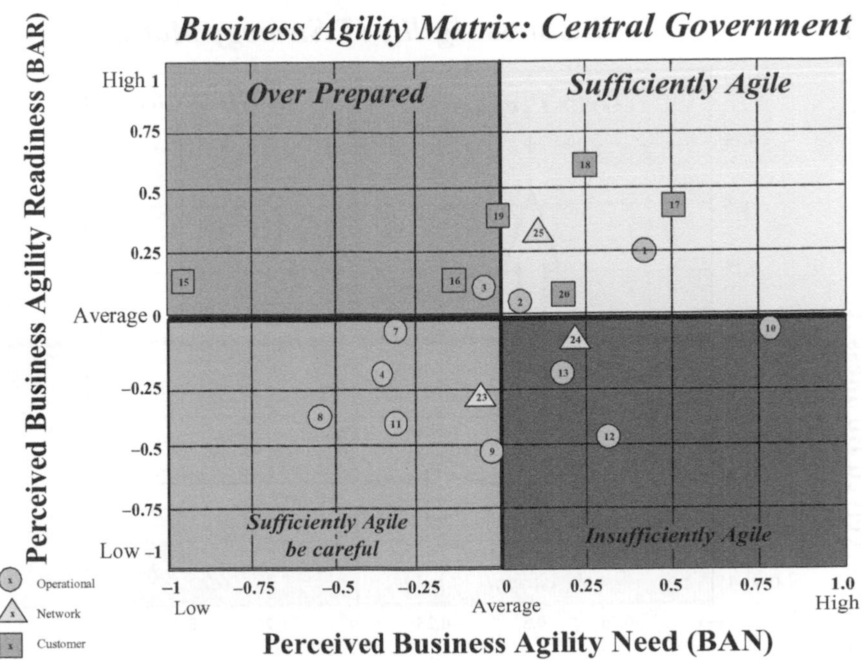

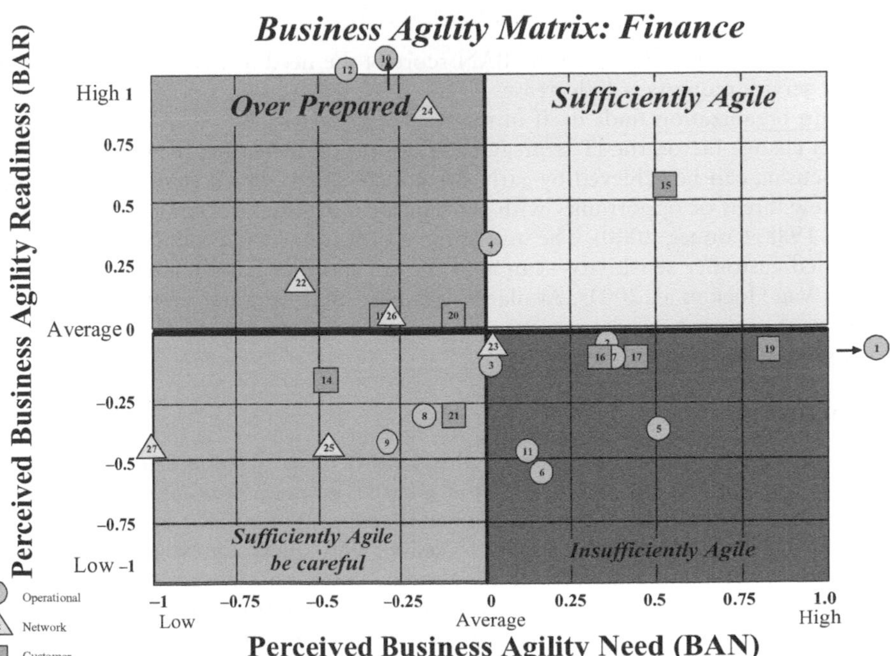

Figure 5.4

Business Agility IT Strategy Matrix

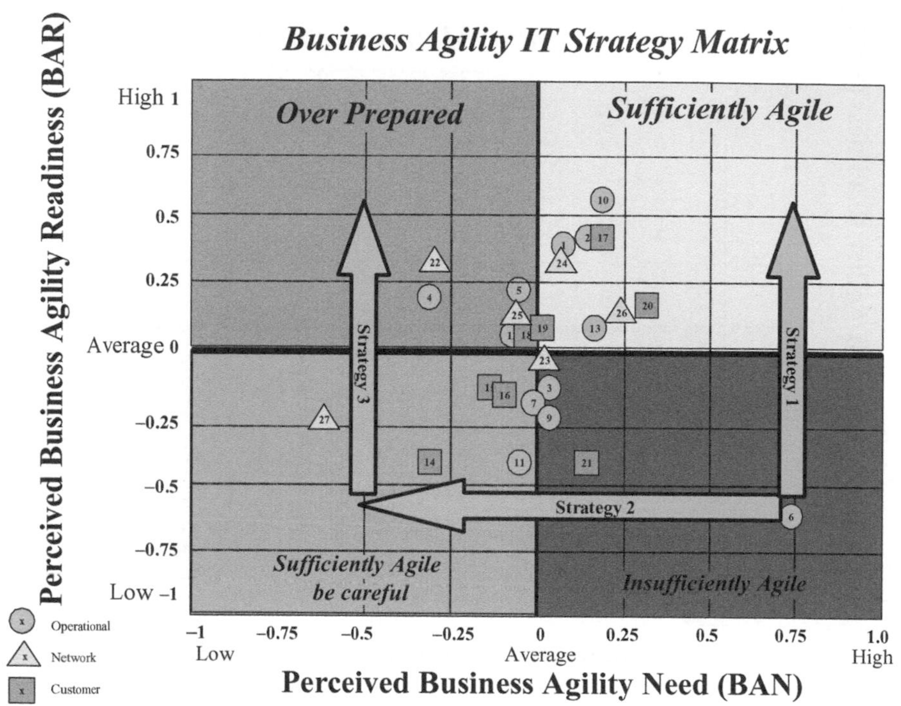

service requests and therefore the BAN score of the need to quickly respond to customer service requests will decrease.

If an organization finds itself in the *Sufficiently Agile, Be Careful quadrant* for a certain change factor, the IT strategy should focus on increasing the sensing capabilities. Sensing can be achieved by early detection systems, which alert at the first signs of a new threat or opportunity with procedures to determine a proper response (Daft et al., 1988; Conner, 2000). The involvement of customers in product development—so-called customer sensitivity—can also be an important basis for sensing (Maskell, 2001; Van Hoek et al, 2001). Available, complete, pertinent, and easy-to-access information on customer needs, anxieties, and service requirements via IT is a key enabler for agility (Christopher, 1992).

Conclusion

The central research question of this chapter was: *What are the contributing factors that require business agility, and what IT strategies can be implemented for enhancing business agility*? First we defined the concept of business agility. Our definition is "Business agility is the ability to sense highly uncertain external and internal changes and respond reactively or proactively, based on innovation of the internal operational processes, involving the customer in exploration and exploitation while leveraging the capabilities of partners in the business network."

This study shows that some change factors are generic, but some are dependent on public or private domains. The emerging price war and the need for lower priced products and services combined with fast-changing customer requests dramatically influence all business sectors analyzed. Companies face severe difficulties in coping with the required changes. In many cases, this requires a totally different way of organizing the company and its business network. Additionally, new regulation is causing high BAN in almost all sectors analyzed. Furthermore, various change factors are sector-specific. Given the differences between different sectors on the relative scores for change factors on BAN and BAR, sector-specific benchmarks are needed for organizations to assess and compare their BAN and BAR scores on various change factors.

The results also indicate that BAN is not just created by uncertainty about external changes. Many internal changes (such as mergers and acquisitions, changes in systems and procedures, digitalization of documents, and e-signatures) require organizations to increase their BAR scores. This is reflected in the BAG scores we found for various change factors with a more internal origin in different sectors.

BAR in general is organization-specific, although the same types of challenges in increasing business agility IT capabilities are found in all organizations analyzed. Respondents are very worried about the pace at which responses to the changes can be implemented. To a large degree, this can be explained by the existing organizational structures, cultures, and legacy infrastructures.

The highest BAG scores were found in logistics and energy, while changes requiring agility on the operational and the customer dimension caused larger gaps than the business network dimension. The highest BAG scores on the operational dimension were found within logistics and energy, on the customer dimension in energy and finance, and on the business network dimension in other public arenas.

Depending on the position of a change factor in the Business Agility Matrix, three generic IT strategies were defined. If an organization finds itself in the *Insufficiently Agile quadrant* for a certain change factor, two possible IT strategies can be used. In the first strategy, IT is used to increase the BAR. This includes increasing both the sensing and respond capabilities (Dove, 2001). In the second strategy, IT is used to decrease the BAN. If an organization finds itself in the *Sufficiently Agile, Be Careful quadrant* for a certain change factor, the IT strategy should focus on increasing the sensing capabilities.

References

Brown, S. and Bessant, J. (2003). The manufacturing strategy-capabilities links in mass customization and agile manufacturing: An exploratory study. *International Journal of Operations & Production Management*, 23 (7–8), 707–730.

Canter, J. (2000). *An agility-based OODA model for the e-commerce/e-business enterprise*. Retrieved from: http://www.belisarius.com/modern_business_strategy/canter/canter.htm.

Christopher, M. (1992). *Logistics & Supply Chain Management: Strategies for Reducing Cost and Improving Service*. London, UK: Pitman.

Conner, D. R. (2000). How to create a nimble organization. *National Productivity Review*, 19 (4), 69–74.

Conboy, K. B., Fitzgerald. (2004). Towards a conceptual framework of agile methods: A study of agility in different disciplines. In *Proceedings of the 2004 ACM workshop on interdisciplinary software engineering research*. Newport Beach, CA, pp. 37–44.

D'aveni, R., Richard A., Gunther, R. E. (1994). *Hypercompetition: Managing the Dynamics of Strategic Maneuvering*. New York: The Free Press.

Daft, R. L., Sormunen, J., and Parks, D. (1988). Chief executive scanning, environmental characteristics, and company performance: An empirical study. *Strategic Management Journal*, 9 (2), 123–139.

Dove, R. (2001). *Response Ability: The Language, Structure and Culture of the Agile Enterprise*. New York: Wiley.

Goldman, S., et al. (1991). *21st Century Manufacturing Enterprise Strategy*. Bethlehem, PA: Iacocca Institute, Lehigh University.

Goldman, S., Nagel, R., and Preiss, K. (1995). *Agile Competitors and Virtual Organizations*. New York: Van Nostrand Reinhold.

Hooper, M. J., Steeple, D., and Winters, C. N. (2001). Costing customer value: An approach for the agile enterprise. *International Journal of Operations and Production Management*, 21 (5), 630–644.

Kidd, P. T. (1994). *Agile Manufacturing: Forging New Frontiers*. Wokingham, UK: Addison-Wesley.

Kidd, P. T. (1995). *Agile Corporations: Business Enterprises in the 21st Century—An Executive Guide*. Macclesfield, UK: Cheshire Henbury.

Konsynski, B. and Tiwana, A. (2004). The improvisation-efficiency paradox in inter-firm electronic networks: Governance and architecture considerations. *Journal of Information Technology*, 19 (4), 234–243.

Maskell, B. (2001). The age of agile manufacturing. *Supply Chain Management: An International Journal*, 6 (1), 5–11.

Mason-Jones, R. and Towill, D. R. (1999). Total cycle time compression and the agile supply chain. *International Journal of Production Economics*, Special Issue 62 (1–2), 61–73.

Milliken, F. J. (1987). Three types of perceived uncertainty about environment: State, effect, and response uncertainty. *Academy of Management Review*. 12 (1), 133–143.

Preiss, K., Goldman, S. L., and Nagel, R. N. (1996). *Cooperate to compete: Building agile business relationships*. New York: Van Nostrand Reinhold.

Ramasesh, R., Kulkarni, S., and Jayakumar, M. (2001). Agility in manufacturing systems: An exploratory modeling framework and simulation. *Integrated Manufacturing Systems*, 12 (7), 534–548.

Sambamurthy, V., Bharadwaj, A., and Grover, V. (2003). Shaping agility through digital options: Reconceptualizing the role of information technology in contemporary firms. *MIS Quarterly*, 27(2), 237–263.

Schrage, M. (2004). The struggle to define agility: It's all about the Execution. *CIO Magazine*, Aug. 15th, 2004. Retrieved from: http://www.cio.com/archive/081504/schrage.html.

Sharifi, H. and Zhang, Z. (1999). A methodology for achieving agility in manufacturing organizations: An introduction. *International Journal of Production Economics*, 62 (1–2), 7–22.

Swafford, P. M. (2003). Theoretical development and empirical investigation of supply chain agility. *Dissertation*, Georgia Institute of Technology, Atlanta, April, pp. 1–138.

van Hillegersberg, J., Boeke, R., and Van den Heuvel, W. J. (2005). The potential of web services to enable Smart Business Networks. In *Smart Business Networks* (P. H. M. Vervest, E. V. Heck, K. Preiss, L. F. Pau, eds.). Berlin-Heidelberg: Springer-Verlag, pp. 349–362.

van Hoek, R. I., Harrison, A., and Christopher, M. (2001). Measuring agile capabilities in the supply chain. *International Journal of Operations & Production Management*, 21 (1/2), 126–147.

Vervest, P. and Dunn, A. (2000). *How to Win Customers in the Digital World: Total Action or Fatal Inaction*. Berlin-Heidelberg: Springer-Verlag.

Vervest, P. H. M., Heck, E. V., Preiss, K., and Pau, L. F. (eds.) (2005). *Smart Business Networks*. Berlin-Heidelberg: Springer-Verlag.

Wadhwa, S. and Rao, K. S. (2003). Flexibility and agility for enterprise synchronization: Knowledge and innovation management towards flexagility. *Studies in Informatics and Control*, 12 (2), 111–128.

Weill, P., Subramani, M., and Broadbent, M. (2002). *IT Infrastructure for Strategic Agility.* MIT CISR Working Paper, No. 329, Center for Information Systems Research, Sloan School of Management.

Yusuf, Y. Y., et al. (2004). Agile supply chain capabilities: Determinants of competitive objectives. *European Journal of Operational Research,* 159 (2), 379–392.

Zhang, Z. and Sharifi, H. (2000). A methodology for achieving agility in manufacturing organizations. *International Journal of Operations & Production Management,* 20 (4), 496–513.

Achieving Economic Returns from IS Support for Strategic Flexibility: The Roles of Firm-Specific, Complementary Organizational Culture and Structure

Michael J. Zhang

As strategic flexibility is widely viewed as a critical organizational capability that enables firms to achieve and maintain competitive advantage and superior performance, a great deal of attention has been devoted to the roles of Information Systems (IS) in supporting and enabling strategic flexibility (Sanchez, 1995; Upton, 1995; Lei, Hitt, and Goldhar, 1996; Byrd, 2001; Sambamurthy, Bharadwaj, and Grover, 2003). While the extant literature is replete with conceptual frameworks, anecdotes, and case studies suggesting that firms may use Information Systems (IS) to support strategic flexibility for competitive advantage, empirical work assessing the impacts of IS support for strategic flexibility on the bottom-line performance of firms is generally lacking. Without systematic assessments of the bottom-line impacts of IS support for strategic flexibility, it remains unclear whether firms can actually achieve economic returns from such IS deployment. Furthermore, IS researchers who have examined IS impacts on competitive performance from the resource-based view of competitive advantage have increasingly entertained the notion that firms need to bundle IS with certain firm-specific and hard-to-copy organizational resources in order to reap economic returns from their IS investments (Feeny and Ives, 1990; Clemons and Row; 1991; Powell and Dent-Micallef, 1997; Wade and Hulland, 2004). The existing research on the performance impacts of IS support for strategic flexibility has also recognized the roles of certain organiza-

Figure 6.1

Research Model

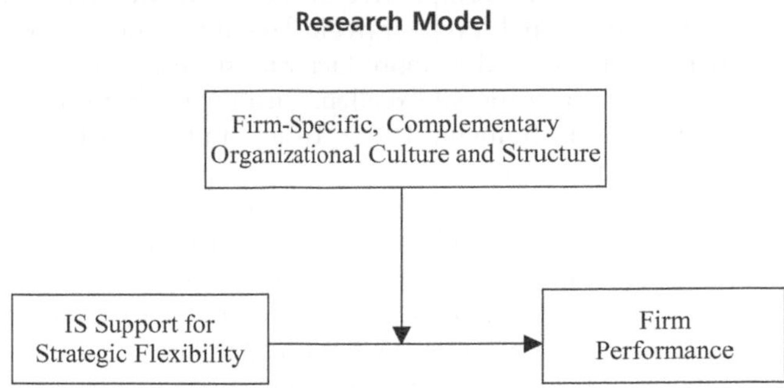

tional resources that complement such IS support (Upton, 1995; Lei, Hitt, and Goldhar, 1996), but it lacks empirical studies investigating the interactions between IS support for strategic flexibility and firm-specific, complementary organizational resources in influencing the bottom-line performance of firms.

In this chapter, I present the findings from a field study that assessed the performance impacts of IS support for strategic flexibility. In particular, the study drew upon the resource-based view of competitive advantage to examine and test the roles of firm-specific, complementary organizational culture and structure in determining the performance impacts of IS support for strategic flexibility. By firm-specific, complementary organizational culture and structure, I refer to firm-specific organizational culture and structure, which facilitate the development and exploitation of IS to support strategic flexibility. Discerning the moderating effects of firm-specific, complementary organizational culture and structure would enhance our understanding of the conditions under which firms are more likely to achieve economic returns from IS-based strategic flexibility (Figure 6.1).

Theory and Hypothesis

Strategic Flexibility and Its Competitive Value

The subject of flexibility has been dealt with extensively in several disciplines (e.g., manufacturing management, economics, strategic management, and IS management), and various conceptualizations of flexibility have been advanced during the past two decades, reflecting a wide range of research interests and theoretical perspectives. There are a number of excellent reviews of different definitions and typologies of flexibility, especially in the manufacturing management literature (e.g., Sethi and Sethi, 1990; Hyun and Ahn, 1992; Gerwin, 1993; Upton, 1994). In keeping with the current strategic perspective of flexibility (Sanchez, 1995; Hitt, Keats, and DeMarie, 1998), I adopted a broad (strategic) view of flexibility, referring to a set of organizational abilities to proact or respond quickly to a changing competitive environment and thereby develop and/or maintain competitive advantage, in this study. Indeed, the concept of strategic flexibility has been increasingly embraced by researchers in fields such as strategic management, manufacturing management, and IS management, given the growing recognition of the strategic significance of strategic flexibility to firms competing in today's changing business environments (Boynton, 1993; Gerwin, 1993; Sanchez, 1995; Hitt, Keats, and DeMarie, 1998).

Research examining the strategic impact of strategic flexibility has shown that strategic flexibility contributes to competitive advantage at different organizational levels. At the tactical or functional level, strategic flexibility is now known to be vital to several value-creating operational or manufacturing strategies, including mass customization, time-to-market, operational excellence, lean manufacturing, and stockless inventory (Stalk, Evans, and Shulman, 1992; Treacy and Wiersema, 1993; Kotha, 1995; Byrd, 2001). At the business level, strategic flexibility enables a firm to avoid the trade-off between low cost and differentiation and offer high-quality products or services at low cost (Boynton, 1993; Lei, Hitt, and Goldhar, 1996). At the corporate level, since the development and implementation of strategic flexibility involve constant improvements in the firm's organizational processes and technologies as well as continuous learning of new organizational knowledge, capabilities, and skills (Hayes and Pisano, 1994; Goldhar and Lei, 1995), strategic management researchers rooted in the resource-based view of competitive advantage consider strategic flexibility as a higher-order (dynamic) capability that enables the firm to adapt and change over time to maintain its long-term competitiveness (Amit and Schoemaker, 1993; Collis, 1994; Teece, Pisano, and Shuen, 1997; Eisenhardt and Martin, 2000).

IS Support for Strategic Flexibility

It is evident in the literature that the development of strategic flexibility requires support from other organizational resources and capabilities. Manufacturing management and IS management research linking IS to operational flexibility indicates that IS are an indispensable factor in achieving strategic flexibility (Boynton, 1993; Sanchez, 1995; Upton, 1995; Lei, Hitt, and Goldhar, 1996; Byrd, 2001). Research on the flexibility impacts of advanced manufacturing technologies (AMT) has shown that the computer-aided design (CAD) system, through its support for product design, engineering, simulation, testing, and rapid prototyping, enables a firm to significantly reduce its costs of creating and evaluating different product designs and shorten product design cycles (Sanchez, 1995; Lei, Hitt, and Goldhar, 1996; Hitt, Keats, and DeMarie, 1998). Moreover, flexible manufacturing systems (FMS) using computer-aided manufacturing (CAM) technology can greatly increase the speed of introducing new tools and dyes as well as integrating previously separated workstations and machining centers into an interdependent manufacturing system (Clark, 1989; Lei, Hitt, and Goldhar, 1996).

As a result of using IS-based AMT, firms can radically reduce the cost versus variety and speed versus variety trade-offs, thus achieving economies of scope—"the capacity to efficiently and quickly produce any of a range of parts or products within a family" (Zammuto and O'Connor, 1992, p. 702). In other words, firms can derive the simultaneous benefits of greater product variety, faster response, and increased productivity from IS (Chase and Garvin, 1989; Pine, 1993; Hayes and Pisano, 1994; Goldhar and Lei, 1995). Economies of scale can also be gained from the IS-derived economies of scope in that the multi-product operations supported by CAD and CAM eliminate the risk of rendering the investment in a high-volume, single-product plant obsolete due to changes in market demand (Bakos and Treacy, 1986; Goldhar and Lei, 1995). Because of these operational benefits, IS-based operational flexibility has been found instrumental to the development of mass customization (a widely recognized value-creating organizational capability), whereby firms customize products of high variety to customers' special needs at low costs (Pine, Victor, and Boynton, 1993; Kotha, 1995; Byrd, 2001).

While research on IS support for strategic flexibility has mostly focused on the use of IS in manufacturing settings, there is emerging anecdotal evidence that service firms can also benefit from using IS to achieve strategic flexibility. Boynton, Victor, and Pine (1993) reported an IS (dubbed as the CS90) designed by Westpac (a South Pacific financial service conglomerate) to consolidate its knowledge and expertise about the processes of developing new financial products into a set of highly flexible software modules. By allowing Westpac to combine different sources of its knowledge rapidly and efficiently, the system enabled the company to handle a greater variety and range of customer and marketplace needs at low cost and fast speed. In a more recent study, Sawhney (2001) described how Thomson Financial (a subsidiary of Thomson Corporation, an electronic information provider) used IS to increase its market responsiveness and new product offering speed. Thomson Financial accomplished this through installing a software called "middleware," which allowed the company to represent legacy IS applications and products as "objects" (modular components) that can be easily combined and flexibly assembled to create tailored solutions for the customers.

Moderating Roles of Firm-Specific, Complementary Organizational Culture and Structure

While IS can be used to achieve strategic flexibility, some may argue that such IS deployment is subject to easy imitation because many IS lack characteristics that are unique or difficult to copy (Mata, Fuerst, and Barney, 1995). However, drawing on the notion of complementary assets—resources whose presence enhances the values of other resources (Teece, 1986), IS researchers rooted in the resource-based view of competitive advantage have recently argued that firms with certain firm-specific, hard-to-copy resources that complement their IS are in a better position to defend their IS-derived advantage than those that lack such resources (Feeny and Ives, 1990; Clemons and Row, 1991; Lado and Zhang, 1998; Bharadwaj, 2000). This argument has received some empirical support from two recent studies that found IS complemented by other intangible organizational resources yielded competitive advantage (Powell and Dent-Micallef, 1997; Bharadwaj, 2000).

It is well recognized in the IS literature that organizational culture and structure are instrumental in enabling a firm to benefit from IS support for strategic flexibility (Upton, 1995; Lei, Hitt, and Goldhar, 1996; Hitt, Keats, and DeMarie, 1998). In the case of organizational culture, Hitt, Keats, and DeMarie (1998) note that firms with strong values that encourage and reward innovation are more likely to increase the use of IS to improve strategic flexibility. In his study of the problems with using computer-integrated manufacturing (CIM) to achieve operational flexibility, Upton (1995) found that firms placing little value on responsiveness to customers and stressing high utilization of machines in their measurement and reward systems experienced difficulty in obtaining operational benefits from CIM. Research on IS implementation and adoption problems has also documented the absence of a supportive organizational culture as a major cause of many system failures. Several empirical studies, for instance, have found relatively low system use among firms lacking a culture and reward systems that support IS adoption (Zuboff, 1988; Constant, Sproull, and Kiesler, 1996; Goodman and Darr, 1998). Besides affecting the economic impacts of IS support for strategic flexibility, organizational culture makes it difficult for competitors to imitate the IS it complements because organizational culture tends to be firm-specific, intangible, and costly to imitate (Barney, 1986).

Organizational structure is important to the effectiveness of IS support for strategic flexibility in that organizational structure affects how well a firm manages cross-functional coordination, which many researchers view as crucial to the firm's ability to increase the value of IS support for strategic flexibility (Ahmed, Hardaker, and Carpenter, 1996; Lei, Hitt, and Goldhar, 1996; Hitt, Keats, and DeMarie, 1998). Smooth cross-functional coordination within and across firms promotes effective acquisition and sharing of critical information and knowledge needed for quick detection of market and product changes, redesign of business processes and workflows, and development of new insights and skills (Lei, Hitt, and Goldhar, 1996; Hitt, Keats, and DeMarie, 1998; Bharadwaj, 2000). Without well-coordinated functional activities, the firm is unlikely to derive competitive advantage from flexibility because compartmentalized processes and decision making hinder the firm's ability to "create a holistic sense of direction and utilize response flexibility to build advantages" (Ahmed, Hardaker, and Carpenter, 1996: 565).

In order to maximize the value of investments in IS support for strategic flexibility, a firm must develop or adopt an organizational structure that not only integrates different functional activities into self-contained and highly autonomous units that are allowed to optimize and change internally, but also balances the requirement for strong interdependence among functions with external linkages with suppliers and customers (Ahmed, Hardaker, and Carpenter, 1996; Lei, Hitt, and Goldhar, 1996; Hitt, Keats, and DeMarie, 1998). Firms that are successful in developing and adopting such an organizational structure may enjoy sustainable economic returns from IS support for strategic flexibility since smooth cross-functional coordination is embedded in firm-specific and socially complex organizational routines (Badaracco, 1991), and balancing internal cross-functional coordination and cross-firm integration is a highly complex task (Lei, Hitt, and Goldhar, 1996).

Hypothesis: The interaction between IS support for strategic flexibility and firm-specific, complementary organizational culture and structure is positively related to firm performance.

The Field Study

Sample and Data Collection

The data for this study were obtained from two sources. The data tapping the independent variables were gathered via a mail survey administered in 1998, and the data about the performance and control variables were obtained from the Research Insight (formerly known as Compustat) database. The target respondents of the survey were senior IS executives in large firms (*Fortune* and *Forbes*) in the United States. Most of the respondents held the positions of either vice presidents of IS or chief information officers. The senior IS executive was chosen as the single informant in this study because of his or her familiarity with both IS and strategic management issues. Several previous studies have found increasing involvement of senior IS executives in the strategic planning and control activities of firms (Applegate and Elam, 1992; Stephens et al., 1992; Earl and Feeny, 1994). Furthermore, a recent study found the information offered by key IS executives consistent with the insights obtained from other senior members of management (Palmer and Markus, 2000). Consequently, IS researchers have increasingly relied on senior IS executives as single informants in gathering data about strategic IS issues (Sethi and King, 1994; Karimi, Gupta, and Somers, 1996; Palmer and Markus, 2000).

The contact information of the senior IS executives was obtained from the Directory of Top Computer Executives compiled by Applied Computer Research Inc. From this source, a sample of 879 firms that had financial data in the Research Insight database was identified. Before being mailed to the target respondents, the survey instrument was pretested and refined for content validity and item clarity with senior IS executives from five Fortune companies headquartered in a Midwestern state. One hundred and one questionnaires were undelivered or returned because the IS executives were no longer with the companies. Twenty-nine firms declined to participate in the study in writing, on the phone, or through email. To boost the response rate, two follow-up mailings and one reminder letter were initiated after the first mailing. Of the 778 firms that received the questionnaires, a total of 164 responses were received, out of which 11 responses were unusable. The effective response rate was thus 20 percent (153 responses). This response rate is comparable to those reported in similar studies using senior IS executives in large firms (Sethi and King, 1994; Powell and Dent-Micallef, 1997; Byrd and Turner, 2001; Kearns and Lederer, 2003).

To test for potential nonresponse bias, the respondent firms were compared to their nonrespondent counterparts with respect to sales and number of employees. T-test results showed no significant differences in both characteristics between the two groups. In keeping with Armstrong and Overton (1977), another nonresponse bias check was conducted by comparing early respondents with late respondents. T-tests of the mean differences for the two explanatory variables failed to reveal any significant differences. Together, these checks provided some evidence for the absence of non-response bias in the data set.

Measures

Independent Variable

In this study, IS support for strategic flexibility was defined as the various types of support a firm's IS provided for the development of strategic flexibility. To measure this variable, three items were adopted from Mahmood and Soon (1991) and another five were developed based on the ideas of Bakos and Treacy (1986), Goldhar and Lei (1995), and Sanchez (1995). For each item, the respondents were asked to indicate the extent to which their IS had provided a particular type of support during the previous three years on a five-point, Likert-type scale with anchors ranging from "very great extent" (= 5) to "no extent" (= 1). To assess the construct validity and unidimensionality of the scale, a principal components factor analysis was performed with varimax rotation on the eight items. The factor analysis results shown in Table 6.1 revealed a single factor explaining about 51 percent of the total variance and thus supported the unidimensionality of the scale. The Cronbach Alpha of this scale is .86.

Moderating Variable

Firm-specific, complementary organizational culture and structure were measured with a two-item scale. The respondents were asked to indicate the extent to which the use and implementation of their IS required unique organizational culture or unique organizational structure on a five-point, Likert-type scale with anchors ranging from "very great extent" (= 5) to "no extent" (= 1). The Cronbach Alpha of this scale is .78.

Table 6.1

Factor Analysis of IS Support for Strategic Flexibility	
Item Description	**Loadings**
1. Reduce the cost of tailoring products/services to market segments	.761
2. Reduce the cost of modifying or adding features to existing products/services	.755
3. Increase the flexibility of business processes	.568
4. Make product-line changeover easy	.747
5. Improve product/service adaptability	.758
6. Allow economies of scale from small production runs	.592
7. Reduce the cost of designing new products/services	.754
8. Shorten product design cycles	.733
Eigen Value	4.06
% of common variance explained	50.78
Cronbach Alpha	.86

Dependent Variables

Two popular measures of profitability (return on sales and return on assets) were employed to measure the bottom-line performance of the sample firms. Both profitability ratios have been frequently used in previous assessments of the strategic impacts of IS (Kettinger et al., 1994; Brown, Gatian, and Hicks, Jr., 1995; Tam, 1998; Li and Ye, 1999). To smooth annual fluctuations and reduce short-term effects to some degree, a three-year average (1997 to 1999) was used for both variables.

Control Variables

Since the firms participating in this study came from a variety of industries, it was necessary to control, to some degree, the different industry conditions under which the firms operated. To control for the industry effects, SIC codes were first used to clas-sify the firms into four groups: 1) manufacturing, 2) transportation and public utilities, 3) wholesale and retail trade, and 4) service. Where a firm operated in more than one industry, the firm's SIC code was determined by identifying the industry from which the firm received the largest percentage of sales and the corresponding SIC code. Three dummy variables (each with values of 0 or 1) were then created for the second (transportation and public utilities), the third (wholesale and retail trade), and the fourth (service) groups of firms. For each dummy variable, a firm was assigned a value of 1 if it belonged to a group.

The fourth control variable was firm size, which has frequently been used in other studies involving firm performance as a dependent variable (Kivijarvi and Saarinen, 1995; Tam, 1998; Li and Ye, 1999). In keeping with Kettinger et al. (1994), firm size was measured as the natural logarithm of the number of full-time employees. The fifth control variable was technological resources. A firm's technological resources may influence its ability to develop IS for sustainable competitive advantage (Kettinger et al., 1994). While a preferable measure of technological resources is R&D intensity, the research insight data for R&D intensity were missing for many firms in the sample. An alternative measure (investment intensity operationalized as invested capital to sales), as recommended by Kettinger et al. (1994), was then used for technological resources. The sixth control variable was organizational slack, which is indicative of a firm's ability to generate cash flow for reinvestment (Chakravarthy, 1986). Organizational slack needs to be controlled due to its potential influence on a firm's financial performance as well as on the firm's ability to invest in and develop IS (Kettinger et al., 1994; Li and Ye, 1999). A traditional ratio, the current ratio (current assets to current liabilities), was used to measure organizational slack (Bourgeois, 1981).

Analyses

To test the research hypothesis, two sets of hierarchical regression analyses were performed, using Return on Sales (ROS) and Return on Assets (ROA) as the dependent variables. In the first stage of each set of the analyses, the six control variables were entered into the regression model as a set. In the second stage, the independent and moderating variables were added to the equation to separate their potential direct effects. In the third stage, the interaction term between the independent variable and the moderating variable was added to the model. Before being used in the model, both variables were mean-centered (by subtracting the means from the variables) to reduce potential multicollinearity between the interaction term and the independent variable or the moderating variable (Aiken and West, 1991).

Results

Table 6.2 displays the results of the hierarchical regression analyses. The research hypothesis predicts that the interaction between IS support for strategic flexibility and firm-specific, complementary organizational culture and structure is positively related to firm performance. As shown in Table 6.2, neither IS support for strategic flexibility nor firm-specific, complementary organizational culture and structure had a direct effect on either ROS or ROA. On the other hand, the interaction term between IS support for strategic flexibility and firm-specific, complementary organizational culture and structure was significant in predicting both ROS ($b = .18$, $p < .01$) and ROA ($b = .17$, $p < .05$) in the expected direction. Taken together, these results provide strong support for the hypothesis.

Discussion

Overview of the Findings and Research Implications

This research was conducted to investigate the moderating roles of firm-specific, complementary organizational culture and structure on the bottom-line performance impacts of IS support for strategic flexibility. The results showed that IS support for strategic flexibility was positively associated with two common measures of profitability (ROS and ROA) only when IS were complemented by firm-specific organizational culture and structure. While providing evidence for the economic benefits from using IS to achieve strategic flexibility, the findings suggested that the bottom-line impacts of IS for strategic flexibility were subject to the influence of distinctive organizational culture and structure that supported IS. Without supportive organizational culture and structure, IS support for strategic flexibility did not improve firm performance.

Table 6.2

Regression Results[a]						
	ROS			ROA		
Variables	**Model 1**	**Model 2**	**Model 3**	**Model 4**	**Model 5**	**Model 6**
Industry dummy 1	−.09	−.09	−.11	−.10	−.10	−.12
Industry dummy 2	−.13+	−.12	−.10	−.23**	−.25**	−.23**
Industry dummy 3	.20*	.19*	.19*	−.27**	−.27**	−.27**
Firm size (log of employees)	.10	.09	.10	.18*	.17*	.18*
Current assets to current liabilities	−.03	−.02	−.02	.04	.05	.05
Invested capital to sales	.44***	.45***	.45***	.02	.02	.02
IS support for strategic flexibility		.11	.10		.02	.02
Firm-specific, complementary organizational culture and structure		.02	.02		.10	.10
Firm-specific, complementary organizational culture and structure			.18**			.17*
R^2	.33	.35	.38	.11	.13	.16
ΔR^2		.02	.03		.02	.03
F	12.13***	9.49***	9.59***	3.13**	2.60*	2.91**
ΔF		1.39	7.16**		.99	4.87*

[a] N = 153. Standardized regression coefficients are shown.
+ $p < .10$, * $p < .05$, ** $p < .01$, *** $p < .001$.

This study makes two contributions to research on the strategic value of IS-based strategic flexibility. First, it provides evidence that links IS support for strategic flexibility to the bottom-line performance of firms. This evidence is significant in view of the potential high costs of using IS to achieve strategic flexibility (Upton, 1995; Aggarwal, 1997). Second, the results found herein lend empirical support to the growing recognition that IS investments for strategic flexibility alone do not generate economic returns (Gerwin, 1993; Pine, Victor, and Boynton, 1993; Upton, 1995). Instead, the IS investments must be supported by certain critical organizational resources in order to improve profitability (Lei, Hitt, and Goldhar, 1996; Hitt, Keats, and DeMarie, 1998). Hence, future studies assessing the performance impacts of IS-based strategic flexibility need to incorporate or control the organizational context in which IS support for strategic flexibility is applied.

The current study also contributes to the increasingly popular resource-based approach to examining the strategic impacts of IS by evaluating the roles of firm-specific organizational culture and structure in linking IS support for strategic flexibility to the bottom-line performance of firms. One major resource-based argument is that the potential competitive contributions of IS rely on the presence of certain distinctive organizational resources that complement the IS (Feeny and Ives, 1990; Clemons and Row; 1991; Powell and Dent-Micallef, 1997). However, we currently don't know enough about what represents a relevant set of complementary organizational resources that interact with IS in affecting firm performance (Wade and Hulland, 2004). This research empirically evaluated and verified firm-specific organizational culture and structure as two complementary organizational resources that affected the relationship between one type of IS deployment and the bottom-line performance of firms. Additional research identifying and/or testing the influence of other organizational complements of IS would help advance the resource-based theory of the strategic impacts of IS.

Managerial Implications

The results of this research have significant implications for IS management for strategic flexibility. While firms these days are investing heavily in building and using IS to increase their flexibility to respond to the rapid changes in their business environments (Upton, 1995), the performance impacts of such IS investments depend on the presence of certain firm-specific resources that complement the IS. Firms are in a better position to gain competitive advantage from their IS investments for strategic flexibility if they possess distinctive organizational culture and structure that complement the IS. Accordingly, it is insufficient for a firm to invest in IS that support strategic flexibility if the firm hopes to reap economic returns from such IS investments. The firm also needs to develop distinctive organizational culture and structure that align with its IS investments for strategic flexibility.

The study also implies a bigger role of IS in helping firms gain competitive advantage than that suggested by those who question the strategic value of IS (Mata, Fuerst, and Barney, 1995; Martinsons and Martinsons, 2002). Contrary to the growing skepticism toward whether IS can be more than a "strategic necessity," the findings from the study suggest that IS can be a source of competitive advantage and superior firm performance under certain circumstances, that is, when IS are used to support the development of distinctive organizational capabilities (e.g., strategic flexibility) and complemented by certain firm-specific organizational resources. Therefore, firms and their managers should link their IS investments and deployment closely to the development of their distinctive organizational capabilities and create an environment for maximizing the economic value of IS support for distinctive organizational capabilities.

Limitations of the Study

The findings in this study need to be interpreted within its limitations. The study relied on perceptual data collected from single informants in measuring IS support for strategic flexibility and firm-specific, complementary organizational culture and structure. Data collected in such a manner may be subject to the respondents' cognitive biases and distortions. On the other hand, the use of objective measures for the performance and control variables avoided similar biases and inaccuracies in collecting the data for those variables and reduced the "common variance bias." As another limitation, the response rate for the survey used in this research (20 percent), while comparable to those of similar studies, was relatively low and thus limited the generalizability of the study results. Obtaining high response rates for sensitive information concerning the strategic use of IS continues to be a challenge for researchers.

References

Aggarwal, S. (1997). Flexibility management: The ultimate strategy. *Industrial Management*, (Jan/Feb), 26–31.

Ahmed, P., Hardaker, G., and Carpenter, M. (1996). Integrated flexibility: Key to competition in a turbulent environment. *Long Range Planning*, 29 (4), 562–571.

Aiken, L. and West, S. (1991). *Multiple Regression: Testing and Interpreting Interactions*. Newbury Park, CA: Sage.

Amit, R. and Schoemaker, P. (1993). Strategic assets and organizational rent. *Strategic Management Journal*, 14, 33–46.

Applegate, L. and Elam, J. (1992). New information systems leaders: A changing role in a changing world. *MIS Quarterly*, 16 (4), 469–490.

Armstrong, J. and Overton, T. (1977). Estimating nonresponse bias in mail surveys. *Journal of Marketing Research*, 14, 396. 402.

Badaracco, J. L. (1991). *The Knowledge Link: How Firms Compete Through Strategic Alliances*. Boston, MA: Harvard Business School Press.

Bakos, J. and Treacy, M. (1986). Information technology and corporate strategy: A research perspective. *MIS Quarterly*, 10 (2), 107–119.

Barney, J. B. (1986). Organizational culture: Can it be a source of sustained competitive advantage? *Academy of Management Review*, 11 (3), 656–665.

Bharadwaj, A. (2000). A resource-based perspective on information technology capability and firm performance: An empirical investigation. *MIS Quarterly*, 24 (1), 169–196.

Bourgeois, L. (1981). On measurement of organizational slack. *Academy of Management Review*, 6 (1), 29–40.

Boynton, A. (1993). Achieving dynamic stability through information technology. *California Management Review*, 35 (2), 58–77.

Boynton, A., Victor, B., and Pine, B. (1993). New competitive strategies: Challenge to organizations and information technology. *IBM Systems Journal*, 32 (1), 40–64.

Brown, R., Gatian, A., and Hicks, Jr., J. (1995). Strategic information systems and financial performance. *Journal of Management Information Systems*, 11 (4), 215–248.

Byrd, T. (2001). Information technology: Core competencies, and sustained competitive advantage. *Information Resources Management Journal*, 14 (2), 27–36.

Byrd, T. A. and Turner, D. E. (2001). An exploratory analysis of the value of the skills of IT personnel: Their relationship to IS infrastructure and competitive advantage. *Decision Science*, 32 (1), 21–54.

Chakravarthy, B. (1986). Measuring strategic performance. *Strategic Management Journal*, 7 (5), 437–458.

Chase, R. and Garvin, D. (1989). The service factory. *Harvard Business Review*, 67 (4), 61–69.

Clark, K. (1989). What strategy can do for technology. *Harvard Business Review*, 67 (6), 94–98.

Clemons, E. and Row, M. (1991). Sustaining IT advantage: The role of structural differences. *MIS Quarterly*, 15 (3), 275–292.

Collis, D. (1994). Research Note: How valuable are organizational capabilities? *Strategic Management Journal*, 15 (1), 143–152.

Constant, D., Sproull, L., and Kiesler, S. (1996). The kindness of strangers: On the usefulness of weak ties for technical advice. *Organization Science*, 7 (2), 119–135.

Earl, M. and Feeny, D. (1994). Is your CIO adding value? *MIT Sloan Management Review*, 35 (3), 11–20.

Eisenhardt, K. and Martin, J. (2000). Dynamic capabilities: What are they? *Strategic Management Journal*, 21, 1105–1121.

Feeny, D. F. and Ives, B. (1990). In search of sustainability: Reaping long-term advantage from investments in Information Technology. *Journal of Management Information Systems*, 7 (1), 27–46.

Gerwin, D. (1993). Manufacturing flexibility: A strategic perspective. *Management Science*, 39 (4), 395–410.

Goldhar, J. and Lei, D. (1995). Variety is free: Manufacturing in the twenty-first century. *Academy of Management Executive*, 9 (4), 73–86.

Goodman, P. S. and Darr, E. D. (1998). Computer-aided systems and communities: Mechanisms for organizational learning in distributed environments. *MIS Quarterly*, 22 (4), 417–440.

Hayes, R. and Pisano, G. (1994). Beyond world-class: The new manufacturing strategy. *Harvard Business Review*, 73, 77–86.

Hitt, M., Keats, B., and DeMarie, S. (1998). Navigating in the new competitive landscape: Building strategic flexibility and competitive advantage in the 21st Century. *Academy of Management Executive*, 12 (4), 22–42.

Hyun, J. and Ahn, B. (1992). A unifying framework for manufacturing flexibility. *Manufacturing Review*, 5 (4), 251–260.

Karimi, J., Gupta, Y. P., and Somers, T. M. (1996). The congruence between a firm's competitive strategy and Information Technology leader's rank and role. *Journal of Management Information Systems*, 13 (1), 63–88.

Kearns, G. S. and Lederer, A. L. (2003). A resource-based view of strategic IT alignment: How knowledge sharing creates competitive advantage. *Decision Sciences*, 34 (1), 1–29.

Kettinger, et al. (1994). Strategic information systems revisited: A study in sustainability and performance. *MIS Quarterly*, 18 (1), 31–58.

Kivijarvi, H. and Saarinen, T. (1995). Investment in information systems and the financial performance of the firm. *Information & Management*, 28, 143–163.

Kotha, S. (1995). Mass customization: Implementing the emerging paradigm for competitive advantage. *Strategic Management Journal*, 16, 21–42.

Lado, A. and Zhang, M. (1998). Expert systems, knowledge development and utilization, and sustained competitive advantage: A resource-based model. *Journal of Management*, 24 (4), 489–509.

Lei, D., Hitt, M., and Goldhar, J. (1996). Advanced manufacturing technology: Organizational design and strategic flexibility. *Organization Studies*, 17 (3), 501–523.

Li, M. and Ye, R. (1999). Information technology and firm performance: Linking with environmental, strategic and managerial contexts. *Information & Management*, 35 (1), 43–51.

Mahmood, M. and Soon, S. (1991). A comprehensive model for measuring the potential impact of Information Technology on organizational strategic variables. *Decision Sciences*, 22 (4), 869–897.

Martinsons, M. G. and Martinsons, V. (2002). Rethinking the value of IT, again. *Communications of the ACM*, 45 (7), 25–26.

Mata, F., Fuerst, W., and Barney, J. (1995). Information Technology and sustained competitive advantage: A resource-based analysis. *MIS Quarterly*, 19 (4), 487–505.

Palmer, J. and Markus, M. (2000). The performance impacts of quick response and strategic alignment in specialty retailing. *Management Science*, 11 (3), 241–259.

Pine, B. (1993). *Mass Customization: The New Frontier in Business Competition*. Boston, MA: Harvard Business School Press.

Pine, B. J., Victor, B., and Boynton, A. (1993). Making mass customization work. *Harvard Business Review*, 71 (5), 108–119.

Powell, T. and Dent-Micallef, A. (1997). Information Technology as competitive advantage: The role of human, business, and technology resources. *Strategic Management Journal*, 18 (5), 375–405.

Sambamurthy, V., Bharadwaj, A., and Grover, V. (2003). Shaping agility through digital options: Reconceptualizing the role of Information Technology in contemporary firms. *MIS Quarterly*, 27 (2): 237–263.

Sanchez, R. (1995). Strategic flexibility in product competition. *Strategic Management Journal*, 16, 135–159.

Sawhney, M. (2001). Don't homogenize, synchronize. *Harvard Business Review*, 79 (7), 101–108.

Sethi, A. and Sethi, S. (1990). Flexibility in manufacturing: A survey. *International Journal of Flexible Manufacturing Systems*, 2 (4), 289–328.

Sethi, V. and King, W. (1994). Development of measures to assess the extent to which an Information Technology application provides competitive advantage. *Management Science*, 40 (12), 1601–1627.

Stalk, G., Evans, P., and Shulman, L. (1992). Competing on capabilities: The new rules of corporate strategy. *Harvard Business Review*, 70 (2), 57–69.

Stephens, C. S., et al. (1992). Executive or functional manager? The nature of the CIO's job. *MIS Quarterly*, 16 (4), 449–467.

Tam, K. Y. (1998). The impact of Information Technology investments on firm performance and evaluation: Evidence from newly industrialized economies. *Information Systems Research*, 9 (1), 85–98.

Teece, D. (1986). Profiting from technological innovations: Implications for integration, collaboration, licensing, and public policy. *Research Policy*, 15 (6), 285–305.

Teece, D., Pisano, G., and Shuen, A. (1997). Dynamic capabilities and strategic management. *Strategic Management Journal*, 18 (7), 509–533.

Treacy, M. and Wiersema, F. (1993). Customer intimacy and other value disciplines. *Harvard Business Review*, 71, 84–93.

Upton, D. (1994). The management of manufacturing flexibility. *California Management Review*, 36 (2), 72–86.

Upton, D. (1995). What really makes factories flexible? *Harvard Business Review*, 73 (4), 74–84.

Wade, M. and Hulland, J. (2004). The resource-based view and information systems research: Review, extension, and suggestions for future research. *MIS Quarterly*, 28 (1), 107–142.

Zammuto, R. and O'Connor, E. (1992). Gaining advanced manufacturing technologies' benefits: The roles of organizational design and culture. *Academy of Management Review*, 17 (4), 701–728.

Zuboff, S. (1988). *In the Age of the Smart Machine: The future of work and power*. New York: Basic Books.

7

Balancing Stability and Flexibility: The Case of the California Energy Commission

Miguel Gabriel Custodio, Alan Thorogood, and Philip Yetton

The concept of agility first appeared in the business literature when a group of researchers coined the term *agile manufacturing* at Lehigh University (Iacocca Institute, 1991). Since then, the concept has spread across various disciplines, including software development, in the forms of "agile methods" and "agile systems." However, despite more than a decade of studies, agility is still in its infancy with its dominant logic still underdeveloped. According to Conboy and Fitzgerald (2004), most of the agility concepts are adaptations of elements such as flexibility and leanness, which originated earlier. In developing their definition of agility, Conboy and Fitzgerald draw on the concepts of flexibility and leanness to define agility as: "*the continual readiness of an entity to rapidly or inherently, proactively or reactively, embrace change, through high quality, simplistic, economical components and relationships with its environment*" (p. 40).

Organizations invest in Information Technology (IT) to drive current business performance, enable future business initiatives, and create business flexibility and agility (Weill and Broadbent, 1997; Weill, Subramani, and Broadbent, 2002; Ross, 2003). These benefits are well explored by both academics and practitioners (Brynjolfson and Hitt, 2000; Ross and Beath, 2002). They present two distinct and opposing views in relation to the impact of IT investment on organizational agility. One view is that IT can stabilize and facilitate business processes but can also obstruct the functional flexibility of organizations, making them slow and cumbersome in the face of emerging threats and opportunities. Such IT systems execute business policies and decisions that are hardwired by rigid, predefined process flows (Zoufaly, 2002). The development methods establish a legacy that dictates attitudes, behaviors, and understanding that are relevant to the past, with the organization becoming a "slave to the system" (Ward and Peppard, 2002).

The other view portrays IT applications as disruptive influences, often dislodging efficiently working processes and functions and leading to widespread instability that reduces or even eliminates the effectiveness of the organization's competitive efforts

(Lyytinen and Rose, 2003). Business and IT-focused media are replete with examples of systems implementations that fractured the operating infrastructure (Schrage, 2005). These turbulent episodes often leave organizations reeling in their efforts to recover, making them vulnerable to competitive attacks, and to the internal and external cascade of problems resulting from the initial intervention and subsequent recovery attempts. For an example of turbulent change, see Custodio, Thorogood, and Yetton (2005).

These two competing views need resolution for managers who face a continually changing technology-driven business environment. "Being agile" is a compelling catch cry but may lead to a complex and confusing interaction between stability and flexibility. CIOs and business executives ask: "How can we establish stability without resorting to a rigid and restrictive legacy?" and "How can flexibility deliver predictable and consistent performance?" To be stable is to be robust and strong—consistent behavior even in a changing business environment, while being flexible is being limber and responsive—adapting to new challenges. Despite their opposing nature, these characteristics of stability and flexibility are, in combination, the defining elements of agility.

Agile Systems

Information technology has changed significantly since the mid 1980s. Contemporary application architecture promotes the separation of data, logic, workflow, and presentation layers to achieve distributed processing and component reusability (Wilkes and Veryard, 2004). The need for speedy implementation of business applications has also led to software development techniques that advocate less formal, faster, and more flexible methods of development. In the mid 1990s, attempts to formalize the knowledge that characterizes agile systems began to take form (Dove, 1996). Among many differing definitions, agile systems are associated with "response-ability," or the ability to both proactively and reactively respond to opportunities and needs (Dove, 2005).

Agile systems are highly adaptive IT-driven business applications. However, they are more than just technology: a "system" is an assemblage of interrelated elements comprising a unified whole (*Oxford English Dictionary*, 2004). This "unified whole" includes processes, resources (people and materials), technologies (hardware, software, etc.), and information to perform a particular function. In IT operations, this means designing and building adaptive business applications, and defining and implementing the infrastructure and operating platforms to deliver information-related services to the entire organization. The agility of a particular business system is only as good as the stability, responsiveness, and adaptability of the operating environment for maintaining and using the system.

A Model of IT Agility

In the academic and management literature, the agility-flexibility links receive more attention than the agility-stability links. Indeed, some researchers and journalists use the two terms, *agility* and *flexibility* synonymously. In contrast to the explicit links between agility and flexibility, there is only an implicit link between agility and stability. The literature also shows confusion in the separation of flexibility from stability. For example, in an early study, Hashimoto (1980) refers to robustness or resilience as attributes of flexibility. He argues that, to be truly flexible, a system must not only be able to adapt to change, but must also be able to withstand change. However, robustness and resilience are different constructs. According to Haberfellner and de Weck (2005), robustness signifies the ability to perform without changes under a variety of circumstances and usually relates to stability. Resilience, on the other hand, depicts adaptability—the ability to change autonomously to follow changes in the environment. This trait normally relates to flexibility. The IT Agility model developed here helps to resolve this confusion by explicitly mapping IT along the two dimensions of *stability* and *flexibility* (Figure 7.1).

The model identifies four quadrants that represent various agility conditions, namely: *chaotic, rigid, fluid,* and *agile* (see Figure 7.1). When stability and flexibility are both low, performance becomes *chaotic*, reflecting the absence of strategic direction in determining objectives and execution. Existing operations are unreliable, and future developments are risky because the infrastructure is fragile and complex. The causes may be a lack of knowledge, guidelines, competence, or shared interest in any objectives.

A *fluid* state has high levels of flexibility but low platform stability. While reactive capabilities to changing demands are often available, erratic ad hoc actions may adversely affect outcomes. Knowledge, interest, and competence may be present but, without a guiding foundation, they will be ineffective in delivering sustainable results. A *rigid* state represents stable but constrained conditions that limit the ability to leverage capabilities in taking advantage of emerging opportunities or dealing with arising threats. Despite establishing a stable form of operation, the guiding foundations restrict the use of existing knowledge and capabilities, which diminishes interest in exploring potentially valuable innovative actions.

Figure 7.1

Contextual Constraints on Agile Performance in Dynamic and Turbulent Environments

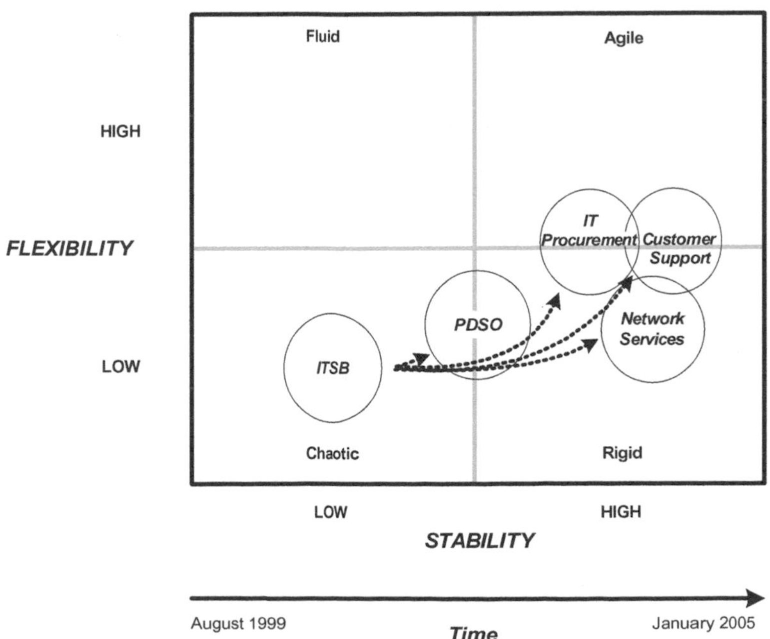

An *agile* state refers to a stable and flexible state, sufficiently dynamic to deal with shifting business demands but with dependable practices and repeatable results. In this condition, the operating platform or infrastructure optimizes knowledge management, dynamic capabilities, and the motivation to capture business innovations. A major question then becomes: *What is the trajectory followed around the quadrants?*

Practitioners measure stability using a variety of techniques. Traditional stability measures include the percentage of uptime, with Five-Nines (99.999 percent) a frequent goal. Over the medium term and long term, stability measures include conformance to architectural standards. Variation from the standards causes "drift," which results in a more complex infrastructure and often requires re-centralization of IT to achieve stability (Ciborra, 2000).

There are also many measures of flexibility. In the short term, these include the capacity to deliver acceptable response times under changing loads. Seasonal, daily, or hourly variations in load can quickly bring a system down unless that system can flex with the demand. Over the medium term, parameterization allows systems to change without undergoing lengthy software development life cycles. In the long term, certain technical and organizational principles can support new developments and decommissioning of old systems. Service-oriented technology architectures encourage decoupling of systems. In this way, organizations can change one system and affect fewer supporting systems than would be the case with alternative architectures. At a socio-technical level, organic organizations have less complex formal structures (Burns and Stalker, 1961), which makes them accommodating to change (Brown and Eisenhardt, 1997).

In terms of the IT Agility model, organizations use a variety of tools to define the degree of stability and flexibility for each of the services they offer. The following section uses a case study to explore the model and to demonstrate how stability and flexibility are prerequisites for *agile* IT operations.

California Energy Commission

California Energy Commission (CEC) is an ideal case with which to examine the development and benefits of agile systems. Over the years, CEC had reacted to constantly changing legislation by quickly developing new IT systems and rapidly altering old ones. The result was a fragmented infrastructure with incompatible systems, developed with a variety of approaches.

Background Information

The CEC is a government entity that plans and regulates energy-related activities in the most populous state of the United States. Created in 1974, the CEC's role grew to include overseeing funding programs to support public-interest energy research; advancing energy science and energy technology through research, development, and demonstration; and providing market support to existing, new, and emerging renewable technologies (California Energy Commission, 2006). The CEC abides by the policies and procedures set forth by the California state government and the U.S. federal government in conducting its activities. The California state government provides major systems such as human resources, payroll, and accounting from a central service, which it delivers to many California state agencies including the CEC. In addition to these centrally provided administrative systems, the CEC has commission-specified business applications under its own control. To support these applications, the CEC established formal IT operations in 1979 to control the growing number of mission-specific applications. Many specialist applications were developed and implemented, using a variety of methods, protocols and technologies.

Identifying the Issues

Dale Bosley took up the position of Chief Information Officer (CIO) in August 1999. His appointment followed a review of the CEC's IT operations by KPMG, a large accounting and consulting practice. For fifteen years before taking the CIO role, Bosley had been CEC's Chief Financial Officer, which had made him one of the IT unit's major customers and a vocal critic of CEC's IT services.

According to Bosley, IT was in a mess. The Information Technology Services Branch (ITSB) faced the compounded results of two decades of piecemeal development. During that time, there had been no espoused strategy for ITSB, which resulted in a state of constant flux, low levels of performance, and low credibility with the business units. The majority of the ITSB staff had little sense of purpose.

Systems development was more akin to undocumented garage-research "skunk" projects than to service-oriented business applications. The design, development, and implementation of business applications had no discernible organization, accountability, documentation, or business requirements. There were no software development or project management standards and procedures, so almost all choices in the design and implementation of application systems fell to the developers' discretion.

Business managers were withholding input and feedback, so planning and prioritization of business initiatives were ineffective. Active projects had minimal coordination resulting in wide-ranging overlaps and duplications. At the same time, many projects were tightly dependent on each other. For example, while the project to upgrade the building's network cabling was on the verge of collapse due to disputes on billing and inadequate vendor and contract management, other projects were completely dependent on the proposed new high-speed network.

The communications and information-processing infrastructure were constantly at risk; email and other network outages were occurring frequently and lasted for several hours at a time. Technology platforms were in disarray, with some grossly outdated and in need of significant investment.

Not only was the technology a challenge, the organizational design was also problematic. There was no clear definition of individual responsibilities or accountabilities. ITSB's operating structure was vague. Formally, it had a flat organization with no structures defining specific areas of responsibilities. All staff reported directly to one manager. With only one overloaded manager and no chain-of-command, confusion abounded. The informal team leaders had no supervisory authority, which fostered dissent. This environment-induced conflict significantly reduced staff performance and, therefore, that of the IT services.

CEC's business units distrusted ITSB, complaining of lack of service attention and unprofessional attitudes. However, ITSB was, at the time, grossly underresourced to perform even the daily operating tasks, and staff lacked essential technical and operational skills. Furthermore, there were no formal training programs or competence development plans for ITSB staff. Day-to-day workloads had reached unsustainable levels, with most system faults remaining unsolved for unacceptable periods. These conditions contributed to a confrontational atmosphere both internally within ITSB, and between ITSB and the business units.

At a technical level, the majority of the business applications fell short of required functionality and performance, and systems had undocumented process flows and user interfaces. To comply with legislative requirements, the business units developed manual workaround processes and added dedicated resources, which cost a considerable amount of time and effort both to establish and to maintain. Subsequently, during troubleshooting episodes, users would reject ITSB-suggested improvements because of the indirect costs of making a change to the workarounds. Indeed, to avoid expensive revisions of workaround processes, the business users would ask technicians to revert applications back to previous versions. Fundamentally, users believed that ITSB was incapable of delivering IT-based business solutions and services. Some took matters into their own hands and bypassed ITSB completely, hiring third-party IT solution providers to satisfy their specific requirements.

Procurement of IT equipment was also a problem. Although ITSB established standards for desktop hardware specifications as part of a 1998 PC deployment project, it was difficult to enforce those standards. CEC's central purchasing operation, external to ITSB, had few technical capabilities, yet was responsible for equipment ordering. There were many expensive mistakes and long delays. Again, the business units took matters into their own hands, and user-defined non-standard technology platforms had begun appearing throughout the CEC. This made ITSB's technical support role even more challenging.

In the IT review, KPMG recommended three changes:

- Develop a structure for IT governance
- Centralize service provision within ITSB
- Develop and enforce policies and guidelines for effective IT operations

For CEC's executives, the troubles in ITSB indicated a need for a leader with a proven record of accomplishment—someone who understood the intricacies of IT. Bosley was seen as the man for the job. As the CFO, Bosley had led the 1998 PC deployment project—a rare example of a successful IT project. He had also served as the chair of the Information Technology Advisory Committee and had a good understanding of, and firm opinions about, ITSB's situation and performance.

Surmounting the Problems

Bosley knew that regaining the trust of the business units would require a complete transformation of ITSB into a high-performing operation. Soon after taking over, in August 1999, he presented a high-performance vision and initiated a massive overhaul. He convinced the CEC executives to stabilize funding for ITSB and began implementing his version of the KPMG recommendations.

The first item on his agenda was ITSB's internal governance. He split the operation into defined functional areas, namely: customer support, network services, and application development. To each, he assigned dedicated managers accountable for the performance of their respective functional areas. To establish control over IT purchasing, he negotiated moving the IT procurement function directly under his control. He also appointed Atlas Hill, a longtime technical operative, as Assistant Manager of ITSB. Hill was then responsible for much of the internal operations, freeing Bosley to concentrate on strategic issues. Hill also directly oversaw Customer Support, including the Help Desk.

The next agenda item was to transform ITSB into a central, organization-wide IT service provider. With clearly partitioned functional areas, Bosley began to define and allocate responsibilities and accountabilities. This allowed for the careful identification and development of services that were both in demand and cost-effective. With the underlying service processes developed and agreed, Bosley identified the appropriate resources. This required people with the right skills, knowledge, and attitude to deliver at the highest level. In parallel, Bosley identified and procured the necessary tools and equipment. With service definitions, staff and tools in place, along with "rules of engagement" for obtaining IT services, he presented the total IT service package to the CEC management and staff.

The third agenda item, defining policies and guidelines, was mostly completed as a by-product of the other two initiatives—internal governance and service definition. In developing the internal governance and transforming ITSB into a centralized service provider, the new ITSB management team had defined major policies and guidelines. As an example, they developed policies and procedures for outsourcing those critical functions where ITSB had few capabilities, such as the design and deployment of high-speed and secure networks.

KPMG conducted an audit in April 2001 and reported an overall improvement, but with slow progress in some areas. They suggested the application of additional resources to accelerate or at least sustain the rate of change. One area that was lagging was Business Applications—later renamed Project Development and Support Office (PDSO), which had run into many difficulties that the business units felt were due to the complacent and reactive attitudes of its staff. Development projects were late due to mistakes in design and implementation, insufficient programming skills, and unsuitable technology for the required functionality and performance. Early in the transformation, ITSB tried to outsource the development of these applications but, because the standards and policies for design, development, project management, and vendor engagement were not fully defined, the resulting applications were little better than those developed internally. While he explored ways of improving PDSO's performance, Bosley abandoned or suspended most IT-based business projects that had been in the process of development.

Improving PDSO

Over the years, PDSO had been unable to develop the necessary competencies to fulfill its mission of developing IT-based business solutions. PDSO personnel felt that most of the CEC staff saw the unit as a hindrance in the successful implementation of new IT systems and the improvement of existing systems. At the end of 2004, Bosley appointed Rita Gass to lead the transformation of PDSO. Just a few months after her appointment, Bosley regarded the observable improvements in PDSO as revolutionary compared with the slow evolutionary advancement in the rest of ITSB. Her upbeat "let's get it done" attitude had revitalized the PDSO staff.

Gass began by building a communications plan, with PDSO and the business units as audiences. Her objective was to make PDSO's purpose clear. She wrote and communicated the unit's mission not only to her staff but to all CEC personnel. To support the mission, she and her staff reviewed the services they would deliver to their customers and how would they deliver them. This led to the creation of PDSO's internal value chain that identified and defined each service they would provide. Similar to Bosley's approach, the value chain broke down the services into subcomponents to determine the processes, resources, and tools needed to deliver the services. Gass then assigned staff members to the services, based on their respective competencies and brought in contractors to address areas where PDSO staff lacked competencies. Through the process of this redesign, the staff developed a sense of ownership over PDSO's role and clarified their individual contributions to the overall mission.

With the intended services defined, the second item on Gass's agenda was to stabilize the unit's current operations. Unlike Bosley, for whom standards and guidelines had emerged as a by-product of other activities, she explicitly created standards and guidelines for application development and project management. This required a substantial investment of her time but established consistency. Drawing on the processes, tools, and resources identified by the internal value chain, her team defined the rules and conditions for initiating, executing, and controlling application development and other project activities. This framed discussions by setting negotiable and non-negotiable procedures to be observed by all parties. Standards were established for definition and formatting of data to enable applications to share information effectively; coding technologies and methods to improve maintenance; project management methodologies to enforce repeatable execution of project tasks; and training programs to improve technical and operative competencies. Exceptions and justifications were identified that would allow flexibility in the processes, with the provision that these exceptions required appropriate negotiation and review to preserve the efficacy of the entire process.

Stabilization also called for a robust application promotion process and a configuration management system to help enforce the newly developed standards and policies. Gass set up a version-controlled code repository and test environments to fit the standards, processes, and competencies for promoting code all the way from development to production. Code quality significantly improved, leading the way to superior application stability and performance. Gass also documented all of the systems supported by PDSO, which was a considerable task. Her team built a documentation portfolio for each business application, which included details of system design and development; technical specifications; original concept and purpose; and changes deployed over time. Updated routinely, the portfolios showed both current and future states to help identify future servicing needs.

By August 2005, most of the PDSO initiatives were in place. Project completion rates improved and business customers praised the functional improvements and system performance. PDSO staff had begun to enjoy their assignments knowing what their hand-offs were within the different processes and functions. Credibility increased and the business units began to open up to suggestions concerning the future of their business systems. With continued guidance and support from Bosley, Gass succeeded in turning PDSO around in only six months.

Analysis and Discussion

CEC sought to rebuild ITSB's credibility with the business units by establishing stability, while maintaining sufficient flexibility to meet business unit needs. Bosley's objective was to deliver reliable IT and to be responsive to the business. This section analyses the CEC case study within the IT Agility model to show the paths that Bosley used to reposition ITSB and improve credibility within the organization.

The analysis positions the functional areas of ITSB over three periods: before Bosley takes the position as CIO, after Bosley's initial intervention, and after Gass's contribution of transforming PDSO. Comparing ITSB's individual functional areas reveals differing agility needs for each area. Separating the positions by time shows the path-to-fit, which can suggest actionable management recommendations (Sauer and Yetton, 1997).

The Lead-up to Bosley's Takeover

Immediately before Bosley took the position of CIO, in August 1999, the ITSB operations were *chaotic*, with low levels of stability and little flexibility (Figure 7.2). Without a strategy, ITSB staff had no sense of direction. ITSB was highly unstable; it was challenged by the lack of knowledge, competence, interest, and guidance in proactively developing systems and in reacting to errors and faults in production. Development projects were using complex and incompatible technologies with unclear internal reporting lines. Performance was low and unpredictable. Existing business applications were unstable due to the absence of programming and implementation standards, major deficiencies in design (i.e., data, logic, and presentation), use of inappropriate and outdated technologies, and low programming competence. Troubleshooting problems in these applications often opened up a cascade of unpredictable factors that would go unresolved for days or even weeks. The source of the problems could hide inside systems developed by third parties and running on proprietary hardware unfamiliar to ITSB.

IT development was inflexible because it did not have solid groundings in the form of robust operating standards and policies and strong relationships with the business units to fulfill the organization's changing business application needs. Without standards, policies, methods, and shared understandings, both ITSB and the business units discouraged proactive IT-based business initiatives. ITSB projects ran according to individual ITSB staffers' preferences, which were unacceptable to the business units,

Figure 7.2

ITSB Units' Paths to Fit: August 1999 to January 2005

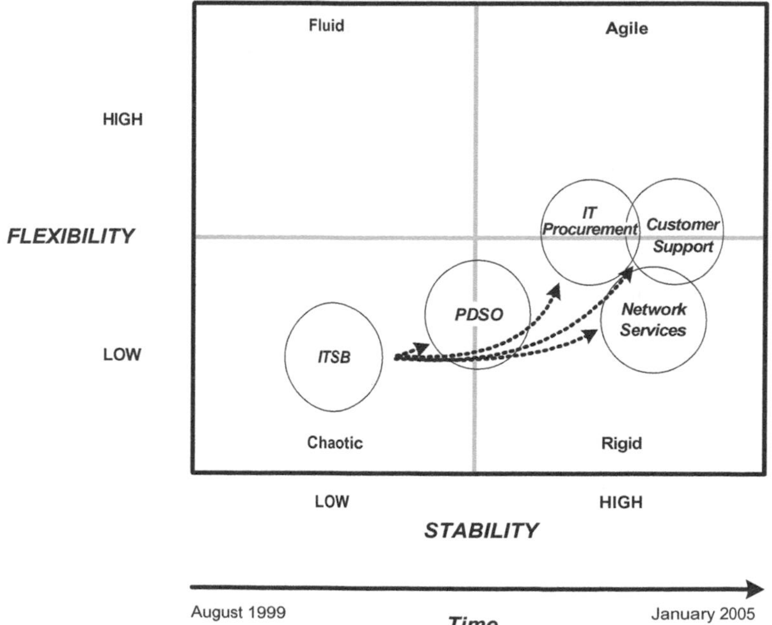

or they were run as undercover skunk works by the business units, which was unacceptable to ITSB. This led to what can be described as a *chaotic deadlock*.

Attempts by both ITSB and the business units to be flexible in the face of changing business needs failed, as new business applications could not be rapidly developed, or existing ones easily adapted to new requirements. Even minor changes to IT were difficult because existing business applications depended on sophisticated workaround processes implemented by the business units to compensate for functional and performance shortcomings. A small change for IT resulted in large changes to the workaround processes. The users were revolting against ITSB to protect CEC and ensure legislative compliance.

IT that is both unstable and inflexible is in the *chaotic* quadrant of the IT Agility model. A platform that works for neither proactive development nor reactive maintenance and operations is difficult to change. A "green-field" replacement was impossible for CEC because the business units had no confidence in ITSB's ability to build new systems. Even though the existing systems were poor, combining them with the workarounds did provide legislative compliance. For the business units, moving to an unknown future without a trusted service provider was unacceptable.

Bosley's Reorganization

Bosley saw ITSB as a portfolio of services rather than a monolithic technology provider. To varying degrees, all CEC's IT services needed to become more stable and more flexible. Figure 7.2 shows that by early 2005, Bosley had reorganized ITSB from a mono-structured operation into a multi-structured one, with each functional area having different agility characteristics. Each of the four areas—customer support, network services, IT procurement, and application development (PDSO)—had different requirements. All needed significant improvement in stability, and some needed more flexibility than the others. In Bosley's reorganization, the functional areas became more stable by adopting policies and procedures, and "rules of engagement" linking ITSB and business units in a structured relationship.

Essentially, the ITSB operations were following a path from *chaotic* to *rigid* to *agile*. Bosley's initial approach was inflexible and resulted in rigid arrangements, which he then relaxed over time to allow for some flexibility, particularly in areas requiring more agility. In ITSB's transition, the first task was to establish some form of stability through an espoused high-performance strategy that in execution delivered new structures, standards, policies, procedures, and resource allocations. Once in place, the teams made adjustments, leaving some elements open to accommodate unforeseen requirements and innovation.

ITSB's path from *chaotic* to *agile* was neither linear nor singular, with different curvilinear trajectories and different distances for each of the functional areas. For example, in Figure 7.2 the transition plots show that PDSO's trajectory was considerably shorter than that of the other functional areas. PDSO was experiencing many delays before Gass took over the unit. Figure 7.2 depicts these delays as a short path of progression.

Gass Transforms PDSO

Gass built considerable flexibility into PDSO to deliver effective services to the business units. She negotiated customization of services with the business units to find an appropriate solution to specific needs. However, not everything was open for negotiation. Many services were non-negotiable and required compliance when developing a business solution (Figure 7.3). For PDSO, agility depended on proficiency in defining the thresholds of negotiability for standards and policies among the services it delivered. Negotiable items allowed input, comment, and adjustments by involved parties. Non-negotiable items enforced compliance.

By establishing this framework, Gass achieved both stability and flexibility, making the organization robust and responsive to its customers. In Figure 7.3, PDSO's data management standards and policies remained mostly non-negotiable. Enforced data formatting, data usage, and data communication standards secured CEC's information assets from corruption, misuse, and abuse. These non-negotiable standards and policies facilitated consistent and effective data sharing among different business applications. For data management, one of the few negotiable aspects involves new data supporting new business initiatives. Applications for new data must include a full justification and must receive proper approvals before implementation. Figure 7.3 shows the *negotiability threshold* of several PDSO services. By comprehensively defining its negotiability threshold for each service, Gass began to define PDSO's *agility profile*.

For Gass, a proactive development team such as PDSO needed to be more flexible to accommodate business needs, compared with other ITSB functional areas. The result was a trajectory that took PDSO steeply into the model's *agile* quadrant by early 2006 (Figure 7.4). PDSO's services were highly interactive and required the unit to be deft and adaptive to deliver effective custom-built solutions. PDSO had to adapt to each business unit's needs and fit its modus operandi to each project, while protecting the infrastructure from high-cost fragmentation. Network Services, in comparison, had less need to adapt to business units or IT-based business projects. Analysis of Network Services showed that most of its operating elements remained static without affecting its business effectiveness. For example, when implemented correctly, a network architecture or topology changes infrequently, but network downtime can bring the business to a halt. Policies governing the CEC's network were

Figure 7.3

PDSO's Agility Profile

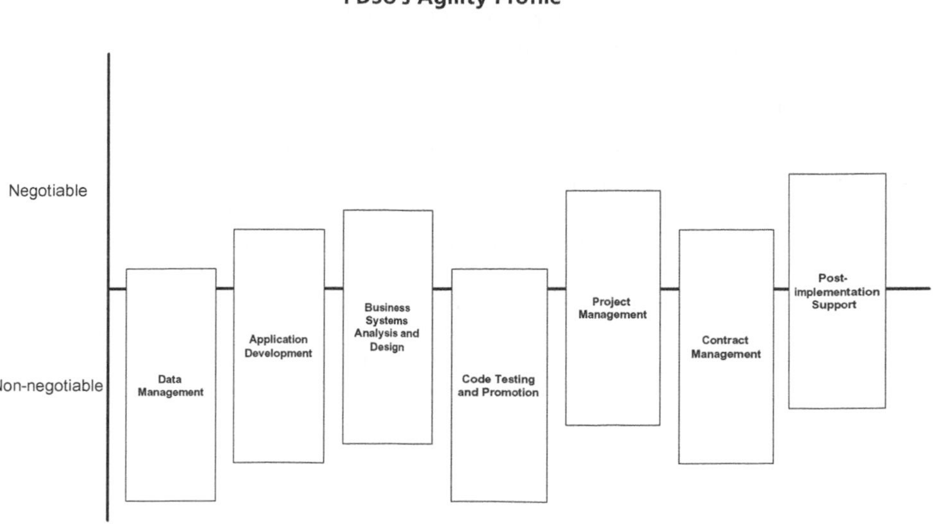

Figure 7.4

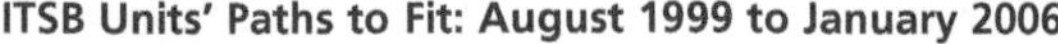

ITSB Units' Paths to Fit: August 1999 to January 2006

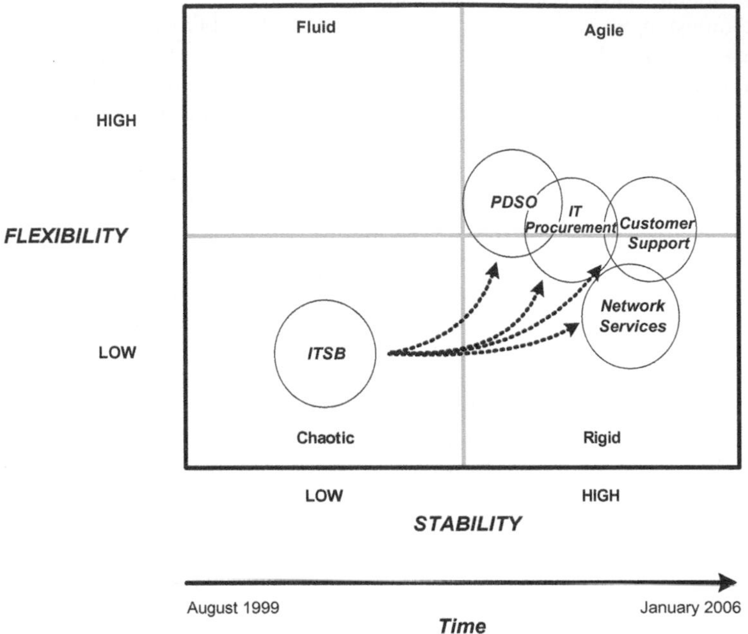

inflexible and restricted adaptations catering to particular business needs because the second-order consequences could be difficult to envision and potentially disastrous in outcome.

In early 2006, ITSB continued to refine its service agility profiles, placing each into a configuration to fit the business service needs. Figure 7.4 depicts the major improvements in PDSO's positioning by January 2006, and the incremental improvements for Customer Support and Network Services.

Discussion

The analysis above shows that CEC's IT agility is a positive function of ITSB's operational stability and flexibility. Without an appropriate combination of stability and flexibility, ITSB's operations had been chaotic and proactive business projects had low success rates and unpredictable outcomes. Under chaotic IT operations, corrective actions were challenged by nonstandard IT, undefined functions and processes, and a demoralized technical staff. CEC's path to regaining control over its IT operations was to focus on stability as a precursor to improving flexibility. Focusing on stability is an established path to success for CIOs (Earl and Feeny, 1994). However, the insight here is that, for PDSO, establishing stability was a prerequisite step in moving to *agile* operations. The alternative paths, moving directly to agility or going via fluidity, would require significant green-field investments. For CEC, the performance history of ITSB precluded large-scale investments, leaving the stability path as the only viable option.

With stability achieved, Gass allowed negotiation over some service deliveries within PDSO. This increased local flexibility to satisfy particular needs of business units and projects. Paradoxically, this also increased stability. Inflexible standards can lead to many exceptions that then cause a loss of control and instability (Ciborra, 2000). For Gass, this meant being responsive to user needs and applying flexibility rather than maintaining barriers that may have led business units to employ independent software developers. The *agility profile* is a key tool in determining how flexibility relates to stability.

Conclusion

This chapter has shown that *agile* IT operations involve a portfolio of IT services with *agility profiles* relevant to each service. Agile IT operations draw on customer support services, network services, and application development services, each requiring socio-technical considerations to differing degrees in designing processes, developing standards, and allocating resources. Moving from the *chaotic* quadrant to the *agile* quadrant of the IT Agility model requires that each service develop an appropriate balance of stability and flexibility.

From the practical perspective, the case shows that using *agility profiles* can help IT operations determine the stability-flexibility balance of their functional units, by establishing the *negotiability thresholds* for the various services they provide. These profiles can help identify the positions and movements of the functional units across the quadrants of the IT Agility model, helping track improvements. The case also shows that increased stability, characterized by trajectories passing through the *rigid* quadrant, was a precursor to becoming *agile*. From the research viewpoint, with agility as the intent, one critical question is: *Are there alternative trajectories that can directly or indirectly lead to the agility quadrant*?

References

Brown, S. L. and Eisenhardt, K. M. (1997). The art of continuous change: Linking complexity theory and time-paced evolution in relentlessly shifting organizations. *Administrative Science Quarterly*, 42 (1), 1.

Brynjolfson, E. and Hitt, L. M. (2000). Beyond computation: Information technology, organizational transformation and business performance. *Journal of Economic Perspectives*, 14 (4), 23–48.

Burns, T. and Stalker, G. M. (1961). *The Management of Innovation*. London, UK: Tavistock Publications.

California Energy Commission. (2006, 08/12/2005). Welcome to the California Energy Commission. Retrieved January 17, 2006, from: http://www.energy.ca.gov/commission/index.html.

Ciborra, C. U. A. (2000). *From Control to Drift: The Dynamics of Corporate Information Infrastructure*. Oxford, UK: Oxford University Press.

Conboy, K. and Fitzgerald, B. (2004). *Toward a Conceptual Framework of Agile Methods: A Study of Agility in Different Disciplines*. ACM Workshop on Interdisciplinary Software Engineering Research, Newport Beach, CA. November 2004.

Custodio, G., Thorogood, A., and Yetton, P. (2005). *24 × 7 @ Full Speed: Accelerated Time to Market*. Americas Conference on Information Systems, Nebraska.

Dove, R. (1996). *Tools for Analyzing and Constructing Agile Capabilities*. Paper presented at the 1996 Agility Forum, Bethlehem, PA.

Dove, R. (2005). *Fundamental Principles for Agile Systems Engineering*. Paper presented at the 2005 Conference on Systems Engineering Research, Hoboken, NJ.

Earl, M. J. and Feeny, D. (1994). Is your CIO adding value? *Sloan Management Review*, 35 (3), 11–20.

Haberfellner, R. and de Weck, O. (2005). *Agile SYSTEMS ENGINEERING versus AGILE SYSTEMS Engineering*. 15th Annual International Symposium of the International Council on Systems Engineering.

Hashimoto, T. (1980). *Robustness, Reliability, Resilience and Vulnerability Criteria for Planning*. Ithaca, New York: Cornell University Press.

Iaccoca Institute (1991). 21st century manufacturing enterprise strategy, An industry-led view. Iaccoca Institute.

Lyytinen, K. and Rose, G. M. (2003). The disruptive nature of information technology innovations: The case of Internet computing in systems development organizations. *MIS Quarterly*, 27 (4), 557.

Oxford English Dictionary. (2004). Oxford, UK: Oxford University Press.

Ross, J. W. (2003). Creating a strategic IT architecture competency: Learning in stages. *MIS Quarterly Executive*, 2 (1), 31–43.

Ross, J. W. and Beath, C. M. (2002). Beyond the business case: New approaches to IT investment. *MIT Sloan Management Review*, 43 (2), 51–59.

Sauer, C. and Yetton, P. W. (1997). *Steps to the Future: Fresh Thinking on the Management of IT-based Organizational Transformation*. San Francisco: Jossey-Bass.

Schrage, M. (2005). IT's hardest puzzle. *CIO*, September 2005.

Ward, J. and Peppard, J. (2002). The evolving role of information systems and technology in organizations: A strategic perspective. In R. Boland (ed.), *Strategic Planning for Information Systems* (3rd ed., pp. 1–59). Chichester, West Sussex: Wiley.

Weill, P. and Broadbent, M. (1997). *Leveraging the New Infrastructure: How Market Leaders Capitalize on Information Technology*. Boston, MA: Harvard Business School Press.

Weill, P., Subramani, M., and Broadbent, M. (2002). Building IT infrastructure for strategic agility. *MIT Sloan Management Review*, 44 (1), 57.

Wilkes, L. and Veryard, R. (2004). Service-oriented architecture: Considerations for agile systems. *Microsoft Architect Journal* 1. Retrieved December 15, 2005, from: http://msdn.microsoft.com/library/default.asp?url=/library/en-us/dnmaj/html/aj2service.asp

Zoufaly, F. (2002). Issue and challenges facing legacy systems. Retrieved December 16, 2005, from: http://www.developer.com/mgmt/article.php/1492531.

Enabling Strategic Agility Through Agile Information Systems: The Roles of Loose Coupling and Web Services Oriented Architecture[1]

John G. Mooney and Dale Ganley

Strategic agility has become a key competency as businesses face increasingly competitive markets (Sanchez, 1995; 1997; Hitt, Keats, and DeMarie, 1998; Prahalad, Krishnan, and Ramaswamy, 2002). However, for many firms, existing Information Technology (IT) infrastructure and systems pose a serious challenge to strategic agility (Sambamurthy, 2000; Weill, Subramani, and Broadbent, 2002). Many of these IT solutions do not allow for the flexibility and dynamism that is necessary in this new environment and the option of replacing these solutions is often not practically feasible. Given these limitations and the reality that strategic agility has become a critical imperative for many businesses, an important question can be raised about how IT can enable rather than constrain strategic agility.

Web services is one response being promoted aggressively by the major traditional software and IT services vendors, including Microsoft (.Net), Hewlett Packard, IBM (WebSphere), Oracle (Application Services), and Sun Microsystems (SunOne). Web services can be described as "a new way of thinking about acquiring and offering business services" (Gartner, 2002), which incorporates Web services component technology with existing IT infrastructure to create "Web Services Oriented Architecture" (wSOA). *CIO Magazine* describes it as a "major new trend in standards-based software technology . . . that lets two or more Web-based applications talk to each other. The . . . Web services' promise is to enable organizations to integrate and reuse software already built, reduce the hassle and expense of systems integration" (Patton, 2002). As both a business innovation and a technological innovation, wSOA provides an approach to achieving more flexible IT infrastructure and solutions than allowed by previous generations of IT (Hagel III, 2002), which can then serve as a platform for agile information systems that can enhance strategic agility. For example, Hagel III and Brown (2001) predicted that the availability of Web services would overturn many traditional assumptions about IT management and enable innovations in business strategy and process.

The goal of this chapter is to examine the opportunities and implications of wSOA for strategic agility. The chapter draws upon theories and concepts of strategic flexibility (Sanchez, 1997; Hitt, Keats, and DeMarie, 1998), loose coupling (Orton and Weick, 1990; Beekun and Glick, 2001), and IT infrastructure management (Weil and Broadbent, 1998; Ross, 2003) to examine the dynamic among wSOA (viewed as loosely coupled technology systems), loose coupling of business processes, and strategy agility.

The underlying thesis of the chapter is that in the context of everincreasing competitive environments, firms require higher levels of strategic agility (Hitt, Keats, and DeMarie, 1998). This in turn demands more agile organization and business processes, which is prompting a move away from "tight integration" toward "loosely coupled" arrangements (Sanchez, 1997). Flexibility in organization and business processes requires more flexible underlying IT infrastructure and systems (Weil and Broadbent, 1998). We propose that wSOA offers an approach to achieving more flexible IT infrastructure and systems than allowed by previous generations of IT (Hagel III, 2002). Consequently, the wSOA phenomenon can be viewed as the adoption of a highly modular, component-based approach to implementing loosely coupled (rather than tightly integrated) IT architectures, thereby enabling the more loosely coupled business processes and organizational arrangements that are necessary for strategic agility.

Web Services Oriented Architecture

A Web service can be defined as an independent and reusable component of functionality that can be invoked "over the Web" from any other component. The World Wide Web Consortium defines a Web service as "a software system identified by a URI [RFC 2396], whose public interfaces and bindings are defined and described using XML. Its definition can be discovered by other software systems. These systems may then interact with the Web service in a manner prescribed by its definition, using XML based messages conveyed by Internet protocols."[2] By using Web services, application developers can produce modules that can be published once, yet invoked from anywhere across the Internet. This standardization of the connection methods combined with the ubiquity of the communications platform increases the potential for reusable modular functionality to a very wide audience. Web services-enabled applications can interact with other applications, or other Web services, to provide a level of connectivity that, up to this point, has only been a promise of the Internet.

[2] http://www.w3.org/TR/ws-gloss.

The design and purposes of Web services are very similar to Electronic Data Interchange (EDI). EDI "refers to the computer-based exchange of standardized business-related information between buyer and supplier firms" (Hart and Saunders, 1997). The concept of standardized business-related information has been retained within Web services; what is new is the method of exchange. With EDI, participants are required to use a middleware platform to translate the data of each idiosyncratic application to a common form, then transport them from application to application, often translating again at the distant end. These middleware platforms are typically expensive configurations of hardware and software, and have resulted in closed, relatively small communities of EDI networks. Thus, the purported benefits of EDI like faster and more reliable data exchange between firms (Wang and Seidmann, 1995) have been constrained to only small groups of companies that can afford to implement the technology. In the n-tier application architecture perspective, wSOA provides the same functionality as the EDI middleware platform concept, without requiring expensive and proprietary systems to implement it. Essentially, the addition of Web services components moves the task of translating the data to a common form (and back) to the application, where the XML-based interface is incorporated. The transportation of the data is covered by the same Internet protocols that are cheaply and almost universally accessible to any firm.

wSOA is the integration of Web services components with other information processing and data storage systems, which may or may not be built with an eye toward inherent agility. This creates an IT environment that is highly modular and extremely malleable at the system level, despite any limitations of the systems that are integrated. The inclusion of business processes that take advantage of the wSOA creates the platform for an agile information system that can assist in meeting strategic goals in a dynamic business environment.

Loose Coupling

Loose coupling can be traced back to the concept of coordination among parts, as described in 1952 in Ashby's *Design for a Brain* (Ashby, 1952). Ashby described systems as being composed of distinct or independent subsystems acting in a coordinated fashion toward a purposeful goal. Mitchell and Zmud (1999) suggest that one of the primary features of a loosely coupled system is its ability to enact change, while limiting or delaying the effect on the interdependent parts. Loose coupling describes a particular state of connection between disparate elements. Orton and Weick (1990) assert that loose coupling "combine[s] the contradictory concepts of connection and autonomy." They further emphasize that the relevant dimensions of a loosely coupled system are *distinctiveness* and *responsiveness*. They extend earlier work (Weick, 1982; Perrow, 1984; Weick, 1985) to define a system with high lethargy and incrementalism (low responsiveness) and high indeterminacy (low distinctiveness) as loosely coupled. Beekun and Glick (2001) redefine loose coupling in terms of strength, directness, consistency, and dependence. Thus, it is clear that a loosely coupled system is interdependent to some degree, but that the components do not act responsively to each other. Loose coupling describes the functionality of loose linkages, which may be tightened to improve control but loosened to enhance cushioning from external jolts (Beekun and Ginn, 1993).

In the context of this chapter, we are concerned with the loose coupling between a firm's business and organization processes, and the loose coupling of the IT systems deployed to support and enable these processes. Two perspectives are valuable for analyzing this set of relationships: the process architecture perspective and the network organization perspective. The process architecture perspective examines how a process is decomposed and how the components interact to configure a system optimally for a given purpose. This emphasizes the direct impact of the loose coupling on the system that the architecture describes. Sanchez (1997) explains how, in the design of organizational processes, a modular approach with loosely coupled components helps to create the ability to reconfigure the system readily by enabling new functional process variations without excess disruption to the functions themselves. The network organization perspective focuses on the relationship that is being loosely coupled, which is implemented by an information system, and thus emphasizes the impact of the loosely coupled IT on the organization. Kerwood (1995) takes this perspective, discussing the new trend toward loosely coupled, cooperative interorganizational forms that are enabled by IT.

The Benefits of Loose Coupling for Strategic Agility

The outcomes of loose coupling vary strongly with the type of relationship it describes. We adapt the perspectives presented by Orton and Weick (1990) to the particular situation of loose coupling between IT-enabled processes. The following discussion represents a consolidation of findings from literature from both the process architecture and network organization perspectives.

Persistence/Buffering

Many theorists have asserted that a primary benefit of a loosely coupled system is to stabilize the system in the face of environmental uncertainty, and to prevent the spread of problems across subcomponents. This is derived from the condition of system modularity, which is directly enabled by loose coupling (Weick, 1985). This does not mean that the system doesn't change, rather that the system is more likely to adapt to change smoothly and at a measured pace. It is for this reason that Perrow (1984) suggested that loosely coupled systems are more desirable in high-risk systems such as nuclear power plants. Even in less critical environments, the ability to easily manage relationships between elements in a system, possible through loose coupling, can be a valuable strategic capability. In organizations facing uncertain environmental conditions, such as a competitive and rapidly changing market environment, the ability to either decouple or loosen their linkages with external elements to moderate the impact of negative events can be highly desirable (Weick, 1982; Perrow, 1984; Orton and Weick, 1990).

Adaptability

Perrow (1984) strongly advocates the adaptability of a loosely coupled system as a great advantage, especially in situations in which the system should be able to adjust to environmental changes. Mitchell and Zmud (1999) suggest that by promoting modularity and therefore the identity, uniqueness, and separateness of elements, loosely coupled strategies foster a greater number of mutations and novel solutions than tight coupling. Weick (1976; 1982) also asserts the diversity of responses that are enabled by loose coupling.

Efficiency

By enabling the linkages between elements to be broken or reconfigured easily, loose coupling can promote optimal efficiency of a system. Weick (1979; 1982) identified the reduction in coordination costs made possible by loose coupling. Furthermore, companies can retain control and support of the modular functions that are integral to their core competencies while outsourcing other activities to specialist organizations, thus increasing the overall efficiency of the organization's operations (Grabowski and Roberts, 1999). Supporting this idea, Ettlie and Reza (1992) find that loosely coupled integrating mechanisms up the value chain were "associated with internal capacity-related performance measures."

At the programmatic level, loose coupling is a correlate of nonredundancy (Burt, 1992). If a program module is built to allow loose coupling with other elements, future functional requirements are much more likely to take advantage of the existing loosely coupled module than build a new, redundant module. As Burt points out, strong ties that may start out as nonredundant are likely to become redundant over time; weak ties are less likely to become redundant. Since nonredundancy reduces the likelihood of errors and increases the ease of correction and modification to a module, loose coupling tends to be associated with programmatic efficiency of a system, especially over time and with increasing complexity. Additionally, Hansen (1999) asserts that maintaining strong ties are significantly more costly than weak ones. Thus, a loosely coupled system is likely to be cheaper to maintain.

Innovation

According to the weak-tie theory originally advanced by Granovetter (1973), loose coupling is efficient for knowledge sharing because it provides access to novel information by bridging otherwise disconnected groups and individuals, while avoiding the pitfalls of redundant information seen in tight coupling. Thus, by stimulating knowledge sharing in an organization, loose coupling can lead to quicker search and transfer of relevant information and faster new product innovation (Hansen, 1999). In contrast, strong ties bind change much more tightly than weak ones, leading to system inertia (Hansen, 1999). Therefore, not only does loose coupling promote the ability to create new ideas, it allows the system to adapt to implement new ideas.

Flexibility

Orton and Weick (1990) state very simply that "looseness produces flexibility." Their logic follows from the observation that task uncertainty can be mitigated through loose structures and incremental adaptation paths, which is the argument that supports the advantages of persistence and buffering. Further, Weick (1988) points out that "loose coupling enables local knowledge to be applied when responding in a timely manner to local conditions. Small deviations can be sensed quickly and corrective actions quickly applied." Thus, loose coupling promotes flexibility by allowing a "diversity of response to unanticipated events" (Mitchell and Zmud, 1999).

Loose coupling can also enable more proactive adaptation of the network. It can expand the options available to support an instance of a linkage. Strong linkages tend to lock the relationship, which lessens any potential competition to support a side to the relationship. Loose coupling enables substitutes for a resource in the relationship to be viable options for switching. Therefore, increasing the independence of the elements in a relationship increases the strategic flexibility (Sanchez, 1997; Beekun and Glick, 2001). Kerwood (1995) makes a similar observation in an intraorganizational situation: the ability to customize systems or products. Systems that are tightly coupled are relatively inflexible and are more constrained to competing on superior economic benefits, such as larger economies of scale or lower costs (Kerwood, 1995).

Sanchez (1997) echoes this when he defines flexibility as the condition of having strategic options that are created through the combined effects of an organization's coordination flexibility in acquiring and using flexible resources. In other words, it is an organization's ability to respond effectively to various aspects of a changing competitive environment. Simply, he asserts that resource flexibility is greater when there is "a larger range of alternative uses for each resource; when the costs and difficulties of switching from one use of a resource to an alternative are lower; and when the time required to switch to an alternative is lower." He associates these conditions with loose coupling in business processes. He states that the modularity that results from loose coupling "greatly facilitates the creation and realization of strategic flexibility by an organization" (Sanchez, 1997).

Web Services and Loose Coupling

Web services offer an alternative approach to "enterprise integration." Instead of tight integration between applications through customized code or proprietary systems, wSOA enables loose coupling of existing systems, from both the process architecture perspective and the network organization perspective. At the process level, it either creates or replaces the middle tier(s) in data exchange hierarchies. It forces modular process architecture upon the system, facilitating access to processes of both coarse and fine granularity. It standardizes the relationship to a finite set of transactions that can be tested and optimized and available to applications across technical boundaries. Consequently, wSOA provides the loose coupling that is required in modular process architectures, and promotes the process-level efficiency benefits that accrue in such an environment.

At the organizational level, wSOA enables the seamless transfer of information across boundaries that are otherwise technically or financially impractical to bridge. It encourages the creation of linkages between otherwise disparate entities while still maintaining a high degree of autonomy between the entities. Where earlier solutions would have required heavily customized and usually proprietary systems such as EDI, wSOA greatly expands the potential for creating relationships between systems separated by strong and powerful boundaries. This is synonymous with loose coupling between organizations or organizational divisions.

An Emerging Framework for wSOA and Strategic Agility

Drawing from the above discussion, we propose that wSOA offers an approach to building and creating loosely coupled IT infrastructure and IT systems. Such systems support the design and operation of loosely coupled (rather than "tightly integrated") business and organization processes, indicated by the attributes of persistence/buffering, adaptability, efficiency, innovation, and flexibility. Together, loosely coupled IT systems and loosely coupled processes enhance the strategic agility of business organizations. Figure 8.1 summarizes the conceptual framework of wSOA and strategic agility.

Preliminary Observations of Web Services Enabled Strategic Agility

Using the conceptual framework identified above, we undertook an extensive search of business and IT professional publications, vendor and client white papers, press announcements, conference presentations, and other Internet-based sources for

Figure 8.1

Conceptual Framework of wSOA and Strategic Agility

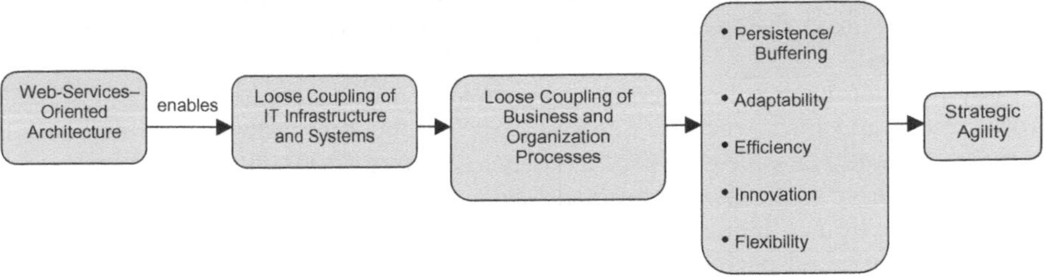

secondary data on Web services adoption. We then examined the nature of the innovations described in these sources to determine whether the initiative fit with the notions of loose coupling as articulated above, and where appropriate, categorized its apparent likely impact under the appropriate categories of loose coupling outcome that are consistent with enhanced strategic agility.

Persistence/Buffering

Buffering of legacy systems is evident in a number of Web services deployments. CUNA Mutual Group, the largest provider of financial services products to credit unions, uses wSOA to transfer information from back-end financial service applications into pages on its Web site. CUNA Mutual operates about 40 secure transaction-processing applications that serve information to customers when they reach self-service data access and entry pages. Most of these back-office applications were written years before Internet access became an issue. The company didn't feel that it was practical to rebuild the applications to dynamically serve the information, but instead used Web services components to automatically format information from the back-end applications (Pallatto, 2002). Similarly, Nationwide, a UK mortgage provider, developed a Web service based business-to-consumer application that reviews mortgage applications that have been forwarded by intermediary mortgage application service providers. Nationwide has developed a library of about 90 XML "recombinant components ... that are getting reused all over the place" to move data back and forth between online data forms and a back-end legacy system (Pallatto, 2002).

Efficiency

MacSweeney (2002a) identifies expense optimization, i.e., the ability to dramatically lower the cost of internal and external legacy integration, thereby increasing the ability to leverage third-party information, applications, and alliances as a key benefit of wSOA for the insurance industry. For example, Fidelity embraced wSOA to create a software infrastructure that lets divisions and external organizations with different computing systems interact and conduct transactions. Productivity has increased because time is not being spent to decide on communication protocols (Junnarkar, 2002). Similarly, MetLife identified a set of core business functions and supported these with common functionality delivered through reusable Web services components, rather than having each business unit develop similar applications to perform the same task (MacSweeney, 2002b). Dell Inc. found that their wSOA approach to supply chain integration motivated suppliers to collaborate more than the earlier tightly linked approaches because it reduces their cost and maintenance burden (Hagel III, 2002). GM has been an early adopter of wSOA to streamline internal processes, which has reduced their vehicle design process from forty-eight to eighteen months (Hanna, 2003).

For Eastman Kodak, lower costs are expected to result from better use of installed applications and infrastructure, improved process and data visibility, and movement toward "a more real-time enterprise" (Foley and Garvey, 2002). By introducing a new and standardized method of automated data exchange, Royal Dutch Shell expects significant reduction in manual efforts for the document exchange with governments, operating units, and partners. These new processes will enable the company to perform business tasks with greater efficiency and improve communication with governments and partners worldwide (IBM, 2002).

Expedia sought a device independent means of providing travel information to its customers via multiple platforms. By using wSOA, Expedia has saved development time and cost in rewriting the interface to new interface devices, thus allowing them to focus on developing their core travel services (Microsoft, 2002a).

Adaptability

MacSweeney (2002a) describes Web services enabled process enhancement in the insurance industry as the ability to enhance core capabilities (underwriting, policy administration, and claims processing) through customizing activities and moving functionality closer to agents and customers. For example, CSE Insurance recently built a wSOA-based insurance policy quotation engine. The component sits on a Web server and is available to a number of current and *future* applications to provide real-time rate information to CSE field agents (Copeland, 2001). Similarly, CitiMortgage Inc. used wSOA to develop a credit authorization utility (Copeland, 2001). Andy Zimmerman, senior system architect, described the benefit of Web services as: "If we've got a component-based application, and market conditions demand that we change it, it's easier to change a component than the whole thing." For example, instead of building a credit card authorization utility for each application that requires one, CitiMortgage would place that component on an application server, enabling different applications to access it as a Web service.

GM's OnStar service allows roughly one million subscribers to obtain a variety of services from roadside assistance to help in locating particular addresses. Their wSOA makes it easier to add or drop services depending on customer preferences (Hagel III, 2002). Dollar Rent-A-Car's first opportunity to adapt its new Web services components interface arose when its marketing department requested the ability for Palm users to place reservations over the Internet. The Web service interface to Dollar's legacy systems was reused without any changes to feed information to the Palm interface (Microsoft, 2002b). Home Depot's traditional point-of-sale system was highly customized and tightly coupled with multiple store systems, including tool rental and special orders. It worked well, but it was tough to tailor the system to respond to business changes. The point-of-sale, tool rental, and special-order systems are built on disparate systems, but they share common functions such as price lookup, tax calculation, tender management, and returns authorizations. These tasks were isolated as Web services that combine existing application functions (*JavaNews*, 2002).

Innovation

J.P. Morgan Chase & Co. employed simple Web services components to rapidly assemble diverse investment information sources in a company portal. The goal was to make customer account data available across all lines of business (Pallatto, 2002). Merrill Lynch has adopted wSOA to implement a new portfolio analysis platform (based on the integration of disparate internal systems and the external systems of key business partners) and to provide access to the new system to internal and external users via a range of Web-accessible devices. John McKinley, former Merrill Lynch CTO, stated that "We had a project that we had estimated at about $800,000 using traditional technology in order to build a series of interfaces to a variety of systems. But by embracing some things we've done to expose our legacy systems as Web services, they did the project for $30,000" (*ASPNews*, 2002). MetLife faced the daunting technical challenge of integrating at least eight front-end, customer-facing systems with more than 15 back-end systems in order to provide a single customer view. It deployed Web services components to let customers view the information from a password-protected area of MetLife's Web site and update information (MacSweeney, 2002b).

Eastman Chemical Co. relies on a new wSOA to improve its collaboration process and provide better presale and postsale processes. The initiative focused on two customer-facing opportunities: streamlining content delivery and sharing the company's value-added intellectual property. Example implementations include a real-time, services-based feed of Eastman's product catalog and "wizard" tools that deliver product knowledge (Stencil Group, 2002). Royal Dutch Shell sees UDDI and wSOA as being important enablers for achieving new levels of performance in the area of inter/intra-company information exchange (IBM, 2002).

Dell Inc. was one of the early adopters of wSOA to improve its supply chain processes, overcoming the technical difficulties of achieving full data sharing and tight systems integration with its supply chain partners, and opting instead "to provide limited visibility through the automatic sharing of simple event acknowledgements, such as notification of potential disruptions of supplies" (Hagel III, 2002). GM implemented a wSOA model to support information exchange with its network of 8000 car dealers, whose IT installations are characterized by significant diversity in standards and performance (Hanna, 2003).

Flexibility

For the insurance industry, MacSweeney (2002a) suggests that reduced expense, reduced time and cost of change, and process enhancement enabled by wSOA will give rise to additional managerial degrees of freedom. Montalbano (2002) reports that a new wSOA solution allows a large insurance company to sell private-label insurance. The solution enables the insurer's business partners to select the services they want to private-label through a "dashboard" based on Web services components. Using the dashboard, the business partners' developers can access the insurer's menu of available services through a GUI, then choose and configure the services they want to offer their own customers. The entire process is transparent to end users.

GM's Web services information exchange will ultimately provide its core business infrastructure for a build-to-order manufacturing and distribution model (Hanna, 2003). Eastman Chemical Co. views its Web services initiatives as helping the company to improve customer service and provide more adaptability for new strategies and business growth (Foley and Garvey, 2002). Dollar Rent-A-Car uses wSOA to expose its reservation system to business partners. This enables them to get new business at lower customer acquisition costs (Microsoft, 2002b). For Nordstrom, wSOA is used to feed inventory information from different divisions inside the company to Nordstrom.com, and to facilitate online sales of used gift cards for payment (Johnston, 2002).

Amazon.com recently launched its Web services initiatives, allowing customers to integrate its vast online content with their own Web site (Lee, 2002). Publishers have been using Amazon.com to monitor their sales, book reviews, and most importantly, their competitors. With the launch of these initiatives, publishers can now integrate the Web services components into their in-house application for report generation and management reporting.

Discussion and Conclusions

Our analysis provides support for our thesis of wSOA enablement of loose coupling, with consequent benefits for strategic agility. Early adoption of wSOA has resulted primarily in *adaptability* and *innovation* benefits. However, *efficiency*, *flexibility*, and *persistence/buffering* benefits are also supported. The common themes across the business examples we survey suggest that the key benefits and outcomes of wSOA deployments include:

Adaptability: improved time to market for products/services for which "IT systems were on the critical path"; simplification (reduced complexity) of corporate-wide IT architecture by reducing multi-tier architectures to fewer layers; creating a capability that will enhance future IT system development activities.

Innovation: Better integration and consistency of information previously stranded on separate islands; better business process integration and consistency (e.g., channel consistency); better business unit integration and coordination, with consequent business benefits such as cross-selling.

Efficiency: Improved developer productivity; faster development times and/or reduced development costs, through the reuse of Web services components such as "foundation services" (e.g., user and data authentication) and other "business services."

Flexibility: Providing a platform/vehicle for fast acquisition of outsourced IT services and business processes; creating more flexible IT systems and an IT infrastructure/architecture that is better positioned to respond to future business needs. In addition, the mechanisms through which these outcomes are emerging appear to be entirely consistent with those predicted by loose coupling. Through loose coupling, the permeation of these attributes across the adopting firms' business and organization processes and underlying IT architecture appear to be providing an effective platform for strategic agility. Thus, the emergence of modular, loosely coupled, Web services-based IT systems for strategic agility is a very rational response to the limitations formed by the tightly integrated, end-to-end, "enterprise systems" for "strategic alignment" that have dominated the information systems design strategy for the past decade. To conclude, we find that loose coupling provides a valuable framework for considering the opportunities of wSOA for strategic agility, and that much of the early adoption of wSOA appears to be consistent with the loose coupling of IT architecture and information systems, and the business processes they support.

Persistence/buffering: Standardization of key business rules and associated functionality, with consequent benefits for business process simplification and consistency.

References

Ashby, W. R. (1952). *Design for a Brain.* New York: Wiley.

ASPNews. (2002). Merrill Lynch is bullish on Web services. *InternetNews.com.* Retrieved from: http://www.internetnews.com/xSP/article.php/1552151.

Beekun, R. I. and Ginn, G. O. (1993). Business strategy and interorganizational linkages within the acute care hospital industry: An expansion of the Miles and Snow topology. *Human Relations*, 46 (11), 1291–1310.

Beekun, R. I. and Glick, W. H. (2001). Organization structure from a loose coupling perspective: A multidimensional approach. *Decision Sciences*, 32 (2), 227–250.

Bradley, S. P. and Nolan, R. L. (1998). *Sense and Respond: Capturing Value in the Network Era.* Boston: Harvard Business School Press.

Burt, R. (1992). *Structural Holes: The Social Structure of Competition.* Cambridge, MA: Harvard University Press.

Copeland, L. (2001). Web services offer flexibility, savings. But architectural hurdles lead to slow adoption of development method. *Computerworld*, June 4, 2001.

Copeland, L. (2001). Web services offers flexibility, savings. *Computerworld*, June 4, 2001. Website: http://www.computerworld.com/softwaretopics/software/appdev/story/0,10801,60990,00.html.

Daft, R. L. and Weick, K. E. (1984). Toward a model of organizations as interpretation systems. *Academy of Management Review*, 9 (2), 284–295.

Ettlie, J. E. and Reza, E. M. (1992). Organizational integration and process innovation. *Academy of Management Journal*, 35 (4), 795–827.

Foley, J. and Garvey, M. J. (2002). Heart of the matter. *InformationWeek*, Nov. 11, 2002.

Gartner. (2002). Untangling Web services. *EXP Club Report*, March 2002.

Grabowski, M. and Roberts, K. H. (1999). Risk mitigation in virtual organizations. *Organization Science*, 10 (6), 704–721.

Granovetter, M. (1973). The strength of weak ties. *American Journal of Sociology*, 78, 1360–1380.

Greenemeier, L. (2002). Web services help MetLife get closer to its customers. *InformationWeek*, May 27, 2002.

Haeckel, S. H. (1999). *Adaptive Enterprise: Creating and Leading Sense-and-Respond Organizations.* Boston: Harvard Business School Press.

Hagel III, J. and Brown, J. S. (2001). Your next IT strategy. *Harvard Business Review*, 79 (9), 105–113.

Hagel III, J. (2002). *Out of the Box: Strategies for Achieving Profits Today & Growth Tomorrow Through Web Services.* Boston: Harvard Business School Press.

Hanna, J. (2003). Web services. *HBS Working Knowledge*, February 3, 2003.

Hansen, M. T. (1999). The search-transfer problem: The role of weak ties in sharing knowledge across organization subunits. *Administrative Science Quarterly*, 44 (1), 82–111.

Hart, P. and Saunders, C. (1997). Power and trust: Critical factors in the adoption and use of electronic data interchange. *Organization Science*, 8 (1), 23–42.

Hatch, J. and Zweig, J. (2001). Strategic flexibility: The key to growth. *Ivey Business Journal*, 65 (4), 44–47.

Hicks, M. (2001). E-biz building blocks. *eWeek*, August 7, 2001.

Hitt, M. A., Keats, B. W., and DeMarie, S. M. (1998). Navigating in the new competitive landscape: Building strategic flexibility and competitive advantage in the 21st century. *Academy of Management Executive*, 12 (4), 22–42.

IBM. (2002). *IBM eBusiness Case Studies.* Retrieved from http://www-306.ibm.com/software/success/cssdb.nsf/CS/LWES-62DV49?OpenDocument&Site=default.

JavaNews. (2002). The Home Depot's latest project: XML Web services. January 2002. Retrieved from: http://industry.java.sun.com/javanews/stories/story2/0,1072,42081,00.html.

Johnston, S. J. (2002). State of Web Services. *InfoWorld*, February 1, 2002.

Junnarkar, S. (2002). Fidelity's plunge into Web Services, ZDNet interview, December 3, 2002.

Kerwood, H. A. (1995). Where do just-in-time manufacturing networks fit? A typology of networks and a framework for analysis. *Human Relations*, 48 (8), 927–953.

Lawton, S. (2002). Custom services: Putting Web services to work. *CIOInsight.com*, April 15, 2002.

Lee, W. (2002). Using Amazon's New Web Services. *O'Reilly OnDotnet.com*, July 2002. Retrieved from: http://www.ondotnet.com/pub/a/dotnet/2002/07/18/amazon.html.

MacSweeney, G. (2002a). Web Services: Here to stay? *Insurance & Technology*, September 2002.

MacSweeney, G. (2002b). MetLife a pioneer in Web Services. *Insurance & Technology*, October 22, 2002.

Microsoft. (2002a). *Web Service Case Studies*. Retrieved from: http://www.microsoft.com/servers/evaluation/casestudies/Expedia.asp.

Microsoft. (2002b). *Web Service Case Studies*. Retrieved from: http://www.microsoft.com/resources/casestudies/CaseStudy.asp?CaseStudyID=11626.

Microsoft. (2003c). *Web Service Case Studies*. Retrieved from: http://www.microsoft.com/resources/casestudies/CaseStudy.asp?CaseStudyID=10815.

Mitchell, V. L. and Zmud, R. W. (1999). The effects of coupling IT and work process strategies in redesign projects. *Organization Science*, 10 (4), 424–438.

Montalbano, E. (2002). Seeing the light: Touting ROI and streamlined business processes, solution providers look to cash in on Web services opportunities. *Computer Reseller News*, December 2002.

Orton, J. D. and Weick, K. E. (1990). Loosely coupled systems: A reconceptualization. *Academy of Management Review*, 15 (2), 203–223.

Pallatto, J. (2002). Web services deliver: J.P. Morgan Chase & Co., CUNA Mutual initiate new applications that pay off. *Internet World*, October 2002. Retrieved from: http://www.internetworld.com/magazine.php?inc=100102/10.01.02feature1.html.

Patton, S. (2002). Web Services in the real world. *CIO Magazine*, April 1, 2002.

Perrow, C. (1984). *Normal accidents: Living with high-risk technologies*. New York: Basic Books.

Prahalad, C. K., Krishnan, M. S., and V. Ramaswamy. (2002). Manager as consumer: The essence of agility. *University of Michigan Business School Working Paper #02-013*, Ann Arbor, MI.

Ross, J. W. (2003). Strategic IT architecture competency. *MIS Quarterly Executive*, 2 (1), 31–43.

Sambamurthy, V. (2000). Business strategy in hypercompetitive environments: Rethinking the logic of IT differentiation. In *Framing the Domains of IT Management* (R. W. Zmud, ed.). Cincinnati: Pinnaflex Education Resources.

Sanchez, R. (1995). Strategic flexibility in product competition. *Strategic Management Journal*, 16 (5), 135–159.

Sanchez, R. (1997). Preparing for an uncertain future—Managing organizations for strategic flexibility. *International Studies of Management & Organizations*, 27 (2), 71–94.

Stencil Group. (2002). The laws of evolution: A pragmatic analysis of the emerging Web services market. *Analysis Memo*, April 2002.

Swanson, E. B. (1994). Information systems innovation among organizations. *Management Science*, 40 (9), 1069–1092.

Teece, D. and Pisano, G. (1994). The dynamic capabilities of firms: An introduction. *Industrial and Corporate Change*, 3 (3), 537–556.

Upton, D. M. (1995). What really makes factories flexible? *Harvard Business Review*, 162 (2), 74–84.

Wang, E. T. G. and Seidmann, A. (1995). Electronic data interchange: Competitive externalities and strategic implementation policies. *Management Science*, 41 (3), 401–418.

Weick, K. E. (1976). Educational organizations as loosely coupled systems. *Administrative Science Quarterly*, 21 (1), 1–19.

Weick K. E. (1979). *The Social Psychology of Organizing*, 2nd edition. Reading, MA: Addison-Wesley.

Weick, K. E. (1982). Management of organizational change among loosely-coupled elements. In *Change in Organizations: New Perspectives on Theory, Research, and Practice* (P. S. Goodman, ed.). San Francisco: Jossey-Bass, pp. 375–408.

Weick, K. (1985). Sources of order in under organized systems: Themes in recent organizational theory. In Lincoln, Y. S. (ed.), *Organizational Theory and Inquiry: The Paradigm Revolution*. Beverly Hills, CA: Sage.

Weick, K. E. (1988). Enacted sensemaking in crisis situations. *Journal of Management Studies*, 25 (4), 305–317.

Weill, P. and Broadbent, M. (1998). *Leveraging the New Infrastructure: How Market Leaders Capitalize on Information Technology*. Boston, MA: Harvard Business School Press.

Weill, P., Subramani, M., and Broadbent, M. (2002). Building IT infrastructure for strategic agility. *Sloan Management Review*, 44 (1), 57–65.

Agile Information Systems as a Double Dream

Silvia Gherardi and Andrea Silli

Open your eyes. What can you see? The information before you must be distributed, transformed, administered. Maybe you need a knowledge management system. Now close your eyes. What can you see? Can you imagine an agile and flexible system that, with a click, lets you communicate with colleagues, share appointments and notes, sense the relevant organizational environment, and access data and documents without having to move? You are dreaming of an Agile Information System (AIS), and perhaps you go off in search of a developer who can help you realize your dream. Users and developers are locked into a double dream, and the object of this dream is the fuzzy image of an AIS. They form a symmetric couple, similar to the characters in Arthur Schnitzel's novel *Dream Story.*[1]

In the book, a man and woman involved in an ambivalent relationship alternate experiences of real life—which resembles a dream—with their dreamed experience, which is so vivid that it seems to be the reality that the other has experienced. The reader who views the double dream from outside feels unease and bewilderment, because he or she is affected on the one hand by the unreality of the real, and on the other hand by the reality of a dream that reflects reality more closely than appears. At the threshold between the real and the dreamed, the two characters, bound together by reciprocal interdependence, negotiate their relationship while interrogating the boundaries between reality and the dream world. They therefore construct the reality of their relationship, and through that relationship they also construct the materiality, and not just the meaning, of the bond between them.

The users and developers of information systems can be considered an interdependent couple caught up in a double dream called AIS. Both have the dream of an AIS, and collaboratively yet conflictually, they materialize and stabilize an artifact that only partly embodies their reciprocal expectations. How does this happen? And above all, how can we learn to move on the threshold between the double dream and its practical applications?

Information systems are often conceived and perceived differently according to whether their constructors or their users are considered. We can represent them as a socio-technical "double dream" that is not necessarily the same for all dreamers, although the context is the same. Designers and users invoke the agility of information systems; they want a design that sharpens the perception by organizations of important signals emitted by the context in which they operate and enhances their ability to process them, which reflects a flexible approach to information transfer, processing, and distribution, and makes systems intuitive and easy to maintain and upgrade. But do they mean the same thing? And what is lost in the negotiation of meaning and in the construction of the artifact?

What is meant by the adjective *agile* applied to an information system can be established by considering the bounded rationality that organizational actors deploy in their decisions. Contrary to what the developers of information system architectures envisage, it is not possible to abstract infinitely reproducible rules and diagrams for use.

Information technologies grant access to a virtual dimension that differs from that of present time and space. Actors use this space in the manner to which they have grown accustomed in their everyday lives. They negotiate their action space, and they exploit games, contingencies, and indeterminacies, using the dynamic concepts of bricolage and situated rationality, rather than the static one of de-contextualized rationality.

A definition of *agility* should recognize that actors act on the basis of factors and conditions that did not exist prior to their decisions but that are dictated by opportunities arising from situated practices. The problems addressed by organizations cannot be broken down into smaller and simpler units that are solvable using universal laws or instruments. Rather, participation and situation enable agility to be interpreted as deriving from interaction among actors, situations, and resources. Therefore a practice-based perspective (Gherardi, 2006) is particularly suited to analysis of the socio-technical development of an agile information artifact. The focus on work practices stems from the assumption that the knowledge necessary for action and the logic of work are situated in the practices that collectively conserve and transmit that knowledge. Hence, when adopting a technology that will reconfigure practices, it is advisable that both actors in the double dream jointly construct a shared representation of the logic of the practice that the AIS will support and modify. Relational theories, such as social embeddedness (Uzzi, 1997) conceive the role of Information Technology (IT) in mediating relationships as based on knowing-in-practice. The paper examined the construction of a virtual office for the collection of municipal taxes in a north Italian valley. To conduct the analysis, we adopt a practice perspective that focuses on interpersonal relationships in practice to shed light on how artifacts are created and used as instantiations of practical knowledge (Schultze and Orlikowski, 2004; Østerlund and Carlile, 2005).

The Dream of Building a Virtual Office

The setting for the case examined is a valley in northern Italy. The area is mountainous with a large number of small villages, many of them with only a few hundred inhabitants, and with histories and public institutions distinct from their neighbors. The study is based on a project entitled Mediasite that is financed by the European Community for the development, introduction, and diffusion of information technologies in "traditional and rural" organizations.

The municipalities concerned were too small for their individual administration to be economically viable. It was therefore decided to centralize certain services in order to economize on resources. The result was a central office that administered seven outlying offices, each with its own database on residents in the corresponding municipality. However, the geography of the valley impeded movement between the central office and the peripheral ones. Because every contact was costly in terms of the traveling required to share data, the managers decided to introduce an information system so that efforts could be coordinated.

In what follows, we shall briefly describe the implementation of an information system conceived as a "virtual office" in which people scattered across a broad and difficult territory were able to work together.

The data collected[2] will be used to reconstruct the process that gave rise to an information system perceived as "agile" by the workers in the tax office with regard to the information instruments available to them. The paper highlights that a technological object acquires meaning only when it comes into contact with the organization for which it has been created, and that it cannot be assumed that this meaning will coincide with the one foreseen by the designers.

The technology used consisted of an "information platform" for the following applications: videoconferencing, shared archives, thematic forum, an electronic calendar for the management of meetings and deadlines, and shared boards for joint work on documents at a distance.

The administrative office in question was responsible for the management of municipal taxes. It collected levies on property and for refuse collection that accounted for a large part of total municipal revenues. For some years, the tax administration had operated under a system termed *Associated Management,* by which was meant that some municipalities no longer had their own tax offices but came under a central office in the "leader" municipality, which managed fiscal matters for each "associate." This system had been introduced to streamline the administrative apparatus so that even very small municipalities could provide their residents with the same services of the same quality as those furnished by larger towns.

The participants in the AIS development project were seven municipalities that used a central Intercommunal Tax Office (ITO) for the collection of municipal taxes. Although in substance the ITO was a single institution, in form it was not logistically contained in a single building.

To administer tax collection, the central office required rates fixed by each municipality according to its economic needs and data on each individual taxpayer. Although large part of these data had been transferred to the central office's archives, many others were still stored in the files of each individual municipality. The work of the ITO consisted in moving information located in different geographical places to the central office for processing.

The Reality and Its Ambivalence

The system was developed jointly by the local authority (involving all officials and municipalities belonging to the ITO) and the University of Trento as the technological and organizational partner. The main concern of the latter was to trial techniques of participative design for the implementation of information systems.

The team selected for the project consisted of information engineers, code developers, and an ethnographer. The intention was to devise a participative methodology

[2] The second author conducted ethnographic research, taking part as a participant observer in the group developing the system. He spent two years in the field and wrote the present case study as part of his doctoral dissertation (Silli, 2004).

for interpretation of the reality observed, and to construct an evolving design practice that involved situated technology and actors.

However, despite the good intentions of the team members, their points of view were not uniform, but influenced by their academic backgrounds. The engineer (who was in charge of the project and development of the technology) and the code developers were interested in producing flow diagrams for the software, so that other administrations could later be involved in the same system, thereby achieving economies of scale. The ethnographer, however, wanted to understand the taxation practices situated in the specific setting studied, and then to understand those practices that would take shape when the technology was in use—practices necessary for a localized design but not necessarily repeatable elsewhere.

Besides the tax officials and the researchers, the indubitable protagonist of the project was the information system, which from the abstract and innovative object that it represented initially, was soon rebaptized "the monster." We shall analyze some phases of its design (in particular, how it was perceived by its users) by getting some applications in the platform to "talk." Their narratives will reveal what development methodology was adopted, and how the logics of ethnography and user modeling came into conflict.

As a technology is developed and appropriated by its users, it becomes a technology-in-use (Suchman et al., 1999), acquiring a specific meaning when embedded in everyday practices that deviate the artifact from the direction that its designers intended. It is this difference that we emphasize by counterposing the terms *technology* and *technology-in-use*. The former denotes the object and its potential in a decontextualized manner; the latter denotes the technology and its potential when it is actually employed by a community of users, and in relation to other instruments, techniques, and practices associated with it.

Understanding the dynamics involved in the implementation of an AIS requires knowledge of the practices that its users adopt. The attitudes of the tax officers toward the ITO varied according to how the newly introduced system of "associated management" would affect their work practices. The officials at the ITO regarded themselves as full-time tax inspectors, while those in the outlying offices (also because the associated management system had relieved them of "tax duty") thought they need only be occasionally involved (psychologically and materially) in the task of levying taxes.

A clerical worker at one of the associated municipalities stressed that:

> *"Finally we've got 'Accounting Department' written above the door, they've taken down the tax sign . . . get it? I now do the municipal accounts, so that everyone gets their wages . . . I sort out what we've got and what we'll need next year. Those at the tax office can work out how to collect the taxes and do the controls!"*[3]

The personal interpretation of the role performed by a tax expert entailed interpretation of the rules regulating the activities of the ITO and the relationships among its associates. The latter believed that they had broad discretionary margins in management of relations between taxpayer and tax office, and between associated offices and the central office. These were margins negotiated over time through informal practices that were strengthened and perpetuated in parallel with those laid down by the formal regulations.

The head of the tax office complained, in contrast to the statement above, that:

---

[3] The statements collected in the field are written in italics.

"Here everyone does what they want, I have to keep tabs on all of them because otherwise you can't understand anything. Some sit in their offices and continue to deal with tax matters as if I didn't exist, others can't wait to delegate work to me and even bring it to me at the central office . . . so they take half a day off and even go and drink an aperitif!"

The situation just described highlights that the future users of the system, which was being designed in participative manner, had different expectations and were involved to different extents. This was because the organizational change about to be introduced by the AIS would have differing impacts on work practices at the central office and the outlying ones, and among the latter, on their conceptions of their role in the tax-collection system. However, these differing attitudes to the ongoing process were not given their due importance. The system began to be shaped in accordance with formal declarations about "how the work should be done," that is, in accordance with prescriptions. In this way, however, "they could forget the aperitif," a metaphor stating that the officials should fulfill their duties.

Technology-in-Use

To show how the dream and reality of the AIS was negotiated as the artifact was being developed, we now describe how the technological applications were constructed in accordance with the ITO office's vision of the world—and therefore with the fact that one of the users had acquired the symbolic role of "he who possesses the problem." These applications were an electronic calendar and a videoconferencing system.

The Calendar

The head of the ITO had to hold periodic meetings with certain officials so he could run his office more efficiently. They exchanged paper-based data and information, took decisions on future strategies, and strengthened relational networks essential for the smooth operation of the tax machinery. The central office telephoned the officials at the associated offices when a meeting was to be held, when important deadlines were approaching, and more generally when it was necessary. Conversely, the outlying offices contacted the ITO when problems arose that they could not handle on their own. This system enabled the officials to deal with tasks that they saw as part of their jobs without having to assume collective responsibility for the entire process of "associated management." As a consequence, also the project developers were caught up by the logic that ambiguously informed the practice. They decided to develop a calendar for the electronic management of requests for meetings. This calendar could be used to convene all those concerned simultaneously, and the development team believed that it would be especially useful because they could add an "availability" function for confirming attendance, and a document attachment tool.

The application appeared to be in line with the specifications stated by the ITO, whose head declared:

"I put in hours of unpaid overtime calling and re-calling colleagues on the telephone to get them to come to meetings."

The initial analysis concentrated on decision-making practices and gave no importance to the meanings that the actions and decisions observed had for the actors. It omitted the "aperitif factor" and neglected the most important component in collaboration among the associate offices: that of being called "only when necessary." For the staff in the outlying municipal offices, any work on tax matters, which they were no longer obliged to do, was acceptable only if it forestalled bigger problems, and if it brought informal benefits like the time off granted to travel among offices.

The design of the electronic calendar ignored this detail, regarding it of little importance and as irrelevant to the movement of information. The design, therefore, did not include a signal to users that they should consult the calendar when it contained information of importance for them. The officials were forced to check periodically for the presence of important deadlines or messages.

The officials at the associated municipalities felt themselves forced to change their perception of their roles *vis-à-vis* the ITO and obliged to perform functions that they had previously been relieved of.

> *"With the associated management system we'd stopped dealing with tax matters and could concentrate on accounts. Now, every day, we've got to deal with tax matters again, logging on to Mediasite even when it's not necessary . . . we'd been relieved of a burden, and now all this technology has dumped it back on us . . . and what's more, it's compulsory!"*

The question that the office workers now asked was whether the technology was working for people, or whether people had to work to maintain the technology. This was the first occasion on which the meaning of the adjective *agile* gave rise to conflict between developers and some of the workers.

A detail deemed of little importance at the design state thus generated a problem in reality. The situation was interpreted as a distortion of the role imposed on the functionaries by the artifact. The AIS obliged the officials once again to perform a function of which they had been institutionally relieved, and it provoked an insurrection that generated new practices intended to restore the *status quo* prior to the advent of Mediasite. It reinforced the detachment of the technology and the tax official's role, undermining the informal mechanism of collaboration between the central office and the outlying ones. In fact, the clerical workers declared:

> *"I won't work with that business, now if they come and look for me, OK, otherwise they can get on with it . . . I've already got enough stuff to do, I really can't do overtime inventing a system to avoid Mediasite!"*

The Videoconferencing System

Besides the calendar as the dream tool for coordination, a second instrument—the videoconferencing application—was designed to facilitate face-to-face communication. This technology was used to exchange data in nonelectronic format, and it eventually came to symbolize the entire Mediasite system.

The news that video cameras would be fitted to the ITO computers, and that they could be used to transmit the user's image to colleagues, generated the greatest expectations, curiosity, and concerns about the project. At the design stage, the videoconferencing application was conceived as an alternative to physical meetings. If used as a scanner, it could be employed to transmit paper-based information, and it would enable the joint creation of images and documents without those involved having to leave their workstations, wherever they were located.

As in the case of the electronic calendar, the developers envisaged that the videoconferencing application would replace the paper exchange of tax data between the ITO and the outlying offices. It would be an alternative to face-to-face meetings and would thus prevent the "loss of resources" that physical transfers entailed. For the users, the videoconferencing system had a wider connotation, and it merged with the identity itself of Mediasite manifested by the presence of the video cameras on the computers.

The officials began a process of identification of the technology that involved materialization of the hopes and fears aroused by the web cams. The concept of *virtual* now acquired a meaning for them:

> *"Virtual is when you can see and talk to someone who isn't there."*

The possibility of organizing and exploiting a dimension parallel to the spatio-temporal present, which could be accessed through the telematic interface and therefore freed from the physicality of meetings and tax responsibilities, was overshadowed by the evocative power of the televiewing of colleagues and, perhaps, taxpayers. In fact, although the videoconferencing system was intended for communication among the ITO members, the officials realized that they could use it to free themselves definitively from their role as tax collectors. By turning the video camera to point at taxpayers at the counter, the latter could communicate directly with the central office, so that the official was relieved of the task of giving information or retrieving it.

> *"Finally, seeing that it's no longer me that does the taxes . . . when someone comes in to ask me something, I call the central office, turn the video camera round, and let them talk to each other while I get on with my work . . ."*

Each user began to attribute to the videoconferencing system the utility and significance that he or she deemed most appropriate, and that did not always correspond to those officially prescribed. For example, the video camera became an object well suited to personal grooming, in that the female workers could project enlarged images of their faces on the computer screen and apply their makeup:

> *"Better than a mirror and simpler to use . . ."*

For others, it became an instrument for the remote monitoring of particular situations:

> *"There's a playground in front of the town hall where there are frequent acts of vandalism. You could do night-time surveillance from the office window, saving the data on the computer, and the next day identify the culprits."*

It was even an instrument for more personal business:

> *"Besides videoconferencing with colleagues, it might be possible to use the video camera to take part in those chat rooms . . . who knows, perhaps you'd find yourself a soul mate!"*

The videoconferencing application ceased being an instrument strictly for work, and the Mediasite a "monster" to be served, as long as the technology could be interpreted from a personal point of view, and put to uses different from those for which it had been designed. The municipal officials looked for a positive and subjective interpretation of the technological artifact in order to avert their fear of the control embodied by the technology. Indeed, one official went so far as to say:

> *"The Mediasite system is a bit like Mediaset.[4] I wouldn't want someone spying on us with the video cameras to check our work. Perhaps we're being monitored by the government!"*

---

[4] Mediaset is the name of the media group owned by the Italian prime minister. In Italian, the pronunciations of Mediasite and Mediaset are very similar, giving rise to an equivocal assonance.

The workers were particularly concerned by the fact that they could be seen via the videoconferencing system, so that they were obliged to maintain what was outwardly rigorous behavior. Dressing in a particular way or fixing one's hair before "going on air" became problems. Even in the absence of video cameras, the officials cultivated their image at work without being consciously aware of doing so. The presence of the video cameras seemingly imposed behavior that in fact was already a consolidated but "invisible" practice. More than one office worker said:

> "*. . . now with the videoconferencing system I have to fix my hair every morning . . . ,*"

And it became a joke:

> "*. . . Comb your hair, the monster is watching you!!!*"

The Reconfiguration of Practices

Technology-in-use evidences an important fact that emerges from the comments by the ITO members: technology brings to the surface the work that was previously hidden or implicit. This decisively influences the effect of technology in organizations: discretionary freedom and margins of individual negotiation are reduced, or even cancelled, by virtual office systems.

From a conceptual and methodological point of view, moving from the study of technology in itself (and its effects) to the study of technology-in-use brings to light all of the "covert work" that users are obliged to do before a technology becomes usable in a particular setting, and because we have a symmetrical conception of the relationship between humans and nonhumans (Latour, 1991), also the "covert work" that the technology does to embody the demands of users and to synchronize with the other technologies that already populate the world of humans. Technologies are not born "usable" and "reliable" regardless of their users; rather, they become usable and reliable when their use in practical settings makes them such. We now see how the dream of an AIS modified everyday work practices and their meanings.

We have already said that each official constructed the meaning of his or her role in a different and personal manner, and in practice not all of them were involved in tax administration in the same way. There were some who intervened in tax cases to replace or overlap with action by the central office; others simply acted as intermediaries between taxpayers and the ITO. Formally, they were all supposed to behave in the latter manner, but in reality each of them had the implicit power, which derived from length of service and relationships with fellow villagers, to utilize the margin of discretionality that they were able to negotiate. Situated in this margin were all of the informal practices that served to produce formally acceptable results. For example, in order to obtain information and models to adopt, the officials had to resort to channels internal to the ITO. But some of them preferred to ask acquaintances external to it (in order to maintain friendships simultaneously with their work, or for personal interest) without this prejudicing the content of the final document or the outcome of the tax case concerned. The documents produced were largely regarded as satisfactory by the associates of the ITO, with flexibility in regard to how they had been produced:

> "*What the heck, I call them at the municipality close by, even if they are not part of our association . . . a friend of mine works there and she's really good. She uses models better than ours . . . and then I never see her, so at least we have a chat and perhaps meet up for a coffee!*"

Obviously, this could not happen under the Mediasite system. All communications were recorded, and the methods used were made public. Moreover, the procedures laid down for producing results were unequivocal and did not permit personal deviations, which remained implicit. Thus the behavior of all workers was standardized on the basis of inflexible rules, so that margins for negotiation shrank, and private practices became public.

Contrary to what one would expect from a participative methodology, a practice did not arise whereby designers, technology, and users united to produce a system embodying the actors' decision-making procedures. Rather, the officials abandoned the Mediasite system. The new practices set in motion by the technology were not intended to integrate previous processes into the new organization of work. Instead, they were practices designed to institutionalize nonuse of the virtual office and to have it more or less tacitly accepted.

Not created as a consequence was stabilization of a "technological practice" as the confluence of shared symbols and meanings in regard to the Mediasite artifact, but rather practices for legitimating its abandonment.

Account was not taken of the meaning appropriation and construction trajectories presented with the electronic calendar and the videoconferencing system, except as "side-issues" or undesired effects produced by Mediaset subsequently to the developers' work. Once the structure of the virtual office had been put in place (in fact, no attempt was made to incorporate into the project the person/technology negotiation performed by the officials), only processes intended to impose the artifact as such, in accordance with the metaphor of the "instruction manual."

From the Dream to the Instruction Manual

From the developers' standpoint:

> *"All right, boys . . . these office-workers haven't understood how they're supposed to work. We'll have to give them an instruction manual to teach them how to follow the procedures. Otherwise the system won't work!"*

From their point of view, the distance between dream and reality was not a distance among the decontextualized technology constructed on the basis of decontextualized work procedures, rather the defect consisted of the human user. Procedures had been mistaken for "situated practices" by both the developers and the users.

From the ITO workers' standpoint:

> *"All right, boys . . . this system's really dangerous. Now we've got to re-learn our jobs and we'll end up wasting time and money for nothing. Just imagine if at my age I'm going to read the instructions for dealing with ICI[5] cases. We should get together some evening, eat pizza and see how we can carry on working with this Mediasite!"*

We conclude our description of the Mediasite case at this point, leaving the reader with the image of a double dream shattered to leave the protagonists in a state of mutual incomprehension, both unable to understand how it could have happened, and how a mistake had been made, and by whom. The Mediasite story did not stop here, in fact, and it was not a case of failure. But we do not intend to discuss it further, neither to analyze it in the light of participative design nor to determine why the

[5] ICI is property tax.

ethnographer's observations did not affect the artifact's design. All of this is obviously possible and relevant, but it is only from the episode recounted that we wish to draw insights with which to set the meaning of the adjective *agile* in relation to design practices.

In a certain sense, the Mediasite story is not surprising, given that studies in the literature calculate that only one-third of information system designs pass from the prototype stage to that of system-in-use (Selwyn, 2003). We have chosen it because the relationship between the Mediasite developers and users is a paradigmatic case of what we have called a *double dream.* A shared desire, a goal that both sides declared valid, and to which they both attributed strong symbolic value, created (how and why we do not know) mutual mistrust and the underutilization of an array of resources. What can we learn from cases of this kind?

Discussion and Reflection

To discuss how a dream like an AIS can become a reality shared by developers and users, we start from the consideration that what constitutes *agile* lies in the eye of the beholder. Whose agility should be incorporated into an IS? Just as the categories of *users* and *nonusers* of an IS fail to cover the entire utilizability range of a system, so the dichotomy between *agile* and *nonagile* should be reframed to decline the concept in relation to a system's future users and their expectations.

If we interpret a technological artifact as a text (Floch, 1990) we find that it has a range of interpretative flexibilities. But this range is not infinite. When the developers of an IS make choices that restrict the artifact's flexibility, they should ask themselves which group of users will benefit from the stabilization effect inscribed in the artifact, and which group will be penalized or forced to reconfigure its work practices in undesired ways. Constructed around the adjective *agile* is conflict over interpretation of the term, so that it becomes a controversial concept whose meaning results from negotiation among users. In the case that we have described, the users—those at the ITO—managed to gain hegemony over the definition of *agile* and to conscript the developers into accepting their definition of reality and their professional view of taxation. The associates were unable to propose an alternative view, nor to mobilize allies in support of different expectations. Thus a group of users set themselves up as the "core group," as those who possessed the problem and consequently knew how the information system should work. The centralization of information and the consequent organization of the technical system reflected a socio-technical world vision based on a rationality situated within a network of power relations. Try to imagine an information system predicated on the world vision of the associates and their expectations of an AIS. Would the result be a different system? We think so!

The conclusion that every artifact embodies its users' world vision is too well known to be reiterated here simplistically. In more specific terms, we may say that it is less important to define what an AIS is or is not theoretically than to pose the question pragmatically in the practice of the participative design of information systems. If, in the user/developer relation, the label "AIS" is a text to be interpreted, and a political text of which several interpretations are not only possible but legitimate, then the range of socio-technical solutions that are both technically and politically possible is extended as well. Is this a democratization of technology? Perhaps, but we do not wish to go that far. Nevertheless, we can certainly say that, once the label "AIS" has been incorporated into design practices, it is a semantic object that furnishes a shared language for the representation and negotiation of its meaning and further realization.

This statement is based on a conception of technology use as a social process of appropriation in situated learning practices. Using technology can be seen as "human agents appropriating technology by assigning shared meanings to it, which influence their appropriation of the interpretative schemes, facilities, and forms designed into the technology, thus allowing those elements to influence their task execution (Orlikowski, 1992). On this definition, the label "AIS" is a knowledge object, around which a process of collective learning gives people better understanding of their differences within work practices that render them similar but also different.

In the case described, the design of two instruments—the electronic calendar and the videoconferencing system—and their practical use marked out terrain for shared learning. As a technological solution to a coordination problem, the calendar made the dependence relation between the center and the associates explosive, because it materialized subordination in the need to consult the calendar to be informed. The artifact asserted that tax administration was the *raison d'être* of the ITO's work, while it was only one work practice among several for the associates. The ITO was dependent on the associates, in fact, but the latter felt themselves controlled, and they resisted a technological design that unreasonably increased their workload. The videoconferencing system was instead terrain for learning alternative uses of the artifact. Fear of control, and the occult work necessary to insert the new system among already-existing practices, was processed ludically and imbued with a tangible meaning. The videoconferencing system made the project tangible as soon as the web cam was visible/showable on entering the office, unlike the data-transmission software, which was entirely unable to involve its users' imaginations.

The ludic aspect that developed around the web cam is well represented by the linguistic exchange that defined the system as the Monster. The jocular remark by the officials: "Comb your hair. The Monster is watching you," expressed domestication of the technology (Silverstone and Haddon, 1996) within the moral economy of that institution. We may say that the first stage in appropriation of the technology consisted of a series of conflicts, negotiations, and compromises over location, ownership, and control; that is, definition of the information system's proper place in the officials' lives. The second stage was its domestication through daily use. What can be learned from this second stage of appropriation? That for an AIS to become such, it must find a place in the collective imagination and expressive life of the community that designs and uses it, and not just in the order of useful and/or functional things.

To summarize, we have identified three distinctive features of an AIS that relate less to its technological construction than to the sociality and knowledge that coalesce around the idea of constructing an AIS, and that substantiate it as a socio-technical system. These three distinctive features of an AIS consist in its nature as:

- A semantic object that establishes a shared language
- An object of knowledge that gives concrete form to knowledge of inter-actor differences and dependencies
- A means to domesticate an IS

References

Floch, J. M. (1990). *Sémiotique, marketing et communication: Sous les signes, les strategies*. Paris: Presses universitaires de France.

Gherardi, S. (2006). *Organizational Knowledge: The Texture of Workplace Learning*. Oxford, UK: Blackwell.

Latour B. (1991). Technology is society made durable. In *The Sociology of Monsters: Essays on power, technology and domination*. The Sociological Review Monograph (J. Law, ed.). London, UK: Routledge, (pp. 103–131).

Østerlund, C. and Carlile, P. (2005). Relations in practice: Sorting through practice theories on knowledge sharing in complex organizations. *The Information Society*, 21 (2), 91–107.

Schnitzler, A. (1926). *Traumnovelle* (orig. ed.). (En. ed.: Dream Story, Sun and Moon classics, 6).

Schultze, U. and Orlikowski, W. (2004). A practice perspective on technology-mediated network relations: The use of Internet-based self-serve technologies. *Information System Research*, 15 (1), 87–106.

Selwyn, N. (2003). Apart from technology: Understanding people's non-use of Information and Communication Technologies in everyday Life. *Technology in Society*, 25 (1), 99–116.

Silli, A. (2002). Brush your hair, the monster is watching you . . . introducing ICTs in public Administration in the North of Italy, *EGOS conference proceedings*. Barcelona, Spain.

Silli, A. (2004). Azione situata ed organizzazione della dimensione virtuale, sistemi informativi quali strumenti per la condivisione di significati online' *(situated action and organisation of virtual dimension, information systems as instruments for shared meanings online)*. Doctoral dissertation.

Silverstone, R. and Haddon, L. (1996). Design and the Domestication of Information and Communication Technologies: Technical Change and Everyday Life. In *Communications by Design: The Politics of Information and Communication Technologies* (R. Mansell and R. Silverstone, eds). Oxford, UK: Oxford University Press.

Suchman L., et al. (1999). *Reconstructing technologies as social practice. American Behavioral Scientist*, 43 (3), pp. 392–408.

Uzzi, B. (1997). Social structure and competition in interfirm networks: The paradox of embeddedness. *Administrative Science Quarterly*, 42 (1), 35–67.

10 Degrees of Agility: Implications for Information Systems Design and Firm Strategy

Tsz-Wai Lui and Gabriele Piccoli

Many have suggested that market globalization, increasing competition and faster-cycle technological innovation require today's organizations to be strategically flexible (Hitt, Keats, and DeMarie, 1998) so as to be more responsive to customers' demands or adopt new approaches to squeeze out waste in the changing marketplace (D'aveni and Gunther, 1994). In this environment, agility becomes critical for firms so that they can be flexible in the face of change, as well as respond to the changes by renewing and creating new competitive advantage (Goldman, Nagel, and Preiss, 1995). Current literature seems to suggest that agility is a binary condition that a firm either has achieved, or it has not (Weill, Subramani, and Broadbent, 2002; Sambamurthy, Bharadwaj, and Grover, 2003). In this chapter, we question this notion and suggest that firms can be characterized on an agility continuum and contend that organizations normally achieve different degrees of agility. Moreover, we suggest that the optimal degree of agility a firm should strive for depends on the environment it is in, including the intensity of market competition and the types and frequency of changes the ecosystem generates. For example, competitive advantage in industries where resource positions are strongly shielded from competitive pressure can be sustained longer than those of industries facing high resource-imitation pressure (Williams, 1992). It follows then that an organization may not need a high level of agility when competition is limited and the cycle time of its ecology is low (Hidding, 2001). Conversely, the competitive advantage of companies in hypercompetitive environments are quickly eroded, forcing the firm to continually innovate and seek new avenues of differentiation and value creation in order to react to the changing environment and seize new market opportunities (Veliyath, 1996). A rational resource allocation perspective suggests that it is crucial for modern organizations to achieve the optimal degree of agility—an objective that implies the ability to define and measure it.

The information systems literature has long shown the importance of alignment of information systems objectives and strategy with those of the business (King, 1978; Henderson and Venkatraman, 1993; Teo and King, 1997)—a condition that is even more important when flexibility and efficacy of information technology are required (Weill, Subramani, and Broadbent, 2002). Executives need to make critical decisions about the optimal Information Technology (IT) investments needed for future strategic agility avoiding both overinvesting, which leads to resources waste, and underinvesting, which leads to achievement of a substandard degree of agility. It follows then that strategic agility is predicated on the firm's ability to create agile information systems. Information systems agility, like strategic agility, is not a binary condition but should instead be conceptualized as a continuum. With investments in information systems agility being costly (Weill, Subramani, and Broadbent, 2002), managers must strive to match the appropriate degree of information systems agility to enable the optimal degree of strategic agility. In other words, if the information system is overagile, resources are wasted; if the information system is underagile, the organization cannot respond to market opportunities or face challenges in a timely manner. Measuring information systems agility becomes a necessary precondition to making appropriate resource allocation decisions.

In this chapter, we define information systems agility, identify its component parts, and propose a technique for measuring degrees of agility in information systems. Our work is grounded in socio-technical theory and uses notions of fuzzy logic to define and compute the measures.

Theoretical Framework

Agility

An agile organization is defined as one that is able to "detect changing markets, rapidly learn to take advantage of these market changes, detect new techniques, adapt these techniques to the organizational culture so as to assimilate them into the organization while maintaining their spirit and using them effectively, meet varying standards in diverse markets, and be able to customize products to individual preferences" (Reich, Konda, and Subrahmanian, 1999, p. 67). The above broad definition subsumes the notion of flexibility, defined as the ability to adjust and find alternative means to achieve anticipated objectives (Knoll and Jarvenpaa, 1994). It differs in that agility requires the ability of not only detecting but also quickly responding to changes in conditions that require the formulation of alternative objectives. Agility is more concisely defined as "the ability to detect opportunities for innovation and seize those competitive market opportunities by assembling requisite assets, knowledge, and relationships with speed and surprise" (Sambamurthy, Bharadwaj, and Grover, 2003, p. 245). An organization is agile when it not only is capable of identifying market opportunities, but also can deploy its assets (tangible and intangible) to react faster than its competitors and seize the available opportunities.

The definition of agility, born out of the need to categorize the organization as a whole, must be extended to information systems since the ability of an organization to be agile subsumes the need to have an agile information system—the necessary enabler of organizational agility. We can therefore think of an agile information system as one that enables the firm to identify needed changes in the information processing functionalities required to succeed in the new environment, and lends itself to the quick and efficient implementation of the needed changes. Socio-technical theory and its conceptualization of the components of an information system provide the basis for better defining and measuring degrees of information systems agility.

Socio-Technical Theory

Socio-technical theory (Trist, 1963) provides the point of departure of our theorizing. An information system, designed to collect, process, store, and distribute information, is a socio-technical work system composed of two subsystems: a technical system and a social system (Bostrom and Heinen, 1977). The technical subsystem encompasses both technology (the tools to transform input into outputs) and process (the procedures enacted to carry out economic activities). The social subsystem encompasses the people who are directly involved in the information system, as well as the hierarchical, reward, and reporting structure in which these people are embedded (Figure 10.1). For example, a hotel can maintain its guest information system by pencil and paper. In this case, pencil and paper represents the technology component of the information systems. Of course, pencil and paper will not create information by themselves. A process of checking-in guests allows front desk agents to acquire, record, and store guest information on a piece of paper by using a pencil. Personnel involved in the information systems are front desk agents and accounting staff, who verify guest information. Information will flow from the front desk to accounting so that the guest will be charged correctly. Evidently, with the increasing widespread adoption of information technologies based on the microprocessor, modern information systems are almost exclusively computer-based. Yet, the conceptualization of these information systems as socio-technical systems still allows us to understand and evaluate how the technology impacts and is impacted by the other three components. It is this interrelationship among the components that makes the measurement of information systems agility less than straightforward.

Socio-technical theory suggests that for an information system to perform its function it requires that its four components are not only present, but interact with one another in a productive manner (O'Hara, Watson, and Kavan, 1999). This is because the four components, while distinct, are interdependent and constantly interacting, such that changes in one component create ripple-effects on the others. When Wyndham International introduced its customer loyalty program "Wyndham ByRequest," aiming at offering a consistent personalized hotel stay experience across the brand to its ByRequest members, it implemented a centralized database of customer preferences that was accessible by employees from all the Wyndham properties (Piccoli and Applegate, 2002). With the introduction of the new technology (the centralized database), changes in processes, people, and structures also occurred. The process of collecting customer data had to be created and employees had to be trained to introduce the new program to customers. The process of housekeeping had to be changed because the rooms in which ByRequest members were arriving had to be prepared not in a standard fashion (i.e., all the same) but according to the personal preference of each member of the program (e.g., preferred location, amenities, drinks, and snacks). A new position, ByRequest manager, was created so that the ByRequest manager could retrieve information about arriving ByRequest members, ensure the customization of their room, greet them personally, and so on. With the hiring of the new positions, the organizational structures and the reporting authority had to be adjusted as well. As seen in the example, the introduction of the new technology caused ripple effects that called for changes in the process to handle the task, the persons' skills, and their roles in the organization—a circumstance normally termed as *systemic effects*.

Recognizing the interdependence of the components of an information system is critical when attempting to measure information system agility. The agility of the information system in fact is not a simple summing of the agility of the four components, but it depends on their nonlinear relationship. For this reason, we propose the use of fuzzy logic to evaluate the overall agility of information systems. Before discussing fuzzy logic, we define agility for each of the four information system components.

Figure 10.1

Information System as a Socio-Technical System

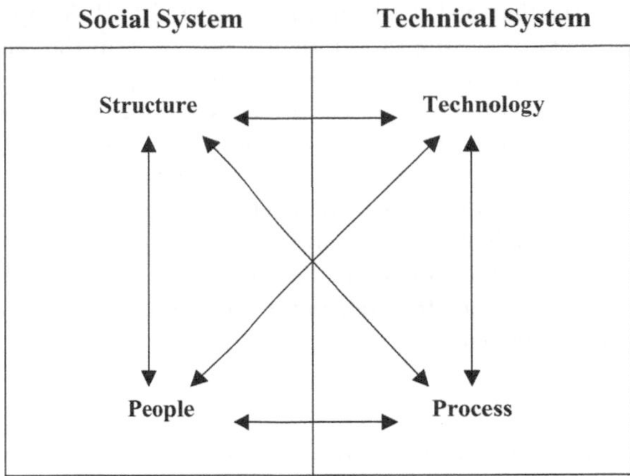

Technology Agility

Technology agility represents the degree of flexibility of the information technology and the extent to which the IT component of the information system lends itself to rapid adjustment when needed. In an effort to conceptualize IT agility, we adopted a relevant subset of dimensions of flexible IT from Knoll and Jarvenpaa's (1994) work: *scalability, adjustability, connectivity, modularity,* and *versatility.* Scalability deals with changes in input conditions. Technology with higher scalability can better accommodate input changes by increasing or decreasing system load while maintaining a steady state in the face of changing conditions so as to remain viable. Adjustability deals with the capability of modifying technologies. Technology with higher adjustability allows it to be modified within a shorter time frame, higher frequency, and higher degree of change. Connectivity deals with the degree to which various IT components can exchange data with one another and automatically trigger events to be completed in one of the connected modules. Technology with higher connectivity enables seamless collaboration within the organization more easily, allowing the firm higher degrees of freedom with respect to information access and fast, effective response to changes in the environment. Modularity refers to the capability to treat IT components independently. Technology with higher modularity enables the addition and/or removal of technology components without significant costs and time delay. IT versatility deals with the ability of the firm's technology core to incorporate new and different technologies that offer a new set of information-processing capabilities.

The above set of characteristics offers a starting point to understanding and measuring the degree of agility achieved by the IT component of a firm's information system. We follow a similar approach to the measurement of the process component below.

Process Agility

We define process agility as the degree of flexibility of the firm's business processes and their ability to adjust in response to changes in the firm's strategy or market conditions. Processes represent the set of steps required to perform an activity or set of activities that transforms inputs into outputs. Process agility can be characterized in terms of three dimensions: *setup times/costs* (Shuiabi, Thomson, and Bhuiyan, 2005), *number of products* (Shuiabi, Thomson, and Bhuiyan, 2005), and *alternative routings* (Fogliatto, Da Silveira, and Royer, 2003). Setup times/costs deal with the time and costs of setting up alternative processes in the face of changes in demand, market conditions, strategy, etc. For example, a process is considered more agile when it can produce different types of products and services without major setup time and cost as demand changes. Number of products captures the fact that a process is more agile when it can handle a greater variety of inputs and generate a greater variety of outputs. Alternative routings deals with different ways to produce a product and services. A process with higher alternative routing is one that is more agile because the input-output transformation process can be carried out in a number of alternative ways. These multiple degrees of freedom in the routing ensure the ability to continue operating as conditions change.

People Agility

We define people agility as the degree to which individuals associated with the information systems possess knowledge and skills that are both varied and easily redeployable in the face of change. Two variables can be used to measure people agility: training level and job rotation.[1] When facing change or unforeseen events, employees in the agile organization are able to sense the change and adjust by using alternative processes and practices (Patten et al., 2005). Training and cross-training programs provide employees with a wide range of skills that allow them to quickly redeploy when needed. Higher levels of training also equip employees with knowledge and capabilities to effectively perform alternative tasks when they are anticipating and reacting to strategy or market changes (Upton, 1995). Job rotation represents the frequency with which employees transfer from existing to new positions, under normal circumstances. Higher frequency of employee job rotation in different positions allows the organization to take rapid action when changes are needed (Tsourveloudis and Valavanis, 2002).

Structure Agility

We define structure agility as the degree of flexibility and decision-making ability afforded to individual members of the information system. Workforce empowerment, distributed decision-making authority, and flatter managerial hierarchies are typical hallmarks of structure agility (Tsourveloudis and Valavanis, 2002). An empowered workforce, and distributed decision-making authority allow employees to take leadership in decision making and to implement the decisions quickly. This is essential because people on the front line are the ones who interact with customers and are typically required to implement changes. The closer decision-making rights are to the locus of change, the quicker the change is likely to be. Flatter managerial hierarchies enhance communication within the organization and speed up the decision-making process in the face of more general and strategic level changes. Moreover, upper management's communication and reinforcement of the vision for agility, and the moni-

---

[1] We assume that the inherent talents of employees are normally distributed within a company. Therefore, the skills levels of employees on variety of jobs are similar.

toring of the requirement that allow agility are essential to increasing the speed of change. Therefore, the commitment and authority from upper management is a major enabler of structure agility (Cohn and Ford, 2003).

Because information systems are subject to systemic effects, measuring the agility of each component is a necessary precondition to gauging the agility of the information system as whole. But measuring the agility of each component is a nontrivial task, as it is combining these measures into an overall information system agility score. Fuzzy logic, a technique pioneered in an effort to enable machines to imitate human reasoning, provides a possible solution. We describe fuzzy logic and its application to our objectives in the next section.

Fuzzy Logic

The theories of logic and mathematics developed by Aristotle and his predecessors dealt with two values: true or false. A proposition cannot be both true and false at the same time. Fuzzy set theory, which allowed the processing of data by allowing partial set membership, was invented in 1965 (Zadeh, 1965). It extended to fuzzy logic, by which computers attempt to mirror human reasoning and judgment. From these beginnings, fuzzy logic has evolved into a technique that was recently used to measure manufacturing flexibility and enterprise agility (Tsourveloudis and Phillis, 1998; Tsourveloudis and Valavanis, 2002). We believe that fuzzy logic can be instrumental in measuring information systems agility.

Three principal features of fuzzy logic make it well suited to measuring the agility of an information system. First, mathematical models are not appropriate to deal with the measurement of agility because they do require the quantification of all variables of interest. They do not allow for imprecision of observed parameters (i.e., how much do you like this flower?). Many of the agility dimensions of the information system components are not easily quantifiable, such as how much one likes a particular flower. Moreover, as mentioned earlier, the agility of an information system cannot be computed as the simple sum of the agility score of its four components, and, because of systemic effects, the same degree of IS agility can be obtained with a virtually limitless blend of each component's agility. For example, a more user-friendly software can be developed to help users who are struggling with an older version. But increased training on the old application is a competing strategy often used to solve the same problem. Arithmetical formulas are not suited to combining the various dimensions of agility. This is similar to a medical diagnosis in which a doctor cannot identify how serious a patient's illness is by simply adding, subtracting, multiplying, or dividing diagnosed clinical symptoms (Zadeh, 1988). A more suitable representation of the manner in which human expertise works should therefore be used to achieve this type of intrinsically imprecise, judgment-based measurement. Unlike classical logic systems, fuzzy logic models the imprecise modes of reasoning that is typical of the human decision-making process in an uncertain and imprecise situation (Zadeh, 1988). Second, fuzzy logic allows for the use of control variables that are linguistic—such as *low, average,* and *high,* which cannot be handled by algebraic formulas (Tsourveloudis and Phillis, 1998). Finally, fuzzy logic is adjustable by the user. Within its context, one can define new variables, values, or even rules and reasoning procedures. The model, therefore, provides a situation-specific measurement and can be easily expanded (Tsourveloudis and Valavanis, 2002).

Fuzzy expert systems apply this linguistic variable concept as a basic concept in fuzzy logic. Linguistic variables will be discussed in detail in the following section. To illustrate the concept of fuzzy logic, we will first discuss linguistic variables, then membership functions, and finally inference rules.

Linguistic Variables

Linguistic variables "provide a means of approximating characterization of phenomenon which are too complex or too ill-defined to be susceptible of description in precise term" (Zadeh 1975a, p. 201). This flexibility is afforded by the fact that linguistic variables, being words or sentences, are not as precise as numerical variables. Thus, the use of linguistic variables forms the basis of "approximate reasoning, the type of reasoning which is neither very precise nor very imprecise" (Zadeh 1975a, p. 205). The values of a linguistic variable can be infinite. For example, the values of the linguistic variable "agility" include "agile, very agile, very very agile, more or less agile, not agile, not very agile, and the like. In this example, *agile* is the *primary term* (atomic term), and *very* and *more or less* are *hedges* (subterms) (Zadeh, 1975b). Combining the primary term and hedges creates the infinite amount of composite values of the linguistic variables.

Membership Functions

A fuzzy variable is notated as "(X, U, R(X:*u*)); where X is the name of the variable; U is a universe of discourse; *u* is a generic name for the elements of U; and R(X:*u*) is a fuzzy subset of U which represent a fuzzy restriction on the values of *u* imposed by X" (Zadeh 1975a, p. 210). A fuzzy restriction on the value of the base variable is characterized by a membership function that associates with each value of the base variable a number in the interval (0, 1), which represents its compatibility with the fuzzy restriction. The degree to which R(X:*u*) is satisfied will be referred to as the compatibility of *u* with R(X). The compatibility function $\mu_{R(X)}(u)$ is the grade of membership of *u* in the restriction R(X). A discrete membership function is notated as $\{\mu_{R(X)}(u)/u\}$. For example, when "Agility" is the name of the variable, High agility can be defined as *High* = {0/0.5, 0.8/0.6, 0.94/0.7, 0.97/0.8, 0.98/0.9, 0.99/1} as shown in Figure 10.2. The continuous membership function of *High* can be expressed as:

$$\mu_{High}(u) = 0 \qquad \text{for } 0 \le u \le 50$$

$$\mu_{High}(u) = \left[\left(1 + \frac{100u - 50}{5}\right)^{-2}\right]^{-1} \qquad \text{for } 50 < u < 100$$

The shapes of membership functions could be triangular, bell shaped, trapezoidal, or exponential. In fuzzy modeling, the membership functions are often empirically chosen. An example is presented in Figure 10.3. Membership functions can be defined as part of the analysis, but there is a trade-off of between the potential higher accuracy of more complex functions and the higher computing overhead they create. Once the membership function of the primary term is set, hedges (e.g., *very, more or less*) and the operations (interaction, union, and complement) of fuzzy sets create a fuzzy set with its own membership function. Hedges modify the fuzzy set. For example, in the phrase "very high," "very" modifies "high." "Very" and "more or less" can be expressed as: Very $X = X^2$ and More or Less $X = X^{1/2}$. Using the example of "High" above (Figure 10.2):

Agility (High) = {0/0.5, 0.80/0.6, 0.94/0.7, 0.97/0.8, 0.98/0.9, 0.99/1}
Agility (Very High) = {0/0.5, 0.64/0.6, 0.88/0.7, 0.94/0.8, 0.97/0.9, 0.98/1}
Agility (More or Less High) = {0/0.5, 0.89/0.6, 0.97/0.7, 0.98/0.8, 0.99/0.9, 1/1}

Three sets operators (*intersection, union,* and *complement*) are essential in fuzzy modeling. Intersection takes the minimum value after an item-by-item comparison between corresponding items ($a \cap b$ = Min (a,b)). Union takes the maximum value after an item-by-item comparison between corresponding items ($a \cup b$ = Max (a,b)). Complement of X is the membership value of x subtracted by 1 ($\bar{X} \equiv 1 - x$). For example, A and B are fuzzy set defined as:

A = {0/0, 0.2/0.1, 0.5/0.2, 0.8/0.3, 1/0.4, 0.7/0.5, 0.3/0.6, 0/0.7, 0/0.8, 0/0.9, 0/1}
B = {0/0, 0/0.1, 0/0.2, 0.2/0.3, 0.4/0.4, 0.6/0.5, 0.8/0.6, 1/0.7, 1/0.8, 1/0.9, 1/1}
$A \cap B$ = {0/0, 0/0.1, 0/0.2, 0.2/0.3, 0.4/0.4, 0.6/0.5, 0.3/0.6, 0/0.7, 0/0.8, 0/0.9, 0/1}
$A \cup B$ = {0/0, 0.2/0.1, 0.5/0.2, 0.8/0.3, 1/0.4, 0.7/0.5, 0.8/0.6, 1/0.7, 1/0.8, 1/0.9, 1/1}
$\bar{A}$ = {1/0, 0.8/0.1, 0.5/0.2, 0.2/0.3, 0/0.4, 0.3/0.5, 0.7/0.6, 1/0.7, 1/0.8, 1/0.9, 1/1}

After understanding the basic concept of fuzzy logic and its operations, we can now use it to model inferences.

Figure 10.2

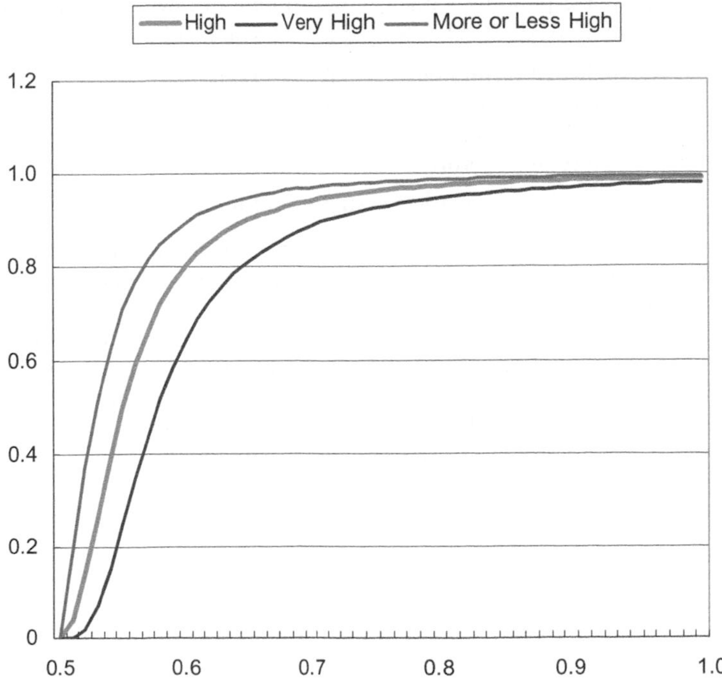

Figure 10.3

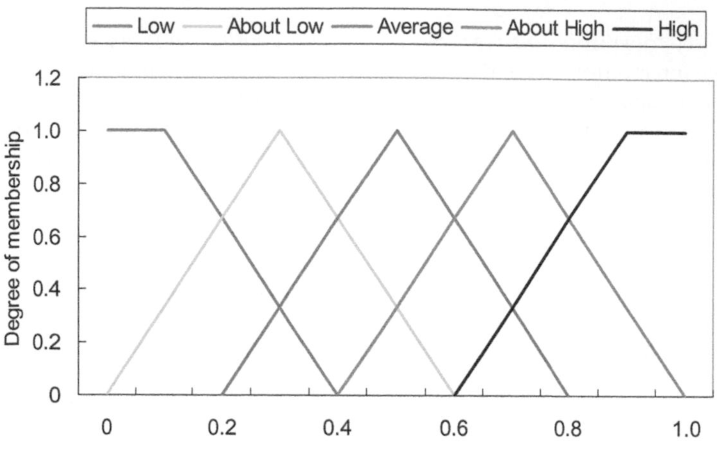

Inference Rules

Multi-antecedent fuzzy IF-THEN rules are used to make inference, where the IF part specifies the conditional statements relating the observable parameters, and the THEN part is the corresponding value of the variable of interest (e.g., agility). One simple, rule-based IF X AND Y, THEN Z approach can be illustrated as:

IF	the agility of technology	is	high
AND	the agility of process	is	average
AND	the agility of people	is	average
AND	the agility of structure	is	average

THEN the agility of the information systems is about high

The above computation is performed by using a *compositional rule of inference* (Zadeh 1975c; Zadeh, 1988). This rule of inference is "solving a simultaneous system of so-called *rational assignment equations* in which linguistic values are assigned to fuzzy restrictions" (Zadeh 1975a, p. 209). To illustrate, we assume a function $y = f(x)$, where f is a given rule to predict y_o from x_o. If we know that statement a implying b is true and also that a is true, we can infer that b is true $(a \wedge (a \Rightarrow b) \Rightarrow b)$. Fuzzy logic allows the statement (a) and implication $(a \Rightarrow b)$ to be slightly different, which generalizes the rule into $a' \wedge (a' \Rightarrow b') \Rightarrow b'$. The inference of b is denoted $b = a \circ f$. For example, we can associate the statement a to "the temperature is high" and the statement b to "turn on the air conditioner." Therefore, when the temperature is high, the air conditioner will be turned on. When the temperature is about high, the air conditioner will be slightly on. Computation is done by using a *max-min rule,* typically performed with dedicated software programs. A simple example with two input variables will be presented in the next section to illustrate a sample computation.

Example[2]

Imagine that we are measuring the agility of one of the components of information systems, for example, people. We observe that the level of training is High *AND* the level of job rotation is About High. The membership functions of High and About High (Figure 10.3) are:

High = {0/0.65, 0.2/0.7, 0.5/0.75, 0.7/0.8, 1/0.9, 1/1}
About High = {0/0.6, 0.4/0.65, 0.7/0.7, 1/0.75, 0.7/0.8, 0/0.9}
Very High = High^2 = {0/0.65, 0.04/0.7, 0.25/0.75, 0.49/0.8, 1/0.9, 1/1}

As mentioned in the previous section, AND is computed using minimum. However, this operation indicated no interaction between two variables, which is not true in this case. For example, given the statement "High AND Low," we computed using only the minimum operator. The result will be $\mu_{High \cap Low} = 0$, which does not reflect the way managers process the information of these given rules. Therefore, instead of just using the minimum operator when computing AND, it can be computed by using intersection (∩) and union (∪) (Dubois and Prade, 1982):

$$\mu_{HighANDAboutHigh}(x) = (1-\gamma)\mu_{High \cap AboutHigh}(x) + \gamma \times \mu_{High \cup AboutHigh}(x) \quad x \in X, \gamma \in [0,1]$$

γ is the grade of compensation and indicates where the actual operator is located between the union ($\gamma = 1$) and intersection ($\gamma = 0$). If the actual operator is union, the result will be the maximum. Otherwise, it will be treated as an intersection, for which the minimum value among two membership functions will be chosen. We can regulate the impact of two variables (training level and job rotation) on people agility by adjusting the γ-parameter. Here, if we assume $\gamma = 0.4$, *High AND About High* = {0.16/0.65, 0.4/0.7, 0.7/0.75, 0.7/0.8, 0.4/0.9, 0.4/1}. The degree of membership when $x = 0.65$ is calculated by $\mu_{HighAndAboutHigh}(0.65) = 0.6 \times 0 + 0.4 \times 0.4 = 0.16$. This is used to form the base rule that "if the two observation variables are *High AND About High*, the agility is *High*." Applying the same computation, the membership of the agility of people when the level of training is very high and the level of job rotation is about high will be *Very High and About High* = {0.16/0.65, 0.304/0.7, 0.55/0.75, 0.5734/0.8, 0.4/0.9, 0.4/1}. Now, we can use the compositional rule of inference $a' \wedge (a' \Rightarrow b') \Rightarrow b'$ and compute the membership function of the agility of people using the max-min rules.

a'	*Very High and About High*
$a' \Rightarrow b'$	*(High and About High) ⇒ High*
The Agility of People	{0.6/0.7, 0.6/0.75, 0.7/0.8, 1/0.9, 1/1}

Notice that the membership function of the agility of the people component is very similar to the membership function of *High*. Therefore, we can infer that the overall agility of the people component of the information system, in this example, is high. Using the same computation, we can infer the agility of the other three components. Combining all four components, we can measure the agility of the information system as a whole.

[2] Due to the strictly illustrative nature of this example, we simply adapted the example presented in Tsourveloudis and Phillis (1998).

Conclusion

This chapter makes the case for why, with growing attention being devoted to strategic and information systems agility, research and practice needs a definition of agility that is not binary, but recognizes that agility is measured on a continuum. Our contribution consists in offering such definition, and in using it to propose a technique to measure the agility of information systems. Our proposed technique suggests identifying the four components of an information system and measuring the agility of each one. It then requires that an overall agility index be computed for the information system. Because of the inherent uncertainty that characterizes the measurement of agility, and the significant judgment involved, we showed that fuzzy logic represents a suitable approach to this measurement.

We hope that the technique we introduced here will prove useful to both managers and researchers as they pursue their work in this area. Being able to compute a reliable measure of information system agility is crucial to avoid overinvesting in agility reaching levels that exceed what is needed by the firm and therefore wasting valuable resources. Moreover, being able to measure agility should allow managers to avoid an equally perilous situation—underinvesting in agility and being therefore unprepared to confront the degree of change in their industry.

References

Ahsan, M. and Ye-Ngo, L. (2005). The relationship between IT infrastructure and strategic agility in organizations. In *Proceedings of the Eleventh Americas Conference on Information Systems* (N. C. Romano, Jr., ed.). Omaha, NE.

Bostrom, R. P. and Heinen, J. S. (1977). MIS problems and failures: A socio-technical perspective. *MIS Quarterly,* 1 (3), 17–32.

Cohn, M. and Ford, D. (2003). Introducing an agile process to an organization. *Computer*, 36 (6), 74–78.

D'aveni, R. and Gunther, R. E. (1994). *Hypercompetition: Managing the Dynamic of Strategic Maneuvering*. New York: Free Press.

Dubois D. and Prade H. (1982). A class of fuzzy measures based on triangular norms: A general framework for the combination of information. *International Journal of General Systems,* 8 (1), 43–61.

Duncan, N. B. (1995). Capturing flexibility of technology infrastructure: A study of resource characteristics and their measure. *Journal of Management Information Systems,* 12 (2), 37–57.

Fogliatto, F. S., Da Silveira, G. J. C., and Royer R. (2003). Flexibility-driven index for measuring mass customization feasibility on industrialized products. *International Journal of Production Research*, 41 (8), 1811–1829.

Goldman, S. L., Nagel, R. N., and Preiss, K. (1995). Agile competitors and virtual organizations: Strategies for enriching the customer. New York: Van Nostrand Reinhold.

Henderson, J. C. and Venkatraman, N. (1993). Strategic alignment: Leveraging information technology for transforming organization. *IBM Systems Journal,* 32 (1), 4–16.

Hidding, G. (2001). Sustaining strategic IT advantage in the information age: How strategy paradigms differ by speed. *The Journal of Strategic Information System,* 10 (3), 201–222.

Hitt, M., Kearts, B., and DeMarie, S. (1998). Navigating in the new competitive landscape: Building strategic flexibility and competitive advantage in the 21st century. *Academy of Management Executive,* 12 (4), 22–41.

King, W. R. (1978). Strategic planning for management information systems. *MIS Quarterly*, 2 (1), 27–37.

Knoll, K. and Jarvenpaa, S. (1994). Information technology alignment or "fit" in highly turbulent environments: The concept of flexibility. *ACM SIGVPR Computer Personnel* (April), 1–14.

O'Hara, M. T., Watson, R. T., and Kavan, C. B. (1999). Managing the three levels of change. *Information Systems Management Journal,* 16 (3), 63–70.

Patten, K., et al. (2005). Leading IT flexibility: Anticipating, agility and adaptability. *Proceedings of the Eleventh Americas Conference on Information Systems.* Omaha, NE.

Piccoli, G. and Applegate, L. M. (2002). Wyndham international: Fostering high-touch with high-tech. *Harvard Business School Publishing, 9-803-092.*

Reich, Y., Konda, S., and Subrahmanian, E., et al. (1999). Building agility for developing agile design information systems. *Research in Engineering Design,* 11 (2), 67–83.

Sambamurthy, V., Bharadwaj, A., and Grover, V. (2003). Shaping agility through digital options: Reconceptualizing the role of information technology in contemporary firms. *MIS Quarterly,* 27 (2), 237–263.

Sanchez, R. (1997). Preparing for an uncertain future: Managing Organizations for Strategic Flexibility. *International Studies of Management and Organizations,* 27 (2), 71–94.

Shuiabi, E., Thomson, V., and Bhuiyan, N. (2005). Entropy as a measure of operational flexibility. *European Journal of Operational Research,* 165 (3), 696–707.

Tapscott, D. and Caston, A. (1993). *Paradigm Shift: The New Promise of Information Technology.* New York: McGraw Hill.

Teo, T. S. H. and King, W. R. (1997). Integration between business planning and information systems: An evolutionary-contingency perspective. *Journal of Management Information Systems,* 14 (1), 185–214.

Trist, E. L. (1963). Organization choice; capabilities of groups at the coal face under changing technologies: The loss, re-discovery, and transformation of a work tradition. London, UK: Tavistock Publications.

Tsourveloudis, N. C. and Phillis, Y. A. (1998). Manufacturing flexibility measurement: A fuzzy logic framework. *IEEE Transactions on Robotics and Automation,* 14 (4), 513–524.

Tsourveloudis, N. C. and Valavanis, K. P. (2002). On the measurement of enterprise agility. *Journal of Intelligent & Robotic Systems,* 33 (3), 329–342.

Upton D. M. (1995). What really makes factories flexible? *Harvard Business Review,* 73 (4), 74–84.

Veliyath, R. (1996). Hypercompetition: Managing the dynamics of strategic maneuvering. *Academy of Management Review,* 21 (1), 291–294.

Weill, P., Subramani, M., and Broadbent M. (2002). Building IT infrastructure for strategic agility. *MIT Sloan Management Review,* 44 (1), 57–65.

Williams, J. R. (1992). How sustainable is your competitive advantage? *California Management Review,* 34 (3), 29–51.

Zadeh L. A. (1965). Fuzzy sets. *Information and Control,* 8 (3), 338–353.

Zadeh, L. A. (1975a). The concept of a linguistic variable and its application to approximate reasoning—Part I. *Information Sciences,* 8 (3), 199–249.

Zadeh, L. A. (1975b). The concept of a linguistic variable and its application to approximate reasoning—Part II. *Information Sciences,* 8 (4), 301–357.

Zadeh, L. A. (1975c). The concept of a linguistic variable and its application to approximate reasoning—Part III. *Information Sciences,* 9 (1), 43–80.

Zadeh, L. A. (1988). Fuzzy logic. *IEEE Computer,* 21 (4), 83–93.

Integration Management for Heterogeneous Information Systems

11

Joachim Schelp and Robert Winter

In large companies where Information Technology (IT) is instrumental for business success (e.g., banking insurance, logistics, telecommunications), complexity and heterogeneity of the Information Systems (IS) landscape tend to be everincreasing. In such a setting, the sustainability of the IT value contribution depends on the ability to manage IS integration effectively and efficiently. Pursuing a goal system should comprise:

- IS agility (flexibility and time-to-market),
- IT business alignment (e.g., business process support),
- An optimal degree of application decoupling (with regard to development and runtime costs)
- Satisfaction of (internal and/or external) IS customers (one of the most important contributions of integration management is to establish a planning and control process for IS architecture)

Based on a literature review, the first two parts of this chapter discuss the goal system of IS integration. The first section focuses on agility, which is often regarded as the most important integration management goal, especially from a business perspective. In the second section, five key areas for IS integration management that contribute to or affect agility are derived: complexity of information systems architecture, degree of coupling between information systems, reuse potential/functional redundancy, integration project expenses, and costs/complexity of the integration infrastructure. For each key management area, performance indicators are proposed that allow such integration management aspects to be measured and ultimately managed.

Agility and Corporate IS

Agility as a business challenge is attributed to a globalizing, accelerating corporate environment (Gandossy, 2003; Cao and Dowlatshahi, 2005). To meet this challenge, many companies are transforming their production structures from standardized mass production to more customer-oriented structures by means of product individualization, higher-quality standards, more adaptive production structures, and shorter product life cycles (Duguay, Landry, and Pasin, 1997; Vokurka and Fliedner, 1998; Maskell, 2001; van Hoek, 2001; McCarthy and Tsinopoulos, 2003).

According to the recent discussion in production management (e.g., Goldman, Nagel, and Preiss, 1995; Sharifi and Zhang, 1999; Yusuf et al., 1999; Zhang and Sharifi, 2000), agility goes beyond flexibility. While flexibility means that a system is able to adapt to expected changes, agility means that a system is also adaptive to unexpected changes (Vokurka and Fliedner, 1998; Becker, 2001). Production management aims to "build in" flexibility by engineering for (re-)configurability of both production structures (e.g., by using CIM and CAD/CAM systems) and products (e.g., by component-based design).

(Re-)configurability, however, provides little help for unexpected changes. As a consequence, agility is recommended (Duguay, Landry, and Pasinal, 1997; Becker, 2001), not only related to production and product structures, but to the entire company. Yusuf, Sarhadi, and Gunasekaran (1999) define this recommendation as follows: "Agility is the successful exploration of competitive bases (speed, flexibility, innovation proactivity, quality and profitability) through the integration of reconfigurable resources and best practices in a knowledge-rich environment to provide customer-driven products and services in a fast changing market environment" (Yusuf, Sarhadi, and Gunasekaran, 1999). It is important to note that agility is not aimed at *reacting* to change, but as a *proactive* means to support change (Goldman, Nagel, and Preiss, 1995).

Corporate IT has an important impact on agility (Sambamurthy, Bharadwaj, and Grover, 2003; Cao and Dowlatshahi, 2005). IT supports faster product development cycles and enhanced flexibility of both production and product structures. In addition, IT can enable the development and implementation of new business models. Considering the discussion in production management, Sambamurthy, Bharadwaj, and Grover (2003) distinguish three types of agility where IT can be supportive:

- *Customer agility:* The ability to learn from customers, identify new business opportunities and implement these opportunities together with customers.
- *Partnering agility:* The ability to leverage business partners' knowledge, competencies, and assets in order to identify and implement new business opportunities.
- *Operational agility:* The ability to execute the identification and implementation of business opportunities quickly, accurately, and cost-efficiently.

Customer agility and partnering agility focus on supporting business processes, either directed at the (mass) customer, such as using consumer portals, or directed at business partners within a supply chain, such as using supply chain management solutions (White, Daniel, and Mohdzain, 2005). Empirical evidence supports that IT can be an enabler for agility (Cao and Dowlatshahi, 2005).

Operational agility focuses on the company's IT and its contribution to agility. IT units support business units by providing agile IT solutions. For analyzing operational agility, there are three starting points:

- The process of developing business opportunities together with business units
- The process of providing IT solutions
- The process of developing IT solutions

As a consequence of the general customer-orientation goal, IT units have to shape their customer (= business) orientation. IT is therefore often recommended to be run as a "business within the business" (Melarkode, From-Poulsen, Warnakulasuriya, 2004). Solutions have to be delivered to (and paid by) the business units based on service-level agreements (Morgan, 2004).

The maturity of development and provision processes for IT solutions defines the extent to which IT/operations units can contribute to a company's agility. In order to engineer for agility, (re-)defining requirements engineering, (re-)defining systems development, and (re-)defining IT operations is not sufficient. Nerur, Mahapatra, and Mangalara (2005) propose that management and organization, people, processes, and technology (in terms of tools and methodology) have to be consistently adjusted. Changes in management and organization should not be limited to team-oriented coordination instead of a hierarchical approach. In addition, organizational culture, leadership, and the incentives system have to be adjusted to enhance collaboration.

IT processes are directly related to IT products/solutions. In order to understand operational agility with regard to IT, the maturity of IT products plays an important role. According to Zarnekow (2004), IT products can be categorized with regard to the dimensions "product complexity" and "business orientation":

- The simplest form of an IT product is the provision of IT resources (e.g., computing power measured in MIPS or storage measured in TB). Such products are of low complexity, but have very little business orientation and therefore provide no basis for effective planning and control purposes.
- A more elaborate IT product is the provision of IT solutions (e.g., a data mart or an enterprise resource management system). Such products have both higher complexity and more business orientation.
- A more business-oriented IT product is the support of business processes (e.g., lead generation for campaign management or rating for a credit check).
- The most complex and most business-oriented form of an IT product is a marketable business service. Examples can be found in the product catalogs of professional IT services (e.g., data-processing centers).

These IT product categories correspond to the IT infrastructure development stages as described by Ahsan and Ye-Ngo (2005): "Application silos" can be found in companies with large amounts of individual software systems that are tailored to certain business units. "Standardized technology" replaces such silos and supports several business units with common IT solutions. The IT infrastructure category "rationalized data" can be characterized as integrated and process-oriented, which corresponds to the third IT product category. The most advanced IT infrastructure type ("modular") requires IT products to be standardized, business-oriented, and marketable. Ahsan and Ye-Ngo propose that the contribution to a company's agility is related to how high and advanced the IT infrastructure development stage is.

Infrastructure, as described in Weill, Subramani, and Broadbental, 2002; Ahsan and Ye-Ngo, 2005; and Umar, 2005, should be understood as a set of integrated applications rather than a specific technology. Many case studies support the assumption that service orientation contributes more to overall agility than single technologies (Coronado Mondragon, Lyons, and Kehoe, 2004).

A modular infrastructure (i.e., loosely coupled services that can be (re-) orchestrated in order to support changing business processes) requires that applications can be integrated and decoupled easily. This requirement is discussed intensely in the literature (e.g., application integration in Arsanjani, 2002; Sutherland and van den Heuvel, 2002; Irani, Themistocleous, and Love, 2003; Schelp and Schwinn, 2005; Schwinn and Winter, 2005). In order to manage IT infrastructure agility, therefore, integration and decoupling of applications have to be managed. A precondition for the effective management of integration/decoupling is that these phenomena can be specified and the extent of integration/decoupling be measured.

Indicators and Performance Measures for Heterogeneous IS Architectures

Among the many factors that influence the agility of an information system, application architecture is the most prominent (Winter, 2003). The application architecture is a set of all applications and their relationships within a company—the application landscape. The structure of a company's application architecture is often in a bad state these days. Reminders can be found from the 1980s (monolithic applications, simple IT products), the 1990s (standard software packages, IT solutions), and from the Internet hype around 2000 (redundant applications addressing the Internet channel, often more simple IT products than IT solutions). Especially around 2000, time to market overrode sustainability and cost efficiency in extending the application architecture. This led to redundancy as many functionalities were reimplemented, not integrated.

The direct influence of the application architecture on the agility of the information system cannot be specified easily. Therefore, the following considerations concentrate on the application landscape's structure with emphasis on the relations between applications. The relations reflect integration needs, so that we can focus on the success factors influencing application integration. Numerous approaches to application integration can be found in the literature, many of them in the field of Enterprise Application Integration (EAI). Schwinn and Winter (2005) analyze both scientific contributions and practitioner papers to identify the success factors discussed in the literature. Table 11.1 summarizes the results. The following success factors were mentioned most often:

- Minimal project expenses (time and costs) for integrating applications into the present application architecture.
- Optimal reuse of software components and minimal functional redundancy.
- Reduction of complexity within the present application architecture.
- Optimal coupling of applications (neither tighter nor looser than necessary).
- Minimal costs for and number of infrastructure components, e.g., middleware components such as message broker or object request broker (ORB).

All of these factors affect the agility of an information system.

The identified success factors as shown in Table 11.1 are described and discussed in more detail in the following sections, and we propose appropriate performance indicators.

Application Architecture Complexity

Historically grown application architectures comprising hundreds of applications (Linthicum, 2000) cannot be managed as a whole, because of a complexity too high and interdependencies too manifold. Therefore, it is necessary to control the complexity by knowingly des-integrating the application architecture. To reduce the complexity, the application architecture can be split up into smaller defined components (building blocks). Among those components we propose loose coupling, and within the components tight coupling. Loose coupling reduces dependencies among the components. That means that changes in one component will not affect the other component (Linthicum, 2000).

One way to des-integrate the application architecture is to define application domains that comprise a defined set of applications. The number of application

Table 11.1

Success Factors for Application Integration in Related Work						
Success factor (horizontal)	**Approach (vertical)**	**Minimal expenses of integration projects**	**Optimal reuse**	**Reduction of complexity**	**Optimal level of coupling**	**Minimal costs for infrastructure**
(Linthicum, 2000)			X	X	X	
(Zahavi, 2000)		X	X	X		X
(Kaib, 2002)		X	X	X	X	X
(Ruh et al., 2001)		X	X	X	X	X
(Cummins, 2002)		X	X	X	X	X
(Fridgen and Heinrich, 2004)				X		X
(Themistocleous and Irani, 2001)		X	X		X	X

domains should be small to keep the advantage of lower complexity. It is important that applications within a domain can be modified without direct effects to other domains.

The most important figure is the degree of des-integration. To measure this figure, the number of loosely coupled controlled links (i.e., links that are directly controlled by architecture management) between application domains is counted. This figure has to be put in relation with the uncontrolled links between the domains. The quotient represents the level of des-integration.

To measure these figures, existing tools such as source code analyzers or application repository managers can be used.

Degree of Coupling

General rules for the degree of coupling are not useful because each application relation is different. Intuitively, tight coupling is appropriate if two applications implement functionalities that belong to the same business process. If two applications implement functionalities of different business processes, loose coupling would be appropriate. The degree of coupling has direct influence on the agility of the information system: Tighter coupling necessarily will result in excess expenses for implementing new or changing existing requirements. If applications are coupled too loosely, runtime overhead may arise and additional middleware components for integration might be needed.

For each application relation, an appropriate level of coupling has to be chosen. Since a common methodology with objective criteria does not exist, it is difficult to derive measurable figures. A potential indicator could be the expenses for implementing changes in "dependent" applications due to modifications of an "independent" application. High expenses indicate too tight coupling. On the other hand, the runtime overhead has to be measured. A high runtime overhead would indicate too loose coupling. However it is difficult to exactly determine the runtime overhead. It usually cannot be measured directly because it is hidden in other maintenance or infrastructure costs. Even if the runtime overhead could be measured, the interpretation of measured values is difficult as no benchmarks exist.

As a consequence, a random sampling of applications and measurement of modification costs "induced" by context changes seem to be the only way to approximate the degree of coupling.

Reuse/Functional Redundancy

The success factor "optimal reuse" claims that every function is only implemented once by an application. If a function only has to be developed and maintained once, lower development and maintenance costs should be achievable. Furthermore, reuse supports the consistency, quality, and flexibility of applications (Cummins, 2002). To achieve a maximum reuse, powerful middleware is needed to deliver the centrally implemented functionality to as many other applications as possible that are running on different platforms. In the design process, a framework is needed to ensure the future reusability of a component (Design-for-Reuse). One important aspect is the granularity of the function. If only large monolithic software components are developed, the potential for reuse is high because a broad functionality or parts of it can be reused. On the other side, dependencies are created, as the frequency of changes is higher and release cycles are shorter. If the components are too modular, the benefit of the reuse is lower and runtime and maintenance overhead increases because many small functions have to be reused—not only one.

Another aspect that should be considered when designing reusable software components is the level of specialization. If only very specialized components are developed, the potential for reuse is low because only few applications or users need this very specialized function. If the components are too general, the potential for reuse should generally be higher, but the benefit for the "re-user" is low as only a very general service can be utilized. Furthermore, additional business logic has to be implemented by the "re-user" which leads to redundancy again.

Another important indicator for the quality of the application architecture is the number and growth of public interfaces. A high amount and a quick growth could indicate redundancy as we believe all functionality should be covered by reusable functions at a time. But fast growth could also be the result of introducing new technologies (e.g., service-oriented architecture). If so, the figure indicates the user acceptance of the new technology.

Integration Project Expenses

It is problematic to determine integration costs on a general level because integration effort is not only dependent on business requirements (e.g., timeliness) and technology support, but also on time. As a consequence, we do not consider single projects, but entire project portfolios over a certain period to measure integration expenses.

Implications to the quality of integration aspects within the application architecture can only be drawn if the integration problem and the expenses are normalized. The integration costs depend on many factors (e.g., the number of interfaces, number of business units involved, quality of existing documentation, etc.) that are hard to determine. As it is very hard to measure the integration complexity, we propose an indicator that compares the entirety of integration efforts: We sum up all integration costs and divide them by the overall integration complexity within a certain period (e.g., one year). If we compare two periods by dividing the quotient from the first year by the quotient of the second year, the result should be smaller than 1. That means that we have implemented more integration complexity with lower expenses.

The only thing we can derive from this figure is the cost-efficiency. However, without benchmarks, we cannot determine useful target values.

Costs and Complexity of the Integration Infrastructure

The number of deployed integration technologies or tools within a company has direct influence on the fixed IT expenditures. As a consequence, the number of utilized tools has an (indirect) influence on IT project costs. If only a few tools are used, they can be supported professionally. Higher numbers of tools lead to uncertainties as developers have to decide which tool is most appropriate for specific requirements. On the other hand, a basic set of technologies is necessary to implement the requirements efficiently and to avoid workarounds by simulating one technology by means of another (e.g., using a message broker to implement a service-oriented architecture).

Possible figures for measuring this factor are infrastructure costs, number of deployed technologies and tools, standardization, or the degree of fulfillment of project requirements by standard technologies and tools.

Influence on Agility

All factors described above influence agility. They contribute to the modular infrastructure asked for in the previous section—loosely coupled services, which can be (re-)combined to support changing business processes. Figure 11.1 illustrates the identified success factors influencing agility and their assumed interdependencies as shown in Schwinn and Winter (2005).

IS Architecture Redesign

Indicators and performance measures were proposed in the preceding section that help to manage IT architecture agility. An effective management system for IT architecture helps to systematically plan for agility, set appropriate priorities for projects, and monitor the transformation. The implementation of a management system alone, however, is not sufficient to transform the IT infrastructure toward more agility. The core of such transformation is a clear application architecture vision and appropriate component (re-)design rules for applications.

Analysis of Existing Application Design

Applications are usually not developed in an "architected" way, i.e., strictly following a set of specific design rules that avoid overlaps, avoid gaps, and are oriented at a specific integration direction (organization/product line, functionality, or information subject).

Figure 11.1

Application Integration Success Factors and Their Interdependencies

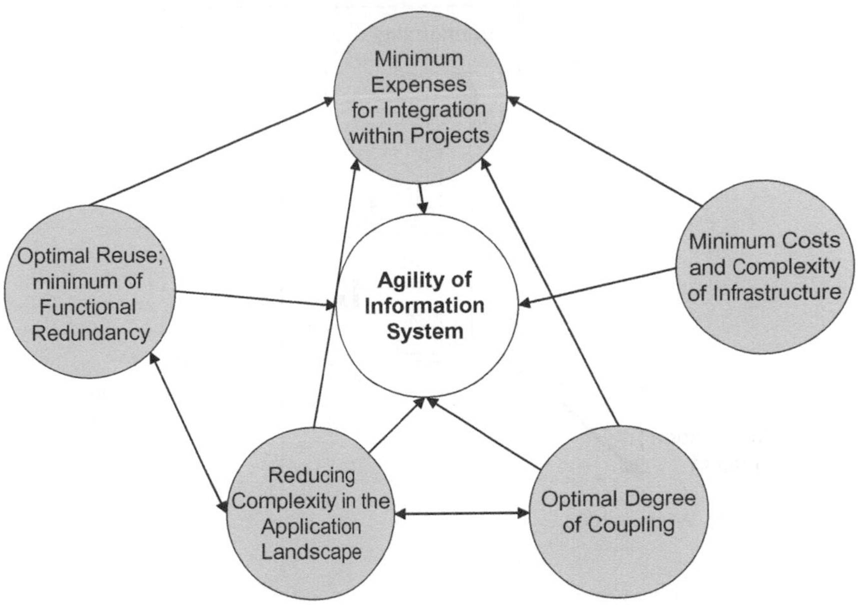

Historically, integration along organizational structures or product lines dominated for a long period. Examples of such applications are a mortgage-processing system (oriented toward a product line) or a securities trading system (oriented toward an organizational unit). With the growing significance of databases and management information systems, many applications have been developed that are integrated along an information subject (e.g., a revenue-controlling system or a risk-management system). More recently, the growing number of distribution and access channels and the business requirement to offer services consistently over multiple channels has led to the development of applications that are integrated around a specific channel (e.g., call center, e-commerce). In addition to "organization/product line," "information subject," and distribution/access channels, selected applications have always tried to encapsulate certain functionalities and make it available for reuse across organizational units, product lines, information subjects, and channels. Examples for functionality reuse are authorization systems, archiving systems, and output management systems. With regard to application architecture, this "functionality reuse" integration type is similar to channel orientation.

Figure 11.2 illustrates a three-dimensional model that is useful to exhibit the different types of integration in application design. A denotes a typical organization/product-line–centered application, B denotes a typical information/subject-centered application, and C denotes a typical channel-centered (or functionality reuse) application.

Figure 11.2 also illustrates a situation that is typically found in most medium and large companies: Since the integration focus changed over time and no consistent

Figure 11.2

Application Architecture Model*

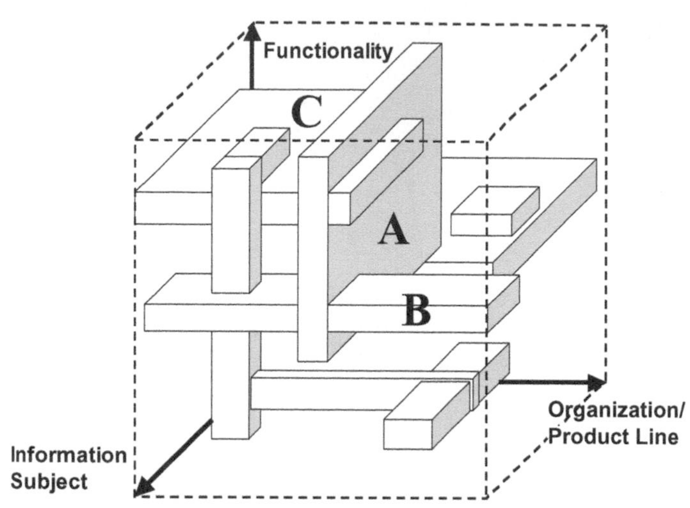

* From Winter, 2003.

architecture design was enforced, many applications overlap (i.e., functionalities or data usages are implemented in more than one application) and many gaps are present (i.e., certain functionalities are not available for every channel or reused by every process) (Winter, 2003).

Please note that the graphical cube representation of A, B, and C does not imply that these (or other) applications are implemented as monolithic pieces of software. Usually, all applications comprise a number of modules, data structures, and/or components that are closely related and therefore integrated by appropriate implementation mechanisms, such as common database, message queues, and so on.

Ideal Application Design

In order to avoid overlaps or gaps and thereby reduce integration costs, applications should be "architected." Business process support, information-centered processing, and functionality reuse (including channel functionalities) should be implemented by different applications. In the proposed model, such architected applications would be completely integrated around only one model dimension, that is, they focus on a small range in only one dimension and extend across a broad range in the two other dimensions (Winter, 2003):

- Organization/product-line–centered applications should integrate all functionalities and all information subjects for a certain organizational unit or product line.
- Information-centered applications should integrate access to a certain information subject across all organizational units/product lines and across all functionalities.

- Functionality-centered applications should make a certain functionality available across all organizational units/product lines and across all information subjects for consistent reuse.

The ideal application architecture that results from strictly architected application design is illustrated in Figure 11.3.

Although being oriented on information subjects and hence having similarities with information-centered applications, analytical applications are represented by a separate component in the model. This is due to the fact that analytical applications support management processes rather than operational processes. As a consequence, different functionalities are implemented, which results in different values regarding the functionality dimension.

Organization/product-line–centered applications are often designated as "vertical" applications. Functionality-centered applications (and particularly channel-oriented applications) are often designated as "horizontal" applications.

In contrast to analytical applications that support management processes, vertical, horizontal, and information-centered applications are often generalized to "operational" applications because they support operational business processes (Winter 2003).

In comparison to non-architected, historically grown application architecture (see Figure 11.2), ideal application design does the following:

- Reduces integration costs by avoiding interfaces that are needed to preserve integrity when application overlaps occur.
- Enhances agility because distribution/access channels can be more flexibly assigned to products/services, and common functionalities can be reused more efficiently.

Figure 11.3

Ideal Application Architecture*

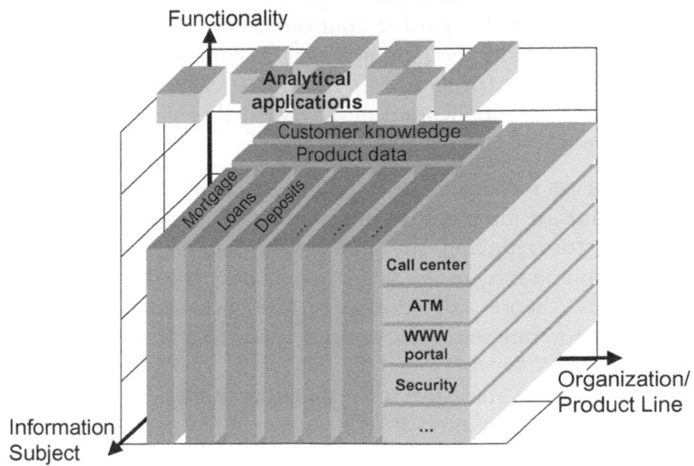

* From Winter, 2003.

The transformation of nonarchitected applications into an ideal or near-ideal application architecture, however, is an expensive and time-consuming process. The separation of information-centered applications and vertical applications (e.g., by extracting product data management and customer data management) has been on the IS architect's agenda since the 1980s and in many companies is still far from being completed. The same holds true for separating vertical applications and horizontal applications (e.g., by extracting quoting and contractual functionalities). However, the expected integration cost savings and agility gains of an architected application architecture are so huge that many companies have started large application rearchitecture projects to realize these benefits.

Application Interfacing and Common Integration Layers

Unfortunately, the separation of business process support, information-centered processing, and functionality reuse creates massive interfacing requirements that lead to high inter-application integration costs. This section investigates how inter-application integration costs can be reduced without invalidating ideal application design.

If applications are created according to the proposed design rules, all intensely coupled modules, data structures, and/or components are aggregated into respective operational or analytical applications, while interfaces are used to implement loose couplings. As a consequence, only a relatively small number of interfaces should be necessary between different applications of the same type. However, for several reasons, a much higher number of interfaces must be implemented between different types of applications (Winter, 2003):

- Analytical applications source their data from operational applications. In the worst case, a data sourcing interface is needed between every analytical application and operational application.
- Horizontal applications provide distribution and access functionalities for vertical applications. Information-centered applications provide information access functionalities for vertical and horizontal applications. In the worst case, an interface is needed between every operational application and every other operational application.
- Operational as well as analytical applications exchange or share data with applications outside the regarded company to support intercompany business processes (e.g., common planning in a supply chain, sharing of customer data in a multi-industry loyalty program). In the theoretically worst case, an interface is needed between every application in the regarded company and every intercompany application.

Although worst-case scenarios are rare, large companies have developed and are maintaining thousands of interfaces to implement such couplings. The most straightforward approach for reducing the number of interfaces between applications is to introduce a common integration layer. Instead of having to develop and maintain $n*(n-1)$ interfaces (theoretically the worst case) between n applications, only n adapters to the common integration layer are needed. This "hub-and-spoke" principle is illustrated in Figure 11.4.

During the last two decades, the software industry has developed three types of common integration layers (Winter, 2003):

- *Data warehouse* (DWH) systems provide a single, consistent information base for analytical applications by integrating (i.e., collecting, transforming, and

Figure 11.4

Individual Interfaces versus Hub-and-Spoke Concept*

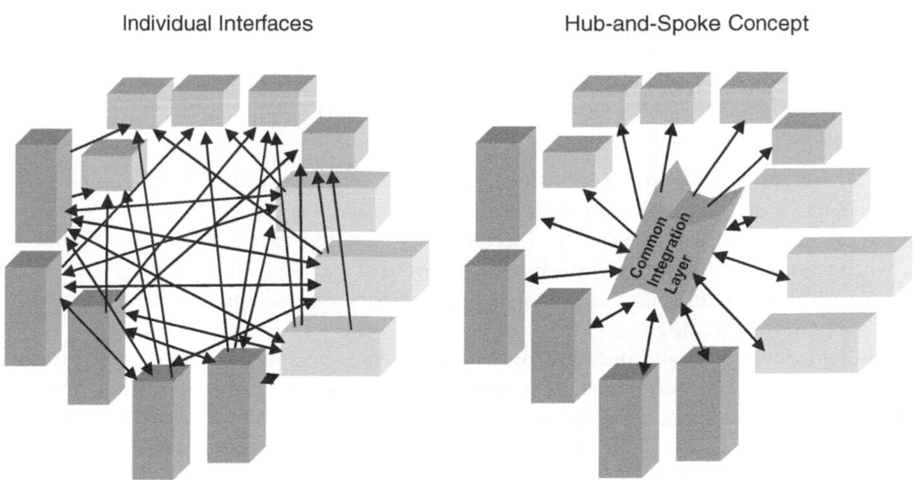

*From Winter, 2003.

cleansing) data from multiple sources. Instead of having to develop and maintain a read-only interface between every analytical application and all its relevant source applications, the DWH system only needs one extraction interface to every relevant operational application and one channeling interface to every supported analytical application or data mart.

- *Enterprise application integration* (EAI) systems provide a platform that can be used to publish and subscribe to data updates or other messages between applications. Besides messaging oriented solutions, functional or process-oriented integration technologies may be used in EAI concepts as well. Their common goal is to overcome the need to develop and maintain a unidirectional or bidirectional interface between every pair of applications that exchanges data or other messages. The EAI system only needs one interface to every relevant operational application, which reduces complexity and costs.
- The *business collaboration infrastructure* (BCI) provides a set of services and standards to exchange data updates and other messages between applications in different companies. Instead of having to develop and maintain a unidirectional or bidirectional interface to/from every application that exchanges data or other messages with an external application, common BCI services and standards can be used.

Although the general integration principle is identical for these three types of common integration layers, their implementation is completely different. DWH systems integrate only by data. EAI systems integrate mostly by message brokering; data-oriented EAI (e.g., by operational data stores) is a complementary implementation technique used for integration with DWH systems and for integration needs that require high data quality and that tolerate delayed data availability (Inmon, Imhoff, and Sousa, 2001). The BCI neither provides significant data nor message brokering. Instead, standards and services are made available that allow for a dynamic and easy configuration of interfaces.

Ideal Application Interfacing

If architected application design is strictly applied and if common interface layers are utilized for application interfacing, the resulting application architecture can be regarded as cost-efficient and agile:

- Intra-application integration costs are optimized because all tightly coupled functionalities/data are integrated, and only loosely coupled functionalities/data are implemented by interfaces. Interapplication integration costs are minimized because the number of interfaces is minimized by using shared, integrated data, publish-and-subscribe mechanisms, common services, and common standards whenever possible.
- Agility is optimized because functionalities have been clustered according to the most appropriate integration dimension (business process support, information centricity, or functionality reuse), thereby creating semantically sound components that have a high potential of being reorchestrated unchanged if business requirements change. Furthermore, integration systems decouple applications so that rearrangements can be made without altering the components.

By applying the proposed application design rules and deploying common integration layers, a generic application architecture is created that can serve as a reference for agile application architecture (Figure 11.5). Messages are denoted by envelope symbols, shared data by disk symbols, and services as well as applications are denoted by cubes.

Figure 11.5

Generic Reference Application Architecture*

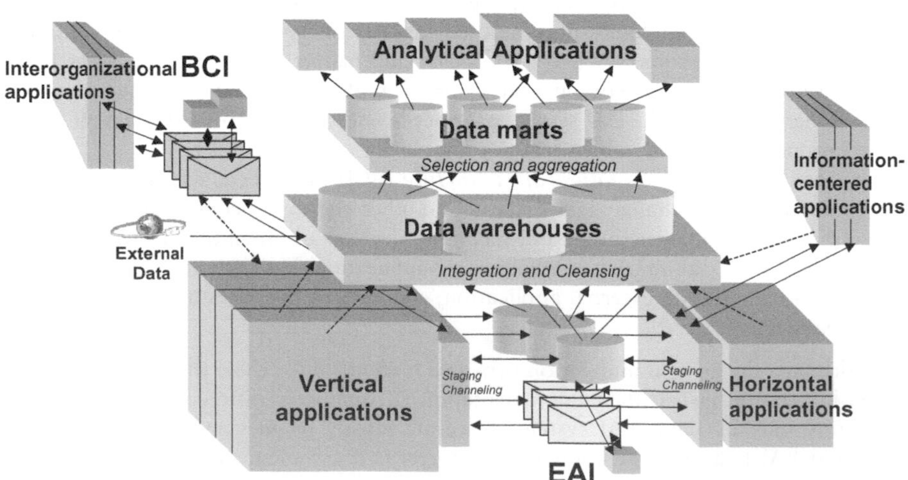

*From Winter, 2003.

Conclusions

Agility is manageable. The architecture of the application landscape has a major impact on IT agility and hence on operations agility. Although application architecture agility cannot be measured (and hence managed) directly, there are indicators for application integration that support agility management: (1) Integration project expenses indicate the flexibility of the information system in financial terms as well as (2) costs and complexity of infrastructure operations do. The complexity of the application landscape can be reduced if (3) functionalities are reused, (4) functional redundancy is minimized, and (5) application coupling is as tight (or loose) as the supported business functionalities require.

An ideal application infrastructure does not have to be monolithic or standardized in terms of integration systems. The previous section showed that there are different integration needs requiring different integration infrastructures: data integration for supporting transactional processes may require operational data stores, whereas data integration for business intelligence may require a data warehouse. Even an EAI infrastructure may be run twice if both data-oriented and message-oriented integration needs are relevant.

Considering the IT contributions to a company's overall agility, it has to be emphasized that not only the technical infrastructure has to be taken into consideration. Empirical studies such as those done by Byrd and Turner (2000) clarify that the human factor is much more important. Especially when considering the still-increasing complexity and the fine-grained structure of functionality clusters (despite all integration efforts), the skill level required to manage such complexity is significant. Redesigning the application landscape has to be accompanied by aligning IT processes and by employing education programs for architects.

Future work should aim at the development of measures for complex application landscapes. A prerequisite for integrated measurement is to connect layer-specific meta models for applications, business models, processes, and (integration) infrastructure components (Schelp and Schwinn, 2005).

References

Ahsan, M. and Ye-Ngo, L. (2005). The relationship between I.T. infrastructure and strategic agility in organizations. In *Proceedings of the Eleventh Americas Conference on Information Systems*, August 11–14, 2005. Omaha, NE, pp. 415–427.

Arsanjani, A. (2002). Developing and integrating. *Developing and Integrating Enterprise Components and Services*, 45 (10), 31–34.

Becker, F. (2001). Organisational agility and the knowledge infrastructure. *Journal of Corporate Real Estate*, 3 (1), 28–37.

Byrd, T. A. and Turner, D. E. (2000). Measuring the flexibility of information technology infrastructure: Exploratory analysis of a construct. *Journal of Management Information Systems*, 17 (1), 167–208.

Cao, Q. and Dowlatshahi, S. (2005). The impact of alignment between virtual enterprise and information technology on business performance in an agile manufacturing environment. *Journal of Operations Management*, 23 (55), 531–550.

Coronado Mondragon, A. E., Lyons, A. C., and Kehoe, D. F. (2004). Assessing the value of information systems in supporting agility in high-tech manufacturing enterprises. *International Journal of Operations & Production Management*, 24 (12), 1219–1246.

Cummins, F. A. (2002). *Enterprise Integration: An Architecture for Enterprise Application and Systems Integration*. New York: Wiley.

Duguay, C. R., Landry, S., and Pasin, F. (1997). From mass production to flexible/agile production. *International Journal of Operations & Production Management*, 17 (12), 1183–1195.

Fridgen, M. and Heinrich, B. (2004). Investitionen in die unternehmensweite Anwendungssystemintegration—Der Einfluss der Kundenzentrierung auf die Gestaltung der Anwendungslandschaft. Working Paper, Universität Augsburg, Lehrstuhl für Betriebswirtschaftslehre, Wirtschaftsinformatik & Financial Engineering, Kernkompetenzzentrum IT & Finanzdienstleistungen. Augsburg.

Gandossy, R. (2003). The need for speed. *Journal of Business Strategy*, 24 (1), 29–33.

Goldman, S. L., Nagel, R. N., and Preiss, K. (1995). Agile competitors and virtual organizations: Strategies for enriching the customer. New York: Van Nostrand Reinhold.

Inmon, W. H., Imhoff, C., and Sousa, R. (2001). *Corporate Information Factory*, 2nd ed. New York: Wiley.

Irani, Z., Themistocleous, M., and Love, P. E. D. (2003). The impact of enterprise application integration on information system lifecycles. *Information Management*, 41 (2), 177–187.

Kaib, M. (2002). *Enterprise Application Integration—Grundlagen, Integrationsprodukte, Anwendungsbeispiele*. Wiesbaden: DUV.

Linthicum, D. S. (2000). *Enterprise Application Integration*. Reading, MA: AWL Direct Sales.

Maskell, B. (2001). The age of agile manufacturing. *Supply Chain Management: An International Journal*, 6 (1), 5–11.

McCarthy, I. and Tsinopoulos, C. (2003). Strategies for agility: An evolutionary and configurational approach. *Integration Manufacturing Systems: An International Journal*, 14 (2), 103–113.

Melarkode, A., From-Poulsen, M., and Warnakulasuriya, S. (2004). Delivering agility through IT. *Business Strategy Review*, 15 (3), 45–50.

Morgan, R. E. (2004). Business agility and internal marketing. *European Business Review*, 16 (5), 464–472.

Nerur, S., Mahapatra, R., and Mangalara, G. (2005). Challenges of migrating to agile methodologies. *Communications of the ACM*, 48 (5), 73–78.

Ruh, W. A., Maginnis, F. X., and Brown, W. J. (2001). *Enterprise Application Integration*. New York: Wiley.

Sambamurthy, V., Bharadwaj, A., and Grover, V. (2003). Shaping agility through digital options: Reconceptualizing the role of Information Technology in contemporary firms. *MIS Quarterly*, 27 (2), 237–263.

Schelp, J. and Schwinn, A. (2005). Extending the business engineering framework for application integration purposes. In *2005 ACM Symposium on Applied Computing*. Santa Fe, New Mexico, pp. 1333–1337.

Schwinn, A. and Winter, R. (2005). Success factors and performance indicators for enterprise application integration. In *Proceedings of the Eleventh Americas Conference on Information Systems*, August 11–14, 2005. Omaha, NE, pp. 2179–2189.

Sharifi, H. and Zhang, Z. (1999). A methodology for achieving agility in manufacturing organisations: An introduction. *International Journal of Production Economics*, 62 (1–2), 7–22.

Sutherland, J. and van den Heuvel, W.-J. (2002). Enterprise application integration and complex adaptive systems. *Communications of the ACM*, 45 (10), 59–64.

Themistocleous, M. and Irani, Z. (2001). Benchmarking the benefits and barriers of application integration. *Benchmarking*, 8 (4), 317–331.

Umar, A. (2005). IT Infrastructure to enable next generation enterprises. *Information Systems Frontiers*, 7 (3), 217–256.

van Hoek, R. I. (2001). Epilogue: Moving forward with agility. *International Journal of Physical Distribution & Logistics Management*, 31 (4), 290–300.

Vokurka, R. J. and Fliedner, G. (1998). The journey toward agility. *Industrial Management & Data Systems*, 98 (4), 165–171.

Weill, P., Subramani, M., and Broadbent, M. (2002). IT infrastructure for strategic agility. Working Paper, Massachusetts Institute of Technology (MIT), Sloan School of Management. Cambridge, MA.

White, A., Daniel, E. M., and Mohdzain, M. (2005). The role of emergent information technologies and systems in enabling supply chain agility. *International Journal of Information Management*, 25 (5), 396–410.

Winter, R. (2003). An architecture model for supporting application integration decisions. In *Proceedings of the Eleventh European Conference on Information Systems*. Naples.

Yusuf, Y. Y., Sarhadi, M., and Gunasekaran, A. (1999). Agile manufacturing: The drivers, concepts and attributes. *International Journal of Production Economics*, 62 (1–2), 33–43.

Zahavi, R. (2000). *Enterprise Application Integration with CORBA*. New York: Wiley.

Zarnekow, R. (2004). *Produktorientiertes informationsmanagement*. In Informationsmanagement—Konzepte und Strategien für die Praxis (R. Zarnekow, W. Brenner, and H. Grohmann, eds.). Heidelberg: Verlag, pp. 41–56.

Zhang, Z. and Sharifi, H. (2000). A methodology for achieving agility in manufacturing organisations. *International Journal of Operations & Production Management*, 20 (4), 496–512.

12

Investigating the Role of Information Systems in Contributing to the Agility of Modern Supply Chains

Adrian E. Coronado M. and Andrew C. Lyons

Agility, as a concept, has to permeate both organizations and supply chains. Supply chain management has been described as an approach for organizations to control and integrate the execution of different business functions associated with product manufacturing, including material procurement and product distribution, with an objective of higher customer satisfaction and lower inventory risk (Das and Abdel-Malek, 2003). However, most companies overlook the idea that supply chains should be agile (Lee, 2004). Top-performing supply chains possess three very different qualities (Lee, 2004). First, great supply chains are agile. They react speedily to sudden changes in demand or supply. Second, they adapt over time as market structures and strategies evolve. Third, they align the interests of all the firms in the supply network so that companies optimize the chain's performance when they maximize their interests.

In the automotive sector, a competitive business environment has obliged vehicle manufacturers to forge closer ties, one outcome of this being the emergence of supplier parks. Supplier parks are a new experiment in production and logistics management (Sako, 2003; Miemczyk et al., 2004). Supplier parks are defined as a cluster of suppliers located adjacent to, or close to, a final assembly plant. In Western Europe, supplier parks play a pivotal role in the European automotive industry. Running a supplier park requires the support of information systems. The Internet, Electronic Data Interchange (EDI), Enterprise Resource Planning/Manufacturing Resource Planning (ERP/MRPII), and proprietary systems among other applications are frequently found in supplier parks. Information systems play a key role in managing the supply chain. ERP systems such as SAP, via Extranets, connect not only different functions within a firm but also among the firm's supply chain partners (i.e., suppliers, distributors, and third-party logistics providers), enabling the partners to share information such as order status, product schedules, and sales records, to integrate major supply chain processes and to plan production, logistics, and marketing promotions (Gunasekaran and Ngai, 2004).

The importance of agility as a business concept and the prominent place of the supply chain in several industry sectors, particularly the automotive sector with its adoption of supplier parks, have provided the motivation to revisit the role and contribution of information systems. Manufacturers need agile supply chains in order to have the ability to produce rapidly at low cost, varying volumes, high quality, and customized products. Information systems can be used to enable the movement of the decoupling point upstream, the efficient handling of higher volumes, and higher component variety with the potential to achieve substantial cost savings.

In this chapter, we use the particularities of the supplier park business model to identify, from an agile point of view, the implications of information systems in the supply chain. The automotive industry was selected in this study because it has been a pioneer in the introduction of improvement philosophies in manufacturing, as well as being information-intensive and in a dynamic business environment.

Supply Chain and Agility

In the manufacturing sector, the current business environment has forced organizations to become more responsive to customers' requirements. Organizations have realized that supply chain plays a critical role in achieving this responsiveness. Agility is critical because in most industries both demand and supply fluctuate more rapidly and widely than they used to. However, most companies continue to focus on the speed and cost of their supply chains without realizing that they pay a big price for disregarding agility (Lee, 2004). The need to accommodate uncertainty in the supply process raises the issue of flexibility (Das and Abdel-Malek, 2003). Manufacturing flexibility is the ability of a system or facility to adjust to changes in its internal or external environment.

Furthermore, this adjustment must occur with little penalty in time, effort, or operational performance. Being flexible is a characteristic of agility. Manufacturing companies are trying to maintain a high level of flexibility and responsiveness to achieve agility and to remain competitive (Gunasekaran, Tirtiroglu, and Wolstencroft, 2002). Several components might be considered salient for developing and running a flexible and responsive supply chain (Duclos, Vokurka, and Lummus, 2003; see Table 12.1).

Table 12.1

Supply Chain Flexibility Dimensions	
Dimension	**Description**
Operations systems flexibility (both manufacturing and service)	Ability to configure assets and operations to react to emerging customer trends (product changes, volume, mix) at each node of the supply chain.
Logistics flexibility	Ability to cost-effectively receive and deliver products as sources of supply and customers change (customer location changes, globalization, postponement).
Supply flexibility	Ability to reconfigure the supply chain, altering the supply of product in line with customer demand.
Information systems flexibility	Ability to align information systems architectures and systems with the changing information needs of the organization as it responds to changing customer demand.

The dimensions of operations, logistics, supply, and information systems shown in Table 12.1 might be closely intertwined. Furthermore, they are key in supporting modern supply chains in competitive business environments.

Several computer-integrated systems and commercial off-the-shelf applications can be used to support agile manufacturing; these include MRP, MRPII, Internet, Computer Aided Design/Computer Aided Engineering (CAD/CAE), ERP, etc. (Gunasekaran, 1998). The benefits of information systems to the agile enterprise include: enterprise-wide concurrent operations that cover all functions of the company, agreed communications and software standards, electronic commerce on international multimedia networks, and better mathematical understanding of representation methods used in design (Gunasekaran, 1998). Information systems helps to manage supply chain activities by offering information about what kind of product is demanded, what is available in the warehouse, what is in the manufacturing process, and what is entering and exiting the physical facilities and customers' sites (Lancioni, Smith, and Oliva, 2000). New technologies like Web services, wireless applications, and advanced software applications also enable for more effective and efficient collaboration and coordination between partners in the supply chain.

Supplier parks comprise integrated supply chains and rely heavily on the use of information systems. Figure 12.1 depicts the type information and material arrangement commonly found in supplier parks. The suppliers located in close proximity to the Original Equipment Manufacturer (OEM) have to have applications that are compatible with the proprietary information systems of the OEM. The files the OEM transmits to the suppliers comprise daily quantities, weekly and monthly forecasts, and final assembly sequences. The use of these applications allows the OEM to manage thousands of part numbers that eventually will give the site the possibility to build

Figure 12.1

Information and Material Flow Found in Supplier Parks

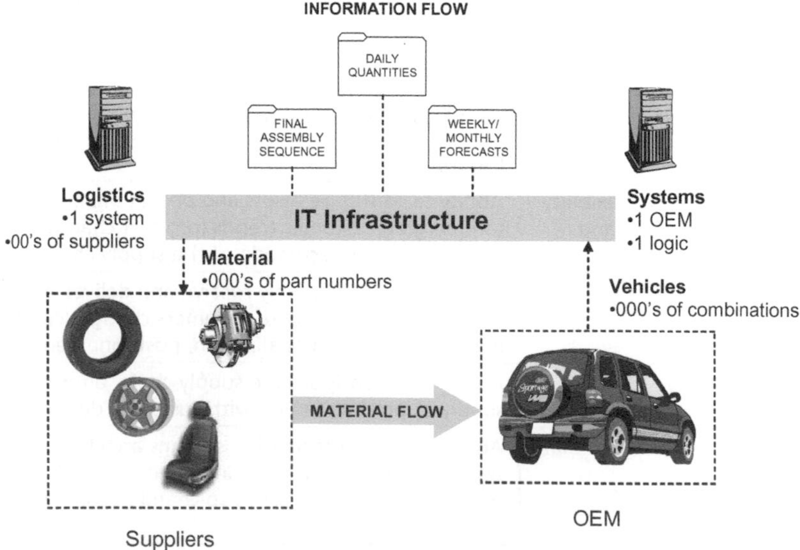

thousands of different vehicle combinations. The EDI process has been the information transmission backbone of manufacturing companies and supply interfaces for many years (Lee, So, and Tang, 2000).

A European Supplier Park

The supplier park configuration presented in this study involves a high-volume manufacturer of passenger vehicles. The production site is owned by a global vehicle manufacturer with operations in five continents. The plant produces four different types of model. Each vehicle is unique and it has a unique place in the final release sequence generated by the OEM. Vehicle options include body color, trim interior, and destination market (left-hand-drive or right-hand-drive), which also determine other vehicle components such as the instrument panel and several interior options. In 2004, over 400,000 units were manufactured on the site.

We chose to study the vehicle seats and headrest supplier for this study. Other first-tier suppliers located in the supplier park that also sequence components include bumpers, instrument panels, and power train components. However, particular characteristics differentiating vehicle seats from other vehicle parts include:

- *Module independence*. The first-tier supplier is entirely responsible for the manufacturing of the seating systems.
- *Complex assembly processes.* The assembly of seats comprises several operations (twelve operations involving flow-line production at the first-tier supplier, front seats only).
- *Complex sequence of use during vehicle assembly*. Usually seating systems are Just-In-Time (JIT) delivered to the point of fit in the vehicle assembly line.
- *Multi-tier in their own right*. Manufacture of seating systems can be composed of up to three tiers of suppliers for one trim option.
- *Relatively costly*. A seating set is one of the most expensive modules delivered by first-tier suppliers.
- *In this case study, the existing geographical proximity between the OEM, the first-tier, and second-tier suppliers*. The geographical proximity means a separation of only a few hundred meters between suppliers.

The development of this case study included visits and periods of time working at the production sites of the companies involved in the value stream chosen (vehicle assembly plant, seat manufacturer, and headrest manufacturer). Figure 12.2 depicts the structure of the supply chain investigated. Although the research involved visiting the OEM, the first-tier and second-tier suppliers, the research focused mainly on the first-tier supplier given its importance in the supply chain. This is not to say the OEM and second-tier suppliers were not important; however, by adopting the principle of modularity and the geographical proximity to the OEM, the first-tier supplier is responsible for building each and every single final module using independent parts and components from second-tier suppliers.

The first-tier supplier (vehicle seats and headrest supplier) is a major supplier to the automotive industry with production locations in Europe, the Americas, and Asia. In the supplier park configuration used in this case study, the first-tier production site is the sole supplier of full seating systems to the OEM and it is located less than 100 meters away from the vehicle assembly line. The site employs about 340 people. A conveyor system is used to deliver the seating systems, in sequence, to the point-of-fit in the assembly line. The organization's production method is JIT with most of the

Figure 12.2

Supply Chain Structure Investigated

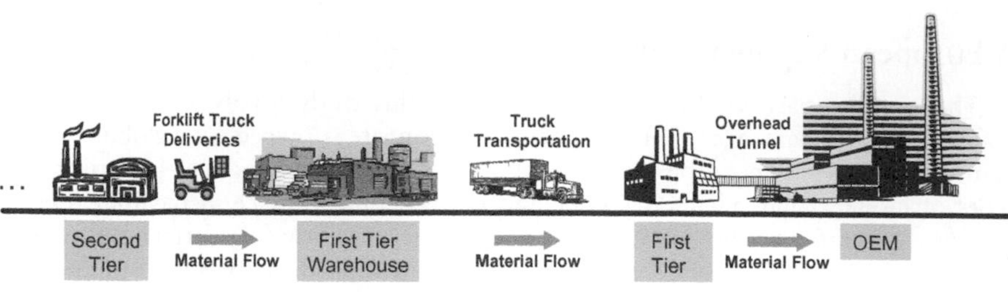

components used to build each seating system sequenced at a local received/goods-in warehouse located three kilometers away from the production site.

The second-tier supplier considered in this study is represented by a local Small-to-Mediums Sized Enterprise (SME) that has been appointed by the OEM as one of the two suppliers of headrests for the seating systems manufactured by the first-tier supplier. The second-tier supplier is located less than 25 meters away from the first-tier's received/goods-in warehouse. The second-tier supplier production accounts for 92 percent of the headrests that go into the second most popular vehicle manufactured by the OEM (monthly volumes of over 10,000 units) with five different colors (cloth) offered. Also, the production site is responsible for cutting and sewing the bags used in 80 percent of the headrests used in the other three vehicle models manufactured by the OEM. Suppliers to the second-tier supplier include manufacturers of foam, cloth, and metal tubes. The foam supplier is located 200 km away from the production site. One of the main cloth suppliers is located within the perimeter of the supplier park.

The second-tier supplier is responsible for the assembly process of the foams with the previously cut and sewn headrest pockets (also done by the second tier). Deliveries from the second tier are done five times a day in batches of 56 units. The fist-tier supplier is responsible for the assembly process of the vehicle seats. Finished vehicle seats are placed on a conveyor system that takes them in sequence directly to the point-of-fit in the assembly line in a one-piece flow.

The first-tier supplier plays a fundamental role in the supplier park structure. This importance lies in the fact that the first-tier supplier is responsible for delivering, to the point-of-fit in the assembly line, final modules comprising several sub-components/parts manufactured by hundreds of different suppliers. First-tier sequenced deliveries of components guarantees JIT production and build-to-order manufacturing in the vehicle assembly plant.

Information Flow in the Supply Chain

From the OEM, aggregated daily seat requirements are communicated to the first-tier supplier via fiber-optic EDI. This daily file describes the requirements for the next ten days, followed by tentative requirements for the coming weeks and months. The assembly of every seat set is triggered by launching its destination vehicle into the final assembly sequence (usually a time window of four to five hours), at which time the actual seat requirement is sent to the first-tier supplier via EDI. A final sequence starts once a painted body is released into the assembly line. Every single seat set manufactured is made to order and it has been allocated to a unique vehicle. The completion of the final assembly sequence represents a built vehicle.

The OEM has two main proprietary systems, labeled Sys1 and Sys2. Figure 12.3 depicts the information architecture found in the supplier park. The first system, Sys1, is an OEM system linked to a single shared database that manages material scheduling inventory management and cost accounting. Customer orders (e.g., dealer orders, personalized orders) are loaded into the system and materials are called in using suppliers' schedules. An additional feature of Sys1 provides schedules with ten-day visibility in daily quantities, and six-month visibility in more tentative weekly and monthly forecasted quantities.

Sys2 is also an OEM proprietary system, holding vehicle orders and scheduling in-plant build information. The system receives customer orders on a daily basis from a central order bank and provides the manufacturing plant with the capability to control and track each vehicle being built. The total process from body construction through to final assembly is monitored by Sys2. An additional feature of Sys2 incorporates a plant vehicle sequencing system that operates to restore disruptions to sequence. In case of a disruption, the system reads body type and substitutes the oldest suitable one to restore the sequence. Suppliers experiencing low levels of inventory for some parts/components may cause disruptions to the final sequence. Because vehicles that are going to be built have already been ordered, the system has to be capable of restoring the sequence with the oldest one once the disruption has been cleared.

The first-tier supplier uses the information from the aggregated daily seat requirements to run its own internal material requirements planning system. The file is loaded each day, and once per week the MRP is run. The first-tier's MRP system is MFG/Pro by QAD Solutions, an application widely used in the industry. The schedules are

Figure 12.3

Information Architecture Observed in the Supplier Park

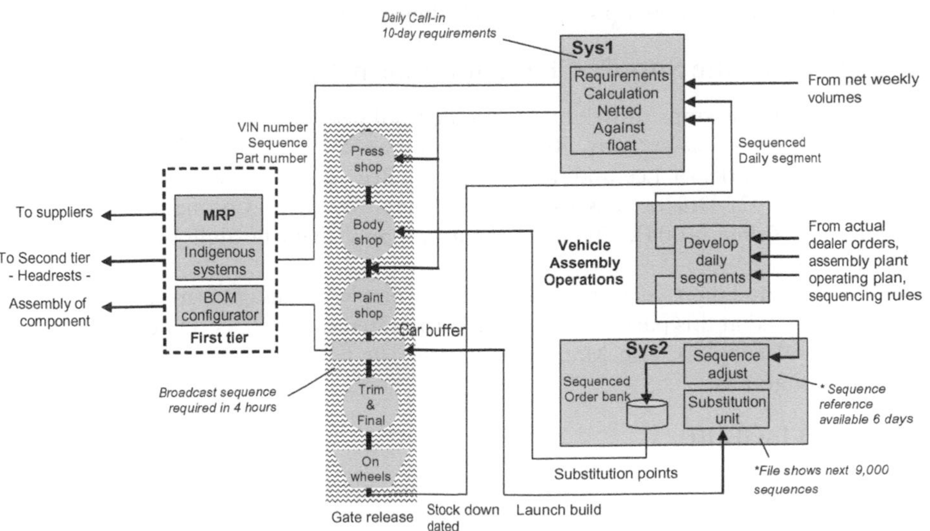

Figure 12.4

Supply Chain Flexibility Assessment

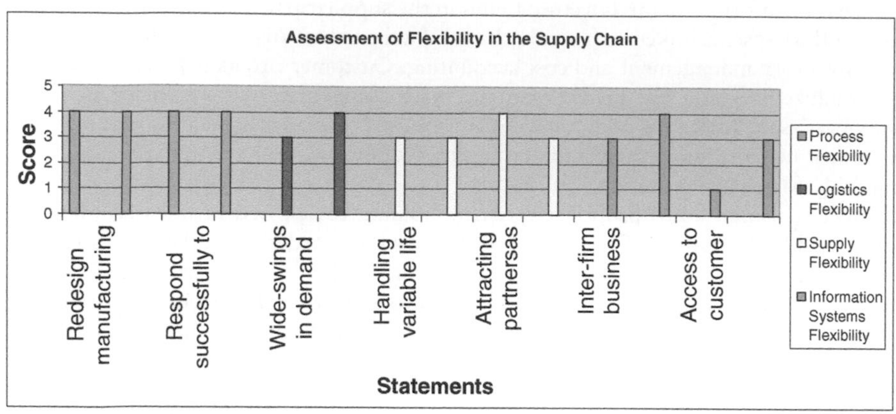

produced for each of the first-tier component suppliers. Schedules are sent to the suppliers via e-mail. These schedules contain daily requirements for the following week, as well as more tentative requirements for the coming weeks and months. To guarantee a reliable flow of information, manufacturing organizations have installed EDI links between them and their customers and their suppliers.

The second-tier supplier shows the particularity of having a system that is linked directly to the OEM's proprietary Sys1 and Sys2 systems. This means that the second-tier supplier is able to receive the files that show production schedules for the coming days as well as receive the vehicle final sequencing, as cars are released into the assembly line. However, that available functionality is not put to work. The policies put in place by the OEM do not allow that. Instead, the second tier needs to input the requirements specified in the file received from the first-tier supplier (output from the MFG/Pro file) into its own production scheduling application.

Flexibility of the Supply Chain and Information Systems

The four dimensions of flexibility included in the study are *process, logistics, supply*, and *information systems*. References to these dimensions of flexibility can be found in the works of Lee and Whang (2000), Lee and Hong (2002), Gunasekaran and Yusuf (2002), Duclos, Vokurka, and Lummus (2003), and Coronado Mondragon, Lyons, and Kehoe (2004). The assessment of supply chain flexibility is presented in Figure 12.4.

A five-point Likert scale ranging from 1 (completely disagree) to 5 (completely agree) was used in this part of the research. The statements were evaluated by the first-tier's Central Supply Chain Management staff. The findings are discussed in the following paragraphs.

Process Flexibility

The manufacturing capabilities of the site are addressed in process flexibility. We asked four statements to be rated:

- *Your organization is capable of redesigning its manufacturing systems to respond to new market requirements.* The rating given to this statement was 4—Agree. The first-tier supplier has to be able to respond to the requirements specified by the OEM, which may vary a few times during the year. For example, it may happen that the OEM may start to offer new options (colors, fabrics, safety) on the seats that go into the vehicles.
- *Your organization is capable of transferring/bringing production from/to other sites in short periods of time.* 4—Agree, was the rating given to this statement. The production site has sister plants in Western Europe. Two of the sister plants serve the same OEM under the same supplier park production scheme. The first and second tiers can cope with other vehicle options that the OEM may decide to move to the present site.
- *Your organization is capable of responding successfully to capacity constraints.* The rating given to this statement was 4—Agree. The production site is able to respond to capacity constraints motivated by lack of/stock-outs of components and operators' absenteeism. The site has developed very flexible manufacturing operations, so it means that it can build in the assembly line all different types of product combinations without experiencing delays that may affect the delivery of finished modules.
- *Your organization is capable of making changes to production volumes.* This statement was rated 4—Agree. Certainly the production site has the capability to increase or diminish daily production rates based on the OEM's daily demand figures. In the past few years, the site has produced over 330,000 seat sets.

Logistics Flexibility

From the flexibility dimensions of the supply chain, we asked two statements that encompass the perception of logistics capabilities to be rated:

- *Your organization is capable of accommodating wide swings in demand over short periods of time.*
- *Your organization is capable of handling a wide-range of products.*

The supplier rated the first statement as 3—Neutral. Based on what was observed, the site is well adapted to the daily demand rate dictated by the OEM. However, the site is not entirely ready to cope with side swing in demand; it may result in high levels of stock to cover against possible stock-out incidents. The second statement was rated 4—Agree. Indeed, the organization is capable of handling hundreds of combinations for all the different types of seat.

Supply Flexibility

For gauging supply flexibility, we asked four statements to be rated:

- *Your organization is capable of handling variable life cycle lengths.* The supplier rated the first statement as 3—Neutral. An explanation for this issue is that the life cycle of every single final module and most of its components are dependent on the life cycle of the vehicle manufactured. Vehicle life cycles are in terms of years.
- *Your organization is capable of downsizing deliveries to your customers.* The supplier rated this statement as 3—Neutral. In the supply chain investigated, every single seating system produced is built-to-order and delivered in sequence

to the point-of-fit in the assembly line, one-piece flow. Altering this condition will not provide benefits to the performance of the entire supply chain. The second-tier supplier can change batch sizes as needed.

- *Your organization is capable of attracting a portfolio of partners that change as customer needs change.* The respondent rating to this condition was 4—Agree. Indeed, given the important role the first-tier supplier plays, the organization is very good at attracting suppliers that possess a high level of expertise in their area.
- *Your organization is capable of establishing flexible relationships with suppliers* (e.g., solicit short-term bids, joint ventures, consortia, and so on). The supplier rated the first statement as 3—Neutral. The main explanation of this response concerns the fact that some of the suppliers to the first-tier supplier are appointed directly by the OEM, therefore predefining the design of the supply chain.

Information Systems Flexibility

Finally, for gauging systems flexibility, we asked four statements to be rated:

- *Inter-firm business synchronization. Your organization's information systems are capable of enabling 100% inter-firm data sharing with your suppliers and customers.* The supplier rated this statement 3—Neutral. Information systems have the potential to provide a direct link to the OEM's systems; however, the potential benefits of sharing data with suppliers are limited by the policies of the OEM that do not promote demand visibility/demand sharing. Suppliers located upstream in the chain cannot use the OEM's customer demand data to generate their own production schedules. It is well-known that demand visibility/information sharing may improve the quality of forecasting and long-term planning to all supply chain parties.
- *Information systems' flexibility supported through automation, computer integrated manufacturing, programs, and interfaces is capable of allowing automation of purchasing between suppliers, operations, and customers.* The rating given to this statement was 4—Agree. It is widely accepted at the OEM's first- and second-tier supplier levels that information systems have enabled the automation of several operations both on the shop-floor and in the office.
- *Upstream tiers in the supply chain are capable of accessing customer demand data.* The rating given to this statement was 2—Disagree. Despite the possibility of making demand data accessible from the OEM up to the second-tier supplier (using existing EDI infrastructure) the reality is that no plans exist to exploit the advantages of full demand visibility along the supply chain.
- *Information systems are capable of incorporating without delay the changing requirements of business partners.* The supplier scored a 3—Neutral. Information systems do not provide an effective way of dealing with changing requirements of customers.

Contribution of IS to Agility

We asked suppliers about their perceptions regarding the contribution of IS to enabling agility in the supply chains. Suppliers were asked to rate the contribution of IS to the following four objectives: (1) achievement of competitive advantage, (2) tasks that could not be done before, (3) the creation of a distinctive proprietary advantage,

Figure 12.5

Ratings Given to Agility Measures

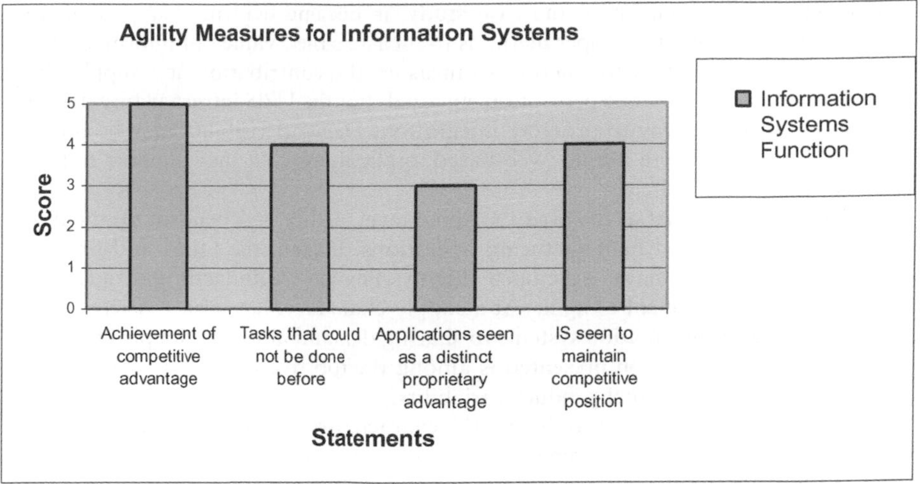

and (4) the maintenance of competitive position. The results of the self-assessment are depicted in Figure 12.5.

- *Achievement of competitive advantage.* The 5—Very Important rating given to this statement shows that information systems are perceived as very important in the achievement of competitive advantage. In this case study, the first and upstream suppliers run commercial applications. The OEM runs proprietary information systems for its manufacturing and supply chains.
- *Tasks that could not be done before.* The rating given to this statement was 4—Important. The respondent perceived information systems as key to perform tasks that were not possible to perform before. Examples include sequenced deliveries of seating systems sets to point of fit.
- *Applications seen as a distinct proprietary advantage.* The respondent rated this statement as 3—Neutral. From this answer, it is clear that organizations do not see information systems as a distinct proprietary advantage. From the first-tier and upwards, most organizations in the automotive industry use commercial solutions that cannot provide an edge over competitors. For example, first-tiers in several industries use MFG/Pro as their daily MRP system.
- *IS are seen to maintain competitive position.* The rating given to this statement was 4—Important. The perception is that information systems are critical to maintain competitive position. It is clear from what has been observed that without the use of IS it would have been impossible to support the JIT, sequenced production that characterizes supplier park arrangements, particularly the relationship existing between the first-tier and the OEM.

In spite of the characteristics of information systems described previously, the responses given to the statements on the contribution to the level of agility demonstrate the perceived importance of information systems on issues regarding competitive advantage, performing new tasks, and maintaining competitive position.

The results of the study demonstrate that within the supplier park supply chain arrangement, achievement of competitive advantage, tasks that could not be done before, and IS seen to maintain competitive position are considered important benefits of information systems.

During the development of the case study, it became evident that participating organizations do not have proper methods to measure the "value" of information systems, not to mention that the metrics to measure the contribution at a supply chain level is nonexistent. Also, the perception emerged that the IT/IS infrastructure does not provide an adequate way to promote integration. Demand visibility may be possible only through EDI. There are no Web-based applications that may support full integration of the supply chain.

The results show that at the organizational level, agility is dependent on the development of flexibility of manufacturing operations. Indeed, the OEM and first- and second-tier suppliers have developed highly flexible manufacturing operations. However, the development of agility at a supply chain level has been restricted by the limited support of information systems to sharing demand along the supply chain. The supplier park configuration presented is among the top five European supplier parks in terms of volume and final product variability.

Based on the results of the study and the characteristics of the supplier park model, we deem that information systems that facilitate demand visibility and information sharing along the supply chain should be considered enhancers of agility. The success of demand visibility and information sharing is dependent on the reliability/consistency of the source generating the information to be made available. Certainly, these characteristics of information systems are critical to achieve agility in the supply chain. On the other hand, we believe that manufacturing flexibility is the foundation of agility for any manufacturing organization. Before agility in the supply chain occurs, agility at an organizational level must be achieved through the development of manufacturing flexibility. Figure 12.6 depicts these statements.

Organizations can develop flexibility at the operational level. However, the entire supply chain where they operate can be negatively affected by undeveloped supply, logistics, and information systems. In Figure 12.6, achieving the agile supply chain is the result of developing operational flexibility in every tier. Furthermore, between tiers the development of logistics, supply and information systems flexibility is what enables the agile supply chain.

Conclusion

The use of the supplier park model has provided a unique supply chain configuration. The findings shown in this work are based on the supplier parks model widely found in the European automotive industry. The arrangement of suppliers in the supplier park—geographic proximity of suppliers to the vehicle assembly plant, the widespread use of JIT, and build-to-order initiatives—motivated a re-evaluation of the concept of agility and the contribution of information systems to the achievement of agility at the supply chain level.

Based on the findings of the study, information systems that enable information sharing and demand visibility should be considered enhancers of agility. In the case study analyzed, the shortcomings experienced with information systems have not prevented the development of manufacturing flexibility at an organizational level. Before agility in the supply chain occurs, agility at an organizational level must be achieved through the development of manufacturing flexibility. Achieving a top-performing supply chain is dependent on information systems that support demand visibility and

Figure 12.6

Information Systems as Enablers of Supply Chain Agility

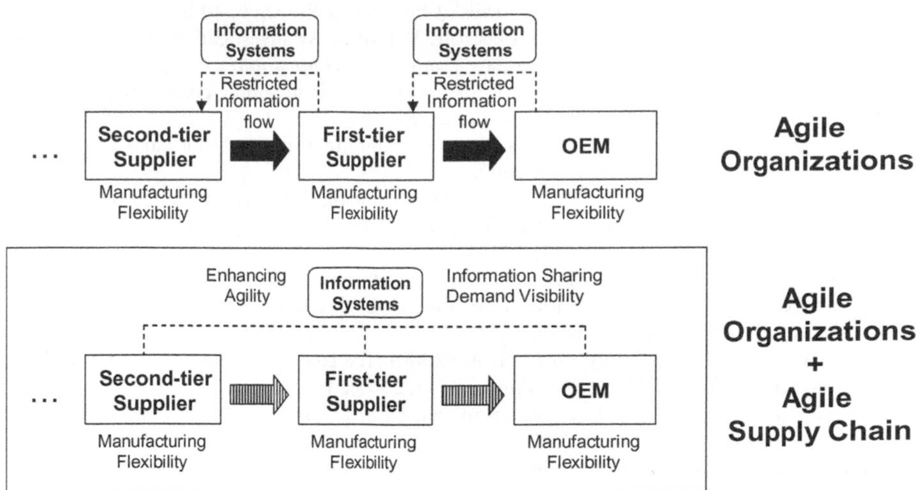

information sharing. Demand visibility reduces demand amplification and eliminates the need for short-term forecasting operations taking place at each tier. The success of demand visibility and information sharing is dependent on the reliability/consistency of the source generating the information made available.

References

Automotive News (2005). Guide to Purchasing 2005. *European Supplier Parks*, 21, 22.

Barrat, M. and Oliveira, A. (2001). Exploring the experience of collaborative planning initiatives. *International Journal of Physical Distribution and Logistics Management*, 31 (4), 266–289.

Bay, B. K., Tang, N., and Bennett, D. (2004). An empirical study of the imperatives for a supply chain implementation project in Seagate Technology International. *Supply Chain Management: An International Journal*, 9 (4), 331–340.

Boyer, K., Frohlich, M., and Hult, M. (2005). *Extending the Supply Chain: How Cutting-Edge Companies Bridge the Critical Last Mile Into Customers' Homes*. New York: Amacom.

Byrd, T. and Davidson, N. (2003). Examining possible antecedents of IT impact on the supply chain and its effect on firm performance. *Information and Management*, 41 (2), 243–255.

Coronado Mondragon, A. E., Lyons, A. C., and Kehoe, D. F. (2004). Assessing the value of information systems in supporting agility in high-tech manufacturing enterprises. *International Journal of Operations and Production Management*, 24 (12), 1219–1246.

Das, S. and Abdel-Malek, L. (2003). Modeling the flexibility of order quantities and lead-times in supply chains. *International Journal of Production Economics*, 85 (2), 171–181.

Duclos, L., Vokurka, R., and Lummus, R. (2003). A conceptual model of supply chain flexibility. *Industrial Management and Data Systems*, 103 (6), 446–456.

Frigant, V. and Lung, Y. (2002). Geographical proximity and supplying relationships in modular production. *International Journal of Urban and Regional Research*, 26 (4), 742–755.

Goldman, S., Nagel, R., and Preiss, K. (1995). *Agile Competitors and Virtual Organizations: Strategies for Enriching the Customer*. New York: Van Nostrand Reinhold.

Gunasekaran, A. (1998). Agile manufacturing: Enablers and an implementation framework. *International Journal of Production Research*, 36 (5), 1223–1247.

Gunasekaran, A., Patel, C., and Tirtiroglu, E. (2001). Performance measures and metrics in a supply chain environment. *International Journal of Operations and Production Management*, 21 (1/2), 71–87.

Gunasekaran, A. and Yusuf, Y. (2002). Agile manufacturing: A taxonomy of strategic and technological imperatives. *International Journal of Production Research*, 40 (6), 1357–1385.

Gunasekaran, A., Tirtiroglu, E., and Wolstencroft, V. (2002). An investigation into the application of agile manufacturing in an aerospace company. *Technovation*, 22 (7), 405–415.

Gunasekaran, A. and Ngai, E. W. (2004). Information systems in supply chain integration and management. *European Journal of Operational Research*, 159 (2), 269–295.

Hariharan, R. and Zipkin, P. (1995). Customer-order information, lead-times and inventories. *Management Science*, 41 (10), 1599–1607.

Howard, M. and Holweg, M. (2004). Investigating the intangible: Lessons learnt from research into automotive inter-organisational IT systems. *International Journal of Automotive Technology and Management*, 4 (4), 354–373.

Huang, G. Q., Lau, J. S. K., and Mak, K. L. (2003). The impacts of sharing production information on supply chain dynamics: A review of the literature. *International Journal of Production Research*, 41 (7), 1483–1517.

Lancioni, R. A., Smith, M. F., and Oliva, T. A. (2000). The role of the Internet in supply chain management. *Industrial Marketing Management*, 29 (1), 45–56.

Lee, H. L., and Whang, S. (2000). Information sharing in a supply chain. *International Journal of Technology Management*, 20 (3/4), 373–387.

Lee, H., So, K. C., and Tang, C. S. (2000). The value of information sharing in a two-level supply chain. *Management Science*, 46 (5), 626–643.

Lee, H. L. (2004). The Triple-A Supply Chain. *Harvard Business Review*, 82 (10), 102–113.

Lee, S. and Hong, S. (2002). An enterprise-wide knowledge management system infrastructure. *Industrial Management and Data Systems*, 102 (1), 17–25.

Miemczyk, J. and Holweg, M. (2004). Building cars to customer order: what does it mean for inbound logistics operations? *Journal of Business Logistics*, 25 (2), 171–197.

Randall, T. (1999). The value of IT in the manufacturing sector. *Compass Business Consulting white paper.* Retrieved July 2003 from: http://www.compassmc.com/

Reich, Y., et al. (1999). Building agility for developing agile design information systems. *Research in Engineering Design*, 11, 67–83.

Rother, M. and Shook, J. (1999). *Learning to See, Version 1.2*. Brookline, MA: Lean Enterprise Institute Inc.

Sako, M. (2003). Modularity and outsourcing: The nature of co-evolution of product architecture and organization architecture in the global automotive industry. In A. Prencipe, A. Davies, and M. Hobday (eds.), *The Business of Systems Integration*. Oxford: Oxford University Press, pp. 229–253.

Smithson, S. and Hirschheim, R. (1998). Analysing information systems evaluation: Another look at an old problem. *European Journal of Information Systems*, 7 (3), 158–174.

Themistocleous, M., Irani, Z., and Love, P. E. (2004). Evaluating the integration of supply chain information systems: A case study. *European Journal of Operational Research*, 159 (2), 393–405.

Thoburn, J., Arunachalam, S., and Gunasekaran, A. (1999). Difficulties arising from dysfunctional information systems in manufacturing SMEs case studies. *International Journal of Agile Management Systems*, 1 (2), 116–126.

Van Hoek, R. I., Harrison, A., and Christopher, M. (2001). Measuring agile capabilities in the supply chain. *International Journal of Operations and Production Management*, 21 (1/2), 126–148.

Williamson, E., Harrison, D., and Jordan, M. (2004). Information systems development within supply chain management. *International Journal of Information Management*, 24 (5), 375–385.

Zhao, X. and Xie, J. (2002). Forecasting errors and the value of information sharing in a supply chain. *International Journal of Production Research*, 40 (2), 311–335.

Clumsy Information Systems: A Critical Review of Enterprise Systems

Sue Newell, Erica L. Wagner, and Gary David

A growing number of companies are investing in enterprise systems (ES) (Scott and Kaindl, 2000). In the United States alone, organizational spending on enterprise hardware is expected to reach $832 million in 2005, increasing to $1.1 billion in 2010; enterprise software spending is expected to increase from $1.2 billion in 2005 to $1.6 billion in 2010; and overall ES spending is predicted to grow 33 percent to more than $7.7 billion by 2010 (*VARBusiness*, 2005). Many individual organizations have spent millions of dollars introducing ES. However, evidence suggests that many organizations do not achieve the expected benefits from their ES (Shanks and Seddon, 2000; Kling, 2003). Enterprise packages are complex technologies, so it is not surprising that implementation projects do not always deliver the hoped-for benefits (Sauer et al., 2001). Thus, while it is not unusual for IT projects to have problems, ES projects are considerably more troubled (Parr and Shanks, 2000), as evidenced by the large number of failed initiatives (Appleton, 1997), especially in organizations that are structurally complex and geographically dispersed (Markus et al., 2000). For example, *Computerworld* reported on October 17, 2005, that two SAP application projects had been halted in the Irish Health Service after they experienced numerous problems in the first four regional installations that were rolled-out. Moreover, the cost of the two projects had escalated from the $10.7 million budgeted to $180 million. *Computerworld* also reported on November 14, 2005, that the U.S. Navy had wasted $1billion since 1998 on four flawed ES pilot projects based on SAP software. Major corporations such as Whirlpool, Hershey, Nestle, and Gore-Tex have similarly struggled with their ES implementations. Overall, the Standish group concluded that 35 percent of ES projects were canceled, 55 percent of ES projects overrun, and only 10 percent were on budget and on time (Calogero, 2000).

Rather than concentrating on outright ES failures, however, this chapter will focus on the problematic nature of ES, even when successfully implemented. More specifically, the chapter will explore two aspects of ES that we see as problematic in relation to developing ES to promote organizational agility—how agile organizations are during the adoption and implementation phases and how agile organizations are in the longer-term as they appropriate and routinize the ES. We will argue that ES are actually the antithesis of agility because of the demands they make on organizations during adoption and implementation and because, when completed, they are infrastructural, meaning that they will provide the information platform for a company for years to come. This platform will be very difficult to change partly because of the sunk costs but also because of the interdependencies that are created, meaning that change in any practice that the infrastructure supports will be very difficult because of its tight coupling with other practices.

Rationale for ES Implementation

IT is seen as an important factor in achieving and maintaining competitive advantage because technology makes it feasible to re-engineer an organization in ways that were not previously possible (Zuboff, 1988). ES exemplify this in the sense that they harness the power of contemporary IT. Cost-efficient database and networking functionality facilitate information integration within centrally located and geographically disparate organizational structures. To understand the promises of ES, we apply a seminal management model that depicts the firm as a value chain of operations (Porter and Millar, 1985). The model provides a visual representation of how business functions are organized where each link in the chain can be seen as a function (e.g., customer service) that adds value to the end product/service. In addition the chain shows the support functions of a company that are necessary but don't add direct value to the final product. Prior to enterprise-wide software, organizations tended toward discrete functional systems each built to support a specific value-adding and support activity (customer service, paying people). While these systems provided a depth of information by function, their design did not provide data across the organization. In other words, there was no horizontal flow of information (Figure 13.1). This created redundancy of data and inefficiencies in terms of business processes.

ES were developed in response to the need for information integration. This was particularly challenging within global businesses where local offices use different systems and technologies (Imra, Murphy, and Simon, 2000). ES provide both a depth of

Figure 13.1

The Value Chain as It Relates to Functional Systems

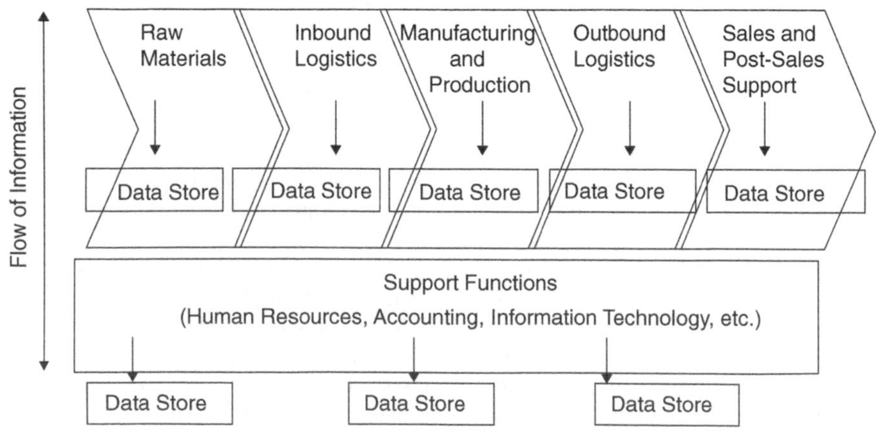

Figure 13.2

The Value Chain as It Relates to ERP Systems

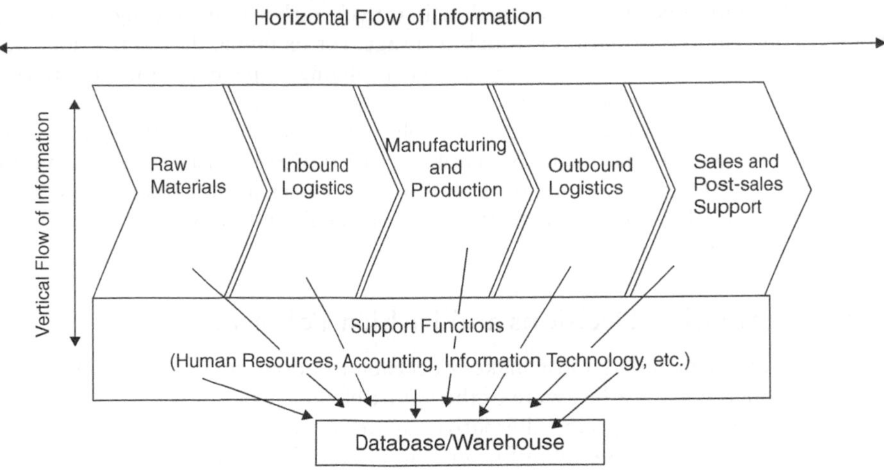

information by function and also a breadth of information horizontally across the value chain because they are designed in an integrated manner around a central data repository (Figure 13.2). Thus, one of the key selling points of an ES is replacing a firm's functional systems with a common IT infrastructure that enables information integration and the streamlining of work practices. Through the installation of required ES modules, such as HR, logistics, and sales, information generated by different business functions can be effectively collected, processed, and distributed via a central data warehouse. This eliminates the duplication of data and redundancies associated with inefficient work processes (Davenport, 1998).

Yet, as we observed in the introduction, many companies do not obtain these expected benefits upon implementing an ES. A number of reasons for this have been considered in the literature, for example, in relation to the constraining effects of politics (Markus, 1983) and culture (Cooper, 1994). In reality, there are likely to be many reasons why ES projects fail to achieve the transformational impact intended. Here we consider factors related to the decision-making processes associated with ES adoption and use because such a focus highlights the extent to which ES are able to support (or not) an agile organization.

Robertson, Swan, and Newell (1996) describe adoption and use of a new technology in terms of a series of decision episodes. Initially, there is *agenda formation* when the idea of adopting a new technology is first seriously discussed within an organization and a decision is taken to adopt (or not) the technology. Once this decision is made, the next episode relates to *selection,* where decisions are made about the particular variant of the technology to adopt and how to configure this to support the needs of the organization. Subsequently, *implementation* occurs, and relates to decisions that are made around the initial installation of the system and its associated organizational changes. These first three decision episodes thus relate to why the organization decides to adopt an ES, how it chooses to design (configure) and implement the technology, and the associated organizational changes that result. The final series of decisions relate to usage and the decisions that affect the appropriation of the technology so that it becomes embedded within organizational routines that prescribe organizational practice.

These decision episodes are engaged in iteratively rather than flowing in a linear fashion, from agenda formation through to usage. For example, decisions made during the selection episode may be revisited when, during implementation, unforeseen problems with configuration decisions emerge. Nevertheless, it is possible to consider decisions during each of these episodes to explore how they influence the agility of an ES. Thus, in the rest of this chapter, we consider each of these decision episodes in turn and analyze why ES may not transform business processes in the kinds of ways that are suggested and how, even where they do, this might not support the long-term agility of an organization.

Agenda Formation Decisions and Fashion-Following

Organizational members must make a decision to adopt an enterprise system. In order to do this, they must be aware of the nature of enterprise software and how this differs from functionally specific alternatives as well as understand how it can benefit the organization. The traditional diffusion of innovation literature (e.g., Rogers, 1962, 1995) assumes that this kind of decision is based on information that is provided to an organization by the supply side (ES vendors and management consultants) and by individuals from other organizations who have already adopted the technology (early adopters of ES). The organization thus gains access to information about ES through a variety of mass media and personal communication channels. This information is by-and-large assumed to be objective, providing members of the adopting organization with details about the characteristics and features of the new technology—its relative advantage, compatibility, and so on. The adopting organization is assumed to use this information to undertake a rational cost-benefit analysis of the relative advantages of this new technology over their in-house technologies or alternatives available on the market. Users will make the decision to adopt, in this case an ES, where it is decided that the ES is more technically efficient and will provide the organization with a relative advantage over what it could gain from the alternatives.

This rational view of how decisions are made during the agenda formation episode underestimates the impact of wider institutional influences and ignores the vested interests of supply side representatives who present a particular rhetoric about their products. In order to assess the ability of ES to meet an agenda of agile business operations, we must adopt a critical perspective related to the manner in which agenda formation occurs. This discussion follows.

First, in relation to wider institutional influences, DiMaggio and Powell (1983) point to the pressures toward isomorphism that exist within an industry or cluster of interacting organizations. Isomorphism refers to the constraining pressures that are present within an industry or cluster for organizations to adopt similar technologies. They identify three different sources of pressure for isomorphism. First, organizations may adopt similar technologies because they attempt to mimic or copy successful organizations (mimetic pressures). Thus, once a large player in a particular industry adopts ES, other smaller players may follow. Second, organizations may adopt similar technologies because they are under pressure from others (e.g., suppliers, customers) on which they are dependent to adopt certain technologies (coercive pressures). Thus, an organization that adopts ES may put pressure on its suppliers to adopt the same technology because this makes it easier for them to interact with their suppliers. Third, organizations may adopt similar technologies simply because they seek to establish legitimacy for themselves, given norms that develop within a particular institutional context (normative pressures). Thus, as the adoption of a new technology "takes off," organizations that have not adopted may feel under pressure to adopt in order to demonstrate that they are up-to-date with the latest technologies, an important consideration very often in terms of how they are valued by the stock market.

Abrahamson (1996) develops this neo-institutional perspective into an analysis of organizational fashions, where he points to the bandwagon effect that occurs as a new "best practice" recipe for success sweeps across an organizational field, promoted by fashion setters, including technology suppliers and consultants, and readily accepted by users. Thus, in relation to the second point about rhetoric, the fashion perspective on technology diffusion recognizes that the supply side (fashion setters) have a vested interest in promoting a particular version of a new technology, highlighting its radical and positive features, often in a way that exaggerates how transformational but simple it will be to implement, rather than its limitations and the likely complexity of implementation. Individuals within potential adopting organizations do recognize the bias in communications received directly from vendors and consultants and may seek information from what they perceive to be more neutral channels. One important channel in this respect is information received through a professional network. However, this information may be less neutral than believed because in many cases it is the vendors and consultants who give the presentations and write papers for the professional publications, even though they may be a minority of the membership (Swan, Newell, and Robertson, 1999). Thus, even from this "neutral" channel, the information provided may oversell the positive and underemphasize the negative. Moreover, even information obtained through personal networks may overestimate the advantages of the new technology and underestimate the difficulties of implementation. This is because adopters may be keen to encourage other users to adopt the ES they have selected to ensure that the software vendor continues to develop the package or, more simply, because adopters need to justify why they have gone through the painful process of adoption. This type of post-hoc rationalization is psychologically useful for maintaining positive self-esteem (Drummond and Chell, 2001). Thus, while Rogers' (1995) diffusion theory emphasizes that technologies will diffuse more broadly if they are compatible with existing technologies and not too complex, adoption decisions are made based on perceptions of compatibility and complexity as presented by the fashion-setting supply side rather than objective characteristics of the technology. Thus, even though an ES is highly complex and not compatible with existing technologies or organizational processes, potential adopters may not understand this because of the type of information they receive from the supply side.

The fashion perspective, however, does not assume that these new best practices are simply pushed onto gullible managers; instead it recognizes that managers are actively looking for new techniques that will help them respond to problems encountered as a result of changes in the external environment. Certainly, the adoption of ES, following on the previous best practices of MRP and MRPII (Swan, Newell, and Robertson, 1999) is seen to be a solution to managing increasingly distributed and networked organizational forms. This need for a solution was coupled, in the ES case, with fears about the "millennium bug" that spread like a contagion and led many firms to follow others in replacing their legacy systems with an ES as part of their Y2K project.

The main point of this section is to demonstrate that decisions made during the agenda formation episode, when organizations are thinking about whether or not to adopt ES, may not necessarily be based primarily on a rational analysis of costs and benefits (Walsham, 2002). Rather, these decisions are influenced by what is happening in other organizations; by a supply-side rhetoric about the benefits of an ES (a rhetoric that underestimates the disadvantages and difficulties); and by managers either being persuaded that there is no other choice because "ERP" is a precursor to business success in the twenty-first century—a mission critical software (Davenport, 1998) or more simply by their search for the "holy-grail"—the quick-fix solution to very complex problems related to distributed and networked organizations. To the extent that these factors influence decisions, whether or not the adopted ES system allows the organization responsively to meet its current or future problems/opportunities is not the primary driver for decisions.

The motivation for the decision to adopt may also have knock-on effects for the decisions that are made during the selection episode. Achieving the transformational benefits of an ES investment depends on changing organizational processes to exploit the integrating potential of the system. This means that organizations will need to make decisions during the selection episode about organizational change and the configuration of the technology that actually exploits the ES. Where organizations adopt a new technology because of the isomorphic or fashion-following processes discussed above, there is more likelihood that they will not exploit the full functionality of the technology because they are less ready to make the radical changes to their organizations that are often necessary in order to achieve the benefits of the ES integrated functionality. This is discussed in the next section.

Selection Decisions and the Status Quo

ES implementation is in essence about transplanting the architecture embedded in the software into the adopting organization (Lee and Lee, 2000). Simply computerizing existing organizational processes will not surface the benefits of such a system (Lee and Lee, 2000). Rather, the transformational benefits of an ES emerge from its potential to combine information across processes that have traditionally been independent. In order to exploit this potential, substantial changes to existing organizational processes will need to be made affecting an unprecedented amount of people across the enterprise. The standardization of business processes across functional areas requires a re-engineering effort that focuses on exploiting the benefits of an integrated IT system. Yet, in reality, studies have shown that, rather than contributing to significant organizational change, the implementation of IT often produces only incremental change that merely reinforces the status quo (Orlikowski, 1991). A study conducted by Newell et al. (2005) demonstrated that this is often also the case in relation to ES, as discussed next.

A case study was undertaken of the experiences of ES consultants working in a large consultancy firm (hereafter called XYZ). XYZ is a very large global organization that manufactures and retails both PC and high-end computer systems. Its consultancy units focus on both general business services and IT-related implementation and support services. Of interest in this chapter were the interviews we conducted with consultants who were specialists in working with firms who were implementing ES systems. In the study, we asked them about approaches taken to ES implementations by the clients with whom they have worked, as well as their experiences working on an ES implementation within XYZ itself. The experience of consultants is useful to consider because consultants have wide-ranging involvement in a variety of companies that are likely to approach their ES adoptions differently. Thus, consultants provide a range of experiences in different organizations.

Among the consultants interviewed, there was general agreement that some degree of re-engineering is essential in an ES implementation in order to achieve the transformational potential:

> "That's the intent [to get them to reengineer upfront]. To fully utilize the SAP functionality, which is a totally integrated system. To fully utilize the functionality of SAP. And often part of using that means making changes . . . which is why we strongly, strongly recommend to try and help facilitate making those changes."

While re-engineering is a high priority among consultants, the consultants noted that often it receives less attention among their client organizations who are implementing an ES, many of whom attempt to avoid re-engineering as much as possible. This tension is demonstrated in the following comment from one of the consultants:

> "I mentioned earlier a lot of times re-engineering and best practices are not always the focal point. They really are not. As much as we would like them to be and we try to drive that, a lot of the time they're not. So they'll look at what standard SAP provides. They'll look at what they have today. And try to go through as least change as possible . . . we, as consultants and as advisors, our challenge is to get them to understand that the answer is not as least change as possible. The answer is take advantage of the opportunity to improve what you have, to re-engineer if that's what you're invested in. Quite frankly that's not always the case . . . Human nature . . . tends to—'I don't want to change—I want to stay with what I have and what's the least painful way that I can do this.' "

One specific example that was provided was of a company that was implementing an enterprise-wide procurement module. They implemented a new process, supported by the ES, to send out orders electronically. However, in the end the company decided against changing their traditional requisition process, of which there were 27 different variants, because finding a common single process was deemed to be too difficult both technically and organizationally. So the company implemented only a small fraction of the procurement's module potential functionality and, according to the consultants, gained in return only a small fraction of the potential benefits from the system.

While these quotes relate to the consultants' experiences with various clients, the consultants also noted this resistance to change within their own organization during ES implementation. Examples were provided about how the ES was delayed because for some of the modules, the departmental representatives simply would not accept the need to change their existing processes. Thus, even in a context where the importance of organizational change for securing the benefits of an ES implementation was well-understood, there were still problems getting this philosophy accepted:

> "The sales team basically stuck their tongue out and said screw you; we ain't going to do this unless you do it our way, which has led to a number of compromises [customizations] in how we actually implemented the package, some of which are good, some of which aren't good."

This indicates that the transformational potential of an ES in relation to its ability to integrate information across functions and geographic areas can be restricted by the motivation and commitment of the adopting organization, who may be following external pressures but seek to implement the system with as little disruption as possible. In these cases, the ES is likely to do little to change the organization, while involving a tremendous amount of upheaval and expense to actually achieve this minimal change. As one of the individuals in one of the companies we have worked with commented, the ES had provided them with an $80 million bookkeeping system that allows them to do what they used to do! While ES adoptions that follow this least-change-as-possible logic may well increase efficiency, this is very unlikely to lead to any kind of organizational transformation, so that even in the immediate aftermath of implementation there is no real change because as the consultants in our study would say, they have not implemented best practice. While this clearly restricts the transformational potential of an ES, there is also a question of what is achieved if best practices are actually followed. We next consider more explicitly what is meant by *best practice.*

Implementation Decisions and Practice versus Process

The idea about not resisting organizational change and adapting the organizational processes to align with the processes embedded in the ES is based on the assumption that ES processes represent *best practices* within a particular industry. Thus, if an organization does not change to follow the ES processes, as many organizations do not according to the consultants at XYZ, they will, by definition, not be following *best industry practice.* The sales pitch behind ES is that if you implement an ES you are implementing best practice within your industry, since ES vendors now promote industry-specific ES configurations. As we have noted above, it may be difficult to get individuals within an organization to accept these acclaimed best practices because they resist changing their existing practices, even when the senior executives have bought into the sales pitch. Moreover, there may be a broader organizational resistance to the idea that the ES represents best practice. In another smaller company that we have been working with (ABC), this resistance was based on a strong belief that they had built up their organization over time and had already in place what for them was best practice. They wanted to implement an ES system that would be more integrative, but they did not want to change the processes that they had spent so much time perfecting. They therefore opted out of an ES vendor relationship that their main customer was attempting to impose on them (an example of coercive pressure that was, in this instance actually resisted). They did this because, having looked at the configuration options in this particular ES, they concluded that it would force them to change their processes in ways that they did not want to change. Instead they opted to work with an ES vendor that wanted to develop its existing ES package specifically for the industry in which ABC worked. The vendor had an ES system for office supply firms and wanted to develop it for furniture suppliers and saw ABC as helping them to do this. Once they started working on the project, both parties came to realize that modifying the software was going to be more difficult than they had imagined at the outset because of differences between the office and furniture supply industries that were not initially appreciated. Nevertheless, at the end of a very difficult implementation, ABC was at least satisfied that the ES they had implemented supported the processes that they defined as "best."

What is more questionable is whether other furniture suppliers would be similarly satisfied with these so-defined best practices that had been based on what ABC considered to be "best." Despite the fact that ES vendors are developing industry-specific solutions, it is questionable whether they are really best practices within any given industry. Indeed, "best" is context- and time-dependent so that what is best now for one particular organization in one particular context may not be best for another organization in a different context, even though they are in the same industry. In particular, the historical and cultural context of an organization cannot be ignored, so that even two organizations operating in very similar current environments may have very different processes that are effective given the evolution of each particular organization. Even within an organization, what is best for one group may not necessarily be best for all; and yet with an integrated system, all need to follow the same processes. This was illustrated in the example of an ES implementation in a university (Wagner and Newell, 2004). In this case, the central administration function attempted to impose their version of best practice in relation to the management of grants onto the faculty department administrators who worked directly for the faculty grant holders. The central finance manager, for example, said:

> "I would say that the mentality that we've had . . . for managing is primitive . . . and it's old-fashioned . . . the corporate world left it . . . years ago . . . faculty think of things fundamentally wrong. We want to move people towards a management model where we're going to ask [them] to put together a time-phased budget and management plan . . . If they don't like it, we ought to fire 'em—and get new users! . . . It's a . . . retreat . . . I taught Karate for years—*you know what*? If you're afraid to fight, you'll never fight! Got to decide to get up there *and get hit* . . . [we're] spending *millions and millions of dollars* to go forward, not to *duplicate what we had* . . . [the university] needs more than a copy of Quicken for each grant—we have 4,000 grants . . . *we don't do that here any more*. I mean—*we just don't!*"

However, the faculty department administrators felt very differently about the processes that the central administrators were attempting to impose on them, believing that they were not only "not best" but that they were actually counter to their needs in terms of dealing with the faculty grant holders. In this context, the faculty departments were able to resist this imposition of best practice and enforced some "bolt-on" customizations that allowed them to continue to use their traditional, old-fashioned processes. Ironically, this case was again of an organization working with a vendor to develop an industry best practice ES, in this case an ES dedicated to the university sector. Yet even in the organization where the best practice was developed, the organization had to add customizations to get the ES accepted and used by its different stakeholders.

Not only does this raise the question of whether a best practice can be defined, it also highlights the difference between the idealized process and actual practice. Organizations can spend much effort in carefully defining *best practice*, only to find that actually people very quickly find ways to circumvent the prescribed processes in the quest to make the system work for them, as was demonstrated by Boudreau and Robey (2005). In the XYZ case, for example, one of the consultants had experienced this when trying to understand the existing processes:

> "There is an interesting difference between the process documents—how they say the job is done and the people at the keyboard actually doing the job—they don't match. You get very clever people who learn their own short-cuts and unless you are a practitioner you don't learn these things."

Another XYZ consultant was, thus, very skeptical of the time often spent in carefully defining *best practice:*

> "[. . .] otherwise you can get a committee working and discussing it for years and they'll come up with something they think is absolutely perfect and it will fall apart within two weeks of going live because there's so much stuff they didn't know, or

> the world moved on, or you know it wasn't supposed to be like that, you told me this field was unique, it's not. I thought it was. And suddenly you have all these other issues."

In other words, while an organization is thus supposedly implementing best practice when implementing an ES, in reality, an ES implementation is oriented around a set of idealized business *processes* that often bear very little resemblance to actual day-to-day *practice* and indeed may inhibit effective practice by oversubscribing what and how work is done. Workers develop work-arounds and shortcuts regardless of what the formal system prescribes (Orlikowski, 1996, 2000; Ciborra, et al., 2000). And as Suchman (1987) observes, in comparing plans (or formal processes and methodological conceptualizations of work) to situated actions (or how work actually gets done as an everyday practical achievement), incongruities between the two can result in significant design flaws in technological systems that actually impede productivity rather than enhance it. Providing users with a tool to support their work, rather than a tool that prescribes their work, may therefore be a more effective approach to the technical design of an ES. In so doing, the organization would be recognizing and valuing the flexibility and the improvisational skills of the users (Orlikowski, 2000). The prescribed processes, on the other hand, can inhibit the users' improvisational skills, which are what often enables work to be carried out in the face of unforeseen circumstances. Yet an organization that has spent millions on an ES implementation is unlikely to abandon the system easily, given all the sunk costs. The ES may then become the organization's future straightjacket, rather than the agile system that is needed in the twenty-first century. This is discussed more fully in the next section.

Usage Decisions and Efficiency versus Flexibility

We raised in the last section the question about best practice. An important additional question in relation to this is "best for when"? A set of processes may be best for a particular organization when it implements the ES, but they may not be best for this organization in the future. As the ES becomes appropriated into the organization so that its use is routine, the transformations that may have been achieved during the implementation episode now become the status quo that will inhibit change in the future. At this point, the ES may be best for the vendor of the ES, locking the organization into a dependent relation for years to come, but this is not necessarily best for the implementing organization as it moves forward in a dynamic environment. We can consider this in relation to the tension between efficiency and flexibility.

As we saw earlier, ES are marketed on the premise that adopting firms can enhance their competitiveness by increasing productivity, reducing cost, and improving information capability. This suggests that while ES may be touted as transformational, the key aspect of transformation that is sought is to increase efficiency—ES can save costs by integrating data across business processes so that blockages and barriers to the fulfillment of a process are smoothed out. Yet, what does this focus of efficiency lead to?

A large body of literature has focused on examining the link between efficiency and flexibility (e.g., Davidow and Malone, 1992; Wright and Snell, 1998). Much of this has concluded that there is a trade-off between efficiency and flexibility (Ghemawat and Costa, 1993). Indeed, the idea of a trade-off between efficiency and flexibility is perhaps the most enduring idea in organization theory (Thompson, 1967). It can be traced back to the development of contingency approaches, in particular the work of Burns and Stalker (1961). Burns and Stalker depicted two distinct types of organizational design that they characterized as mechanistic and organic, and argued that each was appropriate to accomplish different tasks in different environmental situations. Specifically, they argued that mechanistic (or bureaucratic) structures were most appropriate where the environment was stable. This is because in such a situation the goal of the organization is the efficient production of goods and services. Here, there is no need to attempt to develop new products or services, or introduce new organizational processes, because the environment does not require it. However, where the environment is more dynamic so that the organization does need to change its products, services, or processes to adapt to the changing demands, an organic structure is required. Mechanistic structures are characterized by high degrees of standardization, formalization, specialization, and hierarchy; organic structures are characterized by low degrees of each of these aspects of structure. Given these diametrically opposed organizational forms, it became the received wisdom that an organization either had to focus on efficiency or flexibility because flexibility can only be achieved at the cost of efficiency (Hannan and Freeman, 1989).

There are now a few writers who have suggested that it is possible to be simultaneously efficient *and* flexible or "ambidextrous" (Tushman and O'Reilly, 1997; Daft, 1998). Adler, Goldoftas, and Levine (1999) reviewed these different approaches to ambidexterity and highlighted four kinds of organizational mechanisms that the literature postulates as being important for achieving simultaneous efficiency and flexibility. These are meta-routines, job enrichment, switching, and partitioning. Meta-routines are routines to standardize internal processes that focus on flexibility or innovation (Nelson and Winter, 1982), for example, procedures specifying the steps that must be carried out in designing a new product attempt to routinize product innovation. Job enrichment refers to increasing the motivating potential of a job (Hackman and Oldham, 1980) through giving increased autonomy and responsibility, so that the person concerned can be more innovative and flexible even if the tasks are routine. Switching refers to the division of tasks so that a person is given time to spend on some nonroutine tasks (e.g., quality circles), but reverts to routine tasks. Partitioning refers to the division of tasks by groups, so that some groups in an organization concentrate on routine tasks while others concentrate on the nonroutine. So, the R&D department might focus on innovation while the production department focuses on efficiency.

While such ambidexterity is, thus, potentially possible, it is nevertheless the case that ES focus on improving efficiency, as discussed. In one organization (Company A) we found that this focus on efficiency was offset by the simultaneous implementation of an organizational initiative that focused on flexibility (Newell et al., 2002). In this company, the concurrent implementation of an ES with a second-generation knowledge management initiative focused on learning and knowledge generation did provide the opportunity to simultaneously stimulate efficiency and innovation. However, as the case demonstrates, this was not an automatic outcome, but had to be fostered.

Similar to other empirical studies (e.g., Pereira, 1999; Al-Mashari and Zairi, 2000), the implementation of ERP in company A concentrated primarily on the efficiency of producing, gathering, integrating, and managing information. Efficiency improvements were sought by enhancing the information-processing capability of the company, enabled by the systematization and centralization of information management and the adoption of standard approaches to the codification and processing of information. In other words, through a common integrative IT infrastructure, information that used to be functionally concealed became available throughout the organization in a predefined format (Wagle, 1998). Meanwhile, knowledge management (KM) in Company A concentrated on the mobilization of knowledge through the organization of innovation communities as a means of sharing and creating tacit knowledge (Brown

Table 13.1

Impact of ERP and KM Initiatives		
	ERP Initiative	**KM Initiative**
Metaroutines	New set of routines introduced, but once created routines are stabilized	Learning communities created a new routine to continuously stimulate innovation
Enrichment	Inhibited by standardizing processes and routines	Learning communities allowed employees the opportunity to reflect and learn from their experiences
Switching	Minimized to enhance predictability	Learning communities provided opportunity to periodically switch from ERP-defined routines
Partitioning	Pre-existed in company with production divisions focused on efficiency	Pre-existed in company with consultancy division focused on innovation
Shown in terms of Adler et al.'s Four Mechanisms.		

and Duguid, 1991; von Krogh, Ichijo, and Nonaka, 2000). The results indicate, then, that in this company the ERP and KM initiatives were complementary, allowing the organization to improve both its efficiency and innovation capability simultaneously. In relation to the different mechanisms to promote ambidexterity, the ES initiative increased efficiency at the expense of flexibility. However, the KM initiative fostered flexibility that counterbalanced the ES thrust toward efficiency, as described in Table 13.1.

While this case suggests that the efficiency bias of an ES can be counterbalanced with the concurrent implementation of an initiative focused on flexibility, it nevertheless remains the case that an ES alone increases efficiency so that where no counterbalancing technologies are implemented, the ES will reduce rather than increase agility and flexibility.

Conclusions

The focus of much IT innovation has been on increasing control and efficiency; ES, as discussed above, follow this tradition. However, the general thrust of much debate in business is the increasing need for organizations to be adaptable, flexible, and creative. Such flexibility or agility is spurred by chaos rather than control and efficiency. Periodically, in the IS field authors have noted this tension and advocated the design of IT systems that support chaos, foster tension, and support loose coupling and the unpredictable. For example, Hedberg and Jonsson (1978) suggest developing a "semi-confusing information system," Manheim (1988) suggests an "active decision support system," and Mitroff and Linstone (1993) suggest a "dialectical inquiry system." However, the message is never seriously taken forward, because mainstream information systems development is about supporting transaction processing that is predictable and scalable and that can provide orderly and timely data to organizational members. ES fit precisely into this mold. Perhaps this is not surprising since it is much easier to design around control and efficiency because these things are codifiable so that the IT can be designed to support a tangible practice that appears to be efficient, at least in the specific circumstances considered at the time a best practice. Where the IT was designed around independent functions or local practices, this was less problematic as it was easier for users to improvise with the software and their practice. In the case of an ES, this becomes more problematic because the system codifies the processes for the whole enterprise, making it more difficult for individual users to improvise because their practices are so integrated with the practices of others.

Thus, rather than leading to agile information systems, we end up time and again promoting IT that helps to enforce control and efficiency. ES are no different in this respect and cannot be described as systems that promote agility. Even in the short-term, where they do foster transformation (and we have seen that this is not always the case), this is in relation to improved efficiency. In the longer term, they have the potential to become the legacy systems that reduce flexibility and innovation, restricting rather than releasing the improvisational skills of users as they confront new and unpredictable situations that do not fit the standard best practice processes and routines embedded in the ES infrastructure. In this sense, ES are the antithesis of agility; they are the clumsy IT that will restrict the future agility of organizations.

References

Abrahamson, E. (1996). Management fashion. *Academy of Management Review*, 21, 254–285.

Adler, P., Goldoftas, B., and Levine, D. (1999). Flexibility versus efficiency? A case study of model changeovers in the Toyota production system. *Organization Science*, 10, 43–68.

Al-Mashari, M. and Zairi, M. (2000). Supply-chain re-engineering using enterprise resource planning (ERP) systems: An analysis of a SAP R/3 implementation case. *International Journal of Physical Distribution and Logistics*, 30, 296–313.

Appleton, E. (1997). How to survive ERP. *Datamation*, 43 (3), 50–53.

Boudreau, M-C. and Robey, D. (2005). Enacting integrated information technology: A human agency perspective. *Organization Science*, 16 (1), 3–18.

Brown, J. and Duguid, P. (1991). Organizational learning and toward a unified view of working, learning and innovation. *Organization Science*, 2, 40–56.

Burns, T. and Stalker, G. M. (1961). *The Management of Innovation*. London: Tavistock.

Calogero, B. (2000). Who is to blame for ES failure? *ServerWorld Magazine*, June.

Ciborra, C., et al. (2000). *From Control to Drift: The Dynamics of Corporate Information Infrastructures*. Oxford, UK: Oxford University Press.

Cooper, R. (1994). The inertial impact of culture on IT implementation. *Information and Management*, 17–31.

Daft, R. (1998). Essentials of Organization Theory and Design. Cincinnati: South-Western College Publishing.

Davenport, T. (1998). Putting the enterprise into the enterprise system. *Harvard Business Review*, 76 (4), 121–131.

Davidow, W. and Malone, M. (1992). The Virtual Corporation: Structuring and Revitalizing the Corporation for the 21st Century. New York: Harper Business.

DiMaggio, P. and Powell, W. (1983). The iron-cage revisited: Institutional isomorphism and collective rationality in organizational fields. *American Sociological Review*, 48, 147–160.

Drummond, H. and Chell, E. (2001). Life's chances and choices: A study of entrapment in career decisions with reference to Becker's side bets theory. *Personnel Review*, 30 (2), 186–192.

Ghemawat, P. and Costa, R. (1993). The organizational tension between static and dynamic efficiency. *Strategic Management Journal*, 14, 59–73.

Hackman, J. and Oldham, G. (1980). *Work Redesign*. Reading, MA: Addison-Wesley.

Hannan, M. and Freeman, J. (1989). *Organizational Ecology*. Cambridge: Harvard University Press.

Hedberg, B. and Jonsson, S (1978). Designing semi-confusing information systems for organizations in changing environments. *Accounting, Organizations and Society*, 3 (1), 47–64.

Imra, B. F., Murphy, K. E., and Simon, S. J. (2000). Integrating ERP in the Business School Curriculum. *Communications of the ACM*, 43, 39–41.

Kling, R. (2003). Critical professional education about information and communication technologies and social life. *Information Technology and People*, 16 (4), 394–418.

Lee, Z. and Lee, J. (2000). An ERP implementation case study from a knowledge transfer perspective. *Journal of Information Technology*, 15, 281–288.

Manheim, M. (1988). An architecture for active DSS. In *Proceedings of the Twenty-First Hawaii International Conference on System Sciences*, IEEE Computer Society. Volume III, pp. 356–365.

Markus, M. L. (1983). Power, politics and MIS implementation. *Communications of the ACM*, 26, 430–444.

Markus, M. L., et al. (2000). Learning from adopters' experiences with ERP: Problems encountered and success achieved. *Journal of Information Technology*, 15, 245–265.

Mitroff, I. I. and Linstone, H. A. (1993). *The Unbound Mind*. New York: Oxford University Press.

Nelson, R. and Winter, S. (1982). An Evolutionary Theory of Economic Change. Cambridge, MA: Harvard University Press.

Newell, S., et al. (2002). Implementing enterprise resource planning and knowledge management systems: Fostering efficiency and innovation complementarity. *Information and Organization*, 13 (1), 25–52.

Newell, S., et al. (2005). Analyzing different strategies to Enterprise System adoption: Reengineering-led versus quick deployment. *International Journal of Enterprise Information Systems*, 1 (2), 1–16.

Orlikowski, W. (1991). Integrated information environment or matrix of control? The contradictory implications of information technology. *Accounting, Management and Information Technologies*, 1, 9–42.

Orlikowski, W. (1996). Improvising organizational transformation over time: A situated change perspective. *Information Systems Research*, 7 (1), 63–92.

Orlikowski, W. (2000). Using technology and constituting structures: A practice lens for studying technology in organizations. *Organization Science*, 11 (4), 404–428.

Parr, A. and Shanks, G. (2000). A model of ES project implementation. *Journal of Information Technology*, 15, 289–303.

Pereira, R. E. (1999). Resource view theory analysis of SAP as a source of competitive advantage for firms. *Database for Advances in Information Systems*, 30, 38–46.

Porter, M. and Millar, V. (1985). How information gives you competitive advantage. *Harvard Business Review*, 63, 149–160.

Robertson, M., Swan, J., and Newell, S. (1996). The role of networks in the diffusion of technological innovations. *Journal of Management Studies*, 33 (3), 333–359.

Rogers, E. (1962, 1995). *Diffusion of Innovations*, 1st and 3rd ed. New York: Free Press.

Sauer, C., Liu, L., and Johnston, K. (2001). Where project managers are kings. *Project Management Journal*, 32 (4), 39–49.

Suchman, L. (1987). *Plans and Situated Actions: The Problem of Human/Machine Communication*. Cambridge, UK: Cambridge University Press.

Swan, J., Newell, S., and Robertson, M. (1999). Central agencies in the diffusion and design of technology: A comparison of the UK and Sweden. *Organization Studies*, 20 (6), 905–932.

Scott, E. and Kaindl, L. (2000). Enhancing functionality in an enterprise package. *Information and Management*, 37, 111–122.

Shanks, G. and Seddon, P. (2000). Editorial: Enterprise Resource Planning (ERP) Systems. *Journal of Information Technology*, 15 (2), 243–244.

Thompson, J. (1967). *Organizations in Action*. New York: McGraw-Hill.

Tushman, M. L. and O'Reilly, C. A. (1997). *Winning through Innovation*. Boston: Harvard Business School Press.

VARBusiness (2005). ES spending to rise dramatically. October 3, 2005, supplement, p. 4.
von Krogh, G., Ichijo, K., and Nonaka, I. (2000). *Enabling Knowledge Creation.* Oxford, UK: Oxford University Press.
Wagle, D. (1998). The case for ERP systems. *The McKinsey Quarterly*, 9, 130–138.
Wagner, E. and Newell, S. (2004). "Best" for Whom?: The tension between best practice ERP packages and the epistemic cultures of an Ivy League university. *Journal of Strategic Information Systems*, 13 (4), 305–328.
Walsham, G. (2002). Cross-cultural software production and use: A structurational analysis. *MIS Quarterly*, 26 (4), 359–380.
Wright, P. and Snell, S. (1998). Toward a unifying framework for exploring fit and flexibility in strategic human resource management. *Academy of Management Review*, 23, 756–772.
Zuboff, S. (1988). *In the Age of the Smart Machine: The Future of Work and Power*. New York: Basic Books.

14

Enterprise Information Systems and the Preservation of Agility

Anthony Wensley and Eveline van Stijn

Organizations are facing increasingly turbulent environments. Globalization, changing customer expectations, technology, and many other factors are contributing to a significant increase in the complexity and instability of the world in which many organizations operate. As a result of such turbulence and instability, organizations and their managers are becoming increasingly concerned with how to enhance such organizational characteristics as agility and flexibility. In the context of this chapter, we consider that agility refers to the ability of an organization to recognize changes in their environment and respond accordingly. Thus, essentially, an agile organization needs both to be flexible, to be able to change the way it operates, and also to be able to recognize when it needs to change.

In the following chapter, we will investigate organizational agility and flexibility through a technological lens, particularly the part that enterprise systems or Enterprise Resource Planning (ES or ERP) have in effecting and affecting agility and flexibility in organizations. Although our emphasis tends to be toward the negative—how agility and flexibility are impaired through the implementation and use of ES—we freely accept that ES can have positive effects and affects on agility and flexibility. However, we are concerned that too little attention has been paid in the past to the potential negative influences and actions that can be taken to reduce the impact of such influences.

Our theoretical investigation is broadened with an empirically based study. We re-analyze a case that involved the detailed investigation of the implementation and use of an ES in a large university (Ivy University) in order to sketch a more detailed empirical picture as to how organizations may sustain flexibility following the introduction of an ES. The educational setting is an interesting one, because although universities have a history of being highly inflexible, there continues to be many—sometimes highly innovative—changes in education and, in particular, in the administration, management, and logistics surrounding this primary process (Scott and Wagner, 2003; Bondarouk, 2004; Pollock and Cornford, 2004). Although we use a university as our source of insight into practical actions to support and enhance agility, many of the lessons that may be learned are also equally applicable to other organizations.

A Theoretical Framework: Introducing Enterprise Systems, Agility, Interpretative Flexibility, and Workarounds

Introducing an ES means attempting to introduce new standardized, integrated, and formalized practices in the organization. When an ES is implemented, there is a need to ensure the stability and sustainability of the practices. But paradoxically, there is also a need to provide for the alteration and adaptation of these practices as the environment in which the organization operates undergoes change. Working against the possibility of such alteration and adaptation is the perception that once they are implemented, ES are often considered complete and therefore any change is considered to be inappropriate. In addition, adaptation and customization of ES is often either difficult in principle or is made difficult and costly by the vendors of the system.

Understanding agility in this setting involves asking how people sense changes in the organizational environment and can adapt to them by making flexible changes to their day-to-day practices that involve the use of an ES. This means that we can understand agility in terms of the flexibility in enactments and interpretations of routines, and the information used and provided by the ES. Routines can be changed by changing the ways in which routines are actually enacted or by "inventing" new routines or "workarounds." This requires an ability to think through the practices and the role of the ES, to challenge and question the status quo, and to identify alternative ways of enacting routines and the assessment of these different enactments. Thus, agility as a characteristic is partially shaped through workarounds, interpretive flexibility, and reflexivity.

Proposition 1: In order to enhance agility and flexibility, users of ES should be encouraged to question how routines are enacted and actively explore ways in which they can be adapted to new situations.

Proposition 2: In order to enhance agility and flexibility, workarounds should not be dismissed but be investigated to determine whether they reflect limitations of the current ES implementation.

Agility is also dependent on the ability to access appropriate information about the environment. This information establishes the need for change as well as the directions in which such change should take place; clearly ES are a key source of such information, but we should not ignore the potential contribution of other sources such as environmental scanning, informal contacts, and so on. However, in order that such information becomes available to others, it is typically necessary that it be represented in ES. This requires that the information be recognized and classified in some way. Although one of the often stated benefits of ES is their ability to facilitate the collection and dissemination of information, it is important to recognize that this information may lose some of its richness and potential to enable interpretative flexibility. In the following chapter, we will reflect on how this affects the organization's agility.

Proposition 3: In order to preserve agility and flexibility, organizations should actively explore occasions in which users have problems classifying data as it is entered into the system.

Proposition 4: In order to preserve agility and flexibility, organizations should explore ways of preserving ambiguity and uncertainty, where appropriate, in the data that is represented in their ES.

ES and the practices they bring with them are often perceived to become highly inflexible after they are implemented in the organization as the following quotations make plain.

> "ERP packages in particular are solidified technologies whose complexity usually transcends the ability of particular organizations to rework the source code, reprogram or redefine the logic on which any such package is based." (Kallinikos, 2004, p. 11)

Indeed, vendors often deliberately discourage such modifications for a variety of reasons. Most charitably one might suggest that they want to provide systems with predictable and reliable performance. Modifications of such complex systems such as ES will likely lead to unexpected outcomes. Less charitably, vendors seek to sell standardized solutions and thus limit development costs. In fairness, it is argued that such standardized systems provide examples of "best practice" although it is not completely clear what is really meant by this assertion (Van Stijn and Wensley, 2005).

We may also detect a particular philosophy underlying ES that encourages stability and the channeling of variability. In principle, it must be possible to classify everything that an organization needs to pay attention to (events, products, individuals, organizations, plans, etc.) unambiguously and without uncertainty. The adoption of such a philosophy is evidenced by the following quotation:

> "ERP focuses on eliminating rather than enhancing unplanned variations. ERP systems are linear. Changes in organizational processes, procedures and relationships must be programmed into the ERP system, so they are carefully planned and engineered by designated experts. Unconventional responses are considered errors and the range of acceptable diversity carefully proscribed. Spontaneous reorganization and fluid process relationships are not part of ERP functionality at this time." (Lengnick-Hall, Lengnick-Hall, and Abdinnour-Helm, 2004, p. 319)

Proposition 5: In order to preserve agility and flexibility, organizations should actively engage in process audits on a regular basis to determine whether their existing processes are appropriate.

Interestingly, such inflexibility may not cow users of the system. Often as they learn more about the new system, they will begin to identify more precisely how the system might be modified:

> "Proposing new ideas was not a strong issue within the group, especially at the beginning. The users perceived the system as a 'given' and did not come up with suggestions to improve it. However, during the interviews, we found that, in the later stages of using the system, the users had many suggestions. [. . .] These ideas were discussed during the key-user meetings, but only two of them were implemented." (Bondarouk, 2004, pp. 209–210)

We may identify the "inflexibilities" discussed above as arising from a variety of different sources. In the first place, one type of inflexibility arises as a result of the particular way in which individuals have been trained to make use of the system. Not surprisingly, insufficient attention to training and setting expectations of the users of a system can seriously impair the ability of an organization in maintaining, let alone, enhancing, its agility. Individuals may have a very narrow understanding of the system and its performance and thus find it difficult either to see that the system is performing inappropriately or be unable to adapt to a new way of configuring the system. Interestingly, one of purported benefits of ES and integration is that they provide holistic views of the organization. However, such views will only be possible if users have appropriate training:

> "The main complaints were about the lack of understanding what was 'behind the screen.' It was not difficult to click the buttons, but they needed to foresee the

outputs of the transactions: the connection with IPA which, at the beginning, seemed to be a big black box." (Bondarouk, 2004, p. 211)

It is interesting to observe that typically the understanding that it is necessary for users to develop in order to support agility requires a deep understanding of existing systems and their characteristics and capacities.

Proposition 6: In order to preserve agility and flexibility, organizations should examine their training programs to ensure that these support and enhance agility and flexibility rather than undermining them.

An Organization's Experience with Implementing an ERP System

For this chapter, we have opted to re-analyze the Ivy University case, a case study that focuses on introducing ES packages in the university setting. The primary researcher of this case is Erica Wagner, who investigated Ivy University as part of her doctoral studies (Wagner, 2002; Scott and Wagner, 2003; Wagner and Newell, 2004).

Although Ivy is a university, the situation facing Ivy will likely resonate with many business managers and the situations that they have faced when deciding to implement ES.

> "One of the most serious problems faced by Ivy University today is the modernization of its administrative infrastructure in order to manage an increasingly complex financial and regulatory environment. The complexity of Ivy's research, clinical and teaching activities have increased dramatically over the last decade and in such a way that the legacy systems no longer adequately supported the University activities. This situation created a sense of insecurity among the University Officers who were unable to control the financial operations of the institution because of its decentralized operating paradigm. During the early 1990s the University mandated spending for the upgrading of information systems. As a consequence they retained external expertise in the form of management consultants who advised an overhaul of all administrative systems." (Wagner, 2002, p. 73)

Ivy University selected a package by Oracle (also referred to as Vision, a pseudonym), because it was considered to have a good financial backbone, it was used in government and at other universities, and because of a partnership possibility with the vendor.

The University, in particular the central administrators, wanted to improve its financial monitoring of grants, trying to create "more transparent accounting practice in order to manage institutional risk, comply with regulatory bodies, avoid litigious hazards, and act as competent fiduciaries in an increasingly complex operational environment" (Wagner and Newell, 2004, p. 312). We can easily see here a reflection of the need for contemporary business to respond to environmental changes such as those to accounting practices, Sarbanes-Oxley, and a wide range of other environmental factors. However, there is also the perception that the approach that is adopted to responding to particular changes should enhance the organization's ability to respond to change in general.

Proposition 7: In order to enhance agility and flexibility, any changes in processes, procedures, organizational structure, etc., that are instituted to respond to environmental change should be reviewed to determine whether they result in greater or lesser flexibility.

However, such re-engineering of processes in parallel to the ES adoption was difficult, partly because faculty members "are not interested in taking responsibility for administrative activities in order to streamline Ivy's business processes. Their goal is to use the financial resources available creatively over the life of a project to ensure that maximum benefit is derived from the money available in relation to the goals of the research" (Wagner and Newell, 2004, p. 320).

Proposition 8: In order to enhance agility and flexibility, organizations need to develop a culture and incentive structure that encourages individuals to take advantage of flexibility. Actions that result in the appropriate adaptation of processes to new situations should be incentivized.

One of the key issues in developing agility relates to the ability to both modularize the processes within an organization and also, paradoxically, have sufficient, in-depth understanding, so that the modules can be re-configured rapidly and effectively. Such re-configuration required both a broader understanding as to how the modules function together—a meta-understanding of module function—and also a deep understanding of the function of each module itself.

As was noted at Ivy, achieving this complex perspective (difficult enough in a relatively stable environment) is particularly challenging when coupled with the implementation of a major new ES.

> "Departments are very much in silos. They operate like little, independent corporations . . . But what we are trying to do is to prepare people to break down some of those departmental walls and look beyond their departments to build an integrated administration. Knowing that any integrated system is going to be much more complex than the ones they had been used to—not only the systems themselves or the computer systems—but also the new policies, procedures and whatever—we are hoping that we can get everyone on the same page and make a big—a whole administration." (Wagner, 2002, p. 109)—distributed administrator

Clearly, processes are often changed in such a way that there is no going back as is demonstrated by the following quotation:

> "By making a decision to go with Oracle financials, senior management either consciously or semi-consciously—I think it was for former—was making it impossible for [Ivy] to continue doing business in fragmented silos . . . Implementation is about setting up an environment. You make a set of decisions—a set of changes at the top that forces change regardless of whether it's consensus or not—'cause you say—you change their ability to do it any other way." (Wagner, 2002, p. 143)—technical leader

It is also important to recognize that any change will generally not be perceived to be positive by all concerned. In particular, changes to processes may make some information easily available while making other types of information much more difficult to obtain or, indeed to understand as the following observation demonstrates:

> "The work practices inscribed within the legacy grant [Commitment Accounting] practices versus those underpinning the ERP budget application, point to the distinctly different perspectives of central administrators and faculty . . . As such the ERP design was interpreted by faculty as an attempt to align faculty practice with professional managerial values without an adequate understanding of the nature of grant and contract support." (Wagner and Newell, 2004, p. 314)

Flexibility, Agility, and Classification

What also lies at the heart of these problems is not simply the ways in which processes are represented but also, more basically, the ways in which data is classified so that it may be represented by the system. Thus, in the context of Ivy faculty, adopt a different classification system for their expenditures that is incompatible with the standard accounting classification.

From the standpoint of agility, classification can be problematic for a number of reasons. In the first place, adopting a particular approach to classification tends to privilege particular perspectives and ways of interpreting the environment within which an organization operates. Second, an existing classification system makes it difficult to recognize changes in the environment. Individuals who are required to enter data into the system may experience difficulties in entering data into the categories that they have been provided with. However, their response is often to "adapt" the data to fit or simply to place instances into the wrong categories.

A further problem arises if we seek to adopt a new classification. Sometimes the new classification may be a simple mapping from an existing classification, though more commonly the new classification is incommensurable with the existing classification.

> "Most faculty members obtaining grants are also not trained accountants and so do not want complicated accounting statements that they will have difficulty interpreting. [. . .] The legacy systems operating at Ivy, which were based on commitment accounting, provided faculty with both the information they were most interested in—what money they had left—and were simple to use. Commitment accounting was a classification system that worked for Ivy's academic community precisely because it did not attempt to mandate the analytical process of budgeting and management." (Wagner and Newell, 2004, p. 320)

Proposition 9a: In order to enhance agility and flexibility, organizations should actively examine classification problems.

Agility, Flexibility, and Systems Implementation and Use

It seems clear that failure to include the users of ES in their development potentially has many negative consequences. In the first place, it may result in much of the inherent richness and diversity that is present in any organization and supports its resilience and agility. Secondly, it may well be that, even in this case, diversity is retained by default. This occurs as a result of different individuals within the organization interpreting a classification scheme in different ways. The problem with this "preservation" of diversity is that it typically is not recognized; even if it is recognized, it is difficult to determine how the diversity can be captured in a single classification system.

Proposition 9b: In order to enhance agility and flexibility, organizations should investigate ways of maintaining diverse classification schemes.

Proposition 9c: In order to enhance agility and flexibility, organizations should question the extent to which existing classification schemes privilege certain perspectives and exclude or devalue others.

With respect to Ivy, it should be noted that in this project, the future users of the system (those who were to interpret and enact the best practices) were hardly involved at all, which created a lot of resistance in the end when the system went live. It was attempted to partially overcome this by setting up several support centers. The resistance and involvement of some influential people "led the Provost inviting top ERP project leaders to a luncheon in order to speak about the concerns of the science faculty. As a result of this meeting, the Transaction Support Center (TSC) was set up to complete the clerically based, administrative work of science departments. It was emphasized that the knowledge-based work remained the charge of faculty administrators who did not want to lose any of their authority in the ERP-enabled environment. This center was viewed as temporary and working on behalf of Ivy's science-based faculty. A different center—the Business Support Center (BSC) was set up for the smaller non-science departments. This was also seen as a temporary center that helped to shift the effort of translation from the personal assistants in the smaller departments to a central administrative unit. Similarly, Ivy's wealthier professional schools such as Medicine designed their own support mechanisms very similar to the TSC and BSC models" (Wagner and Newell, 2004, p. 317).

As we implement new systems, we have to give considerable thought as to how long we allow for legacy systems to remain in place. In the case of Ivy it was noted that certain concessions were made. "TPB was designed as Ivy's institutional budget system which the core group expected would also satisfy the grant accounting needs previously met by the CA system. Faculty members and their business office staff were frustrated that a business-oriented rationale had been prescribed by the Project team without consulting them about such a significant conceptual shift. They felt insulted that the Commitment Accounting functionality was not considered a priority by the core group and Vision. In the winter (1999–2000), leaders representing faculty and departmental administrators lobbied for changes to both the system and the support structures. In response to this pressure, the core group agreed on three things. First, they agreed to leave the mainframe legacy system running until additional ERP functionality was created. Second, they would meet the faculty functional requirements by designing ERP-based commitments. Third, the BSC and TSC would be left running at least through the end of next fiscal year" (Wagner and Newell, 2004, p. 317).

A concern that one might have in maintaining legacy systems is that they will, at the very least, tend to undermine the commitment to the new system. Worse, they may make it difficult to learn the new system, making it difficult to respond appropriately to changes in the organization's environment. If one chooses to maintain legacy systems, it is necessary to provide systems that capture differences between the legacy systems and the new systems. Such changes should be fully investigated.

What is interesting about this suggestion is that systems should be put in place to provide for the active discussion of "problems" with the new system, even when the legacy system has been fully replaced.

Proposition 10: In order to enhance agility and flexibility, it is recommended that legacy systems be operated in tandem with legacy systems and significant differences between their behavior actively investigated.

Proposition 11: In order to enhance agility and flexibility after the implementation of a new system, appropriate procedures and systems should be put in place to capture problems, and opportunities should be provided to actively explore their nature and importance.

We have noted earlier that it is necessary to develop a culture of agility—this a very old story that simply providing the capabilities for agility does not guarantee that the organization or its employees will actually take advantage of such agility.

It is important that we recognize that as we change and reapportion tasks within a process, it is necessary to recognize that different types of knowledge may be required by different people. This may well require retraining.

> "In other words, the design of the ERP assumed a level of sophistication, and a knowledge base fundamentally at odds with the current arrangement of University work. . . . Therefore, the design of the ERP shifted the nature of expertise needed within Ivy's administration." (Wagner and Newell, 2004, p. 322)

Perhaps more fundamentally, as organizations are restructured, many roles and tasks may be changed and the knowledge necessary to conduct these roles and tasks may change substantially.

Education for Agility

Just how much do individuals working in an organization need to understand about the way in which the organization "works" and how it interacts and responds to its external environment? One of the challenges is to give individuals the mental wherewithall to recognize when change takes place and also have the opportunity to examine and explore this change.

> "To simplify it too much you run the risk of people interpreting the information wrong and doing bad things with it. But to be totally straight about exactly what everything is complicates it to the point that they can't understand what they're looking at." (Wagner, 2002, p. 236)—core group member

One of the problems associated with buying in solutions, especially software solutions, it that we may misunderstand the true characteristics of these systems and also fail to incorporate change mechanisms. Systems should not be static; they should be able to constantly evolve. Thus, systems in themselves are insufficient. Organizations should build internal mechanisms that allow them to recognize change, explore potential responses to change, and develop and implement such responses.

Conclusion

As the case study is limited regarding the actual usage stage, we extrapolate from our data and take a broad view on our findings. In order to identify the nature of existing flexibility, we urge organizations to explore the various ways that individuals create flexibility, primarily through workarounds and interpretative flexibility. Further, in order to ensure that such flexibility is at least preserved when systems are replaced, experienced users should be directly involved in the development of new systems, and opportunities should be provided during implementation and used to actively explore situations in which system behavior is problematic.

Generally speaking, it is also important that organizations develop a culture that supports flexible response, admission of ignorance or uncertainty, and an appreciation, where appropriate, of such activities as workarounds as valuable sources of knowledge and insight.

Workarounds

One of the dominant issues in implementing ES is one of control—the locus of control lies with management, but also shifts in part toward the ES. This is shaped both through the ways in which ES prescribe and proscribe how the practices should be executed—in a normative manner—and the ways in which users are obliged or forced to use the system. Accordingly, behaviors that are required to make the system work, in the sense of workarounds, are seen as negative and subversive. We argue that those behaviors are essential and by prohibiting them, they will become "undercover" behaviors that management is not likely to be aware of. This can create serious problems when change is necessary, as the ways in which management understands the ES routines do not represent the actual work situation.

Interpretive Flexibility

Standardization also implies inertia—you don't standardize and then make it easy to abandon standardization. There is a conviction that often accompanies ES implementations that we can achieve some ideal representation that combines multiple representations—and can be recontextualized in multiply meaningful ways. We contend that this conviction is flawed. In fact, the representations we make use of are, of necessity, incomplete, vague, and ambiguous. However, this is not a drawback; such "limitations" allow for the flexible interpretation of routines and behaviors leading to flexibility and organizational agility. The fixation on a single standard approach to representation results in privileging:

> "Each standard and each category valorizes some point of view and silences another. This is not inherently a bad thing—indeed it is inescapable. But it is an ethical choice, and as such it is dangerous—not bad, but dangerous." (Bowker and Star, 1999, pp. 5–6)

Reflexivity

The integrated nature and higher visibility of information provided by ES establishes a need for higher levels of reflexivity in order to realize organizational benefits with ES (Elmes Strong, and Volkoff, 2005). We have also noted that there is a danger that ES may reduce the richness of the information available to individual decision makers. This may hamper the organization's ability to respond flexibly. It may limit the ability to explore and ask questions or see in what ways the organization (and its environment) may change and evolve. As routines are re-enacted, they may become habitual; you may only look for certain information and ignore information that may suggest that your response, your particular enactment, is inappropriate.

We have provided some initial indications as to how ES in general and ERP systems in particular may reduce the flexibility of organizations and hence impede their agility. We recognize that this position is contentious and we encourage researchers to conduct further research in this area.

References

Bondarouk, T. V. (2004). *Using Group Learning to Enhance the Implementation of Information Technology: The Results of Discourse Analysis*. Unpublished doctoral thesis, Enschede, Netherlands: University of Twente, Enschede.

Bowker, G. and Star, S. L. (1999). *Sorting Things Out: Classification and Its Consequences*. London, UK: MIT Press.

Elmes, M. B., Strong, D. M., and Volkoff, O. (2005). Panoptic empowerment and reflective conformity in enterprise systems-enabled organizations. *Information and Organization*, 15 (1), 1–37.

Kallinikos, J. (2004). Deconstruction information packages: Organizational and behavioural implications of ERP systems. *Information Technology & People*, 17 (1), 8–30.

Lengnick-Hall, C. A., Lengnick-Hall, M. L., and Abdinnour-Helm, S. (2004). The role of social and intellectual capital in achieving competitive advantage through enterprise resource planning (ERP) systems. *Journal of Engineering, Management & Technology*, 21 (4), 307–330.

Pollock, N. and Cornford, J. (2004). ERP systems and the university as a "unique" organisation. *Information Technology & People*, 17 (1), 31–52.

Scott, S. V. and Wagner, E. L. (2003). Networks, negotiations, and new times: The implementation of enterprise resource planning into an academic administration. *Information and Organization*, 13 (4), 285–313.

van Stijn, E. and Wensley, A. K. P. (2005). *Transferring ERP's best practices: An organizational memory mismatch approach*. Paper presented at the European conference on Organizational Knowledge, Learning and Capabilities (OKLC). Boston, MA.

Wagner, E. L. (2002). *Narrating an Organisational Matter of Fact: Negotiating with Enterprise Resource Planning Technology to Achieve Order within a Traditional Academic Administration*. PhD Dissertation. University of London, England.

Wagner, E. L. and Newell, S. (2004). "Best" for whom? The tension between "best practice" ERP packages and diverse epistemic cultures in a university context. *Journal of Strategic Information Systems*, 13 (4), 305–328.

15

Interpretative Flexibility and Hosted ERP Systems[1]

Sarah Cadili and Edgar A. Whitley

The large scale of enterprise resource planning (ERP) systems, coupled with their claims to provide "best practice" support for organizations, raises many new areas of interest. For example, it is common to speak of ERP systems as being *configured* rather than *programmed* and for any implementation problems to be seen as organizational rather than technological failings. As a result, ERP systems are very different from early centralized office data-processing systems or the later desktop computing and end-user computing.

There is a significant body of research devoted to the implementation of ERP systems (e.g., Howcroft and Truex III, 2001, 2002; Newell et al., 2003) as companies have increasingly opted for this generic packaged software in favor of custom-developed systems (Lucas, Walton, and Ginzberg, 1988). The prospect of replacing "home-grown" legacy systems with the integrated business solution offered by ERP systems (such as SAP/r3, PeopleSoft, and Oracle) has proved to be irresistible (Caldwell and Stein, 1998). The momentum that surrounded these "off-the-shelf" software packages in the 1990s is captured by what Ross (1998) terms "The Enterprise Resource Planning Revolution."

The majority of adopting organizations that have joined the "ERP bandwagon" (Kremers and Dissel, 2000) have presumed that with relative ease they can benefit from the alleged "best-of-suite solutions" that are embedded within the business processes of these generic packages (Robey and Boudreau, 1999b). The latest innovation enables global companies to host generic or customized SAP systems through networked servers across multiple sites.

Much of the published research on ERP systems has been about the specific benefits of the technology or particular features of their implementation in individual organizations (Francalanci, 2001; Murphy and Simon, 2002; Ragowksy and Somers, 2002). However, Lee (2000) argues for the information systems research community to try to develop a cumulative and current body of research findings "despite the never-ending onslaught of newly emerging technologies" (Lee 2000, p. viii) by using

[1] Material from this chapter originally appeared in "On the interpretative flexibility of hosted ERP systems," *Journal of Strategic Information Systems*, 14 (2005), 167–195.

the experiences with particular instantiations of the information technologies themselves to produce "contributions to theory" that emerge in the interactive system effects between the technological and the organizational.

- *The aim of this chapter is therefore to contribute to this tradition of conceptualizing the IT artifact through the study of ERP systems.*
- *This chapter presents an interpretive, impressionistic study of the implementation of hosted ERP systems in a division of a large multinational.*

When conceptualizing ERP systems as a form of technological artifact (Orlikowski and Iacono, 2001), a variety of approaches have been adopted in the literature. One common form, given the large-scale nature of the systems, has been adopted by Ciborra and associates (2000) who consider the technology as an information infrastructure and emphasize its large, interconnected nature and installed base (Star and Ruhleder, 1996). Viewing the system as an infrastructure highlights many similarities with institutions (Zucker, 1977; Scott, 2001; Avgerou, 2002;), and this notion is explored critically in the next section.

More generally, this chapter argues that ERP systems can be viewed through multiple lenses rather than through a single deterministic vision of what the system can or cannot do. Opening up the possibility of considering the systems flexibility, consequently opens up the possibility of flexible deployment of the system. In parallel, researchers can study ERP systems through a variety of theoretical lenses.

Literature Review

Technology as Institution

Until recently, the predominant logic employed in IS theory was deterministic (Robey and Boudreau, 1999a) with the assumption of an objective physical and social world that places technology in the role of an external agent that can exert "unidirectional, causal influences over humans and organizations" (Orlikowski, 1992, p. 400). The technological determinist view is a positivistic, technology-led theory of social change in which technology in general is seen as the fundamental premise underlying patterns of social organization (Heilbroner, 1994).

Deterministic theories adopted a narrow and objective lens in an attempt to identify a common relationship between technology and organization—a perspective that was clearly incomplete (Scott, 1987). Institutional theorists have attempted to address this shortcoming by directing "attention to the importance of symbolic aspects of organizations and their environments" (Scott, 1987, p. 507). They reflect and advance the stance that perceives no organization as a mere technical system, but as a social system that exists in an institutional environment that "delimits social reality" (Scott, 1987, p. 507).

Organizations become less expendable as they are infused with value, so participants actively seek to preserve them, promoting the persistence of structure over time (Scott, 1987). The definition of *institutionalization* is extended by Zucker (1977) to describe the point in the process when the meaning of an act or a technology is a "taken for granted" part of social reality. Thus, institutionalization is viewed as a social process by which participants come to accept an "objective and exterior" (Zucker, 1977, p. 728) definition of social reality whose validity is seen to be "independent of the actor's own views or actions" (Scott, 1987, p. 496).

Meyer and Rowan (1977) place great emphasis on the growth of "rational myths" or shared belief systems that give rise to the existence and elaboration of organizational forms. However, Meyer and Rowan recognize that organizations do not necessarily conform to a set of institutionalized beliefs purely because they "constitute reality" or are "taken-for-granted." A variety of processes may cause an organization to alter its structure in ways that make it conform to an institutional pattern (Scott, 1987), including the reward of increased legitimacy. According to Suchman (1995), legitimacy enhances both the stability and the comprehensibility of organizational activities and is intimately related to the process of institutionalization. Scott (2001) introduces three pillars of institutions—the Regulative Pillar, the Normative Pillar, and the Cultural–Cognitive Pillar—and he indicates that each of them provides a different basis for legitimacy and, hence, social conformance.

These pillars should be applicable not only to organizational structures, but to any institutional entity. Recent theory has indicated that information technology itself can assume the properties of an institution or a formative context as it takes shape in relation to other institutions of modern society (Ciborra, 1993, p. 31; Avgerou, 2002). According to this view, the legitimacy surrounding an information infrastructure, for example, is also a reflection of its embeddedness within a system of institutionalized beliefs and social scripts (Suchman, 1995).

Information infrastructures can be regarded as institutions or formative contexts (Ciborra, 1993) on the basis that they "constitute the background condition for action, enforcing constraints, giving direction and meaning, and setting the range of opportunities for undertaking action" (Ciborra and Hanseth, 1998, p. 315). The implication is that as they are "infused with value" they become more taken for granted and less expendable.

Institutional theorists have emphasized that the many dynamics of an organizational environment stem not from technological or material imperatives, but rather from cultural norms, symbols, beliefs, and rituals (Suchman, 1995). Nevertheless, there is an apparent neglect for the capacity of humans to intervene or resist the "overdetermined" (D'Andrade, 1984) structural and technological "constraints" on action. A determinist scenario is therefore implied within institutional theory that places technology and/or structure as the main protagonists, leaving a marginalized role for individual actors in the flow of events.

This logic would appear to collapse in the face of studies that demonstrate inconsistent effects from the same technology within a single organization (Buchanan and Boddy, 1983; Burkhardt and Brass, 1990; Orlikowski and Gash, 1994). In addition, many studies of groupware technologies have demonstrated the ways in which identical technologies are appropriated differently by different groups, thereby producing inconsistent effects (DeSanctis and Poole, 1994). Such contradictory outcomes emphasize the role of human agency and challenge the uniform effects that might have been expected with a deterministic logic.

Although the thrust of institutional theory has been to account for continuity and constraint in social structure, this need not exclude the ability of individual actors to create, maintain, and transform institutions (Scott, 2001). That is to say, structure and agency need not be separated and, indeed, an attempt is made to incorporate both elements in Giddens' Structuration Theory and Actor Network Theory.

Technology as Structure

Structuration Theory is advanced as an integrative meta-theory that incorporates both subjective and objective dimensions of social reality. Giddens (1979) introduces structuration as a social process that involves a reciprocal relationship between human actors and the structural properties of organizations. Although structure is believed to be both constraining and enabling, the theory of structuration rejects the terms in which structure appears as something "outside" or "external" to human action and, instead, structure is understood at a temporal level of analysis, in the "memory traces" (Giddens, 1984) of social actors. As such, structure and action are analytically related through the "duality of structure" to represent how the daily activity of social actors "draws upon and reproduces structural features of wider social systems" (Giddens, 1984, p. 24).

The related concept of agency refers to an actor's "transformative capacity" (Giddens, 1984), the ability to have some effect on the social world by altering the rules or the distribution of resources. There is a recognition that actors are both knowledgeable and reflexive and are thus able to monitor and account for their actions, even if unintended consequences result. This presence of agency "presumes a non-determinant, voluntaristic theory of action" (Scott, 2001, p. 76) that empowers actors "to 'act otherwise' . . . to intervene in the world, or to refrain from such intervention" (Giddens, 1984, p. 14). An element of choice is implicit in action, even where only one feasible option exists, because "awareness of such limitation, in conjunction with wants, supplies the reason for the agent's conduct" (Giddens, 1984, p. 309).

Structuration theory is therefore wholly in support of a more proactive role for individual and organizational actors, as well as a more reciprocal view of institutional processes (Scott, 2001). There is a rejection of the notion that institutions can exert unidirectional forces that can constrain actors in their daily lives, leaving them no option but to comply. Rather, the rules and resources that make up the structural properties of social systems are mediated and reaffirmed by human actors in their ongoing interaction with the world. Institutionalized properties have no objective existence, but are reinforced by the regular action of knowledgeable and reflexive actors (Orlikowski, 1992).

Structuration theory rejects the perspective that technology is an institution or a formative context in its own right. Instead, there is believed to be a reciprocal relationship through which users shape the technology structure that shapes their use. Thus, rather than structures being inscribed into technology and hence considered as external or independent of human agency, they emerge from the repeated and situated interaction with particular technologies (Orlikowski, 2000).

In the Structurational Model of Technology, Orlikowski (1992) proposes that:

> ". . . technology should be considered as one kind of structural property of organisations developing and/or using technology. That is, technology embodies and hence is an instantiation of some of the rules and resources constituting the structure of an organization." (Orlikowski, 1992, p. 405)

Orlikowski therefore equates technology with structure, and as such, she attributes a virtual existence to technology that can only be "made real" through its instantiation during use mode (Dobson, 2001; Orlikowski, 2000). That is to say, it is only through the appropriation of humans that technology can exert any influence.

Structuration theory is undoubtedly useful in defining the role and effects of agency, however in recent years it has been argued that its subjectivist ontology can make it difficult to account for technology as a material artifact that exists independently of social practices (Archer, 1995; Monteiro and Hanseth, 1996; Dobson, 2001).

Structuration theory is premised on the fact that humans and machines are not equivalent, and thus the enduring materiality of machines and their consequent capacity to affect future outcomes is unacknowledged. In effect, technological artifacts become relegated to the status of tools in the hands of knowledgeable human agents.

Pickering (1995, p. 169) argues that "technological innovations can indeed have an impact on the social," but he denies the "autonomy and causal privilege that technological determinism grants to machines." These two statements seemingly contradict each other because, as Kallinikos (2002, p. 287) argues, any effort to describe technology in a way that is "amenable to local reshaping" is frequently deemed deterministic in an indiscriminate manner (Winner, 1993).

Kallinikos (2002) maintains that there is a great diversity across technological artifacts and that whereas some

> "... technologies are embedded in complex and technological and institutional dependencies that limit their contextual adaptability ... others operate in relatively isolated settings, under conditions of considerable manipulability." (Kallinikos, 2002 p. 287)

This statement invites us to explore in more detail the distinctive status of particular technologies in addition to the unique character of situated factors.

An alternative reading of technology and structure is given by actor-network theory (Callon, 1991; Latour, 1996; Law and Hassard, 1998; Hanseth, Aanestad, and Berg, 2004). Methodologically, actor-network theory does not differentiate between human actors and nonhuman actors (such as ERP systems) and presents a performative view of society, where any outcome (such as an institution or system) is a contingent result, produced by the creation of temporary alliances and networks of heterogeneous actors. It therefore makes the researcher sensitive to the many different forms of work needed to create and maintain the network that we call a successful system (Wagner, 2002).

Actor-network theory (ANT) has origins in science studies and semiotics (Latour, 1999) and so shares many similarities with social shaping theories such as the social construction of technology (MacKenzie and Wajcman, 1999). It also, however, has important differences with theories like structuration (Latour, 2004), particularly because of the relative position given to human agency in Giddens' work and the differing views of modernity the two authors have (Latour, 1993). In light of these incompatibilities, this chapter will take a structurational rather than ANT perspective on the topic.

Technology and Interpretive Flexibility

A significant number of commentators have suggested that the malleability of technological artifacts tends to decrease as the degree of interconnectivity and interdependency increases (Hughes, 1994; Davenport, 1998; Orlikowski, 2000; Pozzebon and Pinsonneault, 2001). However, this decreased malleability is attributed to more than just the material constraints of the technology—the "perceived autonomy" (Rose and Truex III, 2000) that humans attribute to complex infrastructures; that is, the extent to which humans behave "as if" these infrastructures have autonomy or intentionality may in itself influence social practice.

The likelihood of technological change therefore becomes increasingly delimited by an agent's ability to understand the potential of a given technology (Orlikowski, 1992), that is, an agent's interpretive flexibility. Social constructionists argue that a given technology has interpretive flexibility (Brey, 1997) that allows for different interpretations of its functional and social-cultural properties (Avgerou, 2002). Technology is hence socially constructed such that perceptions of its properties are largely if not exclusively determined by the interpretive frameworks and negotiations of relevant social groups. "Stabilization" is said to have occurred when different social groups arrive at a similar interpretation of a technology (Pinch and Bijker, 1987). The rhetorical process of agreement on the true nature of a technology results in "closure" when the contents of a stabilized technology are "black-boxed" and then taken for granted (Brey, 1997).

Thus, for example, Pozzebon (2001), addresses prevailing discourses about the rhetorical closure of ERP packages (that is, the idea that a given artifact is not open to change because it is "well-defined, ready to use and able to set out the problem it sets out to solve" (p. 330)). To do this, she proposes to use interpretive flexibility, which she develops from Orlikowski (1992) and is defined as "the degree to which people perceive a given technology as changeable." This, in turn, depends on "(1) the technology's physical properties, (2) the users' knowledge, skills, and perceptions about the technology, and (3) the context in which users and technology interact" (Pozzebon, 2001, p. 331).

The first research issue, therefore, is to find evidence of the differing interpretations of the technology that exist in the organizational context.

The notion of interpretive flexibility has been widely used (Orlikowski, 1992; Hughes, 1994; Davenport, 1998; Rolland, 2000; Chae, 2001; Gow, 2003) to suggest that large information infrastructures tend to be less flexible than information systems due to the fact that they reduce users' interpretive flexibility (Chae, 2001).

This operationalization of interpretive flexibility is drawn from Orlikowksi (1992) who uses the term *interpretive flexibility* to "refer to the degree to which users of a technology are engaged in its constitution . . . during development or use." It is influenced by characteristics of the "material artifact," of the "human agents," and of the "context" (Orlikowski, 1992, p. 409). In particular, Orlikowski argues that the interpretive flexibility of any given technology is not infinite (Orlikowski and Gash, 1994).

An added complexity is the imminence of large-scale packaged software, such as SAP r/3, which has tended to increase the separation between technological design and use (Figure 15.1). According to Orlikowski (1992), the technology designers, influenced by the institutional properties of their organization *(arrow 1)*, construct a technology to meet their strategic goals *(arrow 2)*. Since these designers are involved in the "design mode" of the technology, they will tend to have a higher interpretive flexibility, and will therefore be less likely to treat the technology as "fixed." In the "use mode," technology will appear to influence users *(arrow 3)* as well as the institutional properties of the organization *(arrow 4)*.

The second research issue seeks to apply the time-space discontinuity to ERP systems and to explore the extent to which the hosted nature of the ERP system alters the perceived flexibility of such systems and to understand why a particular hosted implementation is "taken for granted" or has a low interpretive flexibility.

Within the context of researchers drawing upon earlier work of others, Barrett and Walsham (2004) present counterintuitive results. In their study of the use made of Star and Ruhleder's paper (Star and Ruhleder, 1996), they note that there was little use made by later texts of the central theories and concepts that, from the title and content of the paper, were meant to be key contributions.

Bearing these lessons in mind, the next section revisits the original notion of interpretative flexibility, as proposed by Bijker, Hughes, and Pinch (1987). This is not done to argue for a true meaning of words (Wittgenstein, 1976) or to suggest any

Figure 15.1

Analytical Separation of Design and Use for an Inherited Infrastructure*

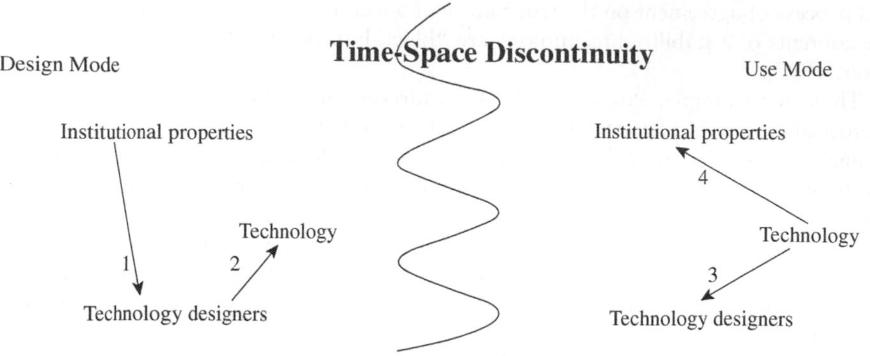

* From Orlikowski, 1992.

deliberate particular slippage in usage (Orlikowski uses interpretive flexibility throughout the paper, apart from one instance of interpretative flexibility (Orlikowski, 1992, p. 421), but to introduce the third research issue of the paper.

Interpretative Flexibility

Most uses of interpretive flexibility refer back to the collection of papers edited by Bijker, Hughes, and Pinch (1987) and particularly the paper by Pinch and Bijker (1987). This draws on work in the sociology of scientific knowledge and particularly the Empirical Programme of Relativism (EPOR) (Collins, 1981). The first stage of EPOR involves demonstration of the interpretative flexibility of scientific statements, that is, the way in which scientific findings are "open to more than one interpretation" (Pinch and Bijker, 1987, p. 27). In particular, they argue that this "shifts the focus for the explanation of scientific developments from the natural world to the social world." Where there is closure as to what the "truth" is in any particular instance, this is the result of consensus, and the second stage of the programme involves understanding the social mechanisms that limit interpretative flexibility. Collins (1981) is even more explicit: the approach "embraces an explicit relativism in which the natural world has a small or nonexistent role in the construction of scientific knowledge" (p. 3).

The fine-grained analysis of ANT lends itself to the discussion as a means of providing a more specific language for describing the "closure" of technical artifacts. According to ANT, closure results from the stabilization (or rhetorical agreement on the meaning or status) of an artifact. Stability is continually negotiated as a social process of aligning a diverse collection of interests (Hanseth and Braa, 1998) via translation (reinterpretation, representation) and inscription (patterns of use and design). Therefore, within a relevant social group, opinion is mobilized by various means, and successful networks of aligned interests are created by enrolling a sufficient body of allies (Walsham, 1997). Using the tenets of ANT to enrich the stages of EPOR, we can state that interpretative flexibility is amenable to social shaping through the alignment of diverse interests into one coherent "truth."

Figure 15.2

The Research Issues

- Is there evidence of differing interpretations of the technology?
- Are these differing interpretations driven by the time-space discontinuity or for other reasons?
- Is the evidence best understood as interpretive or interpretative flexibility?

Thus, the origins of interpretative flexibility do not relate to "the technology's physical properties" or the characteristics of the "material artifact." Thus, it is not appropriate to claim, as Sahay, Palit, and Robey (1994) do, that "information technology is more interpretively flexible than production technology" (p. 250) as this would imply that information technology has some special (material) flexibility that is not found in production technology. Reframing the case from an EPOR perspective, it would be necessary to consider how institutional- and network-based closure mechanisms have limited the interpretative flexibility of production technology in relation to information technology.

Thus the third research issue is to explore the extent to which what is being reported is interpretive flexibility (a materially constrained flexibility in the sense of Orlikowksi and Pozzebon) or interpretative flexibility (as originally described by Collins) and what the implications of these differing viewpoints are.

The three research issues are summarized in Figure 15.2.

Research Methodology

The research strategy was designed to emphasize the perceptions of key stakeholders (Pouloudi and Whitley, 1997), so the researcher adopted an interpretive, qualitative mode of inquiry to capture sensitively the social phenomena under investigation (Cavaye, 1996; Klein and Myers, 1999; Stredwick, 2001). A qualitative approach was adopted to study phenomena in terms of the meanings people bring to them (Denzin and Lincoln, 2000). Methods such as case study, ethnography, and action research can be employed to the study of social and cultural contexts through the eyes of their inhabitants (Wagner, 2002). The case study method is considered to be particularly useful when a natural setting or a focus on contemporary events is needed (Benbasat, Goldstein, and Mead, 1987), and, given the characteristics of the research site, a case research approach was chosen for this study.

A priori knowledge of the case was limited at the outset to a general idea that the accounting department being studied had recently initiated a project to introduce a hosted SAP system. Although this general information enabled the preparation of some initial open-ended questions, the boundaries of the phenomenon remained relatively unclear. That is, the researcher entered the field with a broad area of study but with no specific research question and so hoped to narrow the focus after conducting the initial interviews and observations. Such uncertainty is not uncommon before data collection has commenced (Strauss and Corbin, 1998), and case analysis is a valuable means to develop and refine concepts for further study (Cavaye, 1996).[2]

[2] For details on the research methodology, please see Cadili and Whitley (2005).

Background to the Case

The case firm, Petrolco (name disguised), is one of the largest multi-nationals in the world. The case study is based on the central accounting department (CAD) of a UK branch, being the only Petrolco site that has a nonoutsourced accounting function. The CAD provides its accounting services to 200 companies across all business segments, and this equates to a high level of specificity in their IS requirements. Within the CAD, there are three resource groups: the Processing Group (PG) handles all account "inputs," the Reporting Group (RG) handles the outputs of the accounting function, and the Systems Group (SG) manages the interfaces and data flows between the accounting packages and the rest of the business.

Early in 2003, the CAD was informed that they would be replacing their dispersed accounting systems with a SAP platform. A project group was set up in April 2003 to have the new system ready by January 1, 2004. The current system (Sun Systems) has been in place for almost five years, and CAD expected to upgrade to a new system within the next year. The initiative to introduce the packaged software was instigated by a senior management directive that is prompting business centers worldwide to adopt SAP as the new Petrolco standard. At the beginning of the project, there were two options available to CAD:

- *In-house hosting*: This would involve hosting the SAP server on-site and managing the database administration (DBA) with the existing systems specialists (the server itself would be managed by an outsourced company).
- *Off-site hosting*: This would involve hosting the SAP server at a different site that has already configured the software. There were two main options: one in the United States and the other in Europe.

At the end of July 2003, when the researcher began her investigations at Petrolco, the project was just coming to the end of the first "scoping" phase. This functioned mainly as a business and systems requirements gathering phase. The decision to host the server in-house had already been ruled out by this stage, and the main decision was therefore to choose between the two off-site locations. Each location offered a different configuration of SAP, and neither location matched CAD's requirements perfectly. Part of the scoping exercise was therefore to compile a comparator document that would compare and contrast the features of each location in relation to CAD's business requirements. The comparator was to be presented at the meeting of the Board of Governors in early July when one of the models was to be selected. However, at the meeting the Board requested more information and, at the time the study was completed, the decision had yet to be made.

The European site is based at a downstream and petrochemicals company that was recently acquired by Petrolco, giving them access to five new refineries and the region's largest fuel retailer. The European site was still undergoing a transition to SAP when the project at CAD commenced and they expected to go live with their new system in September 2003. The second location is based at a Petrolco site in the United States, which is home to a huge server farm that hosts most of the SAP instances across the United States.

Evidence and Discussion

This section presents selected excerpts from the interviews that address the research issues. The selection of interview data to present is guided by the research issues in conjunction with the concepts and categories generated from the data analysis.

Issue 1: Is There Evidence of Differing Interpretations?

The Central Accounting Department consisted of three different groups. Each of these groups had differing levels of involvement with the ERP decision, and interviews with members of each group revealed different views of what the technology could and could not do.

The processing group (PG) had a marginalized role within the project, and there was little direct input from the actual users. Instead, team leaders were expected to convey their business requirements in addition to carrying out the testing at a later stage of the project. A user from PG remarked in response to the question "What have you heard about SAP?":

> "Only that it's going to be implemented . . . Somebody who is on the project to implement our system wouldn't dream of thinking about what the Processing people do . . . they never consider that sort of thing."

The majority of the PG tended to see the SAP as an ominous, unchangeable entity:

> "I'm not very positive about the new system, we weren't happy when we got the current system (Sun) but we've had to work with it . . . it doesn't matter what we think, we just have to get on and use it." (User from PG)

The reporting group (RG) also saw the system as unchangeable, but their outlook was "to mimic the existing requirements with as minimal disruption as possible" (Accounting Clerk from RG). The majority of users from RG were unaware of the differences between the hosting options, and, on the whole, users were mainly concerned about changes to their individual work processes:

> "Most people would just accept the way that we have to work as being beyond their control." (Accounting Clerk from RG)

However, an accounting clerk from RG explained that the hosted implementation could constrain his existing way of working:

> "We have certain controls over the (data warehouse) environment and it's driven by us—the problem is that if we go to something that's not in-house, we might not have the same control in terms of what we can get out."

Issue 2: How Important Is the Time-Space Discontinuity?

Orlikowksi's operationalization of the notion of interpretive flexibility emphasizes the time-space discontinuity between the design and use of a system. Thus, the differing interpretations of PG and RG could be a result of the roles they play in the project team. The project team consisted of business and technical personnel from different departments of CAD in addition to the 7 to 8 SAP consultants, all of whom were highly involved throughout the design phase.

This tightly knit culture of the project team encouraged its members to form a shared perception of the new SAP implementation. They also had the power to withhold a certain amount of information from the rest of CAD, as illustrated by the following comment:

> "The core project team are the ones making the decisions . . . it's hard to make decisions when you're trying to get everyone up to speed. . . it's just knowing what people to involve at what stage." (Project Manager)

The comparator document, which was created during the scoping phase of the project, contributed to these shared meanings and perceptions. The comparator provided what was viewed to be an objective view of CAD's business requirements in relation to the functionality offered by the two potential systems (in the United States or Europe).

Thus, it would seem reasonable that those members of CAD not involved in the project team and with limited knowledge of what the system could do would have different interpretations of the technology from those who were more closely involved. It does not, however, help with the explanation of the differences between the responses of RG and PG. For them, the technology was the same (unknown) system, yet their responses were very different. We will return to this point later.

Orlikowski's separation of design/use is further challenged when the focus of attention moved from the decision to go for a hosted ERP system to the choice of which hosting environment to use.

The site in the United States was established in 1967 and houses a large data center, with approximately 600 servers that network most of the Petrolco SAP systems across the country. The U.S. division is not new to hosting SAP implementations, as one member of SG described:

> "In terms of running it, (U.S. site) can do it with their hands tied because they run the whole of U.S. accounting virtually."

This considerable experience with hosting the U.S. implementations was seen as a double-edged sword. There is a sense that since the systems in the United States have "been up and running in the U.S. for so long . . . it's very, very safe." However, the longevity of the infrastructure has fueled the perception that the U.S. system will be less flexible:

> "(U.S. site) is live but very old and . . . we may have to stick with what they're offering or not have them at all." (Project Manager)

The U.S. site has been established for so long that it has become increasingly difficult for them to make changes to their systems without reverberations from their other clients. However, accepting their system as it is could have a huge impact on CAD's work processes and, consequently, their own clients.

The SG representative on the project team confirmed this:

> "They (U.S. site) have got clients set up in a certain way and they require everyone to follow their standards, and obviously that would give us less flexibility."

The project manager disclosed during a telephone interview that if chosen, their system could constrain CAD in a number of ways: They lacked the functionality to handle CAD's billing requirements, and they were reluctant to make changes because their own clients would be affected by alterations to the system.

The European location has been developed very recently, and the majority of development work has taken place in parallel with the project at CAD. The European site is itself a server farm, and there is a project under way to network their SAP instance to a number of countries in Europe. They will host their SAP configuration across Petrolco divisions in Europe, and they will provide the infrastructure and back-up support for all the sites that utilize their hosted implementation. In a sense, they will perform a continental hosting role similar to the U.S. site, but have yet to "go live" with their infrastructure.

They were due to be up and running by September 2003 and this presented a risk, particularly since CAD's own target was for January 2004. However, since the European site was still developing their system, they had as yet no other clients and there has been a general perception that:

"The European site is open and new and we can model it slightly; they are going one way and so we may have to ask them to model it slightly towards us . . . they are still developing it, we feel that we can influence it more so that we can get our bits from it and they can get their bits from it (Project Manager)."

"We don't know what we are inheriting; it's not proven—so how do we know it's a quality solution? Nobody knows yet; it hasn't gone live so it's a big worry and we're trying to rush this thing forward on an unproven system." (SG Team Leader)

Issue 3: On the Role of Materiality and Interpre*ta*tive Flexibility

The distinction between *interpretive* and *interpretative* flexibility can be restated as a discussion of whether the materiality of the technology plays any role. Orlikowski (1992) and Pozzebon (2001) have argued explicitly that material features of the technology do play a role. In contrast, MacKenzie (1987) presents four responses to claims that the interpretative flexibility is more limited for technology. First, he argues that many disagreements take place during the design phase, whereas the criterion of working is an *ex post facto* one; second, even what counts as working is problematic (Collins and Pinch, 1998); third, the range of factors that will typically be required for a technology to work (social, economic, and technological) is so large that it may not be obvious what the cause of failure is; and finally that a working technology does not necessarily confirm the rightness of every decision taken in its design (MacKenzie, 1987).

Thus the representatives from CAD who were not involved in the project gave differing interpretations of what the technology could and could not do, despite receiving the same minimal information about the functionalities and capabilities of the technology. Thus, to paraphrase Collins, the technology has a "small or nonexistent role" in the construction of the interpretations of the ERP system.

Through the development of the comparator document, the project team had access to far more resources about the systems than the rest of CAD, and they were able to make decisions based on these resources. Project members worked closely with the SAP consultants as well as the systems representatives and therefore had more exposure to the technological aspects of the hosted implementations. Nevertheless, the limited explanatory role played by the technology is also clearly visible in the discussion of the various hosting options. In the U.S. case, the experience with hosting previous SAP systems is seen as evidence that they are less likely to be able to allow CAD to modify the system to meet its own needs while the lack of experience with hosting SAP systems in Europe is seen as making them more likely to be flexible. If the materiality of the technology did play an explanatory role, then an equally plausible argument would be that those who were familiar with the technology would be more likely to know what it was capable of achieving.

According to Orlikowski (1992), the key factor influencing interpretive flexibility is the relationship with the design of the system. Pozzebon and Pinsonneault (2001) suggest that interpretive flexibility is "the degree to which people perceive a given technology as changeable" and argue that those involved in the design stages of a system (especially before the system is finalized) are more likely to view a system as changeable than those only exposed to the end product. The project team perceived the system in the United States to be *less* flexible than the European system. This finding is confusing for two reasons: (1) the project team had been equally separated from the configuration of both systems, and (2) both systems "meet the majority of (CAD's) requirements" (SG team leader). If the decision between these two systems was so close, how has this discrepancy in perception occurred?

The logic presented by the project team is that the U.S. instance of SAP was designed over seven years ago and since then numerous clients have been networked to its "existing setup." If CAD selected this model for their main accounting system, they too would be required to "fit in with that setup" (SG team leader). Since the U.S. site is well established, it has become part of a highly interdependent and complex network of players. The increased intricacy and internetworking that has accompanied the growth of the infrastructure has "narrowed the range of alternative uses that may be crafted" with it (Orlikowski, 2000, p. 409). Moreover, as the community using this model grows, stakeholders at the U.S. site realize that any alterations to their system will cause huge coordination problems for their own clients (Hanseth, 2000).

However, the problem is not solely confined to the technical aspects of their infrastructure, as one project member explains: "It's not that they can't change, they've just got a lot of clients all following the same methods." By standardizing the use of their technology, the U.S. stakeholders hope to retain their own and their clients' existing way of doing things, with no discernible changes in work practices or the system itself. This type of enactment is characterized in terms of inertia and has resulted in the reinforcement and preservation of the structural status quo (Orlikowski, 2000). Through these self-reinforcing mechanisms, the system has become a taken-for-granted fixture of the U.S. organization and has become institutionalized (Selznick, 1957; Zucker, 1977).

Stakeholders at the U.S. site therefore perceive their own system to be less malleable. Through a process of negotiation, these stakeholders have influenced how the project team has come to view the system: "We don't have any flexibility with [U.S. site]" (SG team leader).

The distinguishing feature of the European instance of SAP is that it is part of an infrastructure that is still early in its development. The system itself will not "go live" until September 2003 and therefore, adaptations that are made on behalf of CAD will not affect any clients, as illustrated by the following comment:

> "We will have our own unique piece of this machine which is very configurable and we can then do what we like with just that piece. It will not impact or be impacted by other people on that machine." (SG Team Leader)

In addition, the European location has yet to be networked with clients in Europe, and it is therefore situated in an environmental context that is subject to relatively fewer institutional dependencies than the U.S. model. The fact that the European system is still undergoing development also suggests that SAP consultants continue to work with the technical specialists at the European site, which may have lifted their overall sense of the flexibility of the installation.

To a large extent, this high level of interpretative flexibility explains why stakeholders at the European site are more willing to accommodate CAD's requirements. Through an ongoing process of negotiation, these designers have influenced how the project team has come to view the European system: "We have been led to believe that we will have virtually complete control of the machine" (SG team leader).

Conclusion

The interplay between agency, technology, and structure has shifted in emphasis throughout the decades as new theories have emerged. A summary of these changes is depicted in Figure 15.3. The early technological determinist theories placed an undue

Figure 15.3

The Changing Emphasis of Agency, Technology, and Structure

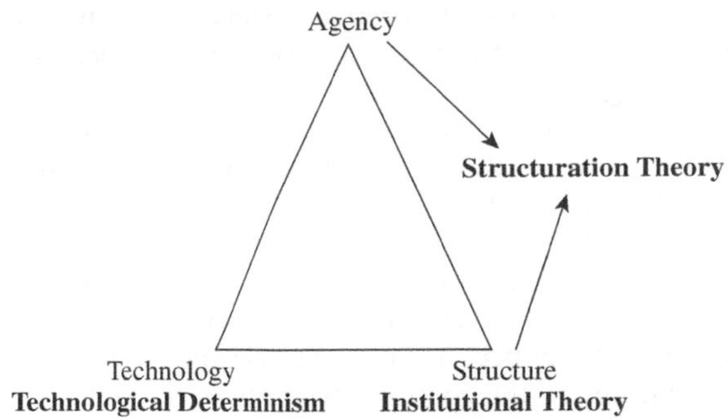

emphasis on the influence of technology with minimal appreciation for the role of structure or agency. In an attempt to correct this imbalance, institutional theorists have stressed relativity and situation dependence and have refocused our attention on the structural influences on society. Yet with the role of interpretation and perception downplayed, humans are rendered passive to the structural forces at work.

Structuration theory is advanced as a compelling and original attempt to incorporate both structure and agency within an interdependent duality. However, its application to technology has instigated a vigorous and sustained debate within the IS field because it has been argued that in describing the structural properties of technology, one diverges from Giddens' (1979) temporal vision of social structure (Walsham and Han, 1991; Archer, 1995; Dobson, 2001). This debate has been fueled by recent claims that large and complex information infrastructures can restrict the malleability of users (Star and Ruhleder, 1996; Volkoff, 1999; Ciborra et al., 2000; Orlikowski, 2000; Dobson, 2001; Pozzebon and Pinsonneault, 2001).

This study has attempted to consolidate Giddens' (1984) conception of the knowledgeable and reflexive human actor and the literature devoted to information infrastructures by emphasizing the role of human perception. Interpretative flexibility represents an agent's knowledge and reflexivity in relation to technology, and hence the conditions that limit the interpretative flexibility of an agent can simultaneously reduce an agent's scope for action.

This research has shown some consistency with existing studies in the field. In particular, it has shown that users of the system who do not have detailed knowledge of the new technology are likely to have different interpretations of it from those who are involved in design decisions. The results also show some divergence with the literature, particularly with regard to the hosted nature of the ERP systems. Here, analytical distinctions between design and use are no longer as convenient or informative as they once were (Orlikowski, 1992).

By providing an alternative explanation of the reasons for these differing perceptions, the paper argues that information systems researchers will benefit from returning to the original understanding of interpretative flexibility that specifically does not include any consideration of material features of the technology rather than relying on the adapted notion of interpretive flexibility that somehow claims a significant role for the specifics of the technology.

The findings of this research indicate that as an information infrastructure grows larger and more interconnected its malleability is perceived to decrease. In addition, the time-space discontinuity between the design and use of hosted implementations can encourage client organizations to adopt a similar perception to the technology as the host. That is to say, the host's interpretive flexibility, influenced by the size, complexity, and interconnectivity of their information infrastructure, can influence client perceptions via processes of negotiation. Information infrastructures do not impose a deterministic force upon agents and their organizations. Rather, constraint is perceived and propagated in the minds of those in contact with the technology, influencing the eventual interaction with material agency.

More generally, the paper has shown that there are many differing interpretations of the same hosted technologies and has argued that these differing perceptions are not due to specific features of the technology. As a result, they challenge management views of ERP systems that see them as unchangeable and deterministic.

It is recognized that due to the context-specificity of technological artifacts "there is no single, one–size–fits–all conceptualisation . . . that will work for all studies." It is therefore accepted that the findings from this case study are phenomena in their own right and may not necessarily be applicable in a generalized sense (Gadamer, 1975; Mol and Law, 2002; Lee and Baskerville, 2003). Further, the findings of this case study represent a single period of time during the early phase of the project at Petrolco. The research would have been enriched if the case study had been followed through until implementation and perhaps beyond, to analyze changes in the perception of agents.

There is scope for further research to develop the cultural and contextual influences on interpretative flexibility and how this can affect infrastructural development, particularly in light of the trend toward hosted implementations. Indeed, it would be interesting to explore whether the implementation of hosted systems will encourage adopting clients to mimic the organizational structure of the host. The field could also benefit from further empirical work to ascertain the subtle difference in perception toward more general information infrastructures and the newer, hosted breeds.

References

Ancona, D. (1990). Outward bound: Strategies for team survival in an organization. *Academy of Management Review*, 33 (2), 334–365.

Archer, M. (1995). *Realist Social Theory: The Morphogenetic Approach*. Cambridge, UK: Cambridge University Press.

Avgerou, C. (2002). *Information Systems and Global Diversity*. Oxford, UK: Oxford University Press.

Barrett, M. and Walsham, G. (2004). Making contributions from interpretive case studies: Examining processes of construction and use. In *Information Systems Research: Relevant Theory and Informed Practice* (Kaplan, B., et al., eds.) (pp. 293–314). Boston: Kluwer.

Benbasat, I., Goldstein, D. K., and Mead, M. (1987). The case research strategy in studies of information systems. *MIS Quarterly*, 11 (3), 369–386.

Bijker, W. E., Hughes, T. P., and Pinch, T. (eds.) (1987). *The Social Construction of Technological Systems: New Directions in the Sociology and History of Technology*. Cambridge, MA: MIT Press.

Brey, P. (1997). *Philosophy of Technology Meets Social Constructivism. Techne: Journal of the Society for Philosophy and Technology*, 2 (3–4). Retrieved from: http://scholar.lib.vt.edu/ejournals/SPT/v2n3n4/brey.html

Bryant, A. (2002). Grounding systems research: Re-establishing grounded theory. In *Proceedings of the Thirty-Fifth Hawaii International Conference on System Sciences*, Big Island, HI, IEEE Computer Society Press, Vol. 8 (p. 253c).

Buchanan, D. A. and Boddy, D. (1983). Advanced technology and the quality of working life: The effects of computerized controls on biscuit-making operators. *Journal of Occupational Psychology*, 56 (1), 109–119.

Burkhardt, M. E. and Brass, J. D. (1990). Changing patterns or patterns of change: The effects of a change in technology on social network structure and power. *Administrative Science Quarterly*, 35 (1), 104-127.

Cadili, S. and Whitley, E. A. (2005). On the interpretative flexibility of hosted ERP systems. *Journal of Strategic Information Systems*, 14 (2), 167–195.

Caldwell, B. and Stein, T. (1998). Beyond ERP: New IT agenda. *InformationWeek*, November 30, 1998.

Callon, M. (1991). Techno-economic networks and irreversibility. In *A sociology of monsters: Essays on power, technology and domination* (J. Law, ed.) (pp. 132–161). London, UK: Routledge.

Cavaye, A. L. M. (1996). Case study research: A multi-faceted research approach for IS. *Information Systems Journal*, 6 (3), 227–242.

Chae, B. (2001). Technology adaptation: The case of Large-Scale Information Systems. In *International Conference on Information Systems* (Storey, V, Sarkar, S., and DeGross, J. I., eds.) (pp. 581–585). New Orleans, LA.

Charmaz, K. (2000). Grounded theory: Objectivist and constructivist methods. In *Handbook of Qualitative Research*, 2nd ed. (Denzin N. and Lincoln, Y., eds.) (pp. 509–535). London, UK: Sage.

Ciborra, C. U. (1993). *Teams, Markets and Systems: Business Innovation and Information Technology*. Cambridge, UK: Cambridge University Press.

Ciborra, C. U. and Hanseth, O. (1998). From tool to gestell: Agendas for managing the information infrastructure. *Information Technology and People*, 11 (4), 305–327.

Ciborra, C. U., et al. (2000). *From Control to Drift: The Dynamics of Corporate Information Infrastructure*. Oxford, UK: Oxford University Press.

Collins, H. M. (1981). Stages in the empirical programme of relativism. *Social Studies of Science*, 11 (1), 3–10.

Collins, H. and Pinch, T. (1998). *The Golem at Large: What You Should Know About Technology*. Cambridge, UK: Cambridge University Press.

D'Andrade, R. G. (1984). Cultural meaning systems. In *Culture Theory, Essays on Mind, Self and Emotion* (Shweder, R. and LeVine, R., eds.) (pp. 88–119). Cambridge, UK: Cambridge University Press.

Davenport, T. (1998). Putting the enterprise into the enterprise system. *Harvard Business Review*, 76 (4), 121–131.

Denzin, N. and Lincoln, Y. (2000). Introduction: The discipline and practice of qualitative research. In *Handbook of Qualitative Research, 2nd ed.* (Denzin, N. and Lincoln, Y., eds.), (pp. 1–28), Thousand Oaks, CA: Sage.

DeSanctis, G. and Poole, M. S. (1994). Capturing the complexity in advanced technology use: Adaptive structuration theory. *Organization Science*, 5 (2), 121–147.

Dobson, P. J. (2001). Investigating ERP systems using structuration theory—A critique. In *Proceedings of The Second International We-B Conference* (pp. 73–82). Perth/ Western Australia, November 29–30, 2001.

Eisenhardt, K. M. (1989). Building theories from case study research. *Academy of Management Review*, 14 (4), 532–550.

Francalanci, C. (2001). Predicting the implementation effort of ERP projects: Empirical evidence on SAP/R3. *Journal of Information Technology*, 16 (1), 33–48.

Gadamer, H-G. (1975). *Truth and Method*. London, UK: Sheed & Ward.

Giddens, A. (1979). *Central Problems in Social Theory: Action, Structure and Contradiction in Social Analysis*. London, UK: Macmillan.

Giddens, A. (1984). *The Constitution of Society: Outline of the Theory of Structuration*. Berkeley, CA: University of California Press.

Glaser, B. and Strauss, A. (1967). *The Discovery of Grounded Theory: Strategies of Qualitative Research*. London, UK: Weidenfeld and Nicolson.

Goulding, C. (1999). Grounded Theory: Some reflections on paradigm, procedures and misconceptions. *Working Paper*, No. WP006/99. Retrieved from: http://asp2.wlv.ac.uk/wbs/documents/mrc/Working%20Papers%201999/WP006-99%20Goulding.pdf.

Gow, G. (2003). Canadian telecommunications policy and the national disaster mitigation strategy: Observing wireless enhanced 9-1-1. *Unpublished PhD thesis*. British Columbia, Canada: School of Communication, Simon Fraser University.

Hanseth, O. (2000). The economics of standards. In *From Control to Drift: The dynamics of Corporate Information Infrastructure* (Ciborra, C. U., ed.) (pp. 56–70). Oxford, UK: Oxford University Press.

Hanseth, O. and Braa, K. (1998). Technology as traitor: Emergent SAP infrastructure in a global organization. In *Proceedings of International Conference on Information Systems* (R. Hirschheim, R. Newman, M. and DeGross, J. I., eds.) (pp. 188–196). Helsinki, Finland.

Hanseth O, Aanestad, M., and Berg, M. (2004). Special issue on Actor network theory and information systems. *IT and People*, 17 (2).

Heilbroner, R. L. (1994). Do machines make history? In *Does Technology Drive History? The Dilemma of Technological Determinism* (Smith, M. R. and Marx, L., eds.) (pp. 53–65). Cambridge, MA: The MIT Press.

Howcroft, D. and Truex III, D. (2001/2002). Special issue on critical analyses of ERP systems: The macro level. *The Database for Advances in Information Systems*, 32/4–33/1.

Hughes, T. P. (1994). Technological momentum. In *Does Technology Drive History? The Dilemma of Technological Determinism* (Smith, M. R. and Marx, L., eds.) (pp. 101–113). Cambridge, MA: The MIT Press.

Kallinikos, J. (2002). Reopening the black box of Technology artifacts and human agency. In *Twenty-Third International Conference on Information Systems, 2002* (Applegate, L., Galliers, R. D., and Gross, J. I. D., eds.) (pp. 287–294). Barcelona, Spain.

Klein, H. K. and Myers, M. D. (1999). A set of principles for conducting and evaluating interpretive field studies in information systems. *MIS Quarterly*, 23 (1), 67–93.

Kremers, M. and Dissel, H. (2000). Enterprise resource planning: ERP system migrations. *Communications of the ACM*, 43 (4), 53–56.

Latour, B. (trans. C. Porter). (1993). *We Have Never Been Modern*. New York: Harvester Wheatsheaf.

Latour, B. (trans. C. Porter). (1996). *Aramis, or the Love of Technology*. Cambridge, MA: Harvard University Press.

Latour, B. (1999). *Pandora's Hope: Essays on the Reality of Science Studies*. Cambridge, MA: Harvard University Press.

Latour, B. (2004). *Why ANT Is not Compatible with Structuration Theory*. Personal communication.

Law, J. and Hassard, J (eds.). (1998). *Actor Network Theory and After*. Oxford, UK: Blackwell.

Lee, A. S. (2000). Editor's comments: Researchable directions for ERP and other new technologies. *MIS Quarterly*, 24 (1), iii–viii.

Lee, A. S. and Baskerville, R. L. (2003). Generalizing generalizability in information systems research. *Information Systems Research*, 14 (3), 221–243.

Leonard-Barton, D. A. (1990). A dual methodology for case studies: Synergistic use of a longitudinal single site with replicated multiple sites. *Organizational Science*, 1 (3), 248–266.

Lucas, H. C., Walton, E. R., and Ginzberg, M. J. (1988). Implementing packaged software. *MIS Quarterly*, 12 (4), 537–549.

MacKenzie, D. (1987). Missile accuracy: A case study in the social processes of technological change. In *The Social Construction of Technological Systems: New Directions in the Sociology and History of Technology* (Bijker, W. E., Hughes, T. P., and Pinch, T. J., eds.) (pp. 195–222). Cambridge, MA: MIT Press.

MacKenzie, D. and Wajcman, J. (1999). Preface to the second edition. In *The Social Shaping of Technology, 2nd ed.* (MacKenzie, D. and Wajcman, J., eds.) (Second edition) (pp. xiv–xvii). Buckingham, UK: Open University Press.

Martin, P. Y. and Turner, B. A. (1986). Grounded theory and organizational research. *The Journal of Applied Behavioural Science*, 22 (2), 141–157.

Meyer, J. W. and Rowan, B. (1977). Institutional organizations: Formal structure as myth and ceremony. *American Journal of Sociology*, 83 (2), 340–363.

Miles, M. B. (1979). Qualitative data as an attractive nuisance: The problem of analysis. *Administrative Science Quarterly*, 24 (4), 590–601.

Mlcakova, A. and Whitley, E. A. (2004). Configuring peer-to-peer software: An empirical study of how users react to the regulatory features of software. *European Journal of Information Systems*, 13 (2), 95–102.

Mol, A. and Law, J. (2002). Complexities: An introduction. In *Complexities: Social Studies of Knowledge Practices* (Law, J. and Mol, A., eds.) (pp. 1–22). Durham: Duke University Press.

Monteiro, E. and Hanseth, O. (1996). Social shaping of information infrastructure: On being specific about the technology. In *Information technology and changes in organizational work* (Orlikowksi, W. J., et al., eds.) (pp. 325–343). Cambridge, UK: Chapman and Hall.

Murphy, K. and Simon, S. J. (2002). Intangible benefits valuation in ERP projects. *Information Systems Journal*, 12 (4), 301–320.

Newell, S., et al. (2003). Implementing enterprise resource planning and knowledge management systems in tandem: Fostering efficiency and innovation complementarity. *Information and Organization*, 13 (1), 25–52.

Orlikowski, W. J. (1992). The Duality of Technology: Rethinking the Concept of Technology in Organizations. *Organizational Science* 3 (3), 398–427.

Orlikowski, W. J. (1993). CASE tools as organizational change: Investigating incremental and radical changes in systems development. *MIS Quarterly*, 17 (3), 309–340.

Orlikowski, W. J. (2000). Using technology and constituting structures: A practice lens for studying technology in organizations. *Organizational Science*, 11 (4), 404–428.

Orlikowski, W. J. and Gash, D. C. (1994). Technological frames: Making sense of information technology in organizations. *ACM Transactions Information Systems*, 12 (2), 174–207.

Orlikowski, W. J. and Iacono, S. C. (2001). Research commentary: Desperately seeking the "IT" in IT research: A call to theorizing the IT artifact. *Information Systems Research*, 12 (2), 121–134.

Pettigrew, A. M. (1990). Longitudinal fieldwork research on change: Theory and practice. *Organizational Science*, 1 (3), 267–292.

Pickering, A. (1995). *The Mangle of Practice: Time, Agency, and Science*. Chicago: The University of Chicago Press.

Pinch, T. J. and Bijker, W. E. (1987). The social construction of facts and artifacts: Or how the sociology of science and the sociology of technology might benefit each other. In *The Social Construction of Technological Systems: New Directions in the Sociology and History of Technology* (Bijker, W. E., Hughes, T. P., and Pinch, T. J., eds.) (pp. 17–50). Cambridge, MA: The MIT Press.

Pouloudi, A. and Whitley, E. A. (1997). Stakeholder identification in inter-organizational systems: Gaining insights for drug use management systems. *European Journal of Information Systems*, 6 (1), 1–14.

Pozzebon, M. (2001). Demystifying the rhetorical closure of ERP packages. In *Proceedings of the Twenty-Second International Conference on Information Systems (ICIS)* (Storey, V., Sarkar, S., and DeGross, J. I., eds.) (pp. 329–337). New Orleans, LA.

Pozzebon, M. and Pinsonneault, A. (2001). Structuration theory in the IS field: An assessment of research strategies. In *Proceedings of the Ninth European Conference on Information Systems* (Smithson, S., et al., eds.) (pp. 205–216). Bled, Slovenia: Moderna organizacjia.

Ragowksy, A. and Somers, T. M. (2002). Special issue on ERP. *Journal of Management Information Systems*, 19 (1).

Robey, D. and Boudreau, M-C. (1999a). Accounting for the contradictory organizational consequences of information technology: Theoretical directions and methodological implications. *Information Systems Research*, 10 (2), 167–185.

Robey, D. and Boudreau, M-C. (1999b). Organizational transition to enterprise resource planning systems: Theoretical choices for process research. In *Proceedings of the Twentieth International Conference on Information Systems* (De, P. and DeGross, J. I., eds.) (pp. 291–299). Charlotte, NC.

Rolland, K. H. (2000). Challenging the installed base: Deploying a large-scale IS in a global organization. In *Proceedings of the Eighth European Conference on Information Systems* (Hansen, H. R., Bichler, M., and Mahrer, H., eds.) (pp. 583–590). Vienna, Austria.

Rose, J. and Truex III, D. (2000). Machine agency as perceived autonomy: An action perspective. In *Organizational and Social Perspectives on Information Technology* (R. Baskerville, Stage, J., and DeGross, J. I., eds.) (pp. 371–390). Aalborg, Denmark: Kluwer.

Ross, J. (1998). *The ERP Revolution: Surviving versus Thriving*. MIT CISR Working Paper 307, November. Retrieved from http://mitsloan.mit.edu/cisr/papers.php

Sahay, S., Palit, M., and Robey, D. (1994). A relativist approach to studying the social construction of information technology. *European Journal of Information Systems*, 3 (4), 248–258.

Scott, W. R. (1987). The adolescence of institutional theory. *Administrative Science Quarterly*, 32 (4), 493–511.

Scott, W. R. (2001). *Institutions and Organizations* (2nd edition). London, UK: Sage.

Selznick, P. (1957). *Leadership in Administration: A sociological interpretation*. New York: Harper and Row.

Skodel-Wilson, H. and Amber-Hutchinson, S. (1996). Methodological mistakes in grounded theory. *Nursing Research*, 45 (2), 122–124.

Star, S. L. and Ruhleder, K. (1996). Steps toward an ecology of infrastructure: Design and access for large information spaces. *Information Systems Research*, 7 (1), 111–134.

Stern, P. N. (1994). Eroding grounded theory. In *Critical Issues in Qualitative Research Methods* (Morse, J., ed.) (pp. 212–223). Thousand Oaks, CA: Sage.

Strauss, A. and Corbin, J. (1998). *Basics of Qualitative Research: Techniques and Procedures for Developing Grounded Theory* (2nd edition). London, UK: Sage.

Stredwick, R. (2001). *Epistemological boundaries and methodological confusions in postmodern consumer research*. Working Paper WP 001/01. Retrieved from asp2.wlv.ac.uk/wbs/documents/mrc/Working%20Papers%202001/WP001_01_Stredwick.pdf

Suchman, M. C. (1995). Managing legitimacy: Strategic and institutional approaches. *Academy of Management Review*, 20 (3), 571–610.

Volkoff, O. (1999). Using the structurational model of technology to analyze an ERP Implementation. In *Proceedings of the Fifth Americas Conference on Information Systems* (pp. 235–237), August 13–15, 1999. Milwaukee, WI.

Wagner, E. (2002). Narrating an organizational matter of fact: Negotiating with Enterprise Resource Planning Technology to achieve order within a traditional academic administration. *Unpublished PhD Thesis*.

Walsham, G. (1997). Actor-network theory and IS research: Current status and future prospects. In *Information Systems and Qualitative Research* (Lee, A. S., Liebenau, J., and DeGross, J. I., eds.) (pp. 466–480). Philadelphia: Chapman and Hall.

Walsham, G. and Han, C-K. (1991). Structuration theory and information systems research. *Journal of Applied Systems Analysis*, 17 (1), 77–85.

Winner, L. (1993). Upon opening the black box and finding it empty: Social constructivism and the philosophy of technology. *Science, Technology and Human Values*, 18 (3), 362–378.

Wittgenstein, L. (trans. G. Anscombe). (1976). *Philosophical Investigations*. Oxford, UK: Basil Blackwell.

Yin, R. K. (1989). *Case Study Research: Design and Methods*. Beverly Hills, CA: Sage.

Zucker, L. G. (1977). The role of institutionalization in cultural persistence. *American Sociological Review*, 42 (5), 726–743.

Agile Drivers, Capabilities, and Value: An Over-Arching Assessment Framework for Systems Development

Kieran Conboy and Brian Fitzgerald

The formation of the Agile Alliance in 2001 and the publication of the Agile Manifesto (Fowler and Highsmith, 2001) formally introduced agility to the field of Information Systems Development (ISD). Those involved sought to "restore credibility to the word *method*" (Fowler and Highsmith, 2001). The Agile Manifesto presented an industry-led vision for a profound shift in the ISD paradigm, through 12 principles. The Manifesto and its principles represent quite a popular initiative that actually complements the critique of formalized ISD methods over the past decade or so (Baskerville, Travis, and Truex, 1992; Fitzgerald, 1994, 1996), and have been well received by practitioners and academics.

However, there are a number of critical issues in the field, all of which revolve around a lack of rigour and cohesion. First, many definitions of an agile method exist. Researchers often use the same term to refer to different concepts and different terms to refer to the same concept. However, this is not surprising given that Information Systems (IS) researchers cannot even reach consensus on the definitions of the most basic terms such as *information system*, *method*, and *technique*. In fact, Sharafi and Zhang (1999), Towill and Christopher (2002), and Vokurka and Fliedner (1998) have explicitly illustrated this issue in the case of the term *agility*.

Second, many agile methods exist, such as *eXtreme Programming* (*XP*) (Beck, 1999), *Dynamic Systems Development Method* (*DSDM*) (Stapleton, 1997); *SCRUM* (Schwaber and Beedle, 2002); *Crystal* (Cockburn, 2001); *Agile Modelling* (Ambler, 2002); *Feature Driven Design* (Coad, de Luca, and Lefebre, 1999); *Lean Programming* (Poppendieck, 2001), and perhaps even the *Rational Unified Process* (*RUP*) (Kruchten, 2000), all categorized as agile by those that use them. Each of these methods focuses heavily on some of the principles of the agile manifesto and ignore others completely, but yet are portrayed by some, not only as an agile method, but as the best agile method.

Third, some studies have advocated an "a la carte" approach such as "XP Lite," where an existing agile method is "defanged" (Stephens and Rosenberg, 2003), and a subset method used, while others state that "the whole is better than the sum of its parts" and that agile methods are only beneficial when used in their entirety (Beck, 1999). However, even one of the main supporters of this notion has admitted that the system metaphor concept in XP is rarely, if ever used (Fowler, 2001), a sentiment felt by others in the field (Succi and Marchesi, 2001; Khaled et al., 2004). Ironically, if all principles have to be used, and metaphor is not used at all, then no project to date could be classified as truly agile.

Fourth at the other end of the spectrum, there are some, especially those using more traditional ISD methods, who disregard agile methods as unstructured, ad hoc, glorified hacking, with Stephens and Rosenberg (2003) dismissing the existence of an agile method altogether, claiming that it is something that developers can only aspire to, and only hindsight can determine whether an agile method was actually adhered to. Finally, there is a perception among proponents of agile methods that all prior methods were nonagile. Given that changing requirements was a problem identified over a quarter of a century ago (Boehm, Gray, and Seewaldt, 1984), and that methods such as RAD were developed to handle such change, it is obvious that some parts of these dated methods at least contributed to agility. "Elements of agility can certainly be found in many processes, but as the saying goes, "One swallow does not make a summer" (Alleman, 2002).

One reason for such a lack of consensus in the literature is that the principles of agility expressed in the Agile Manifesto (Fowler and Highsmith, 2001) and the various agile methods in existence lack sufficient grounding in management theory, organizational theory, and indeed theory behind all the fields and disciplines that constitute ISD. This is evident from today's range of agile methods, whose principles are primarily operational, and represent a relatively low level of conceptual granularity. Developers are encouraged to refactor, pair program and co-locate, but are not encouraged to think about the higher level objectives of such activities. This bottom-up evolution of agile methods has resulted in mass customization of popular methods such as XP, where practitioners attempt to think about agility at a higher level, so as to replace parts of XP with other method fragments that can achieve similar goals. Many efforts have been made to tailor agile methods to suit a variety of contexts such as large organizations (Bowers et al., 2002; Crispin and House, 2002; Cao et al., 2004; Kahkonen, 2004; Lindvall et al., 2004), start-ups (Auer and Miller, 2002), distributed development environments (Kircher et al., 2001; Stotts et al., 2003), offshoring (Kussmaul, Jack, and Sponsler, 2004), greenfield sites (Rasmusson, 2003), educational environments (Fenwick, 2003; Johnson and Caristi, 2003; McDowell, Werener, and Bullock, 2003; Melnik and Mauer, 2003; Wainer, 2003), open source development (Kircher and Levine, 2001), outsourcing arrangements (Kussmaul, Jack, and Sponsler, 2004), and systems maintenance (Poole and Huisman, 2001).

ISD research has made little ground in finding higher-level representations of the concept of agility. If practitioners have to replace a practice such as daily meetings, co-located teams, or pair programming, they are not sure what criteria should be used to find such a replacement. The primary reason for this is that the field of ISD does not adequately consider the evolution of the concept of agility in fields outside ISD. Agility is not a concept unique to software development. Indeed it first appeared in the mainstream business literature in 1991, when a group of researchers at the Iacocca Institute at Lehigh University introduced the term *agile manufacturing* (Goldman et al., 1991).

However, a review of the agile manufacturing literature indicates that even now, 14 years later, those who study agile manufacturing are having the same problems as those studying agile methods in ISD. There are many diverse and often contradicting definitions of agile manufacturing; the concepts lack a theoretical grounding, and consideration is not given to the differences between overall industry sectors and individual organizations (Burgess, 1994).

This suggests that the search for a definitive, all-encompassing concept of agility may not be found simply through an examination of agility in other fields. Rather, it is to be found through an examination of the underlying concepts of agility, namely flexibility and leanness (Sharafi and Zhang, 1999; Towill and Christopher, 2002), which have much older origins. For example, lean thinking can be traced back to the Toyota Production System in the 1950s with its focus on the reduction and elimination of waste (Ohno, 1988), the production of the Spitfire airplane in World War II (Towill, Childerhouse, and Disney, 2000), and even as far back as the automotive industry in 1915 (Drucker, 1995).

The Proposed Framework of ISD Agility

This chapter is interested in the nature of agility and agile methods in systems development, and more specifically the inconsistency with which these methods are referred to and used. There are many arguments in favor of some unifying framework, not just for ISD agility, but for any field or discipline. Without such a framework or underlying theory, a field may be driven by technology or the events of the day (Weber, 1987); "... progress is but a fortunate combination of circumstances, research is fumbling in the dark, and the dissemination of knowledge is a cumbersome process" (Vatter, 1947). It has also been said that a framework is needed so that researchers can build upon the development of a consistent set of data, and avoid reinventing the wheel (Grimshaw, 1992). It has been shown how the production of scientific fact is characterized as a process of creating cognitive order, or some sort of framework, out of disorder (Latour and Woolgar, 1979). In addition, there is historical evidence of certain fields achieving progress at the expense of others, through the establishment of a core, theoretical structure (Latour, 1988).

The primary objective of this research is to develop an over-arching set of concepts of agility, drawn from across the management, organizational behavior, and manufacturing literature, which can then be applied to all systems development projects to assess the level of agility inherent in these projects, whether they are using traditional methods, agile methods such as XP, or some other in-house method.

Agility, for the purposes of this research is defined as:

> "... the continual readiness of an entity to rapidly or inherently create change, proactively or reactively embrace change, and learn from change, through customer value-adding components and relationships with its environment."

It provides a rich enough basis to accommodate even very complex method instances where "just enough method" requires quite a comprehensive and detailed formalized analysis. The proposed framework, based on the above definition, frames the notion of agility around three concepts depicted in Figure 16.1. A method, or part of a method, must satisfy all three principles before it is deemed to contribute to agility.

The first outlines a broad range of *agile drivers*, also known as sources of change, all of which may impose change on an ISD project. An agile method should address all such drivers, and not view customer requirements as the only source of change, for

Figure 16.1

Agile Drivers, Capabilities, and Value

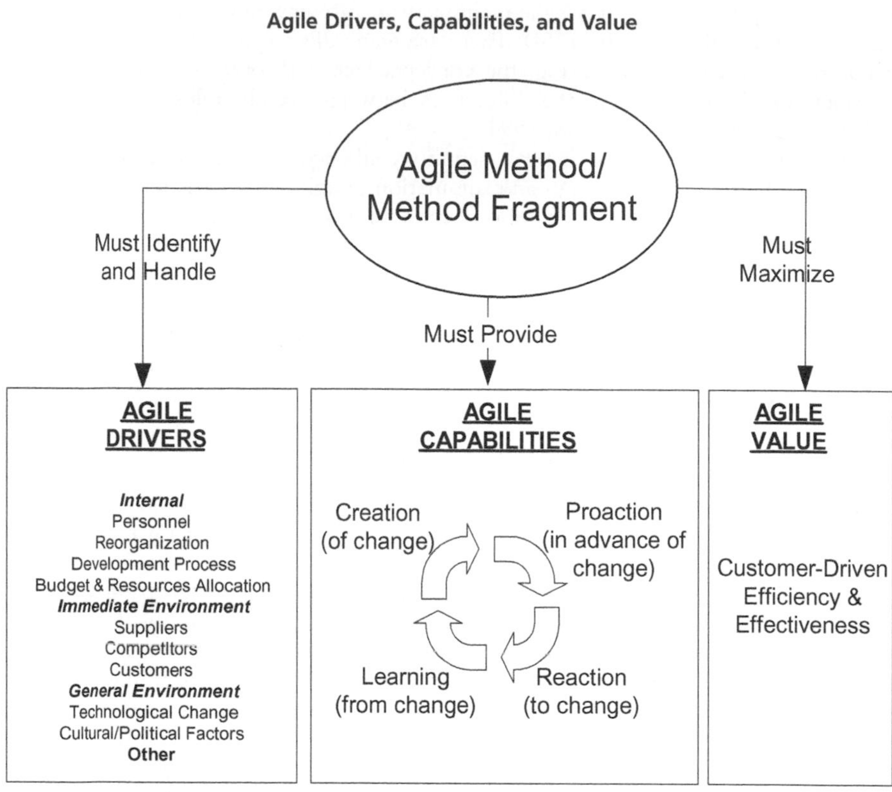

example. Furthermore, an activity is not in itself agile unless it can be explicitly linked to one of these types of change. The second principle describes the many *agile capabilities* an agile method should possess. These should not focus solely on the ability to react to change, as is usually the case in most research involving agility. In addition to *reaction*, it should also contribute to the *creation* of change, *proaction* in advance of change, and *learning* from change. Finally, the third part of the framework, *agile value*, purports that agility is not always a free good. An activity is not in itself agile unless it can be shown that the resources it consumes are less than its benefits.

Agile Drivers

The definition of agility proposed above places the concept of *change* at its core. In ISD, the emergence of agile methods has been explained as arising from the need to handle change (Fowler, 2000; Cockburn, 2001; Fowler and Highsmith, 2001). The rationale behind agile methods such as XP and SCRUM that is most cited is their ability to handle requirement changes, and not necessarily all of the changes that an ISD team may have to face. Therefore, the first part of the framework identifies a more comprehensive set of potential sources of change.

The *internal factors* incorporate changes that originate from actors within the development organization (Burton Swanson, 1988; Teague Jr. and Pidgeon, 1991).

Senior staff members may resign or be absent due to illness, contracts may be terminated (Harker, Eason, and Dobson, 1993; Hoffer, George, and Valacich, 1999; Winklhofer, 2002), or roles and responsibilities may be redefined (Pressman, 1997; Tsoi, 1999; Pfleeger, 2002). Any decisions taken by management to adopt a new development process or make changes to an existing process will naturally have a direct impact on the system being developed (McConnell, 1998) due to the difficulties of learning and growing accustomed to new technologies (Symons, 1988; Jrgensen, 2004). Finally, changes in the allocation of budgets and resources due to shortages or lack of availability (Pressman, 1997) may need to be resolved by the development method (Keil, 2003).

Changing customer requirements is irrefutably a major source of change in ISD (Lederer and Prasad, 1991), and has been described by Forte (1997) as the most common "killer" of software projects. However, this framework lists all of the entities in an ISD team's *immediate environment*, which includes, but is not restricted to, changes arising from the customer. Suppliers can be in the form of software and technology vendors and external consultants or contractors, all of whom may initiate change. For example, products from Oracle or Sybase that are used in the development process will naturally determine certain aspects of the company's development effort. The introduction of a rival feature by a competitor product may also drive change.

The development project's *general environment* consists of entities or trends regarding culture, resources, and politics, which may impact the ISD project, but does not maintain a close day-to-day relationship with the team. Trends such as offshore contracting and the transferral of jobs to low-wage countries such as India have reduced the demand for highly skilled developers and this will lead to a shift in human resource trends in the country in which the company operates (Gibbs, 1994; Cusick, 2003).

A team should analyze these sources of change and identify which are applicable to them and which are not. Some will always be a source of change, such as customer requirements. However, some depend on the context of the project.

Agile Capabilities

Once an ISD team has identified the potential sources of change it faces, it can conduct an analysis of the ability of its current or future activities to handle such change. The literature on agility is complex and often inconsistent. There tends to be overlap between the concepts of agility, flexibility, and leanness. Notwithstanding this, the following conceptualization of agility has been synthesized from the literature.

Creation

Agility focuses on "new ways of running businesses," and "casting off old ways of doing things" (Gunasekaran and Yusuf, 2002). Agility is "aggressively change-embracing" (Goldman, Nagel, and Preiss, 1995) and is "a never-ending quest to do things better than the competition" (Sharp, Irani, and Desai, 1999). Gunasekaran and Yusuf (2002) cite numerous other examples in the agility literature to support this notion (Hong, Payander, and Gruver, 1996; James-Moore, 1996; Kidd, 1996; Gould, 1997). Within the context of supply chains, Vonderembse et al. (2006) conducted a comprehensive theoretical comparison of agile supply chains versus their traditional counterparts, declaring that, while regular chains "serve only current market segments," agile supply chains are always striving to break new ground, "acquiring new competencies, developing new product lines, and opening up new markets." In other words, an agile entity must always strive to "exploit profitable opportunities in a volatile market place" (Naylor et al., 1999) and be a "market winner through excellence and differentiation" (Agrawal, 2005). This concept argues that the concept of agility suggests "distinctly aspirational tendencies" (Stratton and Warburton, 2003), and that a successfully agile entity undertakes "exploration" (Yusuf, Sarhadi, and Gunasekaran, 1999) rather than waiting for change to happen. "When the rate of these changes accelerates, agility emerges as a key element of the organization's capability" (Sharafi et al., 2001).

Proaction

Golden and Powell (2000) discuss the contrast between *proactive* and *reactive* flexibility. This concept recognizes the fact that an entity is not helpless while waiting for change to occur and that steps can be taken *in advance of* change as well as in response to it. The simple example of periodic inspection and preventative maintenance of equipment is a proactive approach to combating machine failure, as opposed to repair and replacement of equipment after failure, which is a reactive one (Gerwin, 1993). *Proactive* versus *reactive* strategies have also been described as *offensive* versus *defensive* strategies (Golden and Powell, 2000) and *initiative* versus *response* (Goldman, Nagel, and Preiss, 1995). In an ISD context, this could be an ISD team taking action to elicit changes before they actually occur. Prototyping is a prime example of this. The delaying of decisions and staging the investment of resources are also examples of proaction.

Reaction

Reaction is the most common interpretation of agility, defined as the ability to adapt to change. Even within this relatively simple component of agility, there exist different notions as to what it represents. For example, the distinction between defensive and offensive strategies raises the issue that, after change occurs, not only can an entity attempt to return to its original state, but it can take advantage of the change to place itself in a better position (Golden and Powell, 2000). The term *adapt to* implies that an entity is homeostatic, and that its only objective in the face of change will be to return to its original state. The term *embrace* implies that the entity may not only try to return to its original state but may capitalize on the change and improve on its position, hence the use of the term in the earlier definition. Reaction in an ISD context refers to the actions taken by the ISD team in response to a change.

Learning

Although a lot of the earlier concepts such as proaction and reaction indicated a large overlap between the terms *flexibility* and *agility*, the concept of learning makes a distinction between them. Observations done by the U.S. Air Force showed that, for a given activity, the hours per unit were found to decrease by a constant percentage each time total repetitions of the activity doubled (Ascher, 1965). This drop in costs was attributed to the learning that takes place every time the worker repeats the task (Huber, 1996). Agility assumes that change is *continuous*, and embracing it is an ongoing activity. Furthermore, an agile entity should learn how to be more creative, proactive, and reactive over time. This assumption was laid down in the key contribution of Goldman, Nagel, and Preiss (1995), where they described agility in general terms as "a continual readiness to change." The flexibility literature makes no reference to continual change as opposed to a once off change. Learning in an ISD context is where the project team learns from the change process so as to be more creative, proactive, and reactive during the next cycle. Learning in this context does not mean learning of skills per se. It only refers to the ability to learn from change.

Learning from Change

Creation, proaction, reaction, and learning are highly abstract principles. A detailed set of exemplars was developed for each one to provide a more tangible expression of the higher-order concepts. This was done through a review of the management, manufacturing, and organizational literature, as well as any related work in ISD. A detailed account of these exemplars is beyond the scope of this chapter, but an example of this can be seen by taking exemplars of one component of the framework, namely *learning from change* (see Table 16.1).

Agile Value

Identifying and handling change, or in other words being agile, requires resources. The development team faces the task of dealing with change while being economical with the cost, time, and diminished quality required to do so. Leanness, already a popular concept in IS development (Poppendieck, 2001), has been defined as "the elimination of waste" (Ohno, 1988; Womack, Jones, and Roos, 1990; Naylor et al., 1999) and "doing more with less" (Towill and Christopher, 2002). Some believe that although agility exhibits similar traits to *leanness* in terms of *simplicity* and *quality*, the literature has identified one major difference in terms of *economy* (Young et al., 2001). Ultimate leanness is to eliminate all waste. Agility requires waste to be eliminated, but "only to the extent where its ability to respond to change is not hindered" (Towill and Christopher, 2002). This does not remove the need to be economical; it only lowers its priority. This part of the framework dispels the notion that an activity can be labeled as completely agile or nonagile. It depends on the context in which it is used. For example, prototyping is a proactive approach to eliciting customer requirements. The cost of developing a prototype and the amount of time taken to run a prototyping session must be weighed against the number of requirements usually elicited by such sessions. Given the law of diminishing returns, running too many sessions will be very costly, and the average number of requirements elicited per session will fall. Therefore, conducting prototyping sessions only contributes to agility if done in moderation.

Through an analysis of the ISD literature, it can be seen that an ISD method can add value in two ways. First, the method can ensure that every part of the system being developed provides some value to the customer. The second means by which a method can add value is through the value attached to the parts of the method itself. Many studies such as Davis (1982), Sullivan (1985), Olle et al. (1991), Kumar and Welke (1992), Brinkkemper (1996), and Harmsen, Brinkkemper, and Oei (1994) have analyzed how organizations select, construct, and deviate from ISD methods. They have concluded that while a method or part of a method may be valuable to one ISD project, it is highly unlikely that all projects will extract the same value, given the diverse nature of systems, customers, developers, and development environments in general. As a result, tailoring of methods is recommended to ensure that each project obtains the most value from a method. A practitioner should not "implement the approach in its entirety," but should "make value judgements on what meets their needs" (Boehm and Turner, 2003).

Table 16.1

Exemplars of Learning from Change			
Construct	**Examper**	**Organizational Behavior Literature**	**Systems Development Literature**
Causal Learning	The development team learns the causes of change that have occurred.		(Salaway, 1997; Stein and Vandenbosch, 1996)
Self-Appraisal	The development team ***internally*** reflects on how creative, proactive, and reactive they were.	(Argyris and Schon, 1978)	(Ciborra and Lanzara, 1994; Wastell and Newman, 1996)
	The development team ***and customers*** reflect on how creative, proactive, and reactive they were.		(Lyytinen and Robey, 1999; Salaway, 1997)
	The development team reflects on how the sequence, longevity, and iteration of tasks contributed to change creation, proaction, and reaction.	(Argyris and Schon, 1978)	(Mathiassen and Purao, 2002; Stein and Vandenbosch, 1996)
	Tasks, task sequence, task longevity, and task iterations are changed to improve change creation, proaction, reaction, and learning in the future.	(Argyris and Schon, 1978; Beer and Walton, 1987)	(Stein and Vandenbosch, 1996)
Unintentional/ Unsystematic Learning	The method facilitates unintentional and unsystematic learning about change.	(Lounamaa and March, 1987; March and Sevon, 1984)	(Ciborra and Lanzara, 1994; Salaway, 1997)
Vicarious Learning (second-hand learning)	The development team learns how other development teams/ projects identify and handle change.	(Levitt and March, 1988)	(Lyytinen and Robey, 1999)
Grafting	New team members are introduced to the team to increase learning or the body of knowledge about change.	(Huber, 1996; Levitt and March, 1988)	(Lyytinen and Robey, 1999)
Information Distribution	Tasks include the distribution of information regarding change ***within*** the development team.	(Huber, 1982; Huber and Daft, 1987)	(Lyytinen and Robey, 1999)
	Tasks include the distribution of information regarding change ***outside*** the development team.	(Huber, 1982; Huber and Daft, 1987)	(Salaway, 1997)
	Information distribution considers the relevance, status, and importance of the information to the recipient(s).	(Huber, 1982)	(Lyytinen and Robey, 1999)

	The sequence, longevity, and iteration of tasks assists the effectiveness of information distribution.	(Huber, 1982)	(Stein and Vandenbosch, 1996)
Cognitive Maps and Framing	Information distributed is framed and referenced to ensure that its relevance and applicability to change is clear.	(Dutton and Jackson, 1987)	(Lyytinen and Robey, 1999)
	Information related to change is distributed separately or is categorized separately to any other type of information being distributed.	(Dutton and Jackson, 1987)	(Lyytinen and Robey, 1999)
Media Richness	The distribution media is rich enough to convey all types and sizes of information related to change.	(Daft and Weick, 1984; Huber, 1996)	
	The distribution media is changed to suit each type and length of change-related information being conveyed.	(Daft and Weick, 1984; Huber, 1996)	
Information Overload	Change-related information being conveyed ***within*** the development team is reduced where appropriate.	(Meier, 1963)	
	Change-related information being conveyed ***outside*** the development team is reduced where appropriate.	(Meier, 1963)	(Salaway, 1997)
Unlearning	The development team discards certain items that have been learned in relation to change, so as to avoid viewing change as a routine occurrence. (Lyytinen and Robey, 1999) refer to "myths-in-use."	(Klein, 1989)	(Lyytinen and Robey, 1999)
Storing and Retrieving Information	The development team documents and stores change-related information for future reference.	(Huber, 1996)	(Lyytinen and Robey, 1999; Stein and Vandenbosch, 1996)
	The development team is encouraged to mentally store "soft" information regarding change.	(Huber, 1996)	(Wastell, 1999)
Training and Rewarding	Developers are trained on how to learn from change and how to be more creative, proactive, and reactive in the future.		(Ciborra and Lanzara, 1994; Lyytinen and Robey, 1999; Mathiassen and Purao, 2002)
	Developers are rewarded for learning from change.		(Lyytinen and Robey, 1999)

Conclusion

A brief look at the literature on agile ISD methods suggests various mechanisms by which the level of agility inherent in a method could be assessed. You could compare your method to the four core values laid out in the *Agile Manifesto*, or to the twelve principles of XP, for example. However, there are a number of limitations of using this approach. Many of the principles of agile methods such as XP are not common across all methods. Therefore, the problem becomes not just trying to adhere to an agile method, but deciding which agile method to follow. Also, because some practices are not possible to implement in every environment, such as co-located teams, using such a myopic assessment approach means that most ISD methods and projects can never be agile.

This chapter identified a number of key components of agility that represent agility at a much higher level of granularity. First, a number of drivers of agility were identified, also known as sources of change. This ensures that when an assessment of agility is made, the assessor identifies which changes are relevant, and then considers the ability of a method to handle all of these changes, and not just changing customer requirements. Four capabilities of agility were also outlined, namely creation, proaction, reaction, and learning from change. This ensures that the assessor does not fall into the trap of equating agility with reaction to change, a common assumption in ISD. Finally, the assessor should look at the extent to which a method delivers business value and value to the customer, and not just value to the developers. This involves an assessment of the extent to which the method is tailored to suit the context of the project, and certainly refutes most agile methods that recommend textbook adoption and a reverence to the method that borders on religious.

These can now be used as the roots upon which a comprehensive assessment of agility can be made. Rather than stating that a method is not agile simply because it does not contain pair-programming, refactoring, or co-located teams, a method can be deemed agile if it links to the higher-level constructs of agility described in this chapter.

References

Alleman, G. (2002). Agile project management methods for it projects. In *The Story of Managing Projects: A Global, Cross-Disciplinary Collection of Perspectives* (Carayannis, E. G. and Kwak, Y. H., eds.). Berkeley, CA: Greenwood Press.

Ambler, S. W. (2002). *Agile Modelling: Best Practices for the Unified Process and Extreme Programming*. New York: Wiley.

Agrawal. (2005). Modelling the metrics of lean, agile and agile supply chain: An ANP-based approach. *European Journal of Operations Research*, forthcoming.

Argyris, C. and Schon, D. (1978). *Organizational Learning: A Theory of Action Perspective*. Reading, MA: Addison-Wesley.

Ascher, H. (1965). *Cost Quality Relationships in the Air Frame Industry*. Santa Monica, CA: Rand Corporation.

Auer, K. and Miller, R. (2002). *Extreme Programming Applied: Playing to Win*. Boston: Addison-Wesley.

Baskerville, R., Travis, J., and Truex, D. P. (1992). Systems without method: The impact of new technologies on information systems development projects. In *Proceedings of the IFIP WG8.2 Working Conference on the Impact of Computer Supported Technologies on Information Systems Development* (Kendall, K., DeGross, J., and Lyytinen, K., eds.), pp. 241–269. North Holland: Elsevier.

Beck, K. (1999). *Extreme Programming Explained: Embrace Change*. Boston: Addison Wesley.

Beer, M. and Walton, A. E. (1987). Organization change and development. *Annual Review of Psychology*, 38 (1), 339–367.

Boehm, B., Gray, T., and Seewaldt, T. (1984). Prototyping versus specifying: A multiproject experiment. *IEEE Transactions on Software Engineering*, SE-10 (3), 290–302.

Boehm, B. and Turner, R. (2003). *Balancing Agility and Discipline: A Guide for the Perplexed*. Boston: Addison-Wesley.

Bowers, J., et al. (2002). *Tailoring XP for Large Mission Critical Software Development*. Paper presented at the XP/Agile Universe, Chicago, IL, August 4–7, 2002.

Brinkkemper, S. (1996). Method engineering: Engineering of information systems development methods and tools. *Information and Software Technology*, 38 (4), 275–280.

Burgess, T. F. (1994). Making the leap to agility: Defining and achieving agile manufacturing through business process redesign and business network redesign. *International Journal of Operations & Production Management*, 14 (11), 23–34.

Burton Swanson, E. (1988). *Information System Implementation: Bridging the Gap between Design and Utilization*. Homewood, IL: Irwin.

Cao, L., et al. (2004). How extreme does extreme programming have to be? In *Adapting XP Practices to Large-Scale Projects*, Thirty-Seventh Hawaii International Conference on System Sciences (HICSS-37 2004), January 5–8, 2004, Track 3—Volume 3 Big Island, HI, IEEE Computer Society.

Ciborra, C. and Lanzara, G. (1994). Formative contexts and information technology: Understanding the dynamics of innovations in organisations. *Accounting, Management and Information Technology*, 4 (2), 61–86.

Coad, P., de Luca, J., and Lefebre, E. (1999). *Java Modeling in Color with UML: Enterprise Components and Process*. New York: Prentice Hall.

Cockburn, A. (2001). *Agile Software Development*. Boston: Addison-Wesley.

Crispin, L. and House, T. (2002). *Testing Extreme Programming*. Boston: Addison-Wesley.

Cusick, J. (2003). How the work of software professionals changes everything. *IEEE Software*, 20 (3), 92–97.

Daft, R. and Weick, K. (1984). Toward a model of organizations as interpretation systems. *Academy of Management Journal*, 9 (2), 284–295.

Davis, G. B. (1982). Strategies for information requirements determination. *IBM Systems Journal*, 21 (1), 4–30.

Drucker, P. (1995). The information that executives truly need. *Harvard Business Review*, 73 (1), 54–62.

Dutton, J. and Jackson, S. (1987). Categorizing strategic issues: Links to organizational action. *Academy of Management Review*, 12 (1), 76–90.

Fenwick, J. (2003). *Adapting XP to an Academic Environment by Phasing in Practices*. Paper presented at the XP/Agile Universe 2003. New Orleans, LA.

Fitzgerald, B. (1994). The systems development dilemma: Whether to adopt formalised systems development methodologies or not? In *Proceedings of the Second European Conference on Information Systems* (W. Baets, ed.) (pp. 691–706). Holland: Nijenrode University Press.

Fitzgerald, B. (1996). Formalized systems development methodologies: A critical perspective. *Information Systems Journal*, 6 (1), 3–23.

Forte, G. (1997). Managing change for rapid development. *IEEE Software*, 14 (2), 120–122.

Fowler, M. (2000). Put your process on a diet. *Software Development*, 8 (12), 32–36.

Fowler, M. (2001). *Extreme Programming Explained*. Boston: Addison-Wesley.

Fowler, M. and Highsmith, J. (2001). The Agile manifesto. *Software Development*, August, 24–28, 2001.

Gerwin, D. (1993). Manufacturing flexibility: A strategic perspective. *Management Science*, 39 (4), 395–410.

Gibbs, W. (1994). Software's chronic crisis. *Scientific American*, 271 (3), 86–95.

Golden, W. and Powell, P. (2000). Towards a definition of flexibility: In search of the Holy Grail? *Omega*, 28, 373–384.

Goldman, S., Nagel, R., and Preiss, K. (1995). *Agile Competitors and Virtual Organizations: Strategies for Enriching the Customer*. New York: Von Nostrand Reinhold.

Goldman, S., et al. (1991). *Iacocca Institute: 21st Century Manufacturing Enterprise Strategy: An Industry Led View* (Vol. 1/2). Bethlehem, PA: Iacocca Institute.

Gould, P. (1997). What is agility? *Manufacturing Engineer*, 76 (1), 28–31.

Grimshaw, D. (1992). Towards a taxonomy of information systems: Or does anyone need a taxi. *Journal of Information Technology*, 7 (1), 30–36.

Gunasekaran, A. and Yusuf, Y. (2002). Agile manufacturing: A taxonomy of strategic and technological imperatives. *International Journal of Production Research*, 40 (6), 1357–1385.

Harker, S., Eason, K., and Dobson, J. (1993). The change and evolution of requirements as a challenge to the practice of software engineering. In Requirements Engineering, 1993, *Proceedings of IEEE International Symposium on Requirements Engineering* (C. Potts, ed.) (pp. 266–272).

Harmsen, F., Brinkkemper, S., and Oei, H. (eds.). (1994). *Situational Method Engineering for Information System Project Approaches*. North-Holland: Elsevier B.V.

Hoffer, J., George, J., and Valacich, J. (1999). *Modern Systems Analysis and Design*: Boston: Addison Wesley Longman.

Hong, M., Payander, S., and Gruver, W. (1996). Modelling and analysis of flexible fixturing systems for agile manufacturing. *The IEEE International Conference on Systems, Management and Cybernetics*, October 1996, Beijing, China.

Huber, G. (1982). Organizational information systems: Determinants of their performance and behavior. *Management Science*, 28 (2), 138–155.

Huber, G. (1996). Organizational learning: The contributing processes and the literatures. In *Organizational Learning* (Cohen, M. and Sproull, L., eds.), Thousand Oaks, CA: Sage.

Huber, G. and Daft, R. (1987). The information environments of organizations. In *Handbook of Organizational Communication: An Interdisciplinary Perspective* (pp. 130–164) (Jablin, F. et al., eds.). Newbury Park, CA: Sage.

James-Moore, S. (1996). Agility is easy but effective agile manufacturing is not. *IEE Colloquium*, 179 (1), 4–10.

Johnson, D. and Caristi, J. (2003). Extreme Programming and the Software Design Course. In *Extreme Programming Perspectives* (M. Marchesi, et al., eds.) pp. 261–271. Boston: Addison Wesley.

Jrgensen, M. (2004). Top-down and bottom-up expert estimation of software development effort. *Information and Software Technology*, 46 (1), 3–16.

Kahkonen, T. (2004). *Agile Methods for Large Organizations: Building Communities of Practice*. In *Proceedings of the Agile Development Conference 2004*, IEEE CS Press (T. Little, ed.), pp. 2–11.

Keil, M. (2003). Software project escalation and de-escalation: What do we know? *Cutter IT Journal*, 16 (12), 5–11.

Khaled, R., et al. (2004). System metaphor in "extreme programming": A semiotic approach. *The Eighth International Workshop on Organisational Semiotics*, June 23–24, 2005, Toulouse, France.

Kidd, P. (1996). Agile manufacturing: A strategy for the 21st century. *IEE Colloquium* (Vol. 74, 61EE). Stevenage, England.

Kircher, M. and Levine, D. (2001). The XP of Tao: Extreme programming of large open-source frameworks. In *Extreme Programming Examined* (Succi, G. and Marchesi, M., eds.). Boston: Addison-Wesley.

Kircher, M., et al. (2001). *Distributed extreme programming*. Paper presented at the *Proceedings of XP2001—eXtreme Programming and Flexible Processes in Software Engineering*. Villasimius, Sardinia, Italy, May 2001.

Klein, J. (1989). Parenthetic learning in organizations: Toward the unlearning of the unlearning model. *Journal of Management Studies*, 26 (1), 291–308.

Kruchten, P. (2000). *The Rational Unified Process: An Introduction*. Boston: Addison Wesley Longman.

Kumar, K. and Welke, R. J. (1992). Methodology engineering: A proposal for situation-specific methodology construction. In *Challenges and Strategies for Research in Systems Development* (Cotterman, W. and Senn, J, eds.), pp. 257–269. Chichester, UK: Wiley.

Kussmaul, C., Jack, R., and Sponsler, B. (2004). *Outsourcing and Offshoring with Agility: A Case Study*. Paper presented at the XP/Agile Universe, Calgary, Canada, August 2004.

Latour, B. (1988). *The Pasteurization of France*. Boston: Harvard University Press.

Latour, B. and Woolgar, S. (1979). *Laboratory Life: The Social Construction of Scientific Facts*. Beverly Hills, CA: Sage.

Lederer, A. and Prasad, J. (1991). The validation of a political model of information systems development cost estimating. In *Proceedings of the 1991 Special Interest Group on Computer Personnel Research Annual Conference*, April 8–9, 1991 (Ferratt, T., ed.), pp. 164–173, Athens, GA.

Levitt, B. and March, J. (1988). Organizational learning. *Annual Review of Sociology*, 14, 319–340.

Lindvall, M., et al. (2004). Agile software development in large organizations. *IEEE Computer*, 37 (12), 26–34.

Lounamaa, P. and March, J. (1987). Adaptive coordination of a learning team. *Management Science*, 33 (1), 107–123.

Lyytinen, K. and Robey, D. (1999). Learning failure in information systems development. *Information Systems Journal*, 9 (2), 85–101.

March, J. and Sevon, G. (1984). Gossip, information and decision-making. In *Advances in information processing in organizations* (Sproull, L. and Larkey, P., eds.). Greenwich, CT: JAI.

Mathiassen, L. and Purao, S. (2002). Educating reflective systems developers. *Information Systems Journal*, 12 (1), 81–102.

McConnell, S. (1998). The power of process. *IEEE Computer*, 31 (5), 100–102.

McDowell, C., Werener, L., and Bullock, H. (2003). *The Impact of Pair Programming on Student Performance, Perception and Persistence*. In *Proceedings of the Twenty-Fifth International Conference on Software Engineering*, May 3–10 (Clarke, L., Dillon, L., and Tichy, W., eds.) (pp. 222–230), Portland, OR.

Meier, R. (1963). Communication overload: Proposals from the study of a university library. *Administrative Science Quarterly*, 4 (1), 521–544.

Melnik, G. and Mauer, F. (2003). *Agile methods in learning environments: Lessons learned*. Paper presented at the XP/Agile Universe, 2003, New Orleans, LA.

Naylor, J., Naim, M., and Berry, D. (1999). Leagility: Integrating the lean and agile manufacturing paradigm in the total supply chain. *Engineering Costs and Production Economics*, 62 (1), 107–118.

Ohno, T. (1988). *The Toyota Production System: Beyond Large Scale Production*. Portland, OR: Productivity Press.

Olle, T., et al. (1991). *Information Systems Methodologies: A Framework for Understanding*: Boston: Addison-Wesley.

Pfleeger, S. (2002). What software engineering can learn from soccer. *IEEE Software*, 19 (6), 64–65.

Poole, C. and Huisman, J. (2001). Using extreme programming in a maintenance environment. *IEEE Software*, 18 (6), 42–50.

Poppendieck, M. (2001). Lean programming. *Software Development*, 9 (5), 71–75.

Pressman, R. (1997). *Software Engineering: A Practitioner's Approach*. New York: McGraw-Hill.

Rasmusson, J. (2003). Introducing XP into greenfield projects: Lessons learned. *IEEE Computer*, 20 (3), 21–28.

Salaway, G. (1997). An organizational learning approach to information systems development. *MIS Quarterly*, 11 (2), 245–264.

Schwaber, K. and Beedle, M. (2002). *Agile Software Development with Scrum*. New York: Prentice-Hall.

Sharifi, H. and Zhang, Z. (1999). A methodology for achieving agility in manufacturing organisations: An introduction. *International Journal of Production Economics*, 62 (1/2), 7–22.

Sharifi, H., et al. (2001). Agile manufacturing: A management and operational framework. In *Proceedings of the Institution of Mechanical Engineers Part B—Journal of Engineering Manufacture*, 215 (6), 857–869.

Sharp, J., Irani, Z., and Desai, S. (1999). Working towards agile manufacturing in the UK industry. *International Journal of Production Economics*, 62 (1), 155–169.

Stapleton, J. (1997). *DSDM: Dynamic Systems Development Method*. Harlow, England: Addison Wesley.

Stein, E. and Vandenbosch, B. (1996). Organizational learning during advanced systems development: Opportunities and obstacles. *Journal of Management Information Systems*, 13 (2), 115–136.

Stephens, M. and Rosenberg, D. (2003). *Extreme Programming Refactored*. Berkeley, CA: Apress.

Stotts, D., et al. (2003). Virtual teaming: Experiments and experiences with distributed pair programming. In *Extreme Programming and Agile Methods: XP/Agile Universe 2003: Third XP Agile Universe Conference*, New Orleans, LA, August 10–13, 2003: proceedings (Wells, D. and Maurer, F., eds.), pp. 129–141. Berlin: Springer.

Stratton, R. and Warburton, R. (2003). The strategic integration of agile and lean supply. *International Journal of Production Economics*, 85 (2), 183–198.

Succi, G. and Marchesi, M. (2001). *Extreme Programming Examined*. Reading, MA: Addison Wesley Longman.

Sullivan, C. H. (1985). Systems planning in the information age. *Sloan Management Review*, 26 (2), 3–11.

Symons, C. (1988). Function point analysis: Difficulties and improvements. *IEEE Transactions on Software Engineering*, 14 (1), 2–11.

Teague Jr., L. and Pidgeon, C. (1991). *Structured Analysis Methods for Computer Information Systems*. New York: Macmillan.

Towill, D. and Christopher, M. (2002). The supply chain strategy conundrum: To be lean or agile or to be lean and agile. *International Journal of Logistics: Research and Applications*, 5 (3), 299–309.

Towill, D., Childerhouse, P., and Disney, S. (2000). Speeding up the progress curve towards effective supply chain management. *Supply Chain Management: An International Journal*, 5 (3), 122–130.

Tsoi, H. (1999). A framework for management software project development. In *Proceedings of the 1999 ACM Symposium on Applied Computing*, San Antonio, Texas, pp. 593–597.

Vatter, W. (1947). *The Fund Theory of Accounting and Its Implications for Financial Reports*. Chicago: The University of Chicago Press.

Vokurka, R. and Fliedner, G. (1998). The journey toward agility. *Journal of Industrial Management and Data Systems*, 98 (4), 165–171.

Vonderembse, et al. (2006). Designing supply chains: Toward theory development. *International Journal of Production Economics*, 100 (2), 223–238.

Wainer, M. (2003). *Adaptations for teaching software development with extreme programming: An experience report*. Extreme Programming and Agile Methods—XP/Agile Universe 2003, pp. 199–207.

Wastell, D. (1999). Learning dysfunctions in information systems development: Overcoming the social defences with transitional objects. *MIS Quarterly*, 23 (4), 581–600.

Wastell, D. and Newman, M. (1996). Information system design, stress and organizational change in the ambulance services: A tale of two cities. *Accounting, Management and Information Technology*, 6 (4), 283–300.

Weber, R. (1987). Towards a theory of artifacts: A paradigmatic base for information systems research. *Journal of Information Systems*, 1, 3–19.

Winklhofer, H. (2002). Information systems project management during organizational change. *Engineering Management Journal*, 14 (2), 33–37.

Womack, J., Jones, D., and Roos, D. (1990). *The machine that changed the world: Based on the Massachusetts Institute of Technology 5-million dollar 5-year study on the future of the automobile.* New York: Rawson Associates.

Young, K., et al. (2001). Agile control systems. In *Proceedings of the Institution of Mechanical Engineers*, 215 (2), 189–195.

Yusuf, Y., Sarhadi, M., and Gunasekaran, A. (1999). Agile manufacturing: The drivers, concepts and attributes. *International Journal of Production Economics*, 62 (1–2), 33–43.

Vigilant Information Systems: The Western Digital Experience[1]

17

Robert J. Houghton, Omar A. El Sawy, Paul Gray, Craig Donegan, and Ashish Joshi

In a cost-conscious and turbulent economy, operating effectively in a lean and high-velocity supply chain is demanding, especially for high-volume suppliers whose large customers change their requirements often. In such dynamic supply chains, Vigilant Information Systems (VIS) are needed, to respond quickly.

To be vigilant means to be alertly watchful. A VIS includes both sensing and responding capabilities. Sensing—to detect change and enhance managerial visibility through multiple levels from the shop floor in the factory to corporate headquarters—comes through real-time dashboards with automated alerting. Responding comes through capabilities that help decision makers at each organizational level reach decisions and take action.

This article describes how Western Digital (WD) built a VIS. The system includes an underlying layer of business intelligence applications that analyze data from numerous sources, and management dashboards that automate the alerting process and provide the means for responding. The dashboards are called "real time," which means they are "sufficiently vigilant for the process being monitored." In other words, "real time" for the factory means "as close to real time as possible," while "real time" for executive management means "once the information was validated and synchronized among data feeds so that noise was filtered out."

Vigilant Information Systems

To understand VIS, it's helpful to understand how these systems differ from traditional information systems, and how the concept of OODA (Observe, Orient, Decide, Act) loops is useful in designing such systems. VIS allow information and business intelligence to be integrated and distilled from various sources to detect changes, initiate alerts, assist with diagnosing and analyzing problems, and support communication for quick action (Walls, Widmeyer, and El Sawy, 1992).

A VIS differs from a traditional system, as shown in Figure 17.1. In a traditional information system, a user initiates a process, by, say, querying an application, causing a database to be accessed. As shown, the database (whether it stores transactions, events, or other data) is passive.

In contrast, in a VIS, the system initiates the process. As shown, the database is active. Each time its data is updated, the data is reanalyzed. If preset conditions are met, the system alerts the user. Thus, VIS provide sense-and-respond capabilities (Haeckel, 1999). They are meant to provide proactive mechanisms, and are designed from strategic and operational plans.

OODA Loops and Vigilant Information Systems

The requirements for VIS can be viewed as coming from the concept of an OODA loop. U.S. Air Force Colonel John Boyd developed the concept of the OODA loop in 1986 (Boyd, 1986; Curts and Campbell, 2001) (see Figure 17.2). He wanted to understand how fighter pilots flying aircraft with inferior maneuverability won air combat engagements (dog fights) against pilots with superior aircraft. He found that the

Figure 17.1

Vigilant versus Traditional Information Systems

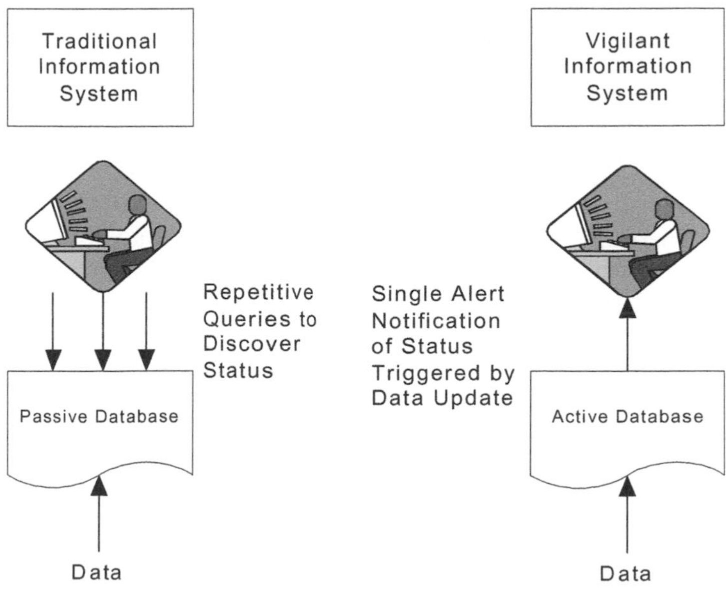

Figure 17.2

The OODA Loop

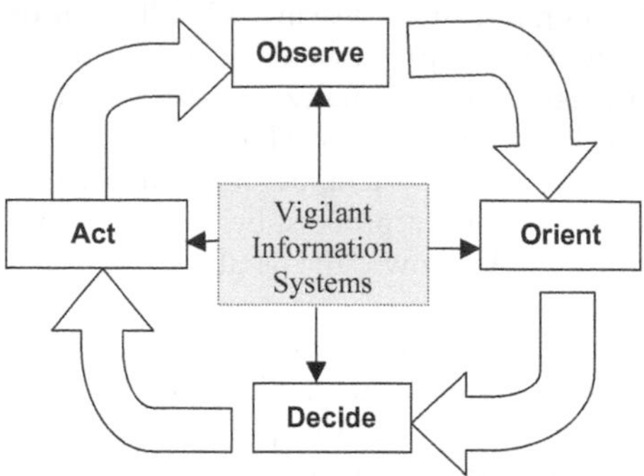

winning pilots compressed the cycle of activities in a dog fight and completed them quicker than their adversaries. Boyd's OODA loop included:

- Observe (see the situation and adversary)
- Orient (size up vulnerabilities and opportunities)
- Decide (choose the combat maneuver to take)
- Act (execute the maneuver)

In 1990 and 1993, respectively, Stalk and Hout and Haeckel and Nolan converted the idea to business use. Haeckel and Nolan's four activities are:

- Observe (see change signals)
- Orient (interpret the signals)
- Decide (formulate an appropriate response)
- Act (execute the selected response)

When changes occur in the business environment, enterprises that can complete OODA loops faster than competitors improve their ability to survive. OODA loops should not only be executed quickly; they should also be flexible and responsive to environmental changes. WD's corporate managers use OODA thinking to react quickly to customer changes. In fact, the goal is to initiate a change in the factories within the same work shift as WD receives requests from customers because being the fastest to respond to new customer requirements in the disk-drive business can increase WD's market share. The OODA loop translates into the following four requirements of VIS:

- *Capabilities for observing:* Provide visibility into the critical business processes in the enterprise's supply chain. Capture key performance indicators (KPIs) in real time. Integrate information from various sources and systems.
- *Capabilities for orienting:* Graphical dashboards that display data. Send alerts to managers. Permit drilling down in data. Permit users to slice-and-dice the data. Provide traffic-light alerts. Report trends.
- *Capabilities for deciding:* Analytics for asking "what-if" questions. Descriptive statistics. Time series comparisons.

- *Capabilities for acting:* Architectures for communicating decisions quickly to approved personnel to take action. Follow-up tracking.

WD applied these concepts to build their VIS.

Business Challenges of WD

WD is a $2 billion global designer and manufacturer of high-performance hard drives for desktop personal computers, corporate networks, enterprise storage, and home entertainment applications. Founded in 1970, WD sells its hard drives to system manufacturers, resellers, and retailers. Headquarters is in Lake Forest, California, about 50 miles south of Los Angeles. Its manufacturing facilities are in Malaysia and Thailand, and it has distribution centers in Europe. WD employs about 10,000 people worldwide. WD's top five business challenges were:

1. Constantly changing customer requirements for more storage space, faster access, and better performance
2. A fiercely competitive global industry that exerts pricing pressures and rapidly changing customer requirements
3. Avoiding business disruption, product returns, excess inventory, and bad scheduling
4. Short product life cycles and rapid obsolescence
5. The need for extremely high quality and reliability in its products

In the early 1990s, the hard drive industry consisted of over 11 manufacturers. It now involves 3 to 5, depending on the product line. WD not only survived but excelled, becoming the third largest volume producer. In 2002, unit volume rose 30 percent over 2001, to 29 million drives, and gross margins improved. It was one of the toughest years in the Information Technology (IT) industry. As part of WD's survival strategy, management demanded a new mode of information delivery. First, they wanted the ability to react more quickly to changes. Second, they wanted integrated information so that they could manage enterprise-wide in a "follow the sun" manner. "Follow the sun" refers to the multiple time zones over which WD operates.

Like many enterprises, information at WD used to be difficult to consolidate because single sources of data were not available. When users ran Enterprise Resource Planning (ERP) reports using different filters, they received different results. The data was not accurate nor was it current. Management and end users had no easy way to see trend data, understand the current state of the business, or use a system to act quickly.

Delivering the needed capabilities meant creating an Information Technology (IT) architecture that supports not only interrupted system availability but also integrates applications and data. To alert managers and analysts of changes in key performance indicators, delays, or supply-demand imbalances (when they happen) required real-time visibility of data in easy-to-use formats, with enough depth that decision makers at different organizational levels could use the same tool. Finally, the systems needed to provide a way for people to take action quickly, because that is when action makes the greatest difference.

The solution is WD's VIS and its real-time management dashboards.

WD's Vigilant Information System

The VIS is complex, so its description is divided into four sections: its overall architecture, three foundation capabilities, revamping WD's business processes, and the management dashboards.

The VIS Architecture

Figure 17.3 shows a four-layer schematic view of the architecture of WD's VIS. Starting from the bottom, in Layer 1 is the raw data, which comes from various sources. That data flows into numerous functional applications (ERP, logistics, and so on) in Layer 2 (observe). Business intelligence systems in Layer 3 analyze each new piece of data to determine whether or not it is within its preset boundaries (orient). Out-of-bounds data initiates an alert to Layer 4, the dashboards, at the top (decide and act).

Three Foundation Capabilities

Three IT capabilities form the foundation for the VIS at WD: the ERP system, the data warehouse, and the Quality Information System (QIS). These systems are considered foundations because together they capture and integrate the data needed for the VIS.

Figure 17.3

Architecture of WD's Vigilant Information Systems

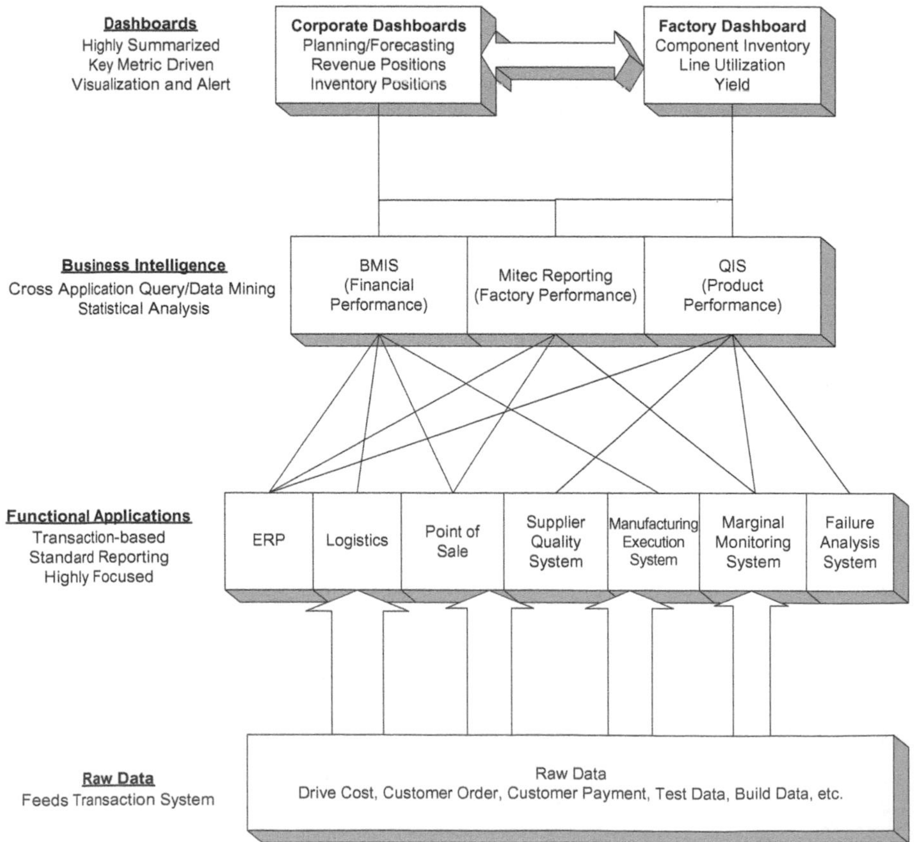

ERP was implemented in 1997, giving managers data about enterprise operations they had never had before. They could, for example, tie together requisitions, purchase orders, sales orders, production runs, and invoices. And they had on-line access to day-to-day workflow and manufacturing processes. The data warehouse was implemented in 1999 and integrated product data from 12 disparate legacy systems. The QIS, implemented in 1999, is in the business intelligence layer and integrates data to provide insights into quality. It is used to trace each hard drive manufactured at WD through its entire life cycle, including components, manufacturing, testing, shipment, and returns. WD's objectives are to maintain high quality, uncover root causes of product failures, and improve future versions of products. QIS can pinpoint component-level defects before hard drives are shipped, and can trace back from failures in the field to the root cause. The data captured by QIS can also be used to make future production decisions, when combined with the data warehouse and R&D's modeling databases.

While these three systems form the foundation for managing operational performance, they did not give executives and managers the visibility into operations that they needed. Specifically:

- A number of legacy systems remained disconnected. Management struggled with combining real-time and historical data from 30+ systems to make strategic and operational decisions. Queries and report generation were expensive, cumbersome, and required many consultants.
- The data refresh rate was inadequate and uneven across systems. Outdated data led to different results (there was no "single truth") and did not support real-time decision making. Management was without the real-time information needed in demand management and distribution (that is, forecasts, billings, backlogs, sell-through). The factories in Malaysia and Thailand could not obtain real-time data on production yields, workstation availability, and component inventories.
- Managers needed better analysis capabilities. They wanted a user-friendly system accessible through the Web that would support standard reporting; detailed, ad-hoc, drill-down queries; graphical reporting capabilities; and executive summary information.

Revamping WD's Business Processes

WD's senior management team, which includes the CIO, looked at how real-time dashboards could best be used. They agreed that the dashboards alone wouldn't change decision making. Take, for example, the five-hour daily production meetings (8:30 A.M. to 1:30 P.M.) where factory management decided what needed to be produced. Not only did these meetings manage production inadequately, but corporate management in California did not know of the decisions made in the meetings. Management realized that these meetings could be much shorter (only two hours, in fact) if the participants used the dashboard data. Furthermore, the executives in California could work with updated production information.

Top management drafted new business policies and processes to put the VIS to work. Three new policies were deemed critical:

- *Align time-based objectives across the enterprise:* WD had to translate strategic enterprise goals into measurable, time-based operational objectives for each department. The result would be consistent metrics.

- *Capture KPIs in real time:* To improve corporate performance, WD needed real-time monitoring—horizontally across organizational groups and vertically within business units. With real-time KPIs, teams could analyze them across groups and business units.
- *Foster cross-team collaborative decision making*: The dashboard environment would need to enable joint decision making collaborative work across teams, departments, enterprises, and geographic areas. Achieving such collaboration took months because the geographically dispersed teams had to decide what information they needed to hand off to R&D, corporate planning, new production groups, the factories, distribution, and customers—so that they could be "virtually there" via their dashboard. This concept was new to some WD executives.

In WD's VIS, the dashboards become managers' eyes and ears into operations. These policies aimed to ensure that decisions and actions were coordinated.

The Management Dashboards

Two real-time dashboard information systems were developed: one for the factory and one for demand planning, distribution, and sales information (the corporate dashboard).The factory dashboards were custom developed in-house and rolled out in late 2000. They are used to monitor such quantities as yields, quality, and production output. The dashboards tap into WD's information flows as shown schematically in Figure 17.4.[2] The four types of factory dashboards and ten types of corporate dashboards are shown at the top. The VIS and its information flows are in the middle. The three constituencies (at the bottom) are the factories in Asia, corporate offices in California, and customers around the globe. Information flows among these components as follows, going from right to left.

- Forecasts of customer demand from WD's distributors and original equipment manufacturers (OEM), on the right, flow into the central corporate business management information system (in the middle).
- Corporate combines these demand forecasts with feedback on production and inventory levels to create build requirements: how many units of which type are to be produced at what time.
- Based on the build requirements, each factory (on the left) determines its supply requirements and commits to building the hard drives. This production data is used for component planning by both first- and second-tier suppliers (on the far left). The product is then manufactured and ready for distribution.
- Products shipped to customers provide data feedback both to the factory and to corporate.

The Factory Dashboards

The manufacturing and engineering staff who run a factory face tight requirements. When working near capacity, a factory can produce as many as 100,000 hard drives per day. Achieving this level of production requires that the production line not be shut down and the disks not require rework. Both cause significant economic loss. Furthermore, to remain competitive, WD continually improves its manufacturing

[2] The dashboards shown at the top of Figure 17.4 are conceptual, not actual.

Figure 17.4

Western Digital's VIS Information Flows

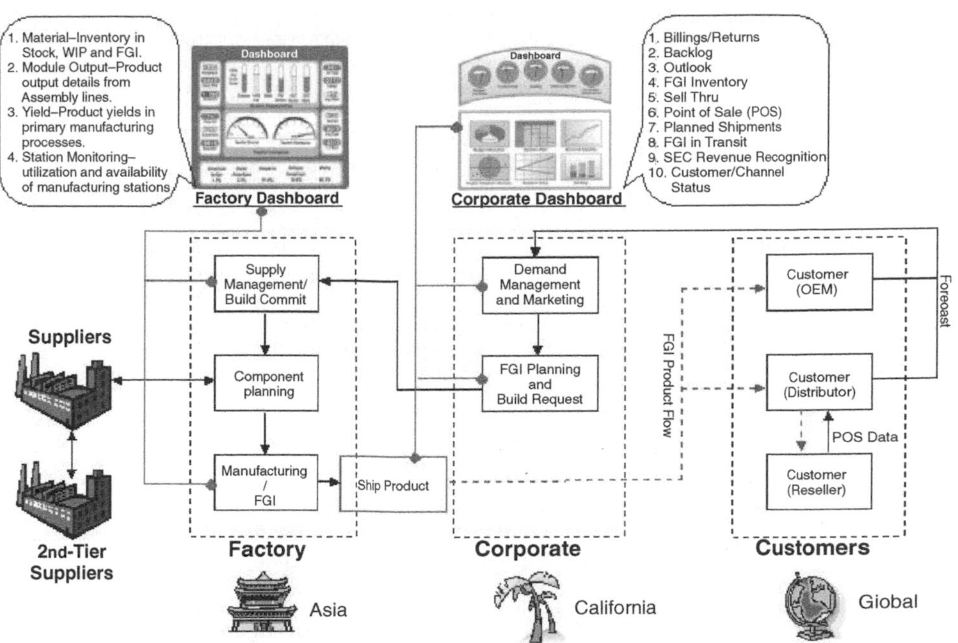

process. An improved process must be monitored to make sure the modifications actually make things better.

To assist factory staff in meeting these demands, the IT department built five factory dashboards. The four core requirements for the factory dashboards were to:

1. *Show KPIs:* Show the health of the factory by providing near-real-time, graphical views of KPIs.
2. *Display metrics:* Show when a KPI goes below 2 sigma of its allowable value.
3. *Allow drill down:* Give staff ways to drill down on each KPI to find the source of a problem.
4. *Issue alerts:* Automatically issue alerts to the individuals responsible for a KPI so they can initiate damage control.

The final requirement, for automated alerts, distinguishes these dashboards from typical executive information systems. Unanticipated events can cascade quickly, requiring fast response, hence the need for automated alerts.

The five dashboards display: yield, material, production output, Single Plug Tester (SPT) monitoring, and quality. Each is described in Figure 17.5. The dashboards allow staff and managers to see KPIs in near real time (that is, as close to real time as appropriate for what is being monitored), so they can recognize and handle problems immediately.

Figure 17.5

Descriptions of the Factory Dashboards

Yield dashboard	Yield is the percentage of units that pass inspection. This dashboard shows yields by product, capacity, cache family, and station level. It also reports cycle time of key processes and at a key manufacturing station, Servo Track Writer (STW).
Material (inventory) dashboard	This dashboard keeps track of inventory in the factory, including the receiving warehouse, work in progress, engineering locations, and finished goods inventory. Targets are set for each location based on the daily manufacturing schedule.
Production output dashboard	This dashboard keeps track of output from all assembly lines, including hard drive and printed circuit board assemblies. These outputs are compared with the targets based on the manufacturing schedule. Because the assembly station is the beginning of the drive manufacturing process, any delay or slip in output can affect the entire manufacturing and shipping operation.
SPT monitor dashboard	This dashboard monitors activities and availabilities of one of the longest processing periods and most important stations in the drive manufacturing process, Single Plug Tester (SPT). Individual drives are tested in SPTs for hours, and hundreds of SPTs are on the factory floor, loaded with drives. SPTs can become bottlenecks unless used to their maximum capacity. This dashboard gives real-time visibility of each SPT, including utilization and the products being run.
Quality dashboard	This dashboard measures the quality of drive production in units of Defective Drives per Million (DDPM). DDPM targets are based on products and customers. Problems with component or tools on the manufacturing line introduce defects. The longer the delay in detecting a problem, the more extensive (and expensive) the effort to repair the affected drives.

Each parameter on a dashboard is assigned a "target value," which, when hit, causes an alert to be issued, often to the pager of the manager in charge of the station or product. The manager then uses a specific Decision Support System (DSS) to analyze the problem. As the vice president and managing director for WD Asia noted:

> "Our factory dashboards provide us with a 'virtual' control room, which, at a few moments' glance, tells us where our trouble spots are so we can respond much more rapidly to issues than before, and we can do it from practically any place in the world."

The Corporate Dashboards

Ten corporate dashboards were created:

- Billings and returns
- Backlog
- Outlook
- Finished goods inventory
- Distributor inventory and sell through
- Point of sale
- Planned shipments

- Finished goods in transit
- Revenue recognition
- Customer/channel status

The dashboards are designed to accommodate all levels of management by varying the level of information aggregation. Each dashboard has its own "data cube," which houses the data for its displays. These data cubes are subsets of WD databases.

An example of one dashboard is the "Distributor Inventory and Sell through Dashboard." "Sell through" refers to goods sold through distributors. Before this dashboard was available, it was difficult and time-consuming to find out how much finished goods inventory distributors had, how many finished goods were sold through the previous week, and how many weeks of inventory they had. The dashboard displays all this information on one screen.

The dashboard required changes in the collection of data. Formerly, the distributors reported their sell through and inventory at the end of each week. That data was entered into regional databases and then consolidated at corporate, where it was imported into an Excel spreadsheet. About one hour later, paper reports were created and distributed, unless errors and new categories caused delays.

Now, inventory and sell-through data is collected automatically into one repository. The data cube, which is used to tabulate the KPIs and present the data, is refreshed every 20 minutes during primary collection times, and once an hour for the remainder of the week. These frequent refreshes help detect new trends. New categories are automatically included, quarterly comparisons are also automatic, and a single email notifies employees of the availability of the report.

Implementation of the dashboards encountered all the usual problems encountered in decision support and executive support systems: poor data, inadequate security safeguards, and user uncertainties about what they really wanted.

How the VIS Accelerates WD's OODA Loops

Each dashboard contains its own set of real-time metrics and KPIs for tracking and analyzing critical operations. Each KPI and metric has a target performance level and a variance setting (some set in advance and some set by the system). Exceeding a setting triggers an alert to the appropriate supervisor or manager.

A well-designed dashboard can help people accelerate the OODA loops of the processes monitored. It can also accelerate OODA loops that span multiple processes and departments. So, to manage the fast cycle environment of its supply chain, WD coupled its dashboards with both performance management and learning, using a nested structure of OODA loops. The factory and corporate dashboards are used in a three-level nesting of OODA loops, as shown in Figure 17.6.

Shop floor OODA loop: The shop floor supervisors in the factory operate in the innermost OODA loop using factory dashboards. When a product or station target is violated, they are immediately alerted via pager or flashing light. Sometimes the problem can be resolved within minutes by diagnosing it through the dashboard.

Factory OODA loop: Production managers operate at the next higher level because they need a broader view of the factory, such as seeing multiple product lines. They also receive alerts when their targets are out of range. But a more important aspect of their job is using the factory dashboards, with a different set of KPIs, to perform "health checks" on the operational performance of the factory (that is, determining that things are working as they should).

Figure 17.6

Nested OODA Loops at Western Digital

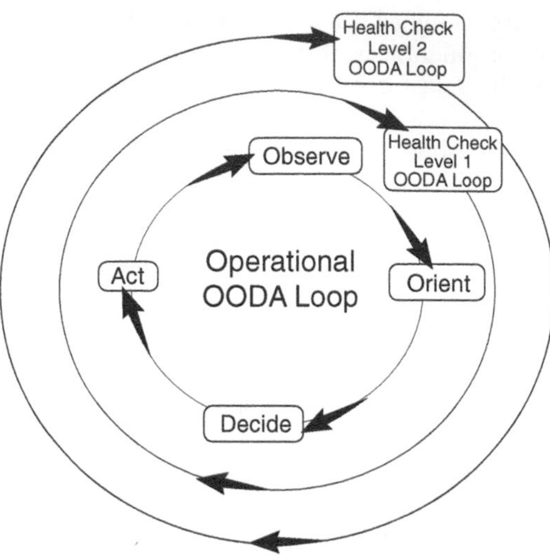

The production managers use the factory dashboards in more of a learning mode. In their daily production meeting, they use the factory dashboards to analyze the previous day's performance and discuss ways to improve processes or avoid problems encountered the day before. Because of the real-time nature of the data, problems already handled by the factory's shop floor supervisors are filtered out, minimizing the information overload on the production managers. They can more easily see the unresolved critical problems, which quickens their OODA loop.

Corporate OODA loop: Like the factory loop, the corporate OODA loop is about learning. It also involves a "health check"—but of the entire enterprise. This loop involves senior executives, and the resulting actions typically have broad implications, for the corporation and the factories.

Although not electronically connected, the factory and corporate dashboard systems are connected through the data they share and the communications and interactions of the managers who use them. The dashboards reduce the physical distances between the factories in Thailand and Malaysia, and corporate management in California. As a result, people can meet virtually and resolve problems quickly. Often, employees or teams send references to a specific screen to another team so that both can discuss the problem and make a decision. To make this possible, managers can give permission for others to see a screen.

By making these connections and conversations easy, WD sped up the OODA loops across the company. People who need either a factory or corporate dashboard can access it from anywhere. This capability very effectively coupled senior executive decisions with operations, and does so by drawing on consistent, real-time, high-quality data. It did not lead to micromanagement by top management. Micromanagement was more prevalent before the dashboards. Previously, every shop floor supervisor, production manager, and supply planner defined his or her data in silos. The data came from redundant sources. Many times this data, if requested at different times, was in conflict with the previous research. Presently, the dashboards allow for everyone to view the same data, at the same time and make decisions that affect the individual's needs, and the production plan as a whole. The system gathers KPIs; the people observe the data and react to the alerts and changes as a team. Micro-intervention isn't needed because the data is more reliable.

The Business Impacts of WD's VIS

More than 225 managers and professionals at all levels of the company now use the dashboards. Their use changed how the OODA loops are managed, resulting in both measurable gains and continuing savings. On a pure cost-savings basis, these systems paid for themselves many times over. However, the real payoff came from quickening the OODA loops and decision cycles in ways that changed WD's strategic capabilities.

Cost Savings

Cost savings came in three forms: better visibility, more efficient querying, and less information overload and faster decision making.

Over the last several quarters, the increased visibility of finished goods inventory allowed WD to increase inventory turns from 22 to 29, decreasing inventory by $25 million in 2002, for annual savings of almost $3 million in inventory carrying costs. By itself, those savings paid for the entire dashboard IT infrastructure. WD's IT organization grouped all the dashboards and the related reporting (business intelligence layer) under the name Business Management Information Systems. When we proposed this solution for fiscal year 2000, we estimated the cost of the capital and expense to be approximately $1.2 million. We then determined the ROI or return on investment to be one year. By decreasing inventory by $25 million in 2002, for annual savings of almost $3 million in inventory carrying costs, we realized the ROI in less than one year. Our savings from improved data gathering and the whole OODA impact paid for the project.

WD's margins more than doubled over the three-plus years since the dashboards were introduced. WD's management attributes the gains in margin to result in large part from the improvements in supply chain management, data visibility, and demand planning, which were realized through the dashboard data. Improved visibility improved demand management, and, on numerous occasions, allowed WD to recapture missing revenue.

Before the dashboards, it cost $1500, on average, for highly paid database administrators to create one of the hundreds of cross-application or cross-database reports requested each year. Now, users create multiple views "on the fly." Report requests dropped from 200 to 50 per quarter, savings about $900,000 per year. Furthermore, use of the dashboards eliminated about 50 percent of the printed paper volume, with an estimated savings of $800,000 per year. Custom reports now take an average of 10 minutes for managers to create, and they can easily combine real-time and historical data.

Executives, managers, and professionals now detect and analyze critical operational problems differently. Production supervisors and engineers no longer need to crunch data from several systems to measure KPIs. The dashboards feed this information to them. They can focus on performing the detailed analysis of trigger violations. Much of the noise and "unreal" problems are filtered out by the system. As a result, daily production meetings at the factories now take 1.5 hours, on average, rather than

3 hours. These meetings involve some 15 supervisors and managers, so time savings alone translates to $350,000 a year—time better spent on other work.

Strategic Advantages

Strategic advantages come from faster analysis and decision making, immediately available information, quicker reflexes, and faster OODA loops, enterprise-wide. Executives using the corporate dashboards to identify KPI problems experience much less information overload. Formerly, they received information in different formats at different times from different managers, making quick, robust analysis difficult. Now, they can make strategic decisions quickly because they no longer need to spend hours trying to interpret the data correctly.

The better business intelligence capabilities helped focus management attention. For example, one WD executive described how one product line can be used to benchmark others:

> "With the dashboard we get one up-to-the-minute snapshot showing a comparison of yields for 16 product lines in the last month on one screen shot or graph, rather than 16 spreadsheets that are difficult to compare. The difficulty is in showing relationships. Dashboards easily show us where the relationships intersect and help us to diagnose problems. Dashboards help provide knowledge rather than just information."

With the dashboards, everyone sees the same information, anytime, anywhere, and updated at the appropriate time intervals. Before the dashboards, a salesperson on the east coast visiting a customer at 8 A.M. could not obtain the most current information because the account manager on the west coast was not at work yet. As expressed by the Senior Director of Sales for Latin America,

> "The comfort zone that management can get to the data almost real-time, anywhere in the world is practically priceless. We have had events where the dashboards were accessed from a customer site and we were able to quickly explain an issue by confirming product shipments, quarter-to-date billings, and sell through volumes on the spot. This type of service and information availability improved our quality image and market share."

The reaction time between receiving data and acting on it was shortened from hours, sometimes days, to minutes. Timely alerts to manufacturing supervisors for "out-of-control" situations reduced waste on the production lines. Analysts can catch demand-supply imbalance problems as they occur (rather than the day after) and react quickly to resolve them and limit damage. As one account manager put it,

> "Instead of sending cumbersome spreadsheets back and forth, we can look at the same data at the same time and make real-time decisions even when we are at different locations. We also eliminated the need to create the spreadsheets."

While many of the business impacts discussed above resulted in measurable gains and millions of dollars in savings, the longer-term benefits are harder to assess quantitatively. Yet, they exist and are clearly strategic.

One benefit is that WD is continuously becoming a more agile competitor, as the OODA loops accelerate at all levels of the enterprise. Tactical OODA loops provide feedback and learning to operational management, which, in turn, feed the executive decision-making OODA loops. WD now ties together executive decision making, supply chain movements, and internal operations into a virtuous circle that can function effectively as various situations unfold. As a result, as an enterprise, WD can learn faster and act with more vigilance, even as the supply chain continues to speed up.

Lessons Learned

The real-time dashboards and their underlying infrastructure changed how WD manages its operations, from the boardroom to the shop floor in the factory. The bottom-line effects of improved visibility, real-time information, and quicker OODA loops occur at all levels of the enterprise. WD is a faster-learning and more vigilant enterprise, so it can operate more leanly. Its ability to link executive decision making with operations in real-time through dashboards gave it a strategic edge as a responsive supply chain partner. WD's experiences provide six lessons.

#1: Design the real-time management dashboards to be the nerve centers of a VIS.

WD's experience shows that management dashboards can become the central point for managing an extended enterprise vigilantly. By providing the means for human-computer interaction, they are a critical component of the VIS architecture. These dashboards may be glitzy, or not. Some may display mainly tables of text. They should provide instant access to information (i.e., observe). But they also should combine event-based alerts (i.e., orient) with company history. And the information should be sharable, to give people ways to track and manage (i.e., decide and act) activities and processes across functions.

#2: Plan and schedule the coordination among teams to use real-time dashboards to manage enterprise-wide.

Dashboards can show real-time metrics, workflow executions, alerts, and various slices from information cubes from other dashboards, providing a holistic picture that allows teams to collaborate more quickly and make decisions. Often these teams are in different functional areas, different geographic locations, and responsible for different business processes. One purpose of providing the information via dashboards should be to eliminate the separation of people in space and time, thereby allowing managers to be "virtually" in the room.

The dashboards' connective integrative view serves to identify problems and opportunities quickly that could otherwise be missed. This coordination is being accomplished at WD by using the corporate dashboards as the focal point of meetings among managers from sales and marketing, distribution, and the factory. These meetings are not ad hoc; they are scheduled daily, weekly, or monthly for specific purposes, such as quality review and production planning. The meetings provide the human coordination and intervention needed to deal with enterprise-wide problems. The goal is to act quickly in a coordinated fashion. To manage enterprise-wide, WD makes sure that people with multiple perspectives are always involved in an OODA loop.

#3: Build a learning loop around each OODA loop to foster group learning because the faster the loop, the more important and frequent the learning reviews need to be.

As cycle times become shorter, errors and exceptions occur more quickly as well. To keep up, enterprises need information systems and management processes that record incidents and retain their history, so that groups can review and learn from them. WD embeds group learning into its OODA loops through its organized "health checks" and review meetings, both of which take place around the dashboards. WD learned that the shorter the cycle times, the more frequent and important the "health checks." Each OODA loop needs its own learning loop, designed specifically for it.

Dashboards and VIS need to be designed and managed to support this use, and the learning loops need to be part of the management culture.

#4: Match the time latency of each OODA loop to the organization's needs and capabilities to become truly vigilant; do not indiscriminately chase zero latency.

At first sight, it would appear that achieving zero latency in any portion of an OODA loop is the Holy Grail. But WD learned that "real time" in practice actually should mean "being sufficiently vigilant for the OODA loop you are in," not zero latency. On the sensing side, the incoming information must be validated; otherwise there is a lot of "noise." Also, the various information feeds need to be synchronized. Both add time to the sensing portion of the loop, but improve the enterprise's ability to be vigilant.

At WD, the OODA loops around the manufacturing process are much faster and closer to real time than the OODA loops around demand management in the supply chain, because validating the information about sales and demand takes longer. Furthermore, some parts of the organization cannot or do not need to act in real time.

The most effective OODA loops provide fresh information when the organization needs to respond. The computer-based sensing portions support the human-based responding portions. There is no point in getting fast sensing (the observe and orient portions of the OODA loop) if no actions can be taken. Likewise, there is no point in being able to respond quickly (the decide and act portions) if there is no fresh information. Investing in sensing capabilities that provide information more frequently than an OODA loop requires may not be the best use of IT funds or management attention. When in concert, the two provide the building blocks for a sense-and-respond enterprise.

#5: Vigilant information systems may need to be justified on some basis other than return on investment.

The real payoff of VIS comes from accelerating OODA loops in ways that change the capabilities of the enterprise. Oftentimes, though, such grand initiatives are difficult to cost-justify. Financial returns are hard to quantify, and risks are high. The Internet bubble increased skepticism about IT-based transformation initiatives.

Sometimes the strategic opportunities of VIS can be quantified, such as the value of increasing the enterprise's ability to respond more quickly to changing customer needs or the value of limiting the enterprise's exposure to suppliers that cannot meet their commitments. CFOs accept estimates that translate these risks into money. At WD, the CIO justified the IT investment in yet another way. To sway the CFO, he illustrated the "impact of not doing it" by pointing out that not investing would hamper WD's ability to meet its supply chain performance commitments.

#6: Implementing an enterprise-wide VIS is a management initiative more than a technology initiative because it requires "active, collaborative engagement" from all top management to instill the needed organizational transformation.

Taking advantage of real-time dashboards and VIS requires transforming an enterprise's management processes. Such a transformation requires more than the usual "getting top management support." It requires the entire top management team to be actively collaborative because they are the one who must model the process of using the new information and knowledge differently to manage and steer the enterprise. Use must start at the top.

At WD, CEO Matt Massengill was one of the first to use the corporate dashboard. He demonstrated his use by taking fresh data from the dashboards to his top management and staff meetings. He used the data to emphasize a point, generate lively conversation, and review numerous KPIs. He set an example for how to use the new gold mine of data to manage differently, thereby sending the message that all top management needed to change their ways of managing as well.

In fact, Massengill adopted the dashboard so completely that he asked that some views be ported to his PDA. The IT team extracted key Billings to Date, Sales by Region, and Orders by Unit—the extracts most important to Massengill and other executives when they are on the road. Generally, the indicators are "all is well." But they are excellent for alerting the executives when production is below expectations. Such information can make all the difference between "go ahead and board the plane" or "get to a phone."

The Future of Vigilant Information Systems

WD's CIO, dashboard teams, and line managers continue to develop the VIS vision, enhance system functionality, and integrate the systems with management practices at WD. Internally, output to wireless devices is planned, as are dashboards for other business processes. Externally, WD plans to build dashboards for collaborating with supply chain partners. Such links will deepen visibility into the supply chain, and thereby widen and accelerate the information inputs into the OODA loops, permitting even better synchronization along the chain. These dashboards will also give suppliers and customers visibility into WD's manufacturing process. Ultimately, the goal is to speed up the entire supply chain's OODA loops.

Figure 17.7 shows four types of real-time management dashboards, based on the amount of "business horsepower" required of their underlying VIS. This horsepower

Figure 17.7

Four Types of Real-time Management Dashboards

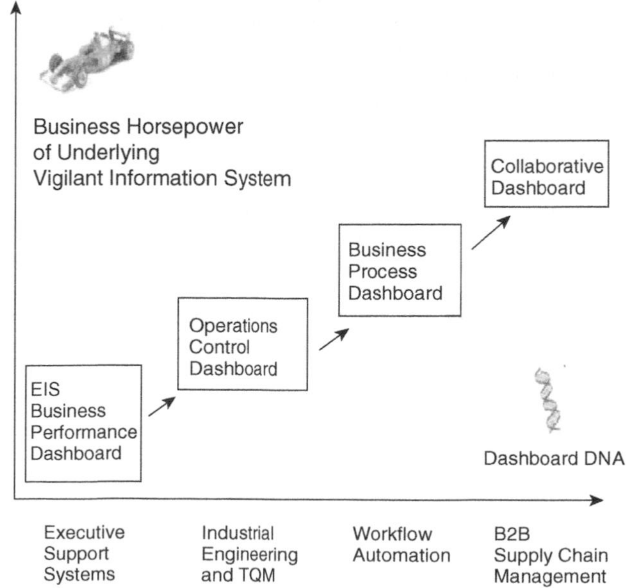

means the ability of the systems to link management decisions to operations and span multiple processes and multiple enterprises. The four are:

- *EIS Business Performance Dashboard:* This dashboard monitors business metrics and key performance indicators. Its roots are in Executive Support Systems (Rockart and DeLong, 1988). The corporate dashboard at WD is of this type.
- *Operations Control Dashboard:* This dashboard is tightly coupled to operational processes, whether in manufacturing or in service operations. Its roots are in industrial engineering and total quality management. The factory dashboard at WD is of this type.
- *Business Process Dashboard:* This dashboard is most commonly used for transactional processes. It monitors business processes across an enterprise while they are executing and can proactively reroute processes and reallocate resources. Its roots are in workflow automation. WD is moving in this direction.
- *Collaborative Dashboard:* This dashboard is shared by multiple partners in a B2B Supply Chain and provides OODA loop synchronization across enterprises. WD is moving in this direction.

Ultimately it is the combination of these real-time dashboards at various levels in an enterprise, and their integration into management processes, that yield the quickest and most effective OODA loops.

As the concept of the real-time enterprise develops, there will be much activity around development of supporting IT architectures and new types of dashboards. WD stitched together its own sense-and-respond IT architecture using generic IT infrastructure components. However a new class of specialized IT architectures is evolving, specifically geared to real-time response. Examples include event-based computing architectures, "publish and subscribe" architectures, and B2B integration architectures. All enable seamless integration of business processes, permitting faster response.

References

Boyd, J. (1986). Patterns of conflict. *Unpublished Manuscript*, USAF.

Curts, R. and Campbell, D. (2001). Avoiding information overload through the understanding of OODA loops. *Proceedings of the Sixth Annual International Command & Control Technology Research Symposium*, 2001.

Haeckel, S. (1999). *Adaptive Enterprise: Creating and Leading Sense-and-Respond Organizations*. Boston: Harvard Business School Press.

Haeckel, S. and Nolan, R. (1993). Managing by wire. *Harvard Business Review*, 71 (5), 122–132.

Rockart, J. F. and DeLong, D. W. (1988). *Executive Support Systems: The Emergence of Top Management Computer Use*. Homewood, IL: Dow Jones-Irwin.

Stalk, G. and Hout, T. (1990). *Competing Against Time: How Time-Based Strategies Deliver Superior Performance*. New York: Free Press.

Walls, J., Widmeyer, G., and El Sawy, O. (1992). Building an information system design theory for vigilant EIS. *Information Systems Research*, 3 (1), 36–59.

18

Coors Brewing Point of Sale Application Suite: An Agile Development Project[1]

Jack Buffington and Donald J. McCubbrey

The primary target market for beer is young adults. While beer sales were relatively flat in the 1990s, sales were expected to grow at 1.5 percent annually as more baby boomers' children reach drinking age. The forecast was based on the observation that "22 year olds drink more than 33 year olds" and that demographics are in the brewing industry's favor for the next 10 years (Tarquinio, 2002).

However, this target market is a difficult one for brewers to reach. Young people demand increasingly creative and innovative approaches to marketing. In addition to television advertisements, timely, relevant, and creative point of sale (POS) materials (e.g., banners, signs, figures, lighted signs, and table tents) in retail outlets are a key component of the marketing mix. Coors depends upon the cooperation of distributors and retailers to place their POS materials in ways that will give Coors products greater visibility with retail customers than those of the competition. Since substantially all retailers and most distributors of Coors products also sell competitors' products, Coors realized that it must win the battle for mindshare not only with those who buy its products at retail, but also with its distributors and retailers who are in a position to influence what the retail customer buys. Produce-to-order (PTO) products are ordered for placement in specific retail locations and are the POS items that consumers see at retailers.

To be effective, many POS materials must be customized for local markets. For example, in March 2002, Coors outbid its major competitors to become the official beer of the National Football League (NFL) through 2007 (MacArthur, 2002). The licensing agreement with the NFL permits it to use the NFL logo on POS materials. However, all POS materials must conform to the terms of the national licensing agreement, which contains many restrictive conditions imposed by the NFL to protect their brand image. At the same time, Coors depends on its distributors and retailers, who are closer to local markets, for input on which POS materials are likely to be most effective. Such input must take into account both assessments on what will appeal to distributors, retailers, and consumers, as well as knowledge of what competitors are doing with their POS programs.

Shortcomings of the Former POS System

Despite its importance in increasing sales, for many years Coors was at a competitive disadvantage with its POS deployment process. The distribution of POS materials was costly and time-consuming, involving paper-based procedures for ordering and fulfillment. Creation of POS materials customized for local markets was outsourced to third parties, some overseas, but the overall process was plagued by weak supporting systems. The systems were time-consuming and hampered by logistical difficulties and high costs.

Prior to the introduction of Coors' electronic POS system, the POS business processes were essentially manual and quite time-bound in ordering, production, and fulfillment. (Coors attempted to replace the manual system with an automated system in the past, but the initiative was not successful.) For example, each year, Coors produced a paper catalog containing both information and images describing available promotional products. Coors brand managers would work with the Company's partner marketing firm to develop the catalogs, which typically ran to 60 pages and contained as many as 400 items. In many cases, significant and expensive efforts would be needed to develop and submit material that missed the catalog print schedule deadline. Due to the lead-time to produce and distribute the catalogs (two months), Coors brand managers were often under severe time pressure to reconcile the need for last-minute ideas to the long lead times needed for catalog production.

Once the catalogs were produced, they were sent to over 600 Coors distributors in the United States and several hundred abroad. If changes were later required, inserts were prepared and sent to distributors for inclusion in the catalog. Obviously, this was not a desirable procedure even though it was a frequent event given the fluid nature of marketing. Once distributors received their catalogs, they would decide which POS materials to order for their local outlets. In many cases, the printed catalog did not contain enough information to permit distributors to make an informed decision and Coors corporate would have to be contacted. These procedures did not readily support the multi-location nature of distributorships, and how decisions were made on POS within their businesses. In addition, the catalogs did not integrate well with Coors' cost-sharing strategy for their distributors. Distributors were given a spending allowance for POS materials by Coors, but Coors' goal was for distributors to exceed their allowance and use some of their own funds for more POS materials. Distributors needed to make separate inquiries to manage their total spending in relation to their spending allowance. The process was cumbersome, and therefore did not support Coors' goal to have distributors order more POS materials.

Distributors often ordered materials at the last possible moment for a given promotion, which tended to introduce errors into the manual process. The distributors would look at the catalog and fill out a form that would be faxed to Coors' marketing partner. A reconciliation process would then occur manually between the marketing partner and distributor and the Coors' field sales department. Since the marketing partner would manually key in orders to be sent to the fulfillment companies, errors occurred, particularly at the last minute. For some of the products, the marketing partner dealt directly with suppliers; in other cases, they dealt with third parties, who dealt with the suppliers. In either case, the many manual handoffs led to significant order errors.

The process flow of the prior system was not well thought out. Whoever was responsible for fulfilling a task in the process owned the process. Systems did not support automation, and processes did not support a viable system. Therefore, most processes were ad hoc and, in many cases, difficult to understand. This point is important, for if distributors did not understand or adhere to the processes for ordering Coors' POS materials it could make them less inclined to favor Coors over other beer companies who are competitive in promoting POS materials. Therefore, while Coors measured POS success solely upon the positive impact of the message on the end user, order creation and fulfillment ease-of-use affected the ultimate success of the programs. A similar set of issues complicated the ordering and ultimate effectiveness of another category of products, Licensed Promotional Materials (LPM). LPM are shirts, hats, and similar items. The LPM system linked to 60 third-party licensees of LPM, who contracted the manufacturing of these materials in developing countries such as China.

Because of the cumbersome customization processes, distributors and retailers tended not to optimize their potential ordering of customized materials and, as a result, noncustomized POS materials were most often used in customer-facing settings. This counterproductive circumstance occurred even though high-quality, targeted POS marketing materials were known to increase sales. Thus, in this highly competitive industry, Coors was not able to realize the benefits of customized POS materials because of inadequate processes, materials, and supporting systems.

Establishment of the e-Business Department

In 2001, after some deliberation, Coors decided that the best way for the Company to gain business benefits from Internet applications was to establish a separate e-Business department.

Establishment of the e-Business department was a crucial decision because, before it was made, business units typically made side deals with technology third parties to deliver solutions. In many cases, the business units opted for third parties with close business relationships with Coors in the area of the business specialty, such as POS. While these companies often fully understood the present-day nature of the business, they frequently did not possess a suitable level of technical expertise to make logical technical and design decisions, or know how to design a more efficient model. In too many cases, the relationships either failed after considerable investment from Coors, led to silo systems that were redundant to others already existing, were "point solutions," and/or were difficult, if not impossible to maintain within the enterprise.

Buffington knew that he needed to achieve a quick success to have an immediate impact and to establish credibility with the business units. Casting about for opportunities, and talking with other managers and executives, it soon became apparent that the POS application would provide significant impact by the e-Business team. Clearly, marketing was critical in the competitive brewing industry, and Coors admittedly fell short in realizing the potential of POS.

POS turned out to be even more important when Coors later signed the NFL contract to be the exclusive beer sponsor for the league. The contract was expensive, and full of upside potential for Coors—potential that could only be realized if a truly effective POS system could support the marketing campaign.

When the e-Business department commenced the new partnership with the Sales department to focus on POS, there was no time to go through a formal process of choosing a vendor, or thinking through the "buy versus build" question. Given that POS fulfillment systems were often specialized within the industry (i.e., built by smaller niche players rather than Enterprise Resource Planning (ERP) companies), the e-Business department felt that it could not risk creating another third-party relationship that could lead to another unsuccessful system. The belief was that process, not technology, would matter most in designing a solution. By owning the responsibility for designing the system, from business to technical, the e-Business team could deal with a critical business need on its own.

Moving Toward Agile Operations

When the decision needed to be made, the options for Coors were to:

- Use a partner who understood the specifics of POS within a three-tier consumer products company
- Use standard ERP software tools[2] for integration
- Build it themselves

While it was the practice of Coors to stay away from home-grown solutions as much as possible, the circumstances did not support such a decision. It was felt that the specialized tool providers could understand certain aspects of the business process, but would still need to customize a significant portion of their software to meet Coors' needs. A primary concern was whether a third-party vendor would be a business or technology specialist, when what Coors needed was a strong focus on integrating the two.

Since Coors is a process manufacturing company, they often found it prudent to use traditional ERP tools to develop add-on business systems. In the case of POS, how-ever, greater integration was needed with the Company's marketing partners than what would be needed with a manufacturing system that was essentially internal. As many of the marketing partners were smaller companies with widely varying Information Technology (IT) capabilities, their technology differed from Coors' (e.g., using Mac versus Windows). The ERP or standard tools[2] within the industry had yet to focus on the specialized set of requirements for the POS application. Furthermore, neither of the options provided Coors with material examples of experience in succeeding in the type and extent of solution that was needed for the company.[3]

In the end, Coors e-Business felt that the most viable option was to design and build a system using existing application tools in-house. Given the philosophy Buffington brought with him was to focus on business and technical requirements and then outsource the actual technical development, it was the stance of e-Business that Coors was best suited to understand and formalize the business process around POS, and that the third-party development company was best suited for cost-effective rapid application development, as long as they were given solid designs.

---

[2] Software applications that aid in development and other generalized functions are commonly called "tools."

[3] Later analysis showed that many of Coors' competitors faced the same problems.

The First Step: Creating a Portal

The e-Business Department began the transformational effort for POS by first creating a portal for its distributors, suppliers, and retailers to use as a collaborative workspace. The portal permitted such functions as targeting, personalization, and data management to be performed with ease and permitted participants to see the value of an Internet-based collaboration mechanism.

The term, *portal* is viewed as a technical problem within the IT sector (Fox 2002). At Coors, however, it was always clear that the reference was less about technology and more about business process. The portal was to become a technical framework that supports the way that Coors conducts business with distributors, suppliers, consumers, employees, shareholders, and other stakeholders. It is foundational, easily supporting whatever initiative is needed at the company quickly, and with the necessary scalability.[4] It is intended to be transparent to the business customer, be reliable, and possess the requisite flexibility to support a fluid competitive environment. The portal, however, was not a popular concept when first discussed with the Sales department, because it seemed to focus more on a foundation for the future than on "needed yesterday" functionality. Within their competitive landscape, business users felt it was a less urgent step when compared to their immediate tactical needs. In the end, their objections were overcome, and the team turned its attention to providing a framework for e-Business through a portal approach.

The specific approach taken was to construct interlocking portals of B2B (business to business), B2E (business to employee), and B2C (business to consumer) that would readily support future initiatives such as POS. Therefore, the POS solution on Coors' B2B portal (primarily for distributors) would not be handled as separate from other critical tasks needed to be performed by distributors electronically. The portals offered distributors one place to interact with the company. As a result, Coors became an "easier to use" company. The portal framework brought forward infrastructure, governance, and structure that allowed for rapid execution on business needs (as was subsequently demonstrated with the POS system). Next, after building a scalable portal foundation, the team turned its attention to rationalizing critical business applications, such as the POS ordering and fulfillment process.

POS System Requirements

All system modules were developed on tight timelines (e.g., only about four months were available in 2002 to roll out the e-POS module needed to support the NFL promotion), and the proper systems and processes were needed to support the POS aspects of this critical promotion. Because of the tight timing, the e-Business department was in much more of a "firefighting" mode than it would have liked. Also, because the POS project was such a critical one for the e-Business department (and the company), they insisted on doing it right by using structured and formalized software development practices that commenced with a deep analysis of the business processes. Although Sales found it difficult to understand why such steps were necessary, by taking the time to document and formalize the business processes properly around POS with the customer, e-Business was able to develop the requirements needed to build the

---

[4] Scalability refers to the notion that an IT system can easily absorb increasing volumes of transactions as demand increases. Additional comments on scalability are included later in the chapter.

Table 18.1

Project Timeline			
Module	**Start Date**	**Completion Date**	**Elapsed Time**
B2B Portal	1/15/2001	4/1/2001	2.5 months
PTO Application	1/1/2002	3/1/2002	2 months
LPM Application	3/1/2002	4/15/2002	1.5 months
e-POS Application	3/15/2002	7/15/2002	4 months
DST Application	1/31/2003	4/15/2003	2.5 months

Key: B2B = business to business
PTO = produce to order
LPM = licensed promotional materials
e-POS = e–point of sale
DST = digital sales tool

system within three months, a short period of time for such an effort. This procedure was an instance of the well-known, but too-seldom-followed paradox of software engineering, that by taking the time to follow structured, disciplined practices in the requirements phase, time is cut from the overall schedule (Leffingwell and Widrig, 2000). The software engineering approach married very busy and focused Sales leaders, e-Business team members, and third-party marketing providers, to software developers separated by an 11.5-hour time difference. Only through a disciplined approach was it possible to integrate all of these parties successfully within tight time frames. Examples of the development time frame for various modules are shown in Table 18.1.

Developing the POS Suite

With the portal addressing the "plumbing" of how Coors does business with its distributors and marketing partners, precious time was saved in developing the POS suite. Furthermore, the POS suite of tools did not need to be introduced. Users were trained as if the suite was a separate idea from other tools provided to distributors on the portal. The concept was to roll out applications like POS in the same way as Microsoft deploys a separate tool within the Windows framework. Because all users understand how to use Windows, less time was needed to be spent understanding how to use specific tools. Therefore, to gain a deep and quick adoption of the POS system, Coors needed to build a suite of tools that corresponded to the specialized business process and standardized workplace provided by the portal. In planning and execution, the realization of this goal was not a trivial matter. Most important, it required constant and effective communication between Coors users, external users, the e-Business team, and the third-party developers.

Phase One

The process of designing and building the POS tools differed from the way Coors developed systems previously. For example, only the foundation of the design, and critical applications were designed and built in Phase One. The primary reason for this decision was time; however, business processes also needed some work before further expansion was to occur. Different assumptions existed relative to customer expectations that needed to be addressed during this first stage. Given the negative experiences of both the Sales department and its distributors with earlier attempts at POS technology solutions, the e-Business team felt that it must focus on meeting basic business process needs and provide strong system performance and reliability. This approach was in contrast to seeking to build all of the functionality in one iteration, hoping that full functionality would win the customers over. The new paradigm was to promise only core functionality that performed well. This thinking was especially important given the atmosphere of anticipation at Coors and its distributors and retailers over the new NFL promotion. This conservative decision was more a function of business process than technology, and it also addressed the credibility issue in proving e-Business as a viable solution partner.

In the design and build of the system, two factors were of paramount importance:

- The longer and deeper involvement in the entire process by the Sales Department
- The earlier and more front-end involvement from the third-party system integrator

Given what was at stake, the business customers from Sales and Coors' marketing partners were willing to involve themselves deeply into the design, even though they were not often asked for this level of participation in technology projects. In many cases, employees of the system integrator were involved in the middle of the deeper business process sessions for knowledge transfer (from Sales to them) and in assessing what could and could not be done within the time frame. This process of including the business customer deeper and later, and the system integrator earlier, was particularly successful given that the plan was to do the actual software development in India. It would have been very difficult for the system integrator to understand the nuances of the POS business process when developing without an initial involvement in the project.

The Produce to Order System Was First

An application system for PTO products was rolled out first. PTO products are those that consumers see at retailers. The PTO system is more than just an ordering system. It links orders to Coors for general management, budgeting, and reporting and from Coors to a single third-party producer of the PTO materials.

Scalability was important because Coors needed to quickly ramp up capacity based upon the success of a single program such as the NFL campaign. Open source was important because it made integration simpler and insulated Coors from subsequent software upgrades associated with proprietary software.

The content management tool needed to be robust enough to support a multitude of different programs yet simple enough to use on top of its open source architecture. Users needed a tool that could be managed from a program standpoint by nontechnical administrators, but be scalable for more dynamic campaigns. The PTO tool was therefore created to the business requirements of the marketing partners who were to use the tool in production. It met their standards from an ease of use and a dynamic tool standpoint. The target user for the "ease of use" criterion was an end user at a marketing partnership with prior experience using paper catalogs but no online experience in creating marketing programs.

Prior attempts for this application did not consider the joint needs of scalability, flexibility, and nontechnical ease of use. In prior versions, programs were hard coded into a tool. As a result, every new marketing program was an application development effort. This proposition was costly and inefficient for Coors and its partners.

Furthermore, prior architecture efforts were limited in functionality to basic ordering procedures, as opposed to a full integration suite of all services and processes that would occur within the POS process. These tools were built as end solutions for specific tactical needs, rather than considerations of total cost of ownership, maintenance, and scalability.

Licensed Promotional Materials Were Added

Next, Coors added LPM to the system. As mentioned earlier, LPM are shirts, hats, and similar materials. LPM support PTO materials and brands. While similar in concept to the PTO system, the LPM system linked to 60 third-party licensees, who contracted the manufacturing of these materials in developing countries such as China.

The technical architecture for LPM was not just similar to that of PTO, it was actually the same. While prior vendor attempts sought to provide the two business processes under separate application paradigms, the e-Business team consolidated them into one.

One reason prior vendors separated the tools was for scalability; not trying to conduct too many transactions within one technical structure. To the contrary, the e-Business team saw enough technical similarities to architect one paradigm for all POS applications, considering scalability to be more of a function of how the "foundation" was built, and opting for more processes and functions to be completed within the dynamic content management tool. This decision was a major win for the business customer who felt that they needed to compromise integration in business processes between PTO, LPM, budgeting, and other systems for the sake of scalability. As Coors built even more applications within the POS application foundation, the tools still meet the system requirements of its users. The lesson from this exercise was that if a strong foundation is built within an application suite, the term scalability can be viewed much differently than before. With a solid technical and business architecture, scalability can be defined as optimizing the use of software and hardware, as opposed to seeking to add more hardware and software when additional business procedures are introduced.

The Portal architecture itself takes basic user procedures such as security, customer targeting, and sign-on away from the tool, which greatly improves its capabilities. Outside the portal, the content management tool provides the flexibility and dynamic ability to create programs. Content management reduces the work that needed to be done at the application level, the level that needs to provide power and scalability to the process.

The E-POS System

The PTO and LPM systems were quite effective, but they lacked the ability to enable distributors and retailers to customize POS materials for local marketing needs while still permitting Coors to maintain central control over what is permitted under its national licensing agreements. Managing POS in the field is especially challenging. Not only must Coors be aware of how its more than 600 distributors use POS so that Coors can maintain integrity (e.g., the image is not being distorted in any unwanted way), it also must ensure that legal requirements are maintained, particularly when celebrities are involved. Naturally, local distributors wanted to use POS materials featuring local teams and players. The PTO and LPM materials did not possess the mass customization features that would permit POS materials to be customized for local markets and ordered through the Coors portal.

After researching alternative options, Coors approached a well-established hardware manufacturer with a request for a secure, streamlined digital imaging system. The hardware manufacturer was beta testing such a system based on sophisticated digital publishing technology, including specialized presses and large-format digital printers. The system facilitated the mass customization Coors was looking for and used:

- The hardware manufacturer's consulting group
- Innovative Web-based software designed and customized by the manufacturer
- A network of partners

Coors' 600 U.S. distributors were given the ability to log on to a Web site and create, download, and print posters, table tents, and other POS materials with branded full-color graphics along with customized messaging and pricing for local markets. The system, dubbed the "e-POS System" enables users to tailor certain Coors POS materials to their own unique requirements while giving Coors positive assurance that national licensing agreements are complied with.

With the e-POS system, each Coors' distributor logs on, selects a design template, chooses from a variety of high-resolution graphics, and customizes the messaging. Orders are validated for conformance to central policies and transmitted to one of 60 fulfillment vendors for fabrication and delivery. The important aspect of the e-POS application is that it permits customer self-service and mass customization while, at the same time, allows Coors corporate to maintain management of the images for license compliance. The system also gave Coors a first-mover advantage over its larger competitors, as its agreement with the hardware manufacturer was exclusive for Coors in the industry. Overall, the POS system provides innovative and widely accepted support for the Company's marketing programs.

The DST Tool Was Last

The last addition to the POS Suite was a "digital sales tool" (DST), developed specifically for retailers by Coors e-Business. Using the DST, retailers can view a layout of their facility (e.g., restaurant or store) online and evaluate alternative placement of POS materials for maximum advantage. The DST is effective in encouraging a retailer demand pull in the POS marketing space. For example, a Coors distributor who was lax in encouraging the use of POS materials now finds its retail customers demanding them.

Conclusions

Business Benefits

The POS application suite improved the ordering process by moving it from a paper-based process to an Internet platform, thus removing time and cost from the process. Distributors and retailers are now able to log on to the Coors portal, tailor POS material to their liking, and place their orders. The system gives the benefits of central control combined with mass customization and timely response. At its peak during the 2002 NFL season, for example, it proved capable of handling more than one completed order per minute, with each order consisting of a large number of individual transactions. The fulfillment cycle time was reduced, as were its associated costs. Finally, the e-POS tool blind-sided the competition, delighted Coors' distributors and retailers, and supported Coors' transformational marketing programs with an equally transformational information system.

The most important aspect of Coors' new POS system is that it strongly supports Coors' marketing approach aimed at the young adult market. As a result, the POS system is widely accepted by Coors' distributors, who view it as a robust growth engine to increase sales in their territories. As a result, Coors' distributors are more excited about the company's products than was the case for some time. The new POS suite allows the distributors to focus on the message of the marketing campaign, rather than the ordering and fulfillment process.

Contribution of Agile Development Methodologies to the Project's Success

The use of agile development methodologies contributed to the success of this critically important project in several ways, as touched on earlier in this chapter and as summarized in the following sections.

- *Balancing tight control and system flexibility.* The contract with the NFL required that Coors maintain tight control over the system's functionality while offering, at the same time, a high degree of flexibility to users to modify the system. The system was designed with a structure (Web style sheets) that permitted users in Marketing, for example, to make changes within acceptable constraints. Current technologies such as .Net and Java offer more options than what was widely available in 2002, but the principle of system structure offering user flexibility within bounds remains the same.
- *Scalability.* Conventional wisdom focuses on scalability as essentially a hardware issue, i.e., how easy is it to add hardware or network capacity to permit a system to handle volume increases? In an agile environment, however, scalability is likely to be a software interface issue as a system grows to absorb additional alliance partners. The original software must, again, be flexible enough to be easily modified to absorb new alliance partners into its ecosystem. This requires careful attention to the way requirements are established and the way that code is written.
- *The organizational context for incremental delivery.* As noted earlier, the adoption of an agile development methodology in this instance "was in contrast to seeking to build all of the functionality in one iteration, hoping that full functionality would win the customers over." IT must understand the business issue well enough to be able to convince the business units that the problem can be decomposed into smaller deliverables. At the same time, the company must be nimble enough to absorb change more rapidly and at more frequent intervals. One key take-away for Coors was that an incremental delivery model is very much dependent on organizational culture and the way it views and accepts change.

Summary

As is usually the case regarding success in information technology, the true success of this project was not strongly correlated to a novel use of technical tools, but rather to the IT department partnering well with business users over a critical need for the company. In 2002, perhaps no area was more critical for Coors' IT to partner with than the firm's Sales and Marketing departments. At that time, Coors was transforming its approach to sales and marketing in an unprecedented way. Looking back, this transformation was seamless despite the rapid changes that took place in the marketing content, the marketing message, and the delivery mechanisms to place these campaigns in front of the target market. Despite the short delivery time demanded of the e-Business and the business departments, the POS suite met its goal for integration with the business. As a result, the initiative was successful from initial marketing concept to fulfillment (i.e., ordering materials and getting them to the end user). Finally, the transition to the new system was seamless, and that is the way it should be: routine business as usual. The only time IT should be exciting is when a project turns into a runaway, an event to be avoided at all costs, as anyone who has been through one can attest.

References

Colias, M. (2000). Colorado Business Awards: Winners hail from old, new economies. *ColoradoBiz*. Retrieved from: http://www.cobizmag.com/.

Coors (2003). Retrieved from: http://www.coors.com.

Fingar, P. and Aronica, R. (2001). *The Death of "e" and the Birth of the Real New Economy*. Tampa, FL: Meghan-Kiffer.

Fox, P. (2002). Portals can open array of services. *Computerworld*, March 4, 2002.

Gilbert, A. (2001). Coors bellies up to the bar for IT on tap. *InformationWeek*, August 27, 2001.

Leffingwell, D. and Widrig, D. (2000). *Managing Software Requirements*. Boston: Addison-Wesley.

MacArthur, K. (2002). Coors wins bid to be NFL's official beer: Beats Miller and Anheuser-Busch for $300 million prize. *Ad Age*, March 26, 2002.

Slater, D. (2002). GM proves e-business matters. *CIO Magazine*, April 1, 2002. Retrieved from: http://www.cio.com/archive/040102/matters.html.

Tarquinio, A. J. (2002). Investing; even in dry spells, the beer is flowing. *New York Times*, November 24, 2002.

Organizational Agility with Mobile ICT? The Case of London Black Cab Work

19

Silvia Elaluf-Calderwood and Carsten Sørensen

The co-evolution of Information and Communication Technology (ICT) and new ways of working constantly challenge the existing order of organizing work. One of the most interesting current technologies is that of mobile ICT comprising mobile (cell) phones, notebook computers, Personal Digital Assistants (PDAs), as well as various forms of convergence between these. The organizational deployment of these technologies marks new opportunities for agile organizing of work activities and associated information. The organization of work is already emerging as less and less reliant on centralized structures and more and more dependent on decentralized networking activities (Nardi, Whittaker, and Schwarz, 2002; Malone, 2004). Emphasis on services rather than products will imply focus on rapid innovation in global teams, close customer contact, and complex adaptation of services to specific needs. Agility for the twenty-first century organization involves strategic choices regarding the mobilization of work activities. Services are produced and consumed concurrently, and more and more work can be accomplished where it makes most sense and not where the PC happens to be. This implies that the death of distance is the birth of context as a strategic resource for the agile organization. Choice of context implies positioning members of the organization where it makes most sense for them to be and that could more often than not be contexts where they will engage in direct human interaction.

The notion of mobile working as an aspect of organizational agility can be a fairly elastic and slippery concept. Mobility can denote everything from simple geographical movement of individuals (Kristoffersen and Ljungberg, 2000) over abstractions of work activities (Luff and Heath, 1998) to the mobilization of society (Urry, 2000). One way of conceptualizing the relationship between ICT and mobility is to characterize the mobilization of interaction (Kakihara and Sørensen, 2002; Kakihara, 2003).

The mobilization of work and interaction raises the issue of the conduct and management of work and the associated technologies deployed to support this. As the application of mobile technologies in remote and mobile work activities denotes mediated interaction, it raises a number of issues of mediation (Olson and Olson, 2000). Furthermore, as the technologies imply a significant strengthening of the direct relationships between individual activities and associated technological support, essential issues of individual discretion and organizational control are evoked (Al-Taitoon, 2005).

The role of ICT support for agile organizing of geographically mobile work naturally involves the combination of supporting the individual in his or her situated decision making and of mobilizing interaction. Mobile ICT supports the individual in managing information locally, seeking information in remote sources, negotiating mutually interdependent participants to coordinating coupled activities, and managing these activities.

This chapter considers the role of mobile ICT for agile organizing of work activities and will highlight some pertinent issues through the detailed discussion of the relationships between London Black Cab work and supporting mobile technologies. London Black Cabs are heavily regulated, and their history goes back to 1620 when they were called Hackney cabs (Bobbit, 2002). They are the only cabs allowed to respond to street hailing, and have traditionally relied entirely on "The Knowledge," an exam that requires them to know and recall from memory up to 400 routes or "runs" in Greater London in order to get a license with the Public Carriage Office. We have studied how complete reliance on The Knowledge is being challenged by emerging mobile technologies supporting Black Cab work. According to the Public Carriage Office (part of Transport for London and responsible for management of the taxi licensing), there are over 20,000 London Black Cabs registered and over 40,000 licensed drivers. Most of the London Black Cabs are independent companies, and, with the emerging competition from mini-cabs where the entry barrier is much lower, agility is essential.

Although still in its early stages, there has been some research of the socio-technical aspects of mobile working (Orr, 1996; Kristoffersen and Ljungberg, 2000; Brown, Green, and Harper, 2001; Wiberg, 2001; Kakihara, 2003; Ling, 2004; Wiredu, 2005). In particular, studies of police work in patrol cars (Manning, 2002; Sørensen and Pica, 2005) and of airplane pilots (Hutchins, 1995) may be relevant for the understanding of vehicle-based working.

In this chapter, we will argue that agile ICT for mobile working emerges from specific contexts where socio-technical arrangements unfold. This is partly due to the interactive nature of the arrangements where the interplay between individual discretion and organizational arrangements forms a range of possible outcomes for any given socio-technical arrangement.

The following section characterizes the institutional arrangements of Black Cab work in London. Then we will briefly outline the research approach and present three socio-technical arrangements of Black Cab work. Later in the chapter, we will discuss and compare these three arrangements in terms of organizational agility in mobile working. Last, we will discuss agile ICT for mobile working and conclude the chapter.

Black Cab Work in London

London Black Cab Service

The history of the London Black Cab is rich and long (Georgano, 2000; Bobbit, 2002). There are two main types of licensed London cabs: licensed Black Cabs and minicabs. The differences are based on the licensing method, fares, and requirements for route planning. To become fully licensed, London Black Cab drivers need to pass The Knowledge. Black Cab drivers or "cabbies" (Townsend, 2003) are proud of this standard of knowledge that allows them so far to be faster than any Global Positioning System (GPS) available (Skok, 1999).

What is The Knowledge? The Knowledge is defined by the Public Carriage Office as "the in depth knowledge of the road network and places of interest in London within a 6 mile radius of Charing Cross Station in Central London (TfL, 2006)." To be accredited with The Knowledge, candidates have to learn from the "Blue Book," a list of routes or runs. The number of routes is currently 320, covering around 25,000 streets. The exam is a basic written exam and a number of one-on-one interviews or "appearances" in which applicants are given the start and finish of an imaginary route and have to describe the shortest route between them.

Most drivers own their vehicles and are proud of their high level of independence when choosing work. Minicab companies, however, have been able to compete with cabbies by hiring drivers who do not have "The Knowledge" but can complement their routes using GPSs. Minicab drivers tend to drive vehicles owned by the minicab company, and they are much less independent than Black Cab drivers when choosing work.

In terms of our arguments concerning organizational agility, it is interesting that in London Black Cab driver work it is still possible to compare live data between traditional and new technology-driven ways of working. In the context of the London Metropolitan area, the use of electronic booking systems in cabs is a relatively new development. Unlike many other cities in the world where the use of GPS is generalized in cabs (Liao, 2003), most radio cab circuits still use inherited systems based on two-way radios and paper-clip bookings. This is the case for both licensed cabs and minicabs (restricted licensing).

The migration to electronic cab booking systems aims to take maximum advantage of the position of the cab at a certain time. Most radio circuits see this positional awareness as a strategic advance when allocating work. When a booking is made, the job is allocated to a driver close to the passenger, reducing the arrival time (of the cab to the passenger) and waiting time (by the cab driver). Drivers do compete with each other for hailing passengers; hence members of the same radio circuit tend to be overzealous when determining whether the allocation of the job has been fair and not subject to the call center dispatcher preferences. The use of computerized booking systems is a means both for optimization and for reducing possible conflicts between drivers.

Black Cab Work Tasks

The cab driver's work can be presented in terms of the interaction of the physical space, the mobile actor, and the technology attached to work (Weilenmann, 2003; Elaluf-Calderwood and Sørensen, 2004). This way of looking at cab drivers' work is complemented by understanding the idea of what mobile work is and what it means in the context of spatially mobile workers.

From the interviews and observations completed, it can be said that when a cab driver works around the city searching for work, the search and its success depends on a number of factors:

- *Physical location*: Where the driver and his or her vehicle are physically located at a certain time.
- *Awareness*: The driver needs to be aware of events on the road such as accidents, congestion, competition from other drivers, etc.
- *Time*: Drivers go to work with a general timetable framework; drivers perceive time either as a compressed unit (e.g., driving while talking to friends) or frag-

mented (e.g., events or actions can occur at discrete intervals of time, such as a conversation followed up between two passenger hails using the mobile phone).

- *Strategic planning*: Cab drivers' decisions, such as how many jobs they wish to take from the electronic booking system, when they will take them and where (e.g., some drivers plan only to take hails in the direction of the driver's home one hour before finishing their work shift, allowing them to get close to home while being paid for it).
- *Situational acts*: When on the road, which hailing situations are preferred by drivers based on the context of work, but also the opposite (which are not preferred and why).
- *Planned acts*: Different from strategic planning as the time intervals when these acts are planned are short and are a function of the randomness of available work.
- *Human factors*: How the cab driver mediates with the mechanical, technological, and human aspects of his work. If the driver is tired, lonely, stressed, or subject to other human emotions, it will affect the way jobs are taken.
- *Role of the technology*: Cab drivers might use one preferred system for obtaining jobs or might choose to be more traditional and work the street hailing of passengers.
- *Emerging practices*: The evolution of the physical space in the city together with new technologies is creating new working practices that cab drivers are taking on-board for their work.
- *Chance to succeed*: This category expresses the randomness of the work, as success might occur "at the first turn of an imaginary fortune wheel" or might take many of the factors listed above in combination. Drivers express their measure of success in different ways currently under analysis.

Research Approach

This chapter reports from an ongoing longitudinal study of London Black Cab work. The empirical data for this chapter is provided by both qualitative interviews with 35 Black Cab drivers from whom deep contextual knowledge was gained, and through 14 hours of videotaped observation of driver behavior (this part of the research is still being developed) in order to obtain deep situational insight. This chapter in particular focuses on a comparison between different technological means for connecting a potential customer to a Black Cab within the normal working conditions of the driver.

The research approach is based on interpretative and ethnographic methods. The interpretative approach aims at understanding the world as it is, created by intersubjective meanings in a social process. It tries to understand a social phenomenon from the perspective of participants in their natural setting. In an interpretative study, the researcher does not try to impose his or her own previous understanding onto the situation. The case study (London Black Cab) presented in this chapter places a significant interpretative value on the narrative as expressed by the object of study. The understanding of the differences between the living situation of the mobile user and the researcher's hypothetical views is of paramount importance. Distinguishing between situated interaction in the world on one hand and interaction thought technologies on the other is at the heart of virtual environments and mobility studies (Luff and Heath, 1998). The strategy defined for the collection of data was the use of one-on-one interviews with drivers from diverse social and cultural backgrounds. There has been research work (still ongoing) in recording everyday situations in which drivers use their computer systems and/or mobile devices. For analytical techniques, the research is done using cognitive approaches, and microanalysis has been applied when required. There is very limited access to logs or records provided for the systems discussed, hence this chapter focuses on how the systems are used (cab drivers, passengers) and not on how the systems work (interfaces, mobile antennas, software, hardware, etc). We will employ the following factors in our comparison of the three arrangements of Black Cab work:

- *Ubiquity*: Identifying the location of drivers closer to the passenger wishing to be transported. This can be an accurate position (by GPS) or an estimated position (by zones).
- *Reachability*: Communication between cab driver and call center or cab driver and passenger should be intelligible enough to provide basic information about the ride.
- *Security*: Passengers and cab drivers value the ability to travel and drive in safety. An added value for any system is the capacity for providing a backup communication media in the case of emergencies.
- *Ergonomics*: From the driver's perspective, a system that minimizes distractions from driving concentration is important; it is also important to note that the billing systems (credit card swap or account register) can also be incorporated into the system.
- *Easy learning*: From the driver's point of view, it is important that the system is easy to use, easy to understand, and allows the rapid location of relevant information. The complexity of this objective is increased by the fact that drivers have different levels of general education and computer knowledge.

These aspects form our defined dimensions of agility in terms of Black Cab work. The dimensions described above were extracted from the data obtained from the interviews and video recording material as direct observations of how Black Cab drivers do their everyday work. Agility is then embedded in their everyday actions, either when working in conventional ways (using The Knowledge and no Mobile ICT) or when Mobile ICT is a driving force.

Agility Arrangements of Black Cab Work

Arrangement A: Traditional Black Cab Work (Figure 19.1)

Traditional Black Cab Work is primarily a knowledge-based activity (Skok, 1999) without or minimal ICT support. The lack of positional awareness with regard to other drivers in an area of the city, and being primarily working in isolation, means that the more knowledge the driver has the more chances he or she has to make more revenue. Black Cab drivers also present themselves as a quality service in which the customer can feel confident to be driven by the best route choice and hence value for money. This is not always the case with other types of taxis available in London. Part of this branding perception is the fact that Black Cab drivers are heavily regulated by the Public Carriage Office and that licensing requirements are so rigorous, as explained earlier.

Agility is primarily obtained through four years of studying The Knowledge (400 routes in Central London) and fine-tuned through years of understanding how to place the taxi in contexts making the most money.

Figure 19.1

Black cab setup for Arrangement A, the traditional Black Cab without mobile ICT (computer or phone support). ***The panel shown is the factory-delivered vehicle drivers get when buying a new Black cab***

Mobile phones have crept into the taxis as a means for keeping in contact with family and friends, and thus helped maintain the work-life/home-life balance. However, they are also used for coordinating Black Cab work either when used to communicate the driver with a call center, or when the driver and passenger establish direct contact for the negotiation of the hail.

Arrangement B: Dispatched Radio Taxi (Figure 19.2)

This is a cab radio call system that has fully migrated to an electronic booking system. Potential passengers book by phone or over the Internet, with no Short Message Service (SMS) accepted. Payment methods are of three types: cash, credit card, and account. The company gives preference to account customers over all other transactions. Customers get an ID number for their booking or an email confirmation. An estimated cost of the journey is also provided on request, and customers are required to state their final destination for this purpose. Customers do not interact with the cab driver until they are picked up at the start of the journey.

Drivers know the location of the customer and their approximate destination. Drivers book in the electronic system based on a virtual zone map. They manually input the zone they wish to be included in. The system automatically assigns them to a virtual queue of cabs, based on order of input of zone. To avoid driver "choose and pick" of jobs from the system, drivers cannot see the destination (or the cost) until the job is accepted. Drivers can have three modes of "location" in the system (if on): p.o.b. (passenger on board), free (no passenger), or c.t.e. (close to end of journey, which allows the driver to be reassigned a place in the queue). There is also the option to be off the system if hailing passengers from the street.

Discrepancies do occur, as passengers are charged from the time the cab arrives to the point of collection, regardless of how long the passenger makes the cab wait, so for the last three years the new computer systems are being provided with a GPS that

Figure 19.2

Black Cab setup for Arrangement B, the dispatcher-based system. *The panel shown has been adapted from the factory-delivered veicle by the addition of a mobile ICT that works as a communication device, computer booking system, and GPS information system.*

can be checked by the call center when there is a dispute. In general the service is good; drivers tend to work a combination of radio jobs and street jobs.

Drivers have mobile phones in their cabs, but it is not the primary mode of communication for work. Most work allocation is negotiated by the computerized system.

Drivers feel very comfortable with their radio circuit passengers as in most cases these will be account passengers—what they call "quality people" (businesspeople), hence knowledge of the journey destination allows the driver to relax somewhat.

Drivers express a level of respect for their passengers in their behavior: trying to make few or no calls on their mobile phones or keeping the radio volume low. Drivers are very receptive to passengers' attitudes and desires (if the passenger wants to chat, the driver will listen and try to be more communicative). This is also true if dealing with cash jobs on late nights, as far as the booking is made through the radio circuit.

In Arrangement B, the agility of the system is a fluid mesh of the individual drivers agility (Arrangement A) and the ability to transcend geographical barriers through sourcing customers to a dispatcher.

Arrangement C: Automatic Customer-Driver Connection (Figure 19.3)

The cab is provided with a GPS that sends the location of the driver in real time to an application server. Passengers call a number using their mobile phone and, based on the location services of the network, the closest cab to the passenger is called directly through the mobile phone in the cab. The driver and passenger negotiate by voice call where the passenger will be picked up, the estimated time of arrival at the destination (for the cab), and in some cases where the passenger wants to go and method of payment.

Figure 19.3

Black cab setup for Arrangement C with automatic matching of customer and cab. ***The panel shown has been adapted with three mobile ICT devices: two cell phones (one for driver's private use, the other for work use), and one mobile billing system connected to a GPS network.***

Street pickups or street hails can also be booked by SMS, in which case the driver calls the passenger to confirm the call (as of this writing, there is no Internet or call center available) using the text header in the SMS message.

The main issue for drivers is that customers do not wait for the cab they booked if there is another one available arriving earlier on. This makes the drivers wary of customers disappearing. It is perceived as a disadvantage that the customer cannot be charged a deposit in advance for the assignment. There are also fluctuations in the precision of the GPSs and how jobs are allocated. There is no queuing; hence the driver has the added tasks of getting information from the passenger, defining the driving route, driving with the passenger, and obtaining his or her payment.

Drivers use their mobile phones as the primary source of communication for job allocation. Job rejection does not affect the chances of getting a new job allocated immediately. However, if the driver answers the call, he is obliged to comply and do the run (travel to the passenger).

This issue depends upon the time of day. At night, drivers are at especially high risk of not finding passengers or not being paid. Hence drivers have a more reserved attitude to jobs and tend to make rounds around the city more frequently than the drivers in Arrangement B. There is no call center associated with the system; hence if a driver gets in trouble the only assistance he or she can reach is using a mobile phone. The GPS is used to locate drivers but does not help them find the optimum route to their destination. This is primarily planned as in Arrangement B using The Knowledge.

The agility in Arrangement B is the direct and automatic connection between the customer and the driver.

Types of ICT Support

The transition from unsupported Black Cab work to Mobile ICT work is a process that has taken several years. ICT has evolved from basic radio circuits with one centralized manned control center, to the current GPS and computer booking cab systems in use. The main differences in the ICT support provided come from the ways the technology is being used 1) to provide work based in contextual location and 2) as a supporting tool in the knowledge used by taxi drivers to optimize their work.

The agility in the ICT support is supporting the knowledge drivers already have and increasing their awareness to other drivers' contextual location when seeking work. The better the ICT support can combine physical location with time location, the better drivers can make the most from the ICT and obtain good results.

Arrangement A is the most social arrangement with some support from mobile phones that seamlessly has crept into the taxi. Arrangement C is the most technologically advanced arrangement of work, and Arrangement B denotes the middle position.

However, this is only a simple reading of the situation and one that merely looks at the surface. Agility in mobile working is not so much about the socio-technical arrangement as such. It depends directly upon how this arrangement unfolds in the concrete context of application. As we saw in Arrangement C, even the most interesting technological opportunities may be thwarted by minor practical barriers. There are problems with support of individual taxi work (not coordination) through GPSs if we assume the driver relinquishes control entirely and simply follows directions when these are far from perfect.

Agile ICT for Mobile Working

Emerging versus Planned Decisions

When using Arrangement B, the passenger exchanges instant connectivity for convenience (if the booked cab does not arrive on time, the radio circuit is able to provide the next closest one in a matter of minutes). When using Arrangement C, the passenger has a level of ubiquity attached to his or her position, and security is exchanged for instant connectivity (the passenger and the driver discuss in real time when and where to be collected).

This way of negotiating position is not unique to the cab business; the police also use diverse methods of communication to create awareness of position and location, and there are similar trade-offs between these methods and instant connectivity (Sørensen and Pica, 2005). In order to understand this without undermining the factors that attract passengers to choose one method over another, we also need to look into the driver's convenience and the ideas provided by mobility studies (Perry et al., 2001).

Many events might occur as the cab driver moves around the city searching for possible passengers, while being shown as available for the radio circuit. *Radio circuit*, the generic name used for *computerized cab circuits*, is seen as a reliable—but not the main or only—source of income for cab drivers. This is in part due to the careful control of the cost of each journey, competing against street hails, which are less carefully recorded and where discrepancies can occur.

With Arrangement B, in which the driver relies on the information provided by the computerized system to obtain work, each time he or she is "live" in the system the driver is allocated a queuing number. This queuing number allows the driver some level of planning (Which job will I take?) based on his or her approximate physical

Table 19.1

Comparison of Arrangements A, B, and C			
	Arrangement A Traditional Black Cab	**Arrangement B Computer Booking System**	**Arrangement C Positional Booking System**
Ubiquity	Driver has no system integrated in the vehicle. Driver determines when the cab is made available. No minimum number of rides per month. Drivers work on their own, loosely associated or informally to other cab drivers.	Driver has the system integrated in the vehicle. Driver determines when the cab is made available. Driver is company shareholder with participation in the working practice decisions. Minimum 30 rides per month are required.	Driver has the system integrated in the vehicle. Driver determines when the cab is made available. Driver pays a flat fee (monthly) for access to the system. No minimum number of rides are required.
Reachability	Based on individual knowledge of the transport, the driver decides working routes and is available for hire accordingly.	Multiple repeaters around London. Good reception. The system has a manual backup and alternative backbone network.	Access is supported by commercial satellites and GPS network. Good reception, but sometimes there are some reachability issues.
Security (from competition)	None. There is a very limited awareness of other drivers' position and behavior. Since bookings are determined by supply and demand, drivers work in a "first-come, first-served basis." Competition is high and intensive.	Good. Access to transactions and locations for driver and passenger are managed by call center. Once a booking is completed, the chances that the job will be taken away from the allocated driver are low. Drivers only can see nonallocated jobs. In most cases, passengers need to provide a credit card for payment.	Reasonable. Communications between driver and passengers are completed using digital mobile networks. There is no assurance that once driver and passenger have agreed to the service, the passenger will wait for a cab. Sometimes passengers will take the first cab that arrives to their position, and not the one booked.

(continues)

Table 19.1

Comparison of Arrangements A, B, and C—*cont'd*				
		Arrangement A Traditional Black Cab	**Arrangement B Computer Booking System**	**Arrangement C Positional Booking System**
Convenience	Driver	Driver has to keep his or her knowledge constantly up-to-date, but is very exposed to unexpected events in the work context.	Driver is given in advance all information for ride by computer system, such as passenger location, destination, cost, and payment.	Driver has to negotiate with passenger the collection time, location, and method of payment. This negotiation can distract the driver from driving well when on the road.
	User	Variable. On most occasions, waiting times in Central London are short, but depending upon supply and demand, and on location of the passenger, waiting times can be very long. Also, driver might refuse to take passenger to destination on the grounds of safety, end of shift, etc.	Passenger can book cab by phone call or Internet. Methods of payment are diverse. Passenger is also provided with estimated time of arrival for booked cab.	Passenger can only book by mobile phone calls. External conditions such as noise of the road can affect the quality of the call. It can take a long time to get passenger details. In some cases, another cab will arrive at the passenger location and the passenger will call to cancel the booking.
Localization		Based on the driver knowledge. It varies during the day and during the week and season. There are fewer taxis available in London during January and August, as most drivers take holiday on those months.	Driver inputs his or her location in the Zone system. GPS is not used to verify the position of the driver unless there is a complaint or dispute. The driver can change the zone system manually at any time.	Driver's location is determined by an advanced GPS system built into the vehicle. This system is a real time feature that cannot be changed manually but only turned off.

Table 19.1

Comparison of Arrangements A, B, and C—*cont'd*				
		Arrangement A Traditional Black Cab	**Arrangement B Computer Booking System**	**Arrangement C Positional Booking System**
Instant Connectivity	Driver	Visual. Driver sees passenger on the road and stops for hail.	Driver is able to correlate a position in a cab queue when waiting for a new job assignment.	There is no queuing system. The nearest cab to the passenger gets the job from the system.
	User	Visual. Passenger gestures for hailing a cab to stop a cab.	A reply is obtained from a call center or Internet page and email confirming booking.	Direct communication with driver and confirmation that it is on its way.
Comparison is from the driver point of view unless otherwise stated.				

vehicle location within the parameters of the system (zones). In some cases, for example, a driver might have a queuing number such as 4, and while waiting to ascend to the top of the queue the driver might decide to take a short run around a physical area or stop at a cab rank for a break.

The driver is more relaxed as the pressures of constantly searching for new passengers is reduced by the greater trust placed in the computer system.

Cab drivers in Arrangement B know in advance their destination or proximity even before they have collected the passenger, allowing them to check routes, verify that there are no road closures, and so on. There is a level of safety associated with the idea of traveling when the destination is known.

With Arrangement C, in which the driver relies on his or her mobile phone to obtain work (besides street hails), the ubiquity is wider. Drivers get accustomed to longer runs on specific routes to maximize the number of passengers transported. However, passengers sometimes take the first cab that is closer to them and the driver loses his ride.

During the interviews, drivers in Arrangement B were reported to say that this uncertainty is the main reason they felt discouraged from trying Arrangement C.

With Arrangement C, drivers argued that using the system was advantageous when working at night; the cab density (number of cabs available) is reduced, passengers are more eager to confirm that the cab is a licensed one (especially female passengers), and passengers are prepared to wait longer times if necessary until one arrives. There is hefty competition from minicabs, but Black Cabs feel backed by their good reputation.

There is a relationship between the spatial distribution of cabs and the passengers that affects the social interaction, the expectations (from driver and passengers) before the journey, during the journey, and at the end of the journey.

With Arrangement C drivers find it more difficult to control their petrol costs: they tend to aim to find the information required for collection of the passenger, but only on collection find out the final destination. Sometimes the journey to the passenger can take as much time as the hail itself due to traffic congestion. Uncertainty becomes part of the space of interaction between the driver and passenger. At some point, the private space of the cab driver is claimed as public by the passenger (during the journey). At the same time, there is an interaction that links the situational acts (collecting a passenger) with the planned ones (where to go, cab driver choosing whether or not to be available), and so on.

Systems and Their Riddles

Black Cab drivers' concerns are driven by a sense of risk, associated with the idea of multiple tasking when driving their vehicles. Hence, there is a need for a simple electronic booking system implementation to be used in their everyday work.

In Arrangement B, drivers claimed that the computer screen was a distraction to their driving, and liked the fact that the system turns off to a black screen after being idle two minutes. They perceived Arrangement B as fair, with little competition between drivers in the radio circuit.

Nevertheless, problems do occur, such as when drivers are on the boundary of one zone and the job allocated is too far within the zone or there are physical obstacles that make the journey not worthwhile (sudden closure of roads or a one-way system). There is also the probability that another driver is closer to the passenger to be collected. Then communication to the call center is required to clear doubts. Misunderstanding can also arise when the description for the collection point or the passenger to be collected is not clear.

In Arrangement C, drivers are concerned with the accuracy of the GPS used. Central London has a high density of mobile masts; hence the accuracy of their most probable position is high. However, there is also greater competition: since the system does not provide a queuing system, two drivers in the same street might both be ideally located for a job or run appearing in the street, yet the allocation of the job is random and there is always a chance that the passenger will take the first taxi that passes close to him regardless of the agreement they might have with another driver.

There are also issues concerning billing and payment. Taxi drivers in Arrangement B know in advance the method of payment (cash, account, credit card) and since their destination is also known they have an advantage when estimating the best route and cost.

Failures occur in the computer systems when no jobs can be allocated. If the system is down, notification is provided to drivers. For drivers in Arrangement B, a broadcast on the two-way radio system announces the problem. For drivers in Arrangement C, a broadcast SMS is the way of announcement.

This type of system failure does not affect the passenger's chance of getting a cab when needed, but it might affect the payment method (if paying by credit card). It will also affect the interactivity between driver and passengers as uncertainty is added to the journey in terms of ubiquity and reachability. In these situations, some drivers switch to street mode until they are sure that the systems do work properly again. Having said this, outages are infrequent.

Computers in vehicles may fail, and in that case both systems have workshops where cabs can be repaired. This activity implies a downtime off the street, which drivers find difficult to accept as it is unplanned time off the road with a cost in their day profits.

Mobile ICT Challenging Mobile Work

The first and main concern for drivers is the competition between drivers using The Knowledge and drivers using GPSs, or in other words licensed cabs versus unlicensed cabs (for now). GPSs in London are not yet able to provide real-time information of what is happening on the very congested London roads. For example, routes closed by the police due to an emergency are only updated in GPSs after a gap in real time. Drivers are aware that this will not be the case when technology will be able to provide location services with real time. The need for The Knowledge is then questioned not only because of the technology but also by other factors such as congestion, more routes defined as one-way systems, and many alleys and shortcuts being closed due to safety measures.

Drivers express this change as a way of making their "skilled" job an unskilled one; anyone with a GPS could do their job. No specific training will be required to do a cab job. This is the case with minicab companies, which are gradually obtaining a bigger share of the cab market. Their costs are reduced because those companies can hire drivers at low rates, who are not required to own their cabs for work.

Drivers see the use of mobile technology as an enhancement of their private and social life, which can continue even when at work. They also appreciate the fact that their passengers seem to be at ease in using the back of their cabs as an extension of their offices, homes, bars, and so on by using mobile technology to be in touch with whom they want. Drivers highlight that as their work is isolated, human interaction is achieved through their mobile phone.

Conclusion

This chapter does not aim to do a theoretical review of the design parameters used in the design of cab systems or to describe state-of-the-art systems, but to analyze how everyday cab drivers adapt their working practices depending upon the technology.

In this chapter, only part of the empirical work completed has been presented. There is still a considerable amount of data to be analyzed under the socio-technical lenses explained in the introduction. Considering the complex spectrum of issues related to time and space faced by cab drivers and their passengers, considerable research remains to be done into how new technologies improve the services provided by the cab drivers to passengers. A first question regarding the evolution of human-to-human resource knowledge (such as The Knowledge) against computer-to-human resources (GPSs) used by cab drivers arises: Will "The Knowledge" be replaced by more advanced GPSs? Will call centers become redundant if smart systems could automatically handle passenger bookings? How will this affect the passenger and driver expectations of the service provided and used?

From the social point of view, there is richness and variety in the cab driver's job, which is affected by the use of mobile ICT. Drivers expressed feelings of isolation when doing their everyday work. Mobile ICT use is allowing drivers to overcome their isolation.

In terms of understanding the relevant factors for mechanisms for executing work with mobile workers, this ongoing research expects to contribute to further research. This can be accomplished by developing a model that maps the factors (listed in the "Research Approach" section above) with the occupational frameworks of time and space, which are currently being blurred through the use of technology such as mobile phones. In doing so, mobile workers can try to make sense of the socio-technical issues arising out of the use of mobile ICT.

References

Al-Taitoon, A. (2005). Making sense of mobile ICT-enabled trading in fast moving financial markets as volatility-control ambivalence: Case study on the organisation of off-premises foreign exchange at a Middle-East Bank. *PhD Dissertation*, London School of Economics and Political Science.

Bobbit, M. (2002). *Taxi: The Story of the London Taxicab*. London, UK: Veloce.

Brown, B., Green, N., and Harper, R. (eds.) (2001). *Wireless World*. London, UK: Springer-Verlag.

Elaluf-Calderwood, S. and Sørensen, C. (2004). Mobile work—Mobile life. In *The Fifth Wireless World Conference* (Green, N., ed.). University of Surrey.

Georgano, G. N. (2000). *The London Taxi*, 2nd ed. London, UK: Shire.

Hutchins, E. (1995). *Cognition in the Wild*. Cambridge, MA: MIT Press.

Kakihara, M. (2003). Emerging work practices of ICT-enabled mobile professionals. *PhD Thesis*. London School of Economics and Political Science.

Kakihara, M. and Sørensen, C. (2002). Mobility: An extended perspective. In *Thirty-Fifth Hawaii International Conference on System Sciences (HICSS-35)*, IEEE (Sprague Jr., R., ed.). Big Island, Hawaii.

Kristoffersen, S. and Ljungberg, F. (2000). Mobility: From stationary to mobile work. In *Planet Internet* (Braa, K., Sørensen, C., and Dahlbom, B., eds.), pp. 41–64. Lund, Sweden: Studentliteratur.

Liao, Z. (2003). Real-Time taxi dispatching using Global Positioning Systems. *Communications of the ACM*, 46 (5), 81–83.

Ling, R. (2004). *The Mobile Connection: The Cell Phone's Impact on Society*. Amsterdam: Morgan Kaufmann.

Luff, P. and Heath, C. (1998). Mobility in collaboration. In *Proceedings of Conference on Computer Supported Cooperative Work*, November 14–18, Seattle, WA, pp. 305–314. New York: ACM Press.

Malone, T. W. (2004). *The Future of Work: How the New Order of Business Will Shape Your Organization, Your Management Style, and Your Life*. Boston: Harvard Business School Press.

Manning, P. K. (2002). *Policing Contingencies*. Chicago: University of Chicago Press.

Nardi, B. A., Whittaker, S., and Schwarz, H. (2002). NetWORKers and their Activity in Intensional Networks. *Computer Supported Cooperative Work*, 11 (1–2), 205–242.

Olson, G. M. and Olson, J. S. (2000). Distance matters. *Human-Computer Interaction*, 15 (2/3), 139–178.

Orr, J. E. (1996). *Talking About Machines: An Ethnography of a Modern Job*. Ithaca, NY: Cornell University Press.

Perry, M., et al. (2001). Dealing with mobility: Understanding access anytime, anywhere. *ACM Transactions on Computer-Human Interaction*, 8 (4), 323–347.

Skok, W. (1999). Knowledge management: London taxi cabs case study. In *Proceeding of the 1999 SIGCPR Conference on Computer Personnel Research*, New Orleans, LA: ACM Press, 94–101.

Sørensen, C. and Pica, D. (2005). Tales from the Police: Mobile Technologies and Contexts of Work. *Information and Organization*, 15 (3), 125–149.

TfL (2006). *Transport for London: Public Carriage Office*. Retrieved from: http://www.tfl.gov.uk/.

Townsend, A. (2003). *Cabbie*. Stroud, UK: Sutton.

Urry, J. (2000). Mobile sociology. *British Journal of Sociology*, 51 (1), 185–203.

Weilenmann, A. (2003). Doing mobility. *PhD Dissertation*, Gothenburg University.

Wiberg, M. (2001). In between Mobile Meetings: Exploring seamless ongoing interaction support for mobile CSCW. *PhD Dissertation*. Department for Informatics, Umeå University.

Wiredu, G. (2005). Mobile computing in work-integrated learning: Problems of remotely distributed activities and technology use. *PhD Dissertation*, London School of Economics and Political Science.

Co-Evolution and Co-Design of Agile Organizations and Information Systems Through Agent-Based Modeling

Mark E. Nissen and Yan Jin

Today's organizational environment is highly dynamic for all enterprises—public and private—and very unpredictable for many. Organizations must adjust, adapt, and even reinvent themselves in response. This requires organizational agility. Information systems (IS) can enable and enhance such agility, or they can impede and degrade it. In a co-evolutionary sense, organizations and IS are closely interrelated, hence the design of one affects the design of the other. The problem is that few organizational designers have the knowledge and authority to design IS, and even fewer IS designers have the knowledge and authority to design organizations. The research described in this chapter addresses the co-evolution and co-design of organizations and IS through agent-based modeling. Building upon recent advances in Computational Organization Theory, we employ state-of-the-art, agent-based methods and tools to design organizations and IS *together*, along with associated work processes, as an integrated socio-technical system. Such an agent-based approach enables many virtual prototypes to be designed, tested, and refined before deciding upon a particular design configuration, and well before beginning the corresponding (re)design of organizations and IS in the operational enterprise. This represents an organizational analog to the manner in which physical artifacts—such as airplanes, bridges, and computers—are designed today: through computational modeling and virtual prototyping. Our agent-based approach is explained and illustrated in this chapter through articulation of a contemporary organization and IS design problem. Through this work, we identify several practical implications for managers of organizations and managers of IS, and we develop a forward-looking agenda for future research along these lines.

Design of Organizations and Information Systems

The term *design* connotes a purposeful, goal-driven, problem-solving activity, which "is concerned with how things ought to be, with devising structure to attain goals" (Simon, 1996, p. 133). In this section, we summarize briefly some key aspects from two areas: 1) the literatures on organizational design and information systems design, and 2) the literatures on co-evolution of organizations and information systems.

Organizational Design and Information Systems Design

The IS field has concentrated upon design almost from its inception (Walls, Widmeyer, and El Sawy, 1992). At this stage in the advance of research and practice, many textbooks have been written to articulate, codify, and teach IS design methods, with most centering on techniques for modeling, visualizing, and analyzing design alternatives (e.g., DeMarco, 1978; Gane and Sarson, 1979) for Information Technology (IT) artifacts. For instance, the use of entity-relationship diagrams (ERDs), dataflow diagrams (DFDs), object models, event-sequence charts, the Unified Modeling Language, architecture diagrams, and the like represents standard practice in IS design today. But as noted above, despite a wealth of research and practice in IS design, a dearth of knowledge and capability exists to address the design of organizations.

As a design science (van Aken, 2004), *organizational design* is prescriptive, and reflects a rational view of organizations (Scott, 2003) that emphasizes fit, for example, with the organization's environment, strategy, and goals (Burton and Obel, 2004). As such, organizational design represents the same kind of purposeful, goal-driven, problem-solving activity associated broadly with IS design (Hevner et al., 2004). But the scope of design is broader when the focus is on organizations than when limited to IT artifacts (Alavi and Leidner, 2001). Indeed, many scholars view organizational design as subsuming IS design, with technologies, organizational structures, personnel systems, and work processes all the focus of purposeful design (Leavitt, 1965). But others (e.g., Orlikowski and Barley, 2002) note that organizational designers treat technology often at only a superficial level, and as noted above, few have sufficient expertise in IS design.

With our present interest in design for the co-evolution of organizations and IS, we draw from both disciplines, seeking in part to integrate and extend organizational design and IS design along the lines of Nissen (2006), but seeking further here to adapt such integrated and extended design to address organizations and IS that must change—often substantially—as they co-evolve. In a sense, this design adaptation mirrors that of design for planned change, which drew great attention in the 1980s via Total Quality Management and in the 1990s through Business Process Reengineering. But in both cases, changes in organizations and IS were planned in advance, and once decided upon, a target design configuration was relatively fixed.

Alternatively, organizations and IS that co-evolve represent moving targets, which change in ways that cannot be forecast reliably on a consistent basis. Hence the nature of design itself—even the integrated design of organizations and IS—may have to adapt to address a co-evolutionary application domain, and such design adaptation must clearly be informed by knowledge of co-evolution. Using the terminology of Information System Design Theory (ISDT; see Walls, Widmeyer, and El Sawy, 1992), both the organization studies and IS fields stand to benefit from research addressing: *meta-requirements* focused on co-evolution; *meta-design* including organizational structures, work processes, and personnel systems, in addition to information technologies; and *kernel theories* that govern design requirements specific to supporting the co-evolution.

Co-Evolution of Organizations and Information Systems

Information systems are developed and applied to serve the purposes of organizations. At the same time, organizations must reinvent themselves in order to take advantage of the evolving IS. In this sense, organizations and IS co-evolve over time attempting to find better fit to each other. Organizations adapt their forms, strategies, and policies in response to the changes of the environment where other organizations and technologies evolve. On the other hand, as new organizational needs and technological innovations evolve, new IS are needed to play new roles, and new IS strategies and policies must be devised for the effectiveness.

Researchers in the field of organization science have studied organizational actions from an evolution and co-evolution perspective (Daft and Lewin, 1990, 1993; March, 1991, 1996; McKelvey, 1997, 1999; Lewin and Volberda, 1999; Lewin, Long, and Carroll, 1999). The key research question here is how do firms co-evolve with their environments (Lewin and Volberda, 1999). Evolution in general is a process in which evolving entities adapt to their changing environment through exploring new possibilities for revolutionary advancement, and exploiting old certainties for high efficiency and competence (Holland, 1975; Kuran, 1988). In the context of organization adaptation, March (1991) associates exploration with complex search, innovation, variation, risk taking, relaxed control, loose discipline, and flexibility. To explore is to experiment with new ideas, strategies, knowledge, and technologies in the hope of finding new and superior alternatives. Exploitation, on the other hand, involves improving existing ideas, technologies, and capabilities with a goal of achieving better efficiency and competence. It has been contended that the long-term survival of an organization depends on its ability to "engage in enough exploitation to ensure the organization's current viability and engage in enough exploration to ensure its future viability" (Levinthal and March, 1993). The balance between exploration and exploitation plays a key role for an organization to survive and for a population of specific types of organizations to evolve (Lewin, Long, and Carroll, 1999).

The development of new technologies in general has also been studied from a co-evolution perspective. Researchers have examined how individuals create the institutional environment that shapes a technology's emergence (Barley, 1986; Weick, 1990). Technologies and institutions interact reciprocally and continuously to shape each other (Rosenkopf and Tushman, 1993). The technological environments (i.e., institutions) are both outcome and medium of the reproduction of technological practices (Giddens, 1979). These environments both constrain and enable the development of new technologies, even as both are created in a co-evolutionary fashion (Garud and Rappa, 1994). When the process of technology development is probed, it becomes clear that technologies are socially constructed, and involve "constant negotiation and renegotiation among and between groups shaping the technology" (Bijker, Hughes, and Pinch, 1987). In this social constructive process, the interactions among individuals' beliefs, artifacts, and evaluation routines play a key role in determining the path of the technology.

Information systems are developed and implemented as technological solutions to achieve some stated operational capabilities and efficiency. From a perspective of designing better IS, the co-evolutionary nature of IS technologies and organizations has two important implications. First, it suggests the mutual constitutive role of IS in shaping organizations and of organizations in shaping IS (Kim and Kaplan, 2005).

Second, to achieve better IS development and adoption results, one needs to elaborate the macro-level concept of co-evolution into micro-level organizational processes and routines so that specific guidance can be generated to support IS design and implementation. In our research, we consider that the co-evolution of IS and organization involves work and work processes that provide a channel for the organization to interact with the bigger ecological environment. More specifically, we propose that IS and organizations including work processes should be co-designed so that best fit between the organizations and IS can be achieved. Co-design is our micro-level elaboration of the macro-level concept of co-evolution. In the following, we present an agent-based approach to co-design of organizations and IS.

An Agent-based Approach to Co-Design of Organizations and Information Systems

In this section, we describe our agent-based approach to co-design of organizations and IS. Drawing heavily from Nissen, Orr, and Levitt (2006) and Nissen and Levitt (2004), we begin with a general discussion of computational organization theory and agent-based modeling approaches to organizational design. We follow then with an overview of the Virtual Design Team (VDT) modeling framework, which is used to represent organizations and IS *together*, and which serves as our co-design platform.

Computational Organization Theory Research

Computational organization theory (COT) is an emerging, multidisciplinary field that integrates aspects of artificial intelligence, organization studies, and system dynamics/simulation (e.g., Carley and Prietula, 1994). Nearly all research in this developing field involves computational tools, which are employed to support computational experimentation and theorem proving through executable models developed to emulate the behaviors of physical organizations (e.g., Carley and Lin, 1997; Levitt, Long, and Carroll, 1999; Burton, Lauridsen, and Obel, 2002).

As the field has matured, several distinct classes of models have evolved for particular purposes, including descriptive models, quasi-realistic models, normative models, and man-machine interaction models for training (Cohen and Cyert, 1965; Burton and Obel, 1995). More recent models have been used for purposes such as developing theory, testing theory and competing hypotheses, fine-tuning laboratory experiments and field studies, reconstructing historical events, extrapolating and analyzing past trends, exploring basic principles, and reasoning about organizational and social phenomena (Carley and Hill, 2001).

Our research through the VDT is a branch of COT, built upon the planned accumulation of collaborative research over almost two decades to develop rich, theory-based models of organizational processes (Levitt, 2004). Using an agent-based representation (Cohen, 1992; Kunz, Levitt, and Jin, 1998), micro-level organizational behaviors have been researched and formalized to reflect well-accepted organization theory (Levitt et al., 1999). Extensive empirical validation projects (e.g., Christiansen, 1993; Thomsen, 1998) have demonstrated the representational fidelity and shown how the qualitative and quantitative behaviors of VDT computational models correspond closely with a diversity of enterprise processes in practice.

The VDT research program continues today with the goal of developing new micro-organization theory, and embedding it in software tools that can be used to design organizations in the same way that engineers design bridges, semiconductors, or airplanes—through computational modeling, analysis, and evaluation of multiple virtual prototypes. Clearly this represents a significant challenge. Micro-theory and analysis tools for designing bridges and airplanes rest on well-understood principles of physics (e.g., involving continuous numerical variables, describing materials whose properties are relatively easy to measure), and analysis of such physical systems yields easily differentiable equations and precise numerical computing. Of course, people, organizations, and business processes differ from bridges, airplanes, and semiconductors, and it is irrational to expect the former to ever be as understandable, analyzable, or predictable as the latter. This represents a fundamental limitation of the approach.

Within the constraints of this limitation, however, we can still take great strides beyond relying upon informal and ambiguous, verbal, theoretical descriptions of organizational behavior. For instance, the domain of organization theory is imbued with a rich, time-tested collection of micro-theories that lend themselves to qualitative representation and analysis. Examples include Galbraith's (1977) information-processing abstraction, March and Simon's (1958) bounded rationality assumption, and Thompson's (1967) task interdependence contingencies. Drawing on this theory, we employ symbolic (i.e., non-numeric) representation and reasoning techniques from established research on artificial intelligence to develop computational models of theoretical phenomena. Once formalized through a computational model, the symbolic representation is "executable," meaning it can be used to emulate organizational dynamics.

Even though the representation has qualitative elements (e.g., lacking the precision offered by numerical models), through commitment to computational modeling, it becomes semi-formal (e.g., most people viewing the model can agree on what it describes), reliable (e.g., the same sets of organizational conditions and environmental factors generate the same sets of behaviors), and explicit (e.g., much ambiguity inherent in natural language is obviated). Particularly when used *in conjunction with* the descriptive natural language theory of our extant literature, this represents a substantial advance.

Additionally, although organizations are inherently less understandable, analyzable, and predictable than physical systems are, and the behavior of people is nondeterministic and difficult to model at the individual level, it is well-known that individual differences tend to average out when aggregated cross-sectionally or longitudinally. Thus, when modeling aggregations of people, such as work groups, departments, or firms, one can augment the kind of symbolic model from above with certain aspects of numerical representation. For instance, the distribution of skill levels in an organization can be approximated—in aggregate—by a Bell Curve; the probability of a given task incurring exceptions and requiring rework can be specified—organization wide—by a distribution; and the irregular attention of a worker to any particular activity or event (e.g., new work task or communication) can be modeled stochastically to approximate collective behavior. As another instance, specific organizational behaviors can be simulated hundreds of times—such as through Monte Carlo techniques—to gain insight into which results are common and expected versus rare and exceptional.

Of course, applying numerical simulation techniques to organizations is hardly new (Law and Kelton, 1991). But this approach enables us to *integrate* the kinds of dynamic, qualitative behaviors emulated by symbolic models with quantitative metrics generated through discrete-event simulation. It is through such integration of qualitative and quantitative models—bolstered by reliance on sound theory and devotion to empirical validation—that our approach diverges most from extant research methods, and offers new insight into the organizational dynamics.

VDT Computational Modeling Environment

The VDT computational modeling environment consists of the elements described in Table 20.1, and has been developed directly from Galbraith's (1977) information processing view of organizations. This view of organizations, described in detail in Jin and Levitt (1996), has two key implications.

The first is ontological: We model knowledge work through interactions of *tasks* to be performed; *actors* communicating with one another and performing tasks; and an *organization structure* that defines actors' roles and constrains their behaviors. Figure 20.1 illustrates this view of tasks, actors, and organization structure. As suggested by the figure, we model the organization structure as a network of reporting relations, which can capture micro-behaviors such as managerial attention, span of control, and empowerment. We represent the task structure as a separate network of activities, which can capture organizational attributes such as expected duration, complexity,

Table 20.1

VDT Model Elements and Element Descriptions	
VDT Model Element	**Element Description**
Tasks	Abstract representation of any work that consumes time is required for project completion and can generate exceptions.
Actors	A person or a group of persons who perform work and process information.
Exceptions	Simulated situations in which an actor needs additional information, requires a decision from a supervisor, or discovers an error that needs correcting.
Milestones	Points in a project in which major business objectives are accomplished, but such markers neither represent tasks nor entail effort.
Successor links	Define an order in which tasks and milestones occur in a model, but they do not constrain these events to occur in a strict sequence. Tasks can also occur in parallel. VDT offers three types of successor links: finish-start, start-start, and finish-finish.
Rework links	Similar to successor links because they connect one task (called the *driver task*) with another (called the *dependent task*). However, rework links also indicate that the dependent task depends on the success of the driver task, and that the project's success is also in some way dependent on this. If the driver fails, some rework time is added to all dependent tasks linked to the driver task by rework links. The volume of rework is then associated with the project error probability settings.
Task assignments	Show which actors are responsible for completing direct and indirect work resulting from a task.
Supervision links	Show which actors supervise which subordinates. In VDT, the supervision structure (also called the *exception-handling hierarchy*) represents a hierarchy of positions, defining to whom a subordinate would go for information or to report an exception.
From Galbraith, J. R. (1977). *Organizational Design*. Reading, MA: Addison-Wesley.	

Figure 20.1

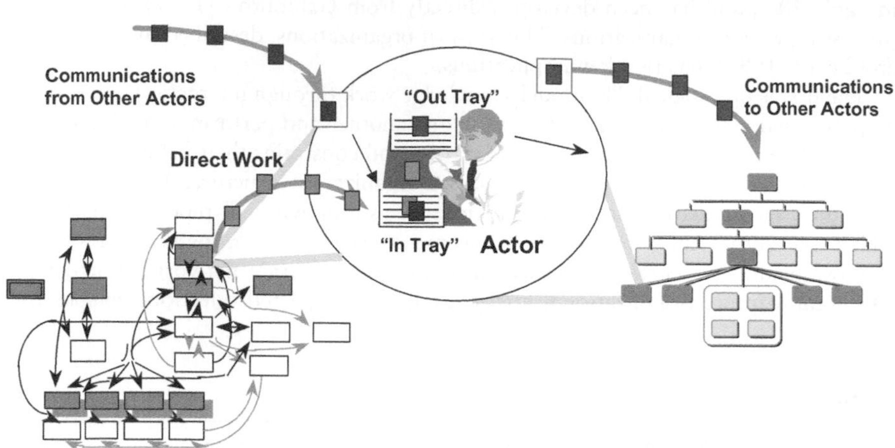

and required skills. Within the organization structure, we further model various *roles* (e.g., marketing analyst, design engineer, manager), which can capture organizational attributes such as skills possessed, levels of experience, and task familiarity. Within the task structure, we further model various sequencing constraints, interdependencies, and quality/rework loops, which can capture considerable variety in terms of how knowledge work is organized and performed.

As also suggested by the figure, each actor within the intertwined organization and task structures has a queue of information tasks to be performed (e.g., assigned work activities, communications from other actors, and meetings to attend) and a queue of information outputs (e.g., completed work products, communications to other actors, and requests for assistance). Each actor processes such tasks according to how well the actor's skill set matches those required for a given activity, the relative priority of the task, the actor's work backlog (i.e., queue length), and how many interruptions divert the actor's attention from the task at hand.

The second implication is computational: Both *direct work* (e.g., planning, design, management) and *indirect work* (e.g., decision wait time, rework, coordination work) are modeled in terms of *work volume*. The work volume construct is used to represent a unit of work (e.g., associated with a task, meeting, or communication) within the task structure. Measuring indirect work enables the quantitative assessment of (virtual) process performance (e.g., through schedule growth, cost growth, and quality). In addition to symbolic execution of VDT models (e.g., qualitatively assessing skill mismatches, task-concurrency difficulties, and decentralization effects) through micro-behaviors derived from organization theory, the discrete-event simulation engine enables (virtual) process performance to be assessed (e.g., quantitatively projecting task duration, cost, rework, and process quality).

Clearly quantitative simulation places an additional burden on the modeler in terms of validating the representation of a knowledge-work process, which generally requires fieldwork to study an organization in action. The VDT modeling environment benefits from extensive fieldwork in many diverse enterprise domains, for example, power plant construction and offshore drilling (Christiansen, 1993), aerospace (Thomsen, 1998), software development (Nogueira, 2000), health care (Cheng and Levitt, 2001; others). Through the process of "backcasting" (predicting known organizational outcomes using only information that was available at the beginning of a project), VDT models of operational enterprises in practice have demonstrated dozens of times that emulated organizational behaviors and results correspond qualitatively and quantitatively to their actual counterparts in the field (Kunz, Levitt, and Jin, 1998).

Viewing VDT as a validated model of project-oriented knowledge work, researchers have begun to use this dynamic modeling environment as a "virtual organizational testbench" to explore a variety of organizational questions, such as effects of distance on performance (Wong and Burton, 2000), or to replicate classic empirical findings (Carroll and Burton, 2000). Thus, the VDT modeling environment has been validated repeatedly and longitudinally as representative of both organization theory and enterprises in practice. This gives us considerable confidence in its results. However, because of its *information* processing view of the organization, the VDT modeling environment was not designed specifically to represent processes associated with flows of *knowledge* through an enterprise.

VDT Computational Model Validation

The VDT computational model has been validated extensively, over a period spanning almost two decades, by a team of more than 30 researchers in the VDT research group at Stanford University (Levitt, 2004). This validation process has involved three primary streams of effort:

1. Internal validation against micro-social science research findings and against observed micro-behaviors in real-world organizations.
2. External validation against the predictions of macro-theory and against the observed macro-experience of real-world organizations.
3. Model cross-docking experiments against the predictions of other computational models with the same input data sets (Levitt, Orr, and Nissen, 2005).

VDT is one of the few extant computational organization models that have been subjected to such a thorough, multi-method trajectory of validation.

VDT Adaptation for Co-Design of Organizations and Information Systems

Despite the many positive aspects of VDT articulated above, drawing principally from extant organization theory, the VDT modeling environment has been developed, validated, and refined to address relatively stable organizations. But as noted above, the context of co-evolution diverges qualitatively from one of stability. Further, the VDT environment has not been developed to address the technical details of IS in detail. But as noted above, technical details matter in organizational design and have been addressed only superficially via most organization design research to date. Hence conventional approaches to using the VDT to support organization design require some adaptation to address our application domain of co-evolving organizations and IS.

As described above, VDT models explicitly the interplay among organization design (e.g., structures, policies, people), technologies (e.g., communication and information sharing tools, training and knowledge storage, technical solutions), and work processes (e.g., tasks, requirements, dependencies). In organization design terms, the designer can effect a contingency perspective via VDT, through which we understand well that no single organization design is appropriate for all environments, technologies, and strategies (Lawrence and Lorsch, 1967; Thompson, 1967; Burton and Obel, 2004). The kind of dynamic and often-unpredictable environment associated with co-evolution can be anticipated using VDT as an organization design platform. For instance, through VDT, design parameters such as *centralization, formalization*, and *meeting requirements,* which have been used in part to represent rigid, *bureaucratic* organizations (Nissen, 2005), can be *modified* to relax organizational constraints for representing more agile organizational forms such as *Adhocracies* (Mintzberg, 1979).

Yet this still represents a fixed organization design point (e.g., either Bureaucracy *or* Adhocracy, but not both) and lacks explicit representation of organizational mechanisms, technologies, and routines required for change from one form to another (i.e., evolution). If we struggle to represent organizational evolution, then we will likely fail to model co-evolution effectively. Indeed, this represents a boundary in our current organization design knowledge, and hence a limit to our representational capability. Likewise, a comparable limit exists in terms of IS design (i.e., representing fixed IS design points, lacking explicit representation of change mechanisms), and our ability to represent technological systems as they evolve. And likewise, if we struggle to represent technological evolution, then we will likely fail to model co-evolution effectively. Indeed, this represents a boundary in our current IS design knowledge, and hence a limit to our representational capability. Clearly, a key aspect to cutting-edge research involves identifying and understanding such knowledge boundaries.

Recapitulating our arguments from above, within these boundaries and limitations, however, we can still make noteworthy advances by designing organizations and IS *together,* to complement, reinforce, and mutually support one another. This is our instantiation of *co-design:* our micro-level elaboration of the macro-level concept of *co-evolution.* For instance, reconsider the contrast between a Bureaucracy and an Adhocracy as qualitatively different organization design points (i.e., distinct organizational forms). We indicate above and demonstrate elsewhere (e.g., Nissen, 2005) how VDT can be used to represent these alternate organizational forms, and how its simulation capability can be used to emulate the dynamic behavior and performance of the different organizational types. But in addition, we integrate explicitly the design of different IS *to fit and accommodate* purposefully, and even *to enable* each distinct organization design point and corresponding organizational form.

Take the Bureaucracy as an example. Centralized decision making, hierarchical information flows, and formalized work processed represent theoretical and empirical hallmarks of this pervasive organizational form. Relatively large-scale, centrally managed, and standardized IS are well-understood for supporting the large, bureaucratic organization in particular, with a predominant emphasis upon synchronous communication (especially via face-to-face meetings). In VDT, we represent the structure and behavior of such IS by specifying model elements that include meeting requirements, supporting technologies such as video teleconferencing and high usage of telephones and memoranda for communication. Hence, the associated IS design is focused on supporting formal processes and centralized decision making through standardized systems and a preponderance of vertical communications. Together, this organization design and IS design are developed in an integrated manner (i.e., via co-design).

Further, we can test the relative fit and performance of this organization-IS co-design (i.e., the Bureaucracy and centralized IS) by changing VDT models to represent an alternate IS design point (e.g., distributed, non-standardized, end-user computing), and by comparing the simulated performance of this alternate organization-IS co-design point. Specifically, in VDT we represent the structure and behavior of such latter IS by changing model elements to eliminate some supporting technologies such as video teleconferencing, but to include others such as email, and to de-emphasize face-to-face meetings and high usage of telephone communication, with correspondingly greater emphasis upon asynchronous messages. Hence, the associated IS design is focused less on supporting formal processes and centralized decision making through standardized systems and a preponderance of vertical communications. Together as above, this organization design and IS design are developed in an integrated manner (i.e., via co-design), but one would not expect for this latter co-design to provide quite as good a fit as the one characterized above. Specifically, we model the Bureaucracy-central-IS design point in one representation and the Bureaucracy–end-user–IS design point as another. This provides the basis for some contingency-theoretic propositions.

The Adhocracy can be taken as a contrasting example. Decentralized decision making, horizontal information flows, and ad-hoc work processed represent theoretical and empirical hallmarks of this alternate organizational form. Relatively small-scale, locally managed, and idiosyncratic IS are well-understood for supporting the small, adhocratic organization in particular. In VDT, we represent the structure and behavior of such IS in the same manner outlined above, but also as above, we vary the organization-IS co-design to represent one that would be expected to fit relatively better than the other. Specifically, we model the Adhocracy-central-IS design point in one representation and the Adhocracy–end-user–IS design point as another. Together, this organization design and IS design are developed in an integrated manner (i.e., via co-design). Also as above, this provides the basis for some contingency-theoretic propositions.

Table 20.2 summarizes the four corresponding propositions. These represent the four, organization-IS co-design points illustrated by our models below. In particular, we show cells corresponding to expected fit and performance for the Bureaucracy versus the Adhocracy *and* for the Centralized IS versus the End-user IS design points. Where Contingency Theory indicates good fit between the design points (e.g., Bureaucracy and Centralized IS, Adhocracy and End-user IS), we indicate this simply by labeling the corresponding table cell "Fit." Likewise, where Contingency Theory indicates poor fit between the design points (e.g., Bureaucracy and End-user IS, Adhocracy and Centralized IS), we indicate this simply by labeling the corresponding table cell "Unfit." Through computational modeling below, we can examine empirically the propositions stemming logically from this table. In particular, we anticipate

Table 20.2

Model Co-Design Fit and Performance Propositions		
Organizational Form	**Centralized IS**	**End-user IS**
Bureaucracy	*Fit*	*Unfit*
Adhocracy	*Unfit*	*Fit*

superior simulated organizational performance where the organization-IS co-design reflects a better fit.

Practical Illustration

In this section we illustrate the use and utility of our adapted, agent-based modeling framework through explanation and elaboration of some alternate models suggesting practical application. Specifically, we summarize how the VDT modeling environment is used to represent the Bureaucracy and Adhocracy organizations, and we detail the experimental manipulations formulated to test the comparative performance of these alternate organizational forms with each of two different IS designs: Centralized and End-user. Beginning with the representation, a commercial version of the VDT modeling environment, called SimVision, is used for modeling and experimentation here. Drawing from our characterization above and from related modeling work (e.g., Nissen, 2005), we represent and parameterize the Bureaucracy and Adhocracy organization designs with each IS design. We first outline the nature of these organization-IS co-design models, after which we summarize their relative performance results produced by the corresponding computational emulations.

Co-Design Models

We can illustrate the Bureaucracy organization using the domain of military operations. This domain is useful to examine for several reasons. First, the military represents an extreme organization along several important dimensions (especially size, complexity, interdependency, geographical coordination, and hazard for failure), and hence represents a particularly challenging co-design problem. Where we are able to develop co-designs that solve organizational and technological problems for this kind of extreme organization, related co-designs for its less-extreme counterparts (e.g., manufacturing, service, and information) tend to be specializations and subsets of those developed for the Military (see Nissen, 2006). Second, the military represents a balanced mix between manual and technological processes. Unlike some domains (e.g., automobile assembly) in which technological support has reached relatively low limits, and others (e.g., software development) in which it remains pervasive and more encompassing, the military domain is neither biased nor predisposed toward one or the other. This helps to illustrate the relative advantages, disadvantages, and fit characteristics associated with alternate organization-IS co-designs.

Mission tasks can be used to represent both the Bureaucracy and Adhocracy computational models. Following current doctrine, the Bureaucracy organization plans and executes its operational tasks in two, sequential phases of two tasks each. Rework is required to correct mistakes made in one particular mission task that affect the performance of another. No communication links exist because task interdependence is predominately pooled and sequential (Thompson, 1967).

Actors are arranged in a three-level hierarchy: Command, Coordination, and Operations. According to Mintzberg's (1979) model, correspondence to the Strategic Apex, Middle Line (and staff functions) and Operating Core, respectively, should be clear. Links between actors and tasks represent job responsibilities. Operations level actors are responsible directly for mission tasks. The Command and Coordination level actors are responsible only indirectly for such mission tasks. But they have their own work tasks. These are unique to the Bureaucracy model. Daily, face-to-face/VTC meetings are also unique also to the Bureaucracy model.

In the Adhocracy organization, the same representational scheme described above applies, and the missions are the same. Alternatively, there are only two layers of organizational hierarchy, representing a flatter organization structure that still preserves the military mandate that someone is always in charge. Other differences between these two co-designs are specified in terms of model parameters as described below.

Table 20.3 summarizes the model parameterization for each of the four co-design points. To preserve continuity for the non-modeler, the discussion here remains at a relatively high level. Briefly, the first five parameters reflect organization design specifications. *Centralization* describes the degree to which information flows and decision making are hierarchical in nature, and *formalization* describes the degree to which work processes and routines reflect documented, standardized procedures. Reflecting both theory and practice, both parameter values are set to "High" for the Bureaucracy and to "Low" for the Adhocracy. *Team experience* describes the degree to which the same people tend to work together over time. The Bureaucracy is noted for treating people as fungible units and for neglecting the human component of teamwork, hence this parameter is specified as "Low," with the opposite for the Adhocracy. *Hierarchical levels* and *meetings* represent the number of hierarchical levels in the organization and the number of regularly scheduled meetings that require attendance, respectively. These parameter settings reflect contrasts between the Bureaucracy and Adhocracy forms also. Clearly these organizational designs reflect ideal types, and may not pertain specifically to any organizational instance in practice. Nonetheless they describe a broad array of organizations that are similar and comparable at the class level.

Table 20.3

Model Parameterization				
SimVision Parameter	**Bureaucracy Centralized IS**	**Bureaucracy End-user IS**	**Adhocracy Centralized IS**	**Adhocracy End-user IS**
Centralization	High	High	Low	Low
Formalization	High	High	Low	Low
Team experience	Low	Low	High	High
Hierarchical levels	3	3	2	2
Meetings	3	3	1	1
Matrix strength	Low	High	Low	High
Communication technology	VTC	Network	VTC	Network
Face-to-face/VTC communication	50%	20%	50%	20%
Telephone communication	20%	10%	20%	10%
Memorandum communication	30%	30%	30%	30%
email communication	0%	40%	0%	40%

The next six parameters reflect IS design specifications. *Matrix strength* is specified here to describe the degree to which people in an organization tend to participate personally in meetings. It is set at "Low" for centralized IS designs and at "High" for end-user designs. This parameter complements *communication technology*, which specifies the kinds of technologies available to support communications. In the case of centralized IS, the predominant communication technology is the video teleconferencing (VTC), whereas email is most pervasive in the end-user design. Clearly judgment is involved with modeling such as this. The beauty of semiformal model representation through our computational approach is that one can be very precise about how a model is specified, and another can understand exactly what modeling assumptions it entails. This provides a substantial contrast to models described solely through natural language, which is ambiguous, and through which the same terms (e.g., *centralized*, *end user*) can be used to mean very different things.

The next four parameters specify the fractions of communications effected through each of four modes: face-to-face/VTC, telephone, memoranda, and email communication, respectively. The parameter settings for the centralized IS design represent the manner in which such IS induce more meetings due to the rigid, largely vertical, and standardized information flows they support principally. Alternatively, the parameter settings for the end-user IS design represent the manner in which such IS enable more horizontal and impromptu communications to take place. As above, these IS designs reflect ideal types and may not pertain specifically to any implementational instance in practice. Nonetheless, they describe a broad array of IS that are similar and comparable at the class level. To reiterate from above, two models—Bureaucracy Centralized and Adhocracy End-user—represent theoretically better fits, and are expected to outperform the other two models—Bureaucracy End-user and Adhocracy Centralized—which represent theoretically poorer fits.

Co-Design Results

Following the 2 × 2 fit matrix from above, we can use the SimVision system to emulate the behavior and performance of four co-design points: 1) Bureaucracy and Centralized IS, 2) Bureaucracy and End-user IS, 3) Adhocracy and Centralized IS, and 4) Adhocracy and End-user IS. Reiterating again from above, we would expect for co-design points 1 and 3 to perform comparatively better than points 2 and 4 do, because they reflect theoretically better fits between organization and IS designs.

Table 20.4 summarizes the comparative performance results. Succinctly, the measure *work volume* quantifies the number of "person-days" of work associated with the modeled activities. Notice that all four models reflect identical results in terms of work volume. This stems from our discussion above and from our model specification that includes the same four mission tasks (e.g., "Air 1," "Surface") in every co-design. We show this to illustrate how our computational approach and tool can be used to *control* for factors such as workload that do not vary across co-designs, and we do not discuss this measure further in terms of comparative performance. All of the other measures in Table 20.4 vary markedly in terms of results.

For ease of comparison and explanation, we highlight in bold the "best" result for each measure. For instance, *duration* measures the number of days required for all mission tasks to be completed, and at 374 days, the Bureaucracy Centralized co-design reflects the fastest performance. Notice that the measure *duration* (days) differs from *work volume* (person-days), because many people work simultaneously on each mission task. As an example, if 10 people work simultaneously on a task for 10 days, then

Table 20.4

Comparative Performance Results				
SimVision Measure	**Bureaucracy Centralized IS**	**Bureaucracy End-user IS**	**Adhocracy Centralized IS**	**Adhocracy End-user IS**
Work volume	4,000	4,000	4,000	4,000
Duration	**374**	453	593	455
Rework	**1,268**	2,892	2,407	1,345
Coordination	599	663	3,333	**542**
Decision wait	250	329	474	**149**
Maximum backlog	**19**	26	48	22

the duration of the task is 10 days, and the work volume for the task is 100 person-days (i.e., 10 people × 10 days). Other performance measures include *rework* (the number of person-days of work required to fix mistakes), *coordination* (the number of person-days associated with coordinate work for the mission), *decision wait* (the number of person-days consumed by people waiting for decisions to be made), and *maximum backlog* (the number of days a particular organization gets behind during the mission). Many other performance measures (not shown) are calculated by SimVision, but do not add appreciably to the comparison here.

In terms of comparative performance, notice that the Bureaucracy Centralized co-design reflects the best performance in terms of three measures: *duration* (374 days), *rework* (1,268 days), and *maximum backlog* (19 days). Notice also that the Adhocracy End-user co-design reflects the best performance in terms of the other two measures: *coordination* (542) and *decision wait* (149). Clearly, lower values reflect better performance along all five of these measured dimensions. At first look, the two co-design points hypothesized to reflect comparatively better fit—Bureaucracy Centralized and Adhocracy End-user—correspond to the best performance for these five measures. But with a multidimensional performance set such as this, it is not straightforward to assess whether any single design point is necessarily *best overall*. For instance, the Bureaucracy Centralized co-design is best in terms of duration, but the Adhocracy End-user co-design is best in terms of decision wait. It is beyond the scope of this chapter to assess how one should trade off performance along one dimension versus that of another. But our use of this multidimensional performance set of measures adds considerable richness to the comparative analysis of the four co-design points.

Alternatively, one can examine readily the comparative performance of organization-IS co-designs. For instance, compare the Bureaucracy performance with each of the two IS designs (i.e., Bureaucracy Centralized vs. Bureaucracy End-user). Here we control for the organization design, and manipulate the IS design. Notice the Bureaucracy Centralized co-design is *superior across all performance measures* to its Bureaucracy End-user counterpart; that is, performance across each of the five measures is better uniformly. Hence the Bureaucracy Centralized co-design *dominates* the Bureaucracy End-user co-design. This comparative performance result is consistent with our co-design fit proposition from above.

As a related instance, compare the Adhocracy performance with each of the two IS designs (i.e., Adhocracy Centralized versus Adhocracy End-user). Here we control again for the organization design, and manipulate the IS design. Notice the Adhocracy Centralized co-design is *inferior across all performance measures* to its Adhocracy End-user counterpart; that is, performance across each of the five measures is worse uniformly. Hence the Adhocracy Centralized co-design *is dominated by* the Adhocracy End-user co-design. This comparative performance result is also consistent with our co-design fit proposition from above. With this agent-based modeling approach to the co-design of organizations and IS, we are able to develop virtual prototypes of different co-design points, and to compare the relative performance of alternate co-designs computationally. This represents a considerable advance in how organizations and IS can be designed *together* as integrated socio-technical systems, and it illustrates the practical value of co-design as such.

Conclusion

Today's organizational environment is highly dynamic for all enterprises—public and private—and very unpredictable for many. Organizations must adjust, adapt, and even re-invent themselves in response. This requires organizational agility. IS can enable and enhance such agility, or they can impede and degrade it. In a co-evolutionary sense, organizations and IS are interrelated closely, hence the design of one affects the design of the other. The problem is that few organizational designers have the knowledge and authority to design IS, and even fewer IS designers have the knowledge and authority to design organizations. The research described in this chapter addresses the co-evolution and co-design of organizations and IS through agent-based modeling. Building upon recent advances in Computational Organization Theory, we employ state-of-the-art, agent-based methods and tools to design organizations and IS *together*, along with the associated work processes, as an integrated socio-technical system. Such agent-based approach enables many virtual prototypes to be designed, tested, and refined before deciding upon a particular design configuration, and well before beginning the corresponding (re)design of organizations and IS in the operational enterprise. This represents an organizational analog to the manner in which physical artifacts—such as airplanes, bridges, and computers—are designed today—through computational modeling and virtual prototyping.

Our agent-based approach is explained and illustrated in this chapter through articulation of a contemporary organization and IS design problem: military combat. Through this work we specify two contrasting organization designs and two contrasting IS designs, and we mix them together to specify four alternate organization-IS co-designs. Drawing from theory as well as practice, we develop a 2×2 matrix of propositions outlining expectations concerning the comparative performance of the four co-designs based upon their relative co-design fit. Then using the behavior emulation capability of our agent-based modeling environment, we assess the comparative performance of the four co-design points, and we identify dominating co-designs corresponding with our expectations. The Bureaucracy Centralized IS co-design is superior—across all performance measures—to its Bureaucracy End-user counterpart, and the Adhocracy Centralized IS co-design is inferior—across all performance measures—to its Adhocracy End-user counterpart.

These results offer immediate practical implications for managers. The design of organizations should be conducted in concert with the design of IS, and vice versa. We know of few—if any—organizations that engage in such co-design as such. Hence the organization that learns to co-design along these lines gains new potential for competitive advantage. If our simulated performance results are representative of the kinds of comparative gains that can be attained by operational organizations in practice, then such competitive advantage can be substantial. For instance, whether organized as Bureaucracy or Adhocracy, having a coherent co-design (i.e., reflecting good fit) can reduce cycle time (i.e., as measured by *duration*) by 20–25%. Speed in the military domain is clearly important, but it is important too in many commercial contexts (e.g., where *time to market, cycle time,* or *service rate* is key). With 20–25% performance improvement possible, a manager would be foolish not to pursue it. Plus, the kinds of agent-based modeling environments demonstrated here are available—beyond the university research lab—today, and hence can be integrated into the work and decision-making processes of organizations spanning a broad array of sectors, types, technologies, and locations. Managers can begin now to design organizations and IS along the same lines that engineers use for airplanes, bridges, and computers. This represents a long-standing dream of ours in terms of practical application.

These results also offer empirical implications for researchers. Two relatively broad design literatures—organizations and IS—can be brought together and integrated through research along the lines of that reported here. This offers potential for new, multidisciplinary research by academic communities that have had only minimal interaction to date. Additionally, using theoretically grounded, empirically validated agent-based models such as ours, researchers can examine the comparative performance of myriad organization-IS co-designs in very short periods of time. This serves to bridge the methodological schism (Nissen and Buettner, 2004) between analytical and laboratory research (e.g., which suffers widely from problems with external validity and generalizability) and methods associated with field research (e.g., which suffer widely from problems with internal validity and control). Indeed, by using agent-based models for *computational experimentation,* one can test organization-IS co-design hypotheses to a degree and at a pace that is unprecedented. Further, such experimentation can be conducted in the comfort of one's office, without the need to develop and run tedious laboratory experiments, and without the necessity of time-consuming field research. Of course, as with every research method, our approach suffers from limitations. But it opens up a whole new paradigm for conducting organization and IS research. Also, it elucidates a micro-level approach to pursuing co-evolution research.

Yet our agent-based models remain insufficient to model *co-evolution* as a phenomenon itself, and we remain unable to emulate the dynamics of organizations and IS as they change and co-evolve. This represents a pressing research question to pursue, one that we are addressing as this chapter is being written. It also signals opportunities for the integration and joint understanding of different kinds of agent-based models, particularly those with good representational expressiveness and fidelity to model organizational environments and ecosystems. Additionally, better models of the technical details associated with various IS technologies could enhance the capabilities of research along these lines considerably. Also, new theoretical and empirical understanding that describes linkages between different organization designs and various IS designs is needed to drive continued computational experimentation and hypothesis testing. There is so much research along these lines to be done. Now that we have available agent-based tools and methods for pursuing such research, we realize how far behind we are. At least we know that we are behind. Many of our colleagues, who hold steadfastly to their comfortable, traditional research methods, appear ignorant—not only of how far behind they are, but of how quickly they are falling further behind as well. In academic research as with business management, our agent-based approach can provide a substantial competitive advantage.

References

Alavi, M. and Leidner, D. E. (2001). Review: Knowledge management and knowledge management systems: Conceptual foundations and research issues. *MIS Quarterly*, 25 (1), 107–136.

Barley, S. (1986). Technology as an occasion for structuring, *Administrative Science Quarterly*, 31, 78–108.

Bijker, W. E., Hughes, T. P., and Pinch, T. J. (1987). *The Social Construction of Technological Systems*. Cambridge, MA: MIT Press.

Burton, R. and Obel, B. (1995). The validity of computational models in organization science: From model realism to purpose of the model. *Computational and Mathematical Organization Theory*, 1 (1), 57–71.

Burton, R. M. and Obel, B. (2004). *Strategic Organizational Diagnosis and Design: The Dynamics of Fit*, 3rd ed. New York: Kluwer.

Burton, R. M., Lauridsen, J., and Obel, B. (2002). Return on assets loss from situational and contingency misfits. *Management Science*, 48 (11), 1461–1485.

Carley, K. M. and Hill, V. (2001). Structural change and learning within organizations. In *Dynamics of Organizational Computational Modeling and Organization Theories* (Lomi, A. and Larsen, E. R., eds.). Cambridge, MA: MIT Press.

Carley, K. M. and Prietula, M. J. (1994). *Computational Organization Theory*. Hillsdale, NJ: Lawrence Erlbaum.

Carley, K. M. and Lin, Z. (1997). A theoretical study of organizational performance under Information distortion. *Management Science*, 43 (7), 976–997.

Carroll, T. and Burton, R. M. (2000). Organizations and complexity: Searching for the edge of chaos. *Computational & Mathematical Organization Theory*, 6 (4), 319–337.

Cheng, C. H. F. and Levitt, R. E. (2001). Contextually changing behavior in medical organizations. *Proceedings of the 2001 Annual Symposium of the American Medical Informatics Association*, November 3–7, 2001, Washington, D.C.

Christiansen, T. R. (1993). Modeling efficiency and effectiveness of coordination in engineering design teams. Unpublished PhD Dissertation. Stanford University.

Cohen, G. P. (1992). The virtual design team: An information processing model of design team management. Unpublished PhD Dissertation. Stanford University.

Cohen, K. J. and Cyert, R. M. (1965). Simulation of organizational behavior. In *Handbook of Organizations* (March, J. G., ed.). Chicago: Rand McNally.

Daft, R. L. and Levwin, A. Y. (1990). Can organization studies begin to break out of the normal science straitjacket? An editorial essay. *Organization Science*, 1 (1), 1–9.

Daft, R. L. and Levwin, A. Y. (1993). Where are the theories for the new organization forms? An editorial essay. *Organization Science*, 4 (4), i–iv.

De Marco, T. (1978). *Structured Analysis and System Specification*. New York: Yourdon Press.

Galbraith, J. R. (1977). *Organizational Design*. Reading, MA: Addison-Wesley.

Gane, C. and Sarson, T. (1979). *Structured Systems Analysis: Tools and Techniques*. Upper Saddle River, NJ: Prentice-Hall.

Garud, R. and Van de Ven, A. H. (1987). Innovation and the emergence of industries. *Best Paper Proceedings, Academy of Management Annual Meeting*, New Orleans, LA.

Garud, R. and Rappa, M. A. (1994). A socio-cognitive model of technology evolution: The case of cochlear implants. *Organization Science*, 5 (3), 344–362.

Giddens, A. (1979). *Central Problems in Social Theory*. Los Angeles: University of California Press.

Hevner, A. R., et al. (2004). Design science in information systems research. *MIS Quarterly*, 28 (1), 75–105.

Holland, J. H. (1975). *Adaptation in Natural and Artificial Systems*. Ann Arbor, MI: University of Michigan Press.

Jin, Y. and Levitt, R. E. (1996). The virtual design team: A computational model of project organizations. *Journal of Computational and Mathematical Organizational Theory*, 2 (3), 171–195.

Kim, R. M. and Kaplan, S. M. (2005). Co-evolution in information systems engagement: Exploration, ambiguity and the emergence of order. In *Proceedings of ALOIS*2005*, March 15–16, 2005, Limerick, Ireland.

Kunz, J. C., Levitt, R. E., and Jin, Y. (1998). The virtual design team: A computational model of project organizations. *Communications of the Association for Computing Machinery*, 41 (11), 84–92.

Kuran, T. (1988). The tenacious past: Theories of personal and collective conservatism. *Journal of Economic Behavior and Organization*, 10, 143–171.

Law, A. M. and Kelton, D. (1991). *Simulation Modeling and Analysis*, 2nd ed. New York: McGraw-Hill.

Lawrence, P. R. and Lorsch, J. W. (1967). *Organization and Environment: Managing Differentiation and Integration*. Boston, Division of Research: Harvard Business School.

Leavitt, H. J. (1965). Applying organizational change in industry: structural, technological and humanistic approaches. In March, J., ed., *Handbook of Organizations*. Chicago: Rand McNally.

Levinthal, D. A. and March, J. G. (1993). The myopia of learning. *Strategic Management Journal*, 14 (Special Issue), 95–112.

Levitt, R. E. (2004). Computational modeling of organizations comes of age. *Journal of Computational and Mathematical Organization Theory*, 10 (2), 127–145.

Levitt, R. E., et al. (1999). Simulating project work processes and organizations: Toward a micro-contingency theory of organizational design. *Management Science*, 45 (11), 1479–1495.

Levitt, R. E., Orr, R. J., and Nissen, M. (2005). Validation of the Virtual Design Team (VDT) computational modeling environment. The Collaboratory for Research on Global Projects, Working Paper #25, 1–15. Retrieved from: http://crgp.stanford.edu/publications/working_papers/WP25.pdf.

Lewin, A. Y., Long, C. P., and Carroll, T. N. (1999). The co-evolution of new organizational forms. *Organization Science*, 10 (5), 535–550.

Lewin, A. Y. and Volberda, H. W. (1999). Prolegomena on coevolution: A framework for research on strategy and new organizational forms. *Organization Science*, 10 (5), 519–534.

March, J. G. (1991). Exploration and exploitation in organizational learning. *Organization Science*, 2, 71–87.

March, J. G. (1996). Continuity and change of theories of organizational action. *Administrative Science Quarterly*, 41, 278–287.

March, J. G. and Simon, H. A. (1958). *Organizations*. New York: Wiley.

McKelvey, B. (1997). Quasi-natural organization science. *Organization Science*, 8 (4), 352–380.

McKelvey, B. (1999). Dynamics of new science leadership: An OB theory of the firm, strategy, and distributed intelligence. *Proceedings of the MESO Conference*, April–May 1999, Duke University, Durham, NC.

Mintzberg, H. (1979). *The Structuring of Organizations*. Englewood Cliffs, NJ: Prentice-Hall.

Nissen, M. E. (2005). Hypothesis testing of Edge Organizations: Specifying computational C2 Models for experimentation. In *Proceedings International Command & Control Research Symposium*, June 2005, McLean, VA.

Nissen, M. E. (2006). Dynamic knowledge patterns to inform design: A field study of knowledge stocks and flows in an extreme organization. *Journal of Management Information Systems*, 22 (3), 225–264.

Nissen, M. E. and Buettner, R. R. (2004). Computational experimentation with the virtual design team: Bridging the chasm between laboratory and field research in C2. In *Proceedings Command and Control Research and Technology Symposium*, June 2004, San Diego, CA.

Nissen, M. E. and Levitt, R. E. (2004). Agent-based modeling of knowledge dynamics. *Knowledge Management Research & Practice*, 2 (3), 169–183.

Nissen, M. E., Orr, R. J., and Levitt, R. E. (2006). Streams of shared knowledge: Computational expansion of organization theory. Working paper.

Nogueira, J. C. (2000). A formal model for risk assessment in software projects. *Doctoral Dissertation*, Department of Computer Science, Monterey, CA: Naval Postgraduate School.

Orlikowski, W. J. and Barley, S. R. (2002). Technology and institutions: What can research on information technology and research on organizations learn from each other? *MIS Quarterly*, 25 (2), 145–165.

Rosenkopf, L. and Tushman, M. L. (1993). On the co-evolution of organization and technology. In (Baum, J. and Singh, J., eds.), *Evolutionary Dynamics of Organizations*. New York: Oxford University Press.

Scott, W. R. (2003). *Organizations: Rational, Natural, and Open Systems, 5th ed.* Englewood Cliffs, NJ: Prentice Hall.

Simon, H. A. (1996). *The Sciences of the Artificial* (3rd edition). Cambridge, MA: MIT Press.

Thompson, J. D. (1967). *Organizations in Action*. New York: McGraw-Hill.

Thomsen, J. (1998). The Virtual Team Alliance (VTA): Modeling the effects of goal incongruency in semi-routine, fast-paced project organizations. Stanford University.

Van Aken, J. E. (2004). Management research based on the paradigm of the design sciences: The quest for field-tested and grounded technological rules. *Journal of Management Studies*, 41 (2), 219–246.

Walls, J. G., Widmeyer, G. W., and El Sawy, O. A. (1992). Building an information systems design theory for vigilant EIS. *Information Systems Research*, 3 (1), 36–59.

Weick, K. (1990). Technology as equivoque. In *Technology and Organizations* (Goodman, P. and Sproull, L., eds.). San Francisco: Jossey-Bass.

Wong, S. S. and Burton, R. M. (2000). Virtual teams: What are their characteristics and impact on team performance? *Computational & Mathematical Organization Theory*, 6 (4), 339–360.

Index

Achieving economic returns from IS support for strategic flexibility, 70–82
analyses and results of study, 77, 78
competitive value, 71–72
factor analysis chart, 76
field study, 74–77
firm-specific organizational culture and structure, moderating roles of, 73–74
limitations of study, 79–80
managerial implications of study, 79
measures for study, 75–77
overview of findings and research implications, 77, 78–79
regression results table, 78
research model diagram, 71
sample and data collection for study, 74–75
theory and hypothesis, 71–74
Act-network theory (ANT), 192, 194
Adhocracy co-design, 275, 276, 277–280, 281
bureaucracy versus, 274
centralized versus end-user, 275, 278–280
comparative performance results, 278
as fixed organization design point, 274
mission tasks, 276
model parameterization chart, 277
performance results, comparative, 279
Agent-based modeling. *See* Co-evolution and co-design of agile organizations and information systems through agent-based modeling
Agile capabilities, 210, 211–213, 216
creation, 211–212
learning, 212–213
learning from change, 213, 214–215
proaction, 212
reaction, 212
Agile decision making, 16–30
challenges, essential. *See* Challenges, essential
characteristics of agility, 25–26
comparison of domains. *See* Domains, comparison of
conclusions, 28
financial management, 26
information systems, 24
investment modeling, 26–27
product planning, 27–28
strategic management, 19
strategic management tasks, 22–24
supporting management, 25
value, providing, 24–25
Agile development project, 239–249
business benefits, 247–248
conclusions, 247–248
contribution to projects success by, 248
digital sales tool, 247
e-business department establishment, 241–242
e-point of sales system, 246–247
moving toward agile operations, 242
point of sale suite development, 244–245
point of sales system requirements, 243–244
point of sale system shortcomings, 240–241
portal creation, 243
produce to order system, 245–246

Agile development project *(Continued)*
promotional materials, licensed, 246
summary, 248–249
timeline of project chart, 244
Agile drivers, 209, 210–211, 216; *see also* Agile drivers, capabilities, and value
Agile drivers, capabilities, and value, 207–221; *see also* Agile capabilities; Agile drivers; Agile value
conclusion, 216
critical issues, 207–208
examples of learning from change table, 214–215
flowchart showing, 210
framework of information system development agility, proposed, 209–210
tailoring agile methods, 208
Agile information organizations (AIOs) components, xii
Agile information systems (AISs) as a double dream, 116–121
building virtual office, dream of, 111–112
calendar, electric, 114–115
discussion and reflection, 119–120
from dream to instruction manual, 118–119
reality and its ambivalence, 112–114
reconfiguration of practices, 117–118
technology-in-use, 113, 114, 117
videoconferencing system, 115–117
Agile Manifesto, 207, 208, 216
Agile manufacturing, 208–209
Agile methods names, 207
Agile organization, xii–xiv
co-evolution and co-design of, 266–284
determining, xii
Agile systems, 84
Agile value, 210, 213
Agility
amount needed, 46–47
capabilities of, 53
characteristics, 25–26
characterizing, 43–44
conception of idea, 52
consumption methods, 47, 48–49
corporate information systems and, 134–136
customer, 135
definitions, 16, 41, 42, 53, 83, 111, 123, 135, 178, 209
education for, 185
element of, defining, 84
flexibility versus, 53, 135
operational, 135
partnering, 135
people, 126
process, 125–126
produced, how, 44, 45, 46
production process diagram, 45
source, 44, 45–46
structure, 126–127
supply chain and, 151–153
technology, 125
theoretical framework, 123
uses, 47, 48–49
Alignment, 2–3, 4–5, 6
Ambidextrous organization, 4, 7, 8, 10, 173
Application architecture complexity, 137, 138

Backcasting, 273
Balanced scorecard, 7
Balancing stability and flexibility case study, 83–96
agile systems, 84
agility profile chart, 93
analysis and discussion, 90
background information, 86–87
chaotic deadlock, 92
conclusions, 95
introduction to case study company, 86–87
issues identification, 87–88
lead-up to case study, 91–92
measuring stability, 86
model of information technology agility, 84–86
outcome discussion, 94–95
problems, surmounting, 88–89
project development and support office, improving, 89–90
reorganization, 92
transforming project development and support office, 92–94
Business case for agility, 52–69
analyses, 62–66
change factor scores table, 56–57
change factors matrices, 65–66
change factors matrix diagram, 63
conceptual framework diagram, 54
conclusions, 66–67
customer, 61–62
definition, 53–54, 66
differences between sections, 58, 59
domains of, 53
findings, 58
flexibility versus agility, 53
framework, 54
implementing, 53
individual change factors and role of information technology importance, 58

matrix, 63–64
methodology, 54, 55–57
needs, readiness, and gap comparisons table, 59
network and partnering agility, 62
operational, 60–61
public versus business, 58
readiness determination, 54
Business process reengineering, 3–4

California Energy Commission case study. *See* Balancing stability and flexibility case study
Challenges, essential, 19–22
addressing, 22
change, 21
focus as path to growth, 21
future, 21
growth as goal, 20
knowledge, 21
relationships among, 20
time, 21
value as foundation for growth, 21
Clumsy nature of enterprise information systems, 163–177
agenda formation decisions and fashion-following, 166–168
conclusions, 174–175
impact of enterprise resource planning and knowledge management initiatives table, 174
implementation decisions and practice versus process, 170–172
rationale for implementation, 164–166
selection decisions and status quo, 168–170
usage decisions and efficiency versus flexibility, 172–174
value chain as it relates to enterprise resource planning, 165
value chain as it relates to functional systems, 164
Co-evolution and co-design of agile organizations and information systems through agent-based modeling, 266–284
approach, 269
computational organization theory (COT) research, 269–270
conclusion, 280–282
design, organizational and information systems, 267–268
information processing view of knowledge work diagram, 272
model paramaterization charge, 279
models, co-design, 276–280
practical illustration, 276
results, co-design, 278–280
virtual design team adaptation for co-design of organizations and information systems, 273–276
virtual design team computational model validation, 273
virtual design team computational modeling environment, 271–273
virtual design team elements and element descriptions, 271
Communities of practice, 35
Coors Brewing point of sale application suite, 239–249; *see also* Agile development project
Corporate information systems and agility, 134–136

Dashboards management, 228–231, 232–233
cost savings and, 233–234
corporate, 228, 230–231
factory, 228, 229–230, 232
lessons learned, 235, 236–237
observe, orient, decide, act loops and, 231
real-time types, 237–238
strategic advantages, 234
Degrees of agility, 122–133
conclusions, 132
example, 131
fuzzy logic, 127–128, 130, 132
inference rules, 130
linguistic variables, 128
membership functions, 128–130
people, 126
process, 125–126
socio-technical theory, 123–125
structure, 126–127
technology, 125
theoretical framework, 123
Domains, comparison of, 16–19
common underlying phenomena, 17, 18
information seeking across domains comparisons, 18
information types versus domains of use, 17
value, providing, 24–25
value of information, 18–19

Electronic data interchange (EDI), 99
Emergence, 3, 10
Enabling strategic agility through agile information systems, 97–109; *see also* Loose coupling; Web services oriented architecture
benefits of loose coupling for strategic agility, 100–102
discussion and conclusions, 106

Enabling strategic agility through agile information systems *(Continued)*
loose coupling, 99–100
observations of web services, preliminary, 102, 103
roles of loose coupling and web services oriented architecture, 97–109
web services and loose coupling, 102
web services oriented architecture, 99–99
web services oriented architecture emerging framework, 102, 103
Enterprise information systems and preservation of agility, 178–187
education for agility, 185
flexibility, agility, and classification, 182–183
flexibility, agility, and systems implementation and use, 183–185
implementing enterprise resource planning system, organization's experience, 181–182
interpretive flexibility, 186
introducing enterprise systems, agility, interpretive flexibility, and workarounds, 179–181
legacy systems, 184
propositions, 179, 180, 181, 182, 183, 184
reflexivity, 186
theoretical framework, 179–181
workarounds, 185
Enterprise resource planning (ERP)
as agile manufacturing support, 152
characteristics of agility and, 26
financial management and, 26
flexibility reduction and, 186
hosted systems and interpretative flexibility. *See* Interpretative flexibility and hosted enterprise resource planning systems
impact of knowledge management and ERP initiatives chart, 174
implementing, an organization's experience with, 181–182
as linear systems, 180
organization's experience with implementing system, 181–182
supplier parks and, 150
viewed as mission critical software, 168
Enterprise systems (ES), 4
critical review, 163–177; *see also* Clumsy information systems
introducing, 179
rationale for implementation, 164–166
spending on, 163
transformational benefits, 168
workarounds, 185
Entrepreneurship, 32, 33
Exploitation strategy, 9, 10
Exploration strategy, 9, 10, 11

Financial management, 26
Flexibility; *see also* Achieving economic returns from information systems support for strategic flexibility; Balancing stability and flexibility case study
agility versus, 53, 135
assessment in supply chain of, 156
complexity and, 42
definition, 53, 123
dimensions of, 156
hosted enterprise resource planning systems and interpretative flexibility. *See* Interpretative flexibility and hosted enterprise resource planning systems
information systems, 151, 158
interpretive, 186, 192–194
interpretive versus interpretative, 199
logistics, 151, 157
loose coupling and, 101–102
manufacturing, 151
need for, 16
operations systems, 151
proactive versus reactive, 212
process, 156, 157
producing agility and, 46
supply, 151, 157–158
technological artifacts and, 119
web services oriented architecture strategic agility and, 105–106
Future information needs, 7, 8
Fuzzy logic, 127–128, 130, 132

Goals setting, xiii
Growth as essential challenge goal, 20–21

Implications for information systems design and firm strategy. *See* Degrees of agility
Information types versus domains of use, 17
Information systems versus IF, 2
Information technology product categories, 136
Integration management for heterogeneous information systems, 134–149
agility and corporate information systems, 134–136
analysis of existing application design, 140, 141–142
application architecture complexity, 137, 138
application architecture model diagrams, 142, 143

application design, ideal, 142–144
application interfacing, ideal, 146
application interfacing and common integration layers, 144–146
application integration success and factors and their interdependencies, 141
architecture redesign, 140
business collaboration infrastructure, 145, 146
conclusions, 147
costs and complexity of infrastructure, 140
coupling, degree of, 138–139
data warehouse systems, 144, 145
enterprise application integration systems, 145, 147
expenses, project, 139–140
generic reference application architecture diagram, 146
indicators and performance measures, 137, 138
individual interfaces versus hub-and-spoke concept diagram, 145
influence on agility, 140, 141
reuse/functional redundancy, 130
success factors for application integration in related work, 138

Interpretative flexibility and hosted enterprise resource planning systems, 188–206
analytical separation of design and use for inherited structure diagram, 194
background to case study, 196
changing emphasis of agency, technology, and structure diagram, 201
conclusion, 200–202
evidence and discussion, 196–200
evidence of differing interpretations question, 197
literature review, 189–194
materiality and interpretative flexibility, role of, 199–200
research methodology, 195
technology and interpretive flexibility, 192–194
technology as institution, 189–190
technology as structure, 190–192
time-space discontinuity importance, 197–199

Investigating role of information systems in contributing to agility of modern supply chains, 150–162
agility and supply chain, 151–153
agility measures for information systems diagram, 159
conclusion, 160
contribution of information systems to agility, 158–160, 161
European supplier park example, 153–154
flexibility, 156, 158
information and material flow in supplier parks diagram, 152
information architecture observed in supplier park diagram, 155
information flow in supply chain, 154–156
information systems as enablers of supply chain agility flowchart, 161
logistics flexibility, 157
process flexibility, 1566, 157
supply flexibility, 157–158

Investment modeling, 26–27

Knowledge, logic of. *See* Logic of knowledge
Knowledge brokers, 10
Knowledge management principles support agile systems. *See* Logic of knowledge
Knowledge management systems, 4, 5–6
Knowledge management to knowledge nurturing, 39–40
Knowledge required to organizations transformations, xiii

Leanness definition, 213
Linguistic variables, 128, 129, 130
Logic of knowledge, 31–40
abhors a vacuum, 33, 35
acts as a fluid, 33, 36–37
changes value, 33, 36
characteristics and implications, 33
collaboration, 34
creation by anyone, 32, 33
distributed cheaply, 33–34
entrepreneurship, 32, 33
guided by spirit, 33, 37–38
increases when shared, 33, 34
as infinite resource, 33, 38–39
from management to nurturing, 39–40
organized hierarchically, 33, 37
reduces conflict, 33, 35–36
transmitted in networks, 33, 35
unique for individuals, 33, 38

London Black Cab case study, 250–265; *see also* Organizational agility with mobile information and communication technology

Loose coupling, 99–100; *see also* Enabling strategic agility through agile information systems case study
adaptability, 100
benefits for strategic agility of, 100–102
degrees of coupling, 138–139

Loose coupling *(Continued)*
  efficiency, 103–104
  flexibility, 101–102
  innovation, 101
  persistence/buffering, 100
  web services and, 102

Mobil working. *See* Organizational agility with mobile information and communication technology case study

Operational agility, 135
Organizational agility with mobile information and communication technology case study, 250–265
  agility arrangements, 254–257, 259–261
  Black Cab work in London, 251–254
  Black Cab work tasks, 252–253
  challenging mobile work, 263
  comparisons of arrangements, 259–261
  conclusion, 263–264
  emerging versus planned decisions, 258, 261–262
  research approach, 253–254
  support types, 258
  systems and their riddles, 262

People agility, 126
Process agility, 125–126
Producing and consuming agility, 41–51
  agile action, 42, 47
  amount of agility needed, 46–47
  business transformation, 43, 47
  characterizing agility, 43–44
  conclusions, 50, 51
  continuous versus discrete agility production diagram, 50
  contrasting agile action, 42, 43
  defining agility, 41, 42
  firefighting, 42, 43, 45, 47
  how consumed, 47, 48–49
  how produced, 44, 45, 46
  overspending and under spending concerns, 47
  platform construction, 43, 47
  relating agility and business development, 48
  relating flexibility, complexity, and agility, 42
  resource allocation matrix, 43
  source of agility, 44, 45–46
Product planning, 27–28

Renting versus owning model for resource management, xiv
Review of enterprise systems, critical. *See* Clumsy information systems

Socio-technical theory, 123–125
Stability. *See* Balancing stability and flexibility case study
Strategic flexibility and economic returns. *See* Achieving economic returns from information systems support for strategic flexibility
Strategic management, 19
  tasks, 22–24
  tools, 22–23
Strategizing for agility, 1–15
  alignment, competitive advantage, enterprise systems, and knowledge management, 2–6
  alignment of, 2–3, 4–5, 6
  business planning advisor, 3–4
  emergence, 3, 10
  enterprise systems, 4
  environmental dynamism, future information needs, and proactive role of information considerations in, 6–8
  environmental dynamism, 7
  exploitation strategy, 9, 10
  exploration strategy, 9, 10, 11
  framework for, 9
  future information needs, 7, 8
  knowledge management systems, 4, 5–6
  proactive role of information, 7, 8
  synthesis, 8–11
Structuration theory, 190–192, 201
Structure agility, 126–127
Supply chains; *see also* Investigating role of information systems in contributing to agility of modern supply chains
  agility and, 151–153
  flexibility assessment, 156
  flexibility dimensions, 151
  information flow in, 154–156
  qualities, 150
Systems development, over-arching framework for. *See* Agile drivers, capabilities, and value

Technological devices, xiii
Technology
  agility, 125
  as institution, 189–190
  interpretive flexibility and, 192–194
  as structure, 190–192
Technology-in-use, 113, 114, 117

Value
of information, 18–19
providing, 24–25
Vehicle-based working. *See* Organizational agility with mobile information and communication technology case study
Vigilant information systems (VIS) case study, 222–238
architecture, 226
business challenges of Western Digital, 225
business impacts of, 233
corporate dashboards, 228, 230–231
cost savings, 233–234
factory dashboards, 228, 229–230, 232
foundations capabilities, three, 226, 227
future of, 237–238
information flowchart for Western Digital, 229
lessons learned, 235–237
management dashboards, 228–231, 237–238; *see also* Dashboards, management
observe, orient, decide, act (OODA) loops and, 223, 231–233, 235–236
revamping Western Digital's business process, 227–228
strategic advantages, 234–235
transitional information systems versus, 223, 224–225
Western Digital's, 225–228
Virtual design team (VDT). *See* Co-evolution and co-design of agile organizations and information systems through agent-based modeling
Virtual office, dream of building, 111–112

Web service definition, 98
Web services oriented architecture (wSOA), 98–99; *see also* Enabling strategic agility through agile information systems
adaptability, 104, 106
definition, 98
efficiency, 103–104, 106
flexibility, 98, 105–106
innovation, 105, 106
loose coupling roles and, 97–109
persistence/buffering, 103, 106
Western Digital (WD) case study, 222–238; *see also* Vigilant information systems
Work in organizations transformations, xiii